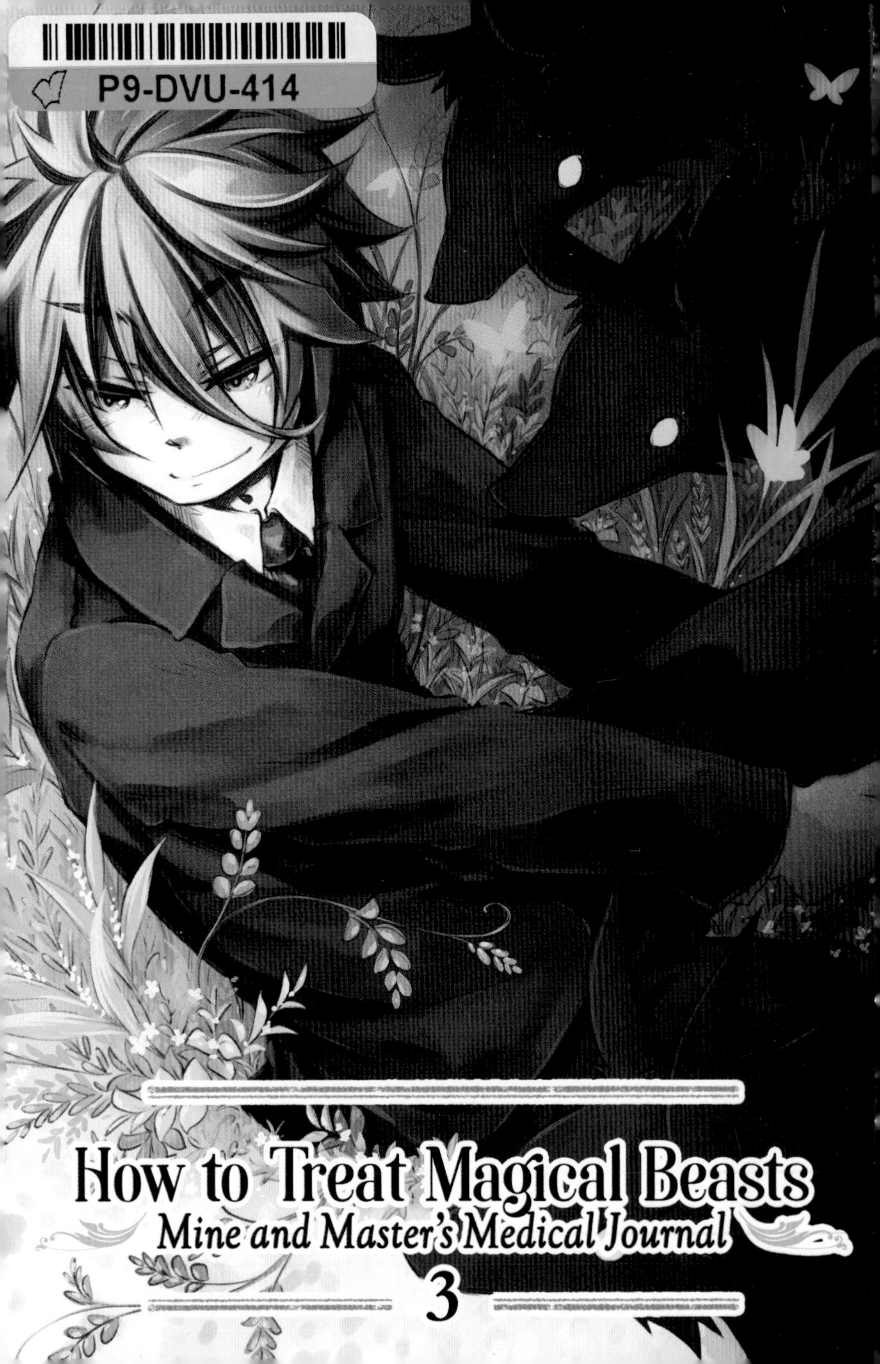

How to Treat Magical Beasts

Mine and Master's Medical Journal

3

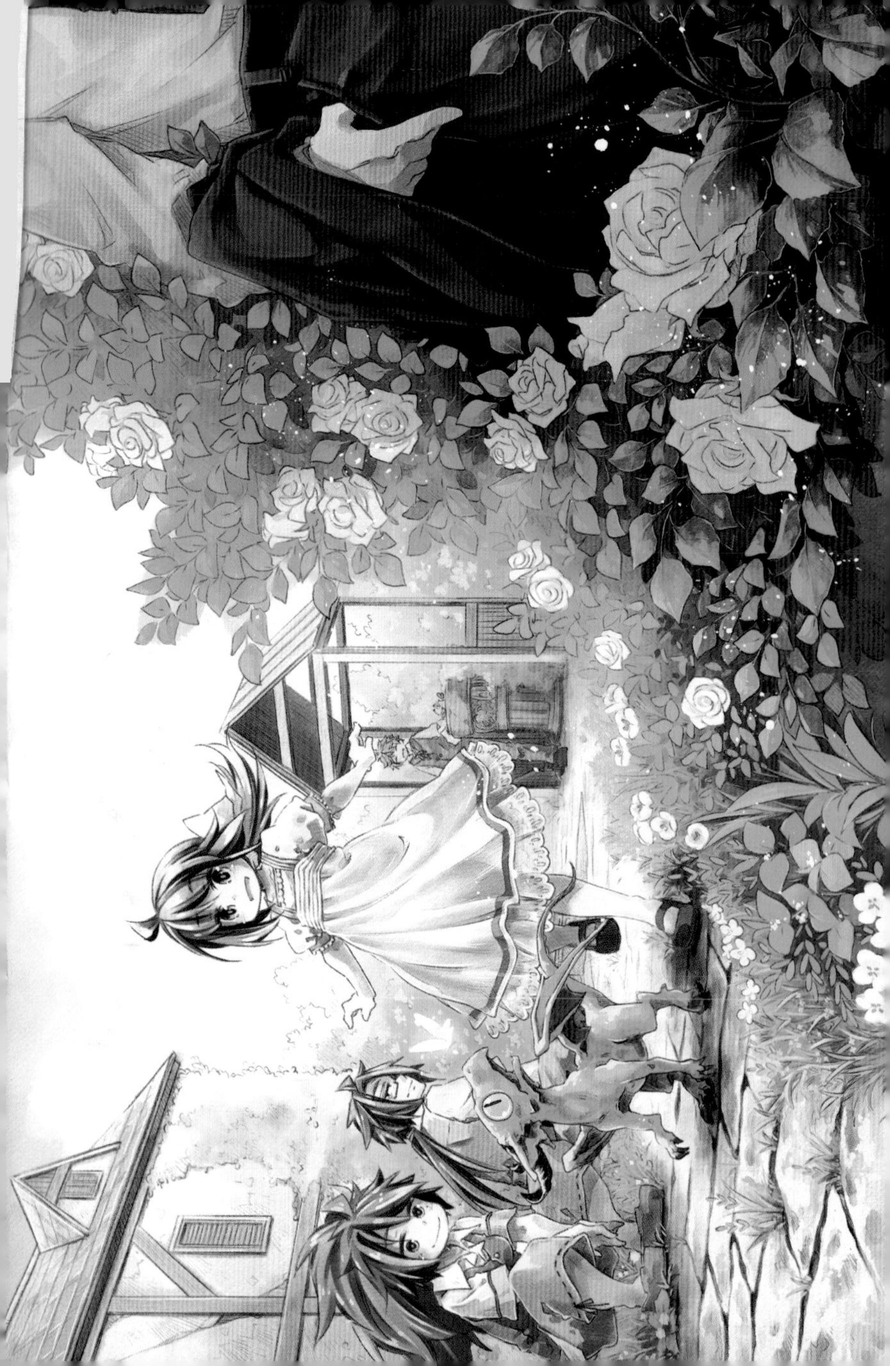

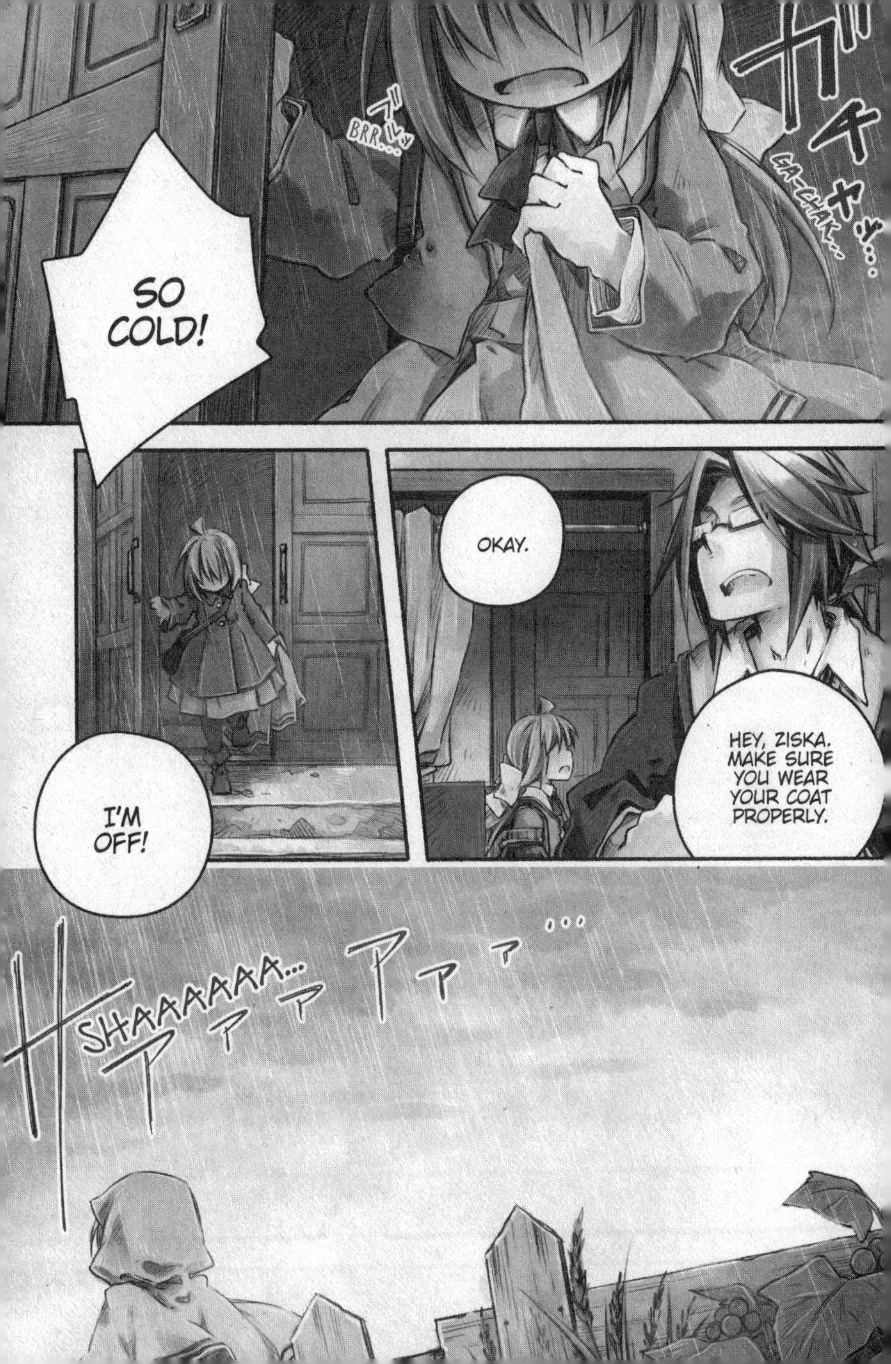
GA-CHAK...
BRR...
SO COLD!
HEY, ZISKA. MAKE SURE YOU WEAR YOUR COAT PROPERLY.
OKAY.
I'M OFF!
SHAAAAAA...

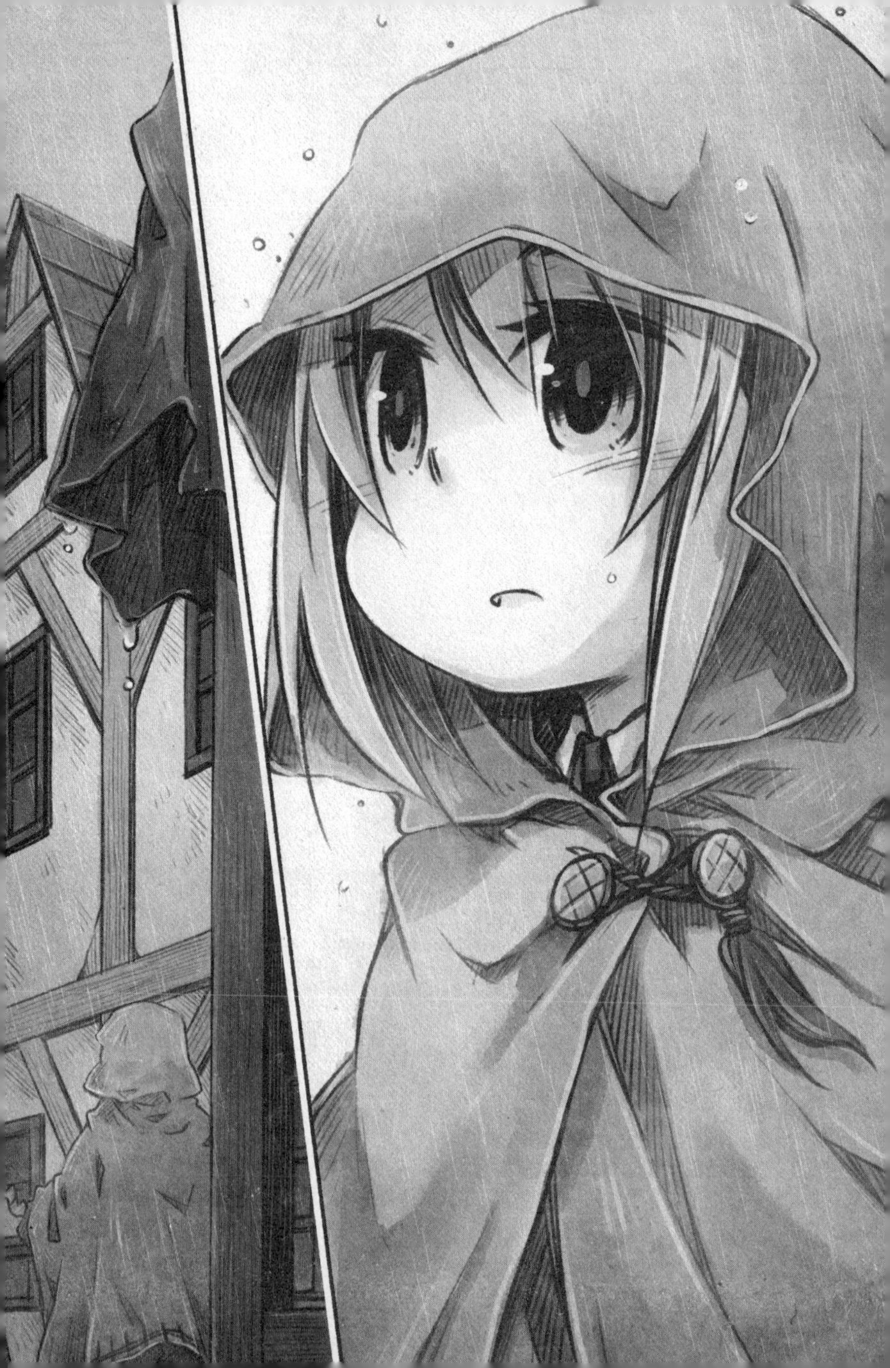

[Case 12: Dark Gray Rain]

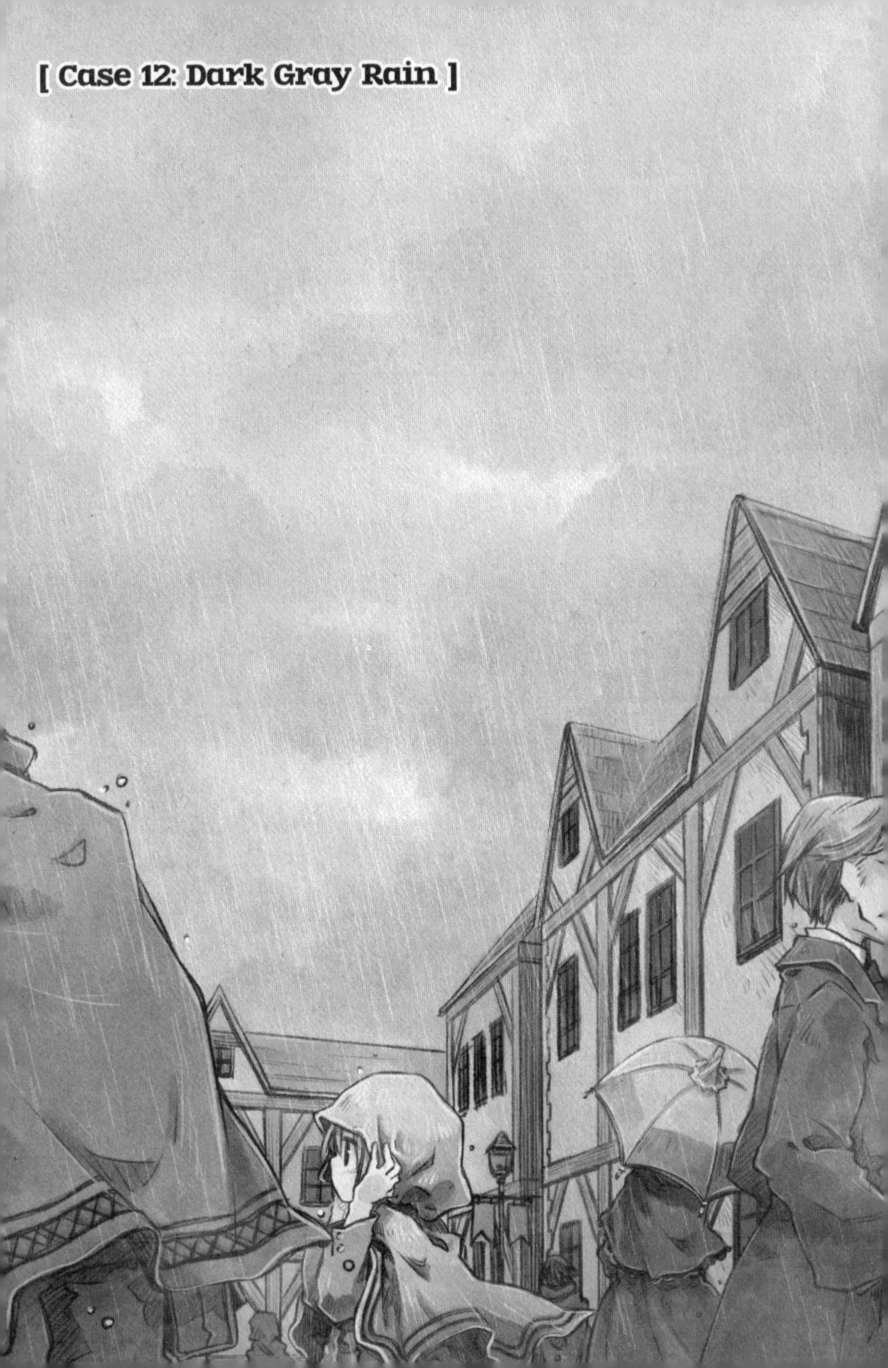

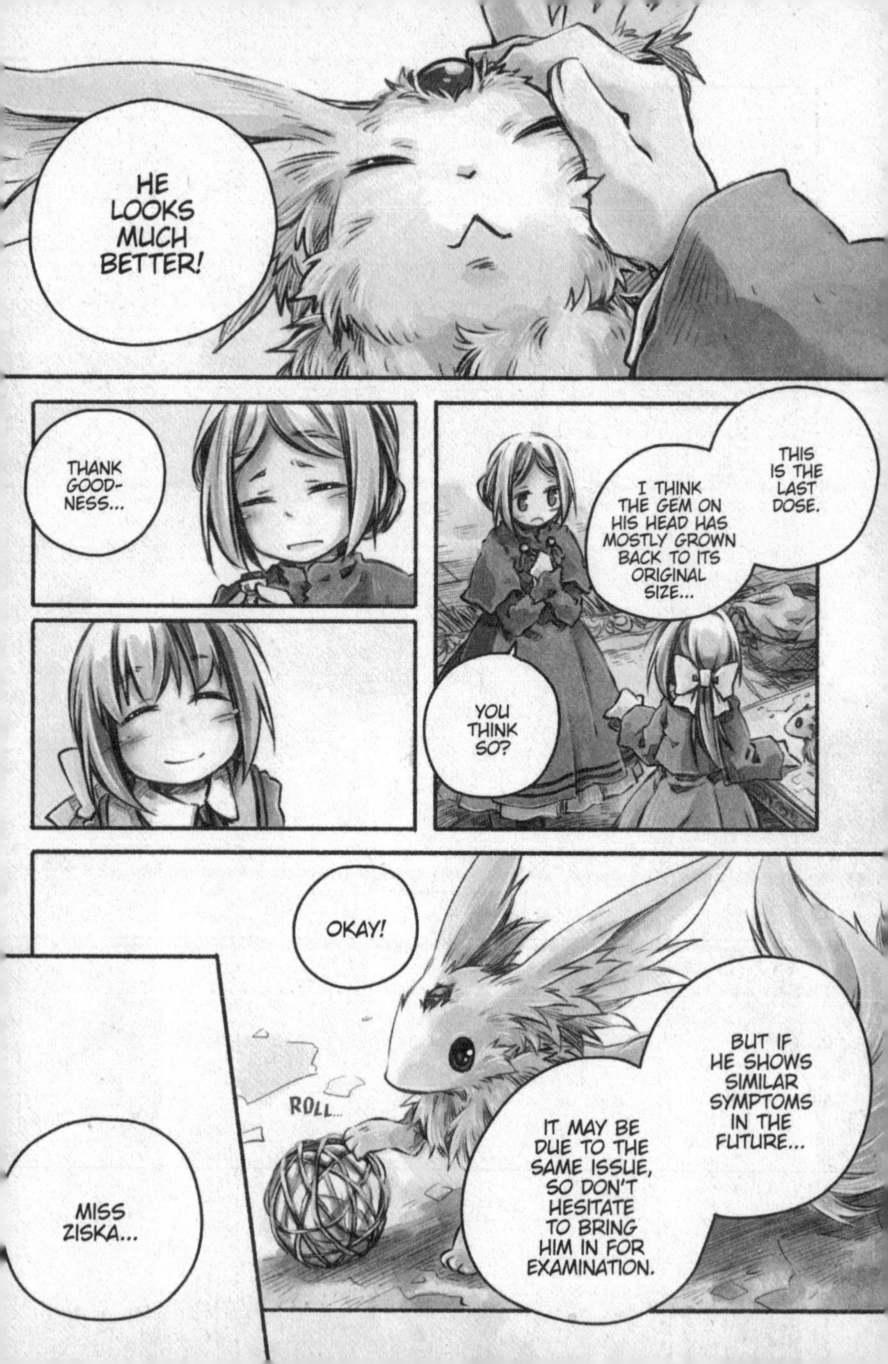
HE LOOKS MUCH BETTER!
THIS IS THE LAST DOSE.
I THINK THE GEM ON HIS HEAD HAS MOSTLY GROWN BACK TO ITS ORIGINAL SIZE...
YOU THINK SO?
THANK GOODNESS...
BUT IF HE SHOWS SIMILAR SYMPTOMS IN THE FUTURE...
IT MAY BE DUE TO THE SAME ISSUE, SO DON'T HESITATE TO BRING HIM IN FOR EXAMINATION.
OKAY!
ROLL...
MISS ZISKA...

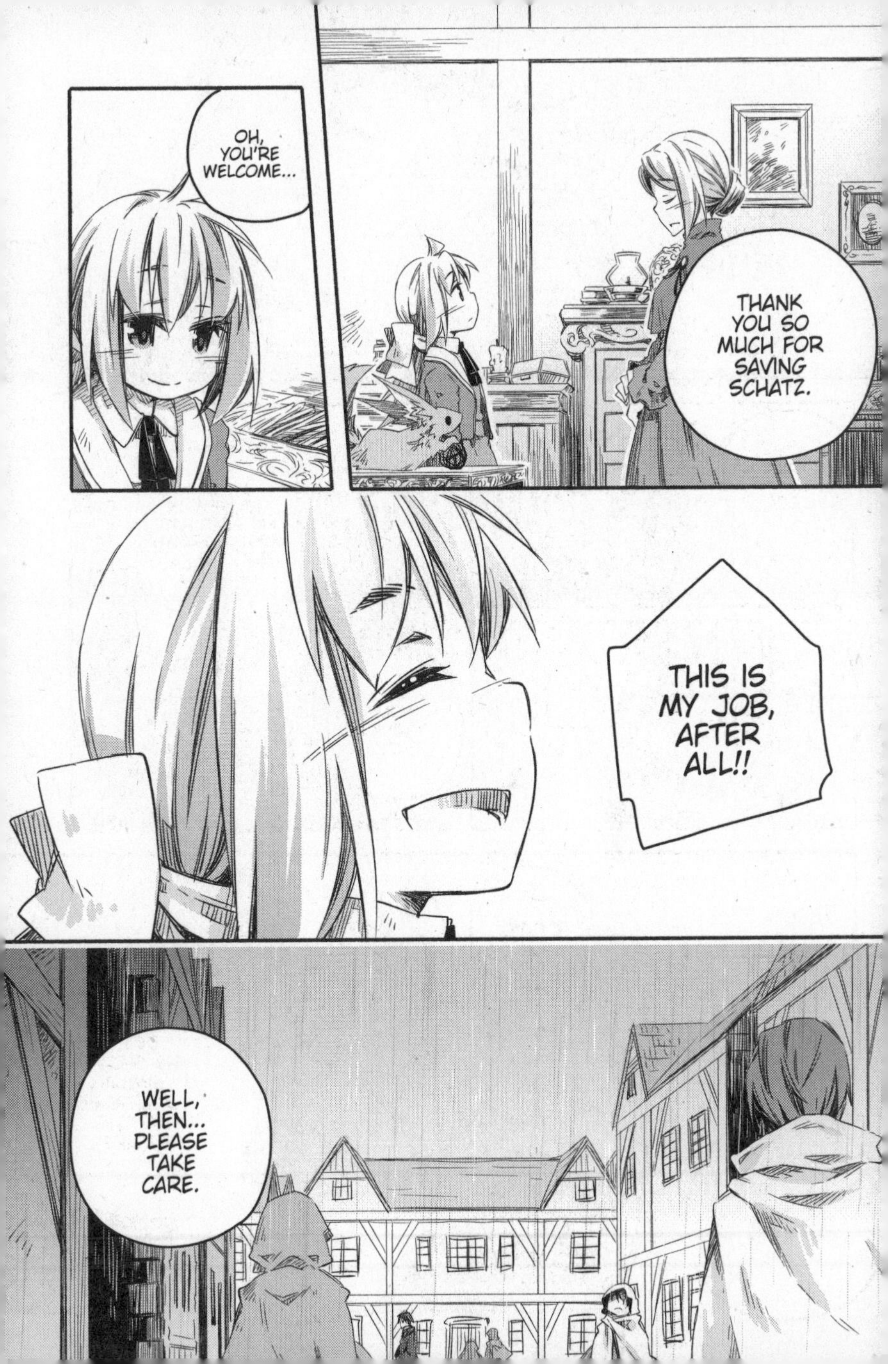
THANK YOU SO MUCH FOR SAVING SCHATZ.
OH, YOU'RE WELCOME...
THIS IS MY JOB, AFTER ALL!!
WELL, THEN... PLEASE TAKE CARE.

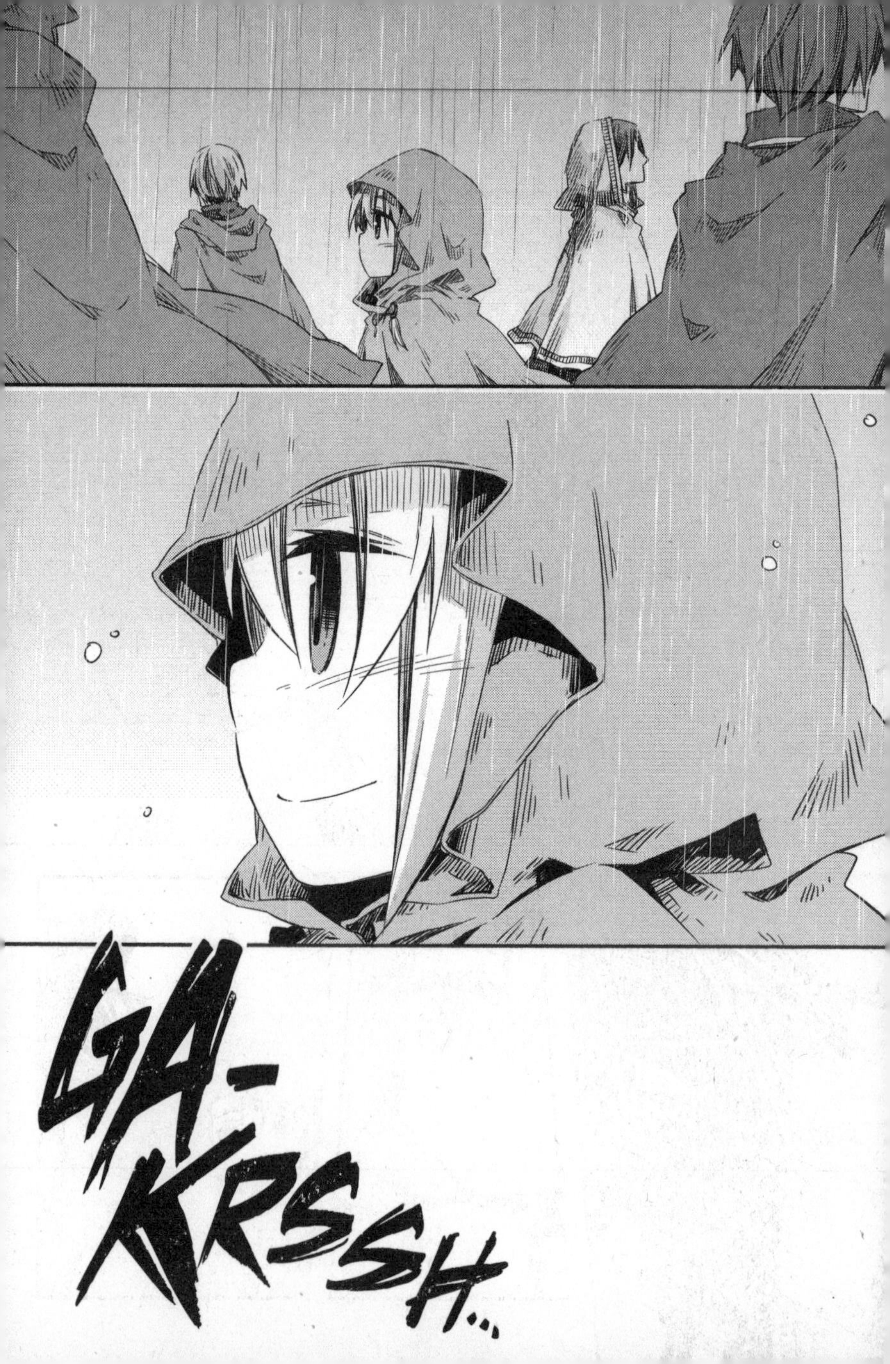
GA-KRSSH...

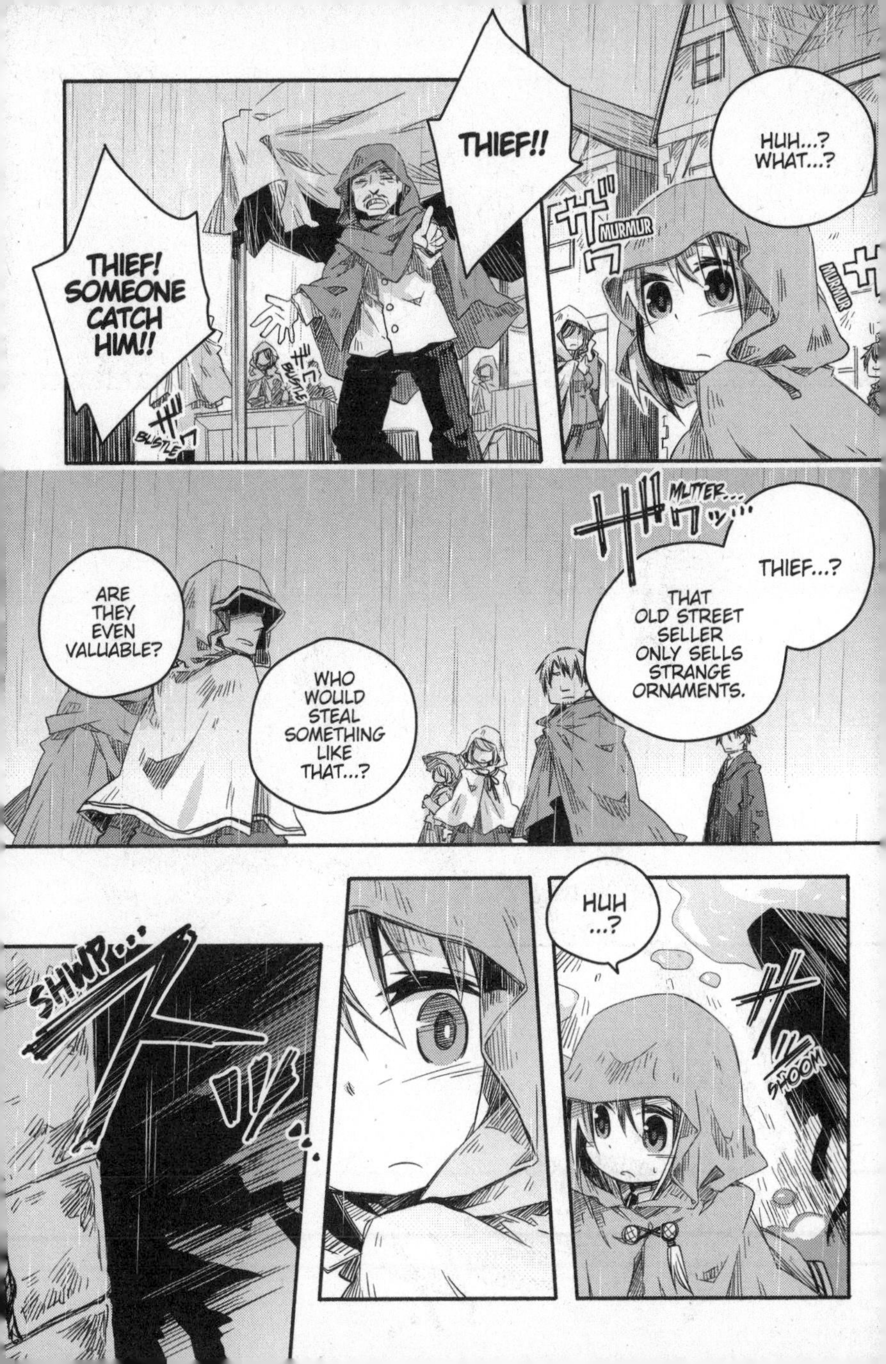
HUH...? WHAT...?
MURMUR
MURMUR
THIEF!!
THIEF! SOMEONE CATCH HIM!!
BUSTLE
BUSTLE
MUTTER...
THIEF...?
THAT OLD STREET SELLER ONLY SELLS STRANGE ORNAMENTS.
WHO WOULD STEAL SOMETHING LIKE THAT...?
ARE THEY EVEN VALUABLE?
HUH ...?
SHOOM
SHWP...

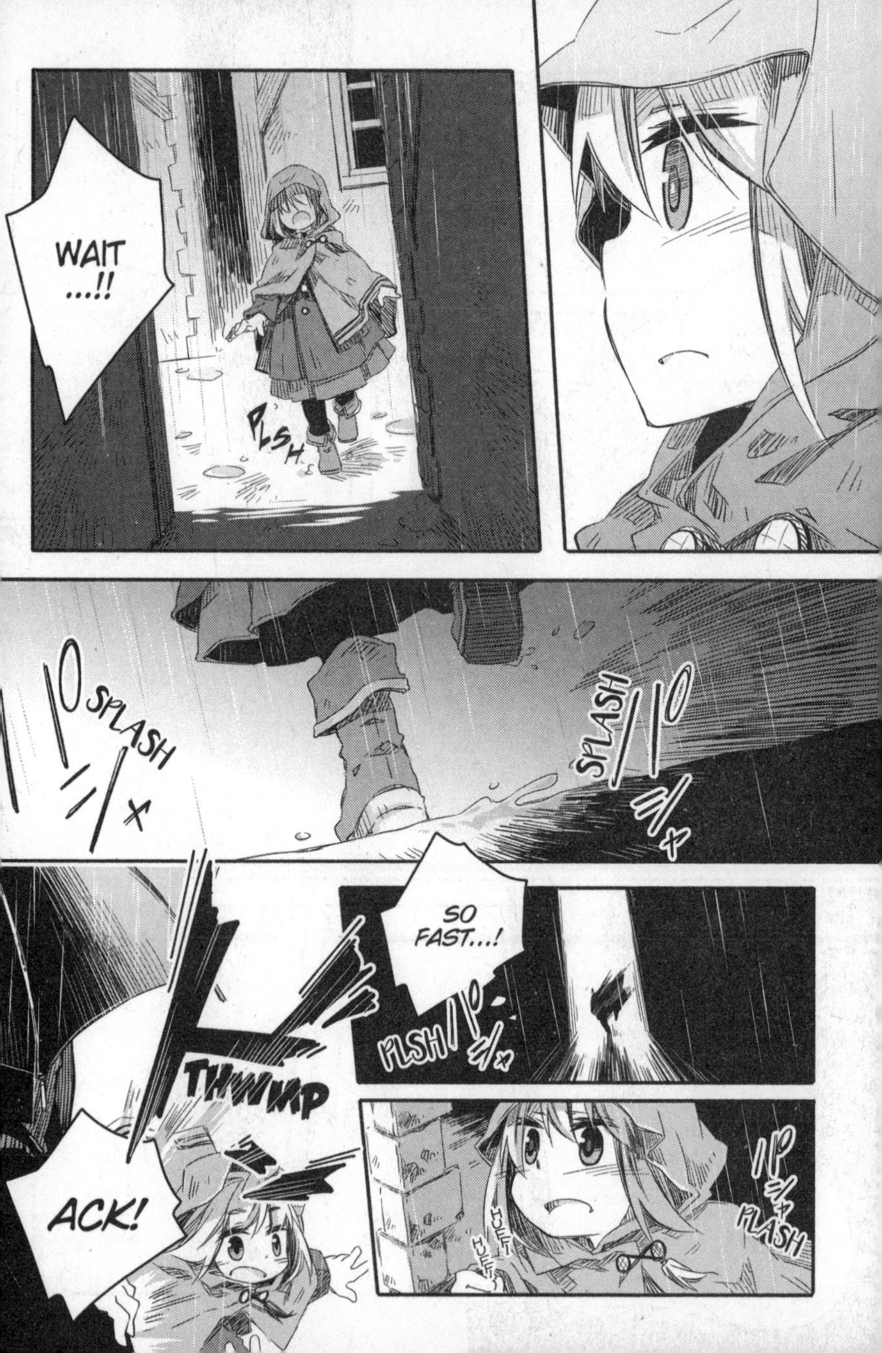
WAIT ...!!
PLSH
SPLASH
SPLASH
SO FAST...!
PLSH
HUFF
HUFF
PLASH
THWUMP
ACK!

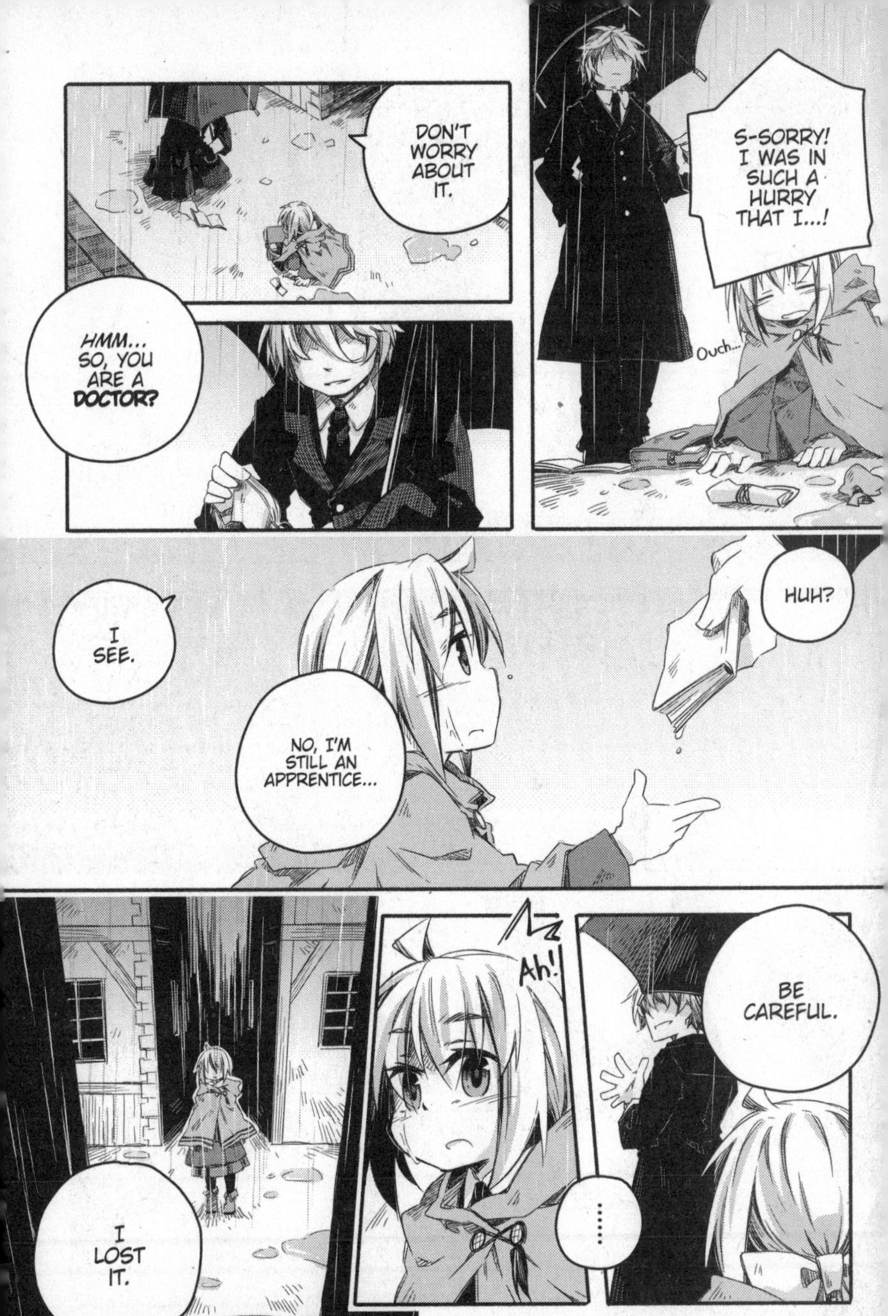
S-SORRY! I WAS IN SUCH A HURRY THAT I...!
Ouch...
DON'T WORRY ABOUT IT.
HMM... SO, YOU ARE A DOCTOR?
HUH?
NO, I'M STILL AN APPRENTICE...
I SEE.
BE CAREFUL.
......
Ah!
I LOST IT.

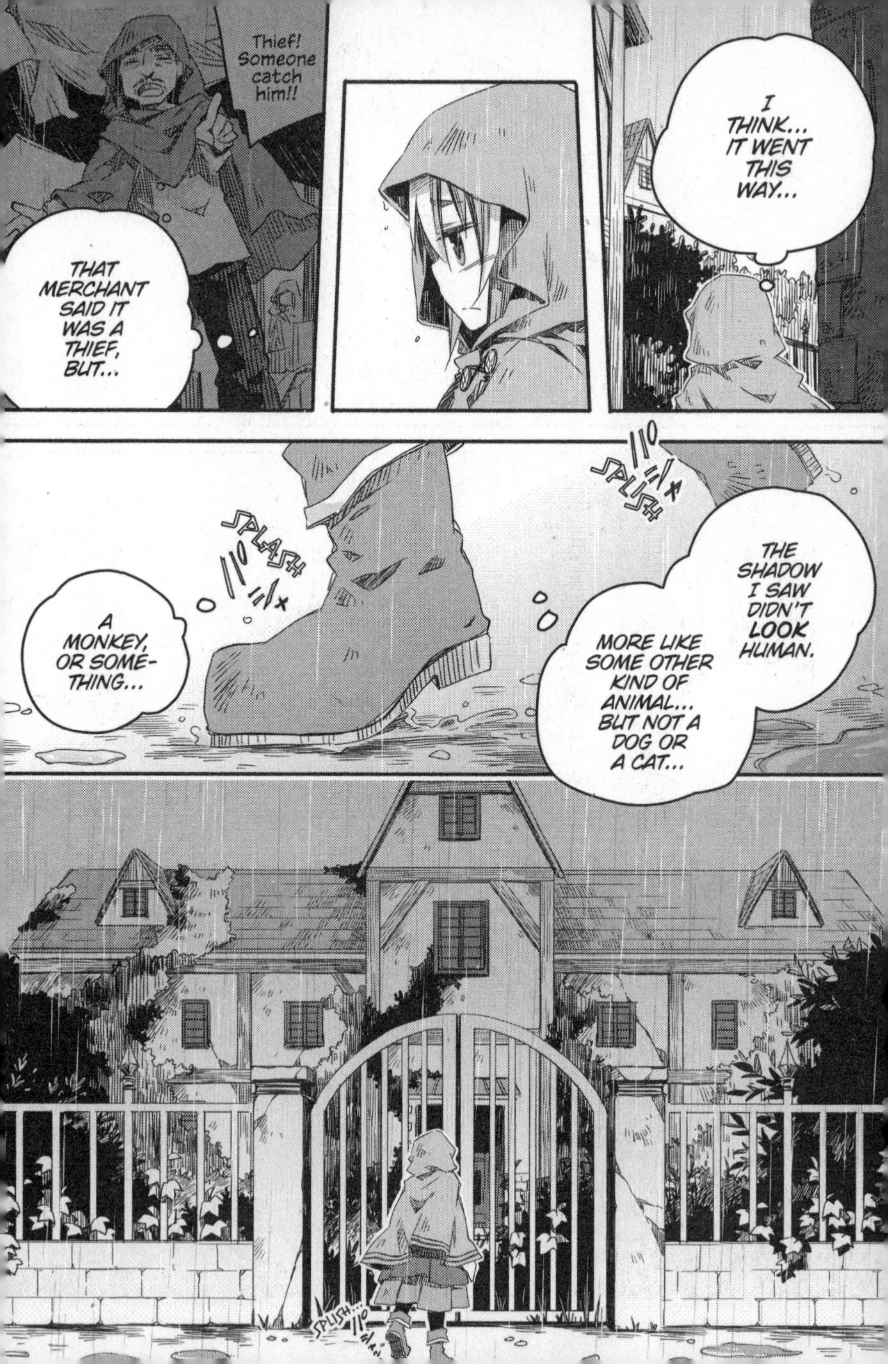
I THINK... IT WENT THIS WAY...
Thief! Someone catch him!!
THAT MERCHANT SAID IT WAS A THIEF, BUT...
SPLASH
THE SHADOW I SAW DIDN'T LOOK HUMAN.
MORE LIKE SOME OTHER KIND OF ANIMAL... BUT NOT A DOG OR A CAT...
SPLASH
A MONKEY, OR SOME-THING...
SPLISH...

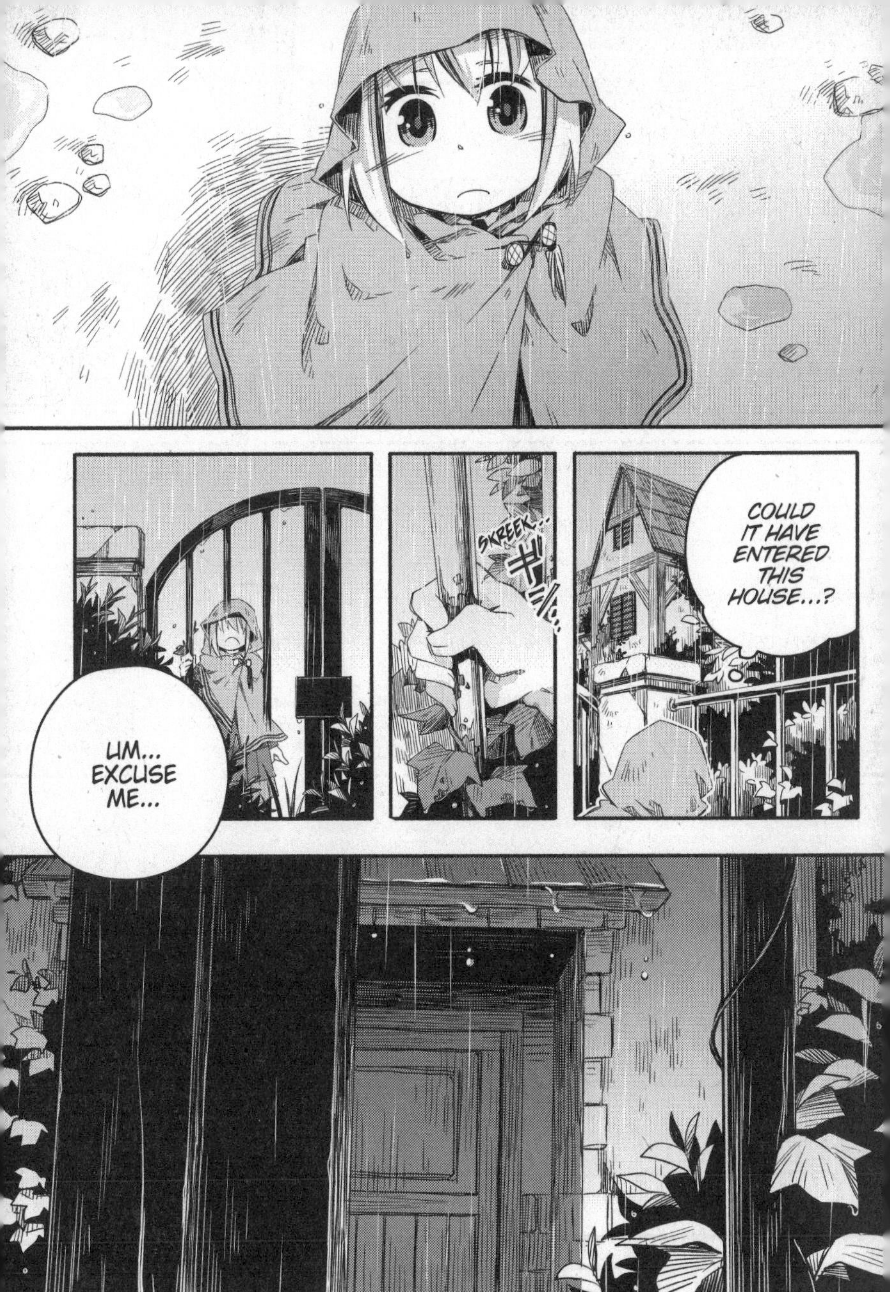
COULD IT HAVE ENTERED THIS HOUSE...?
SKREEK...
UM... EXCUSE ME...

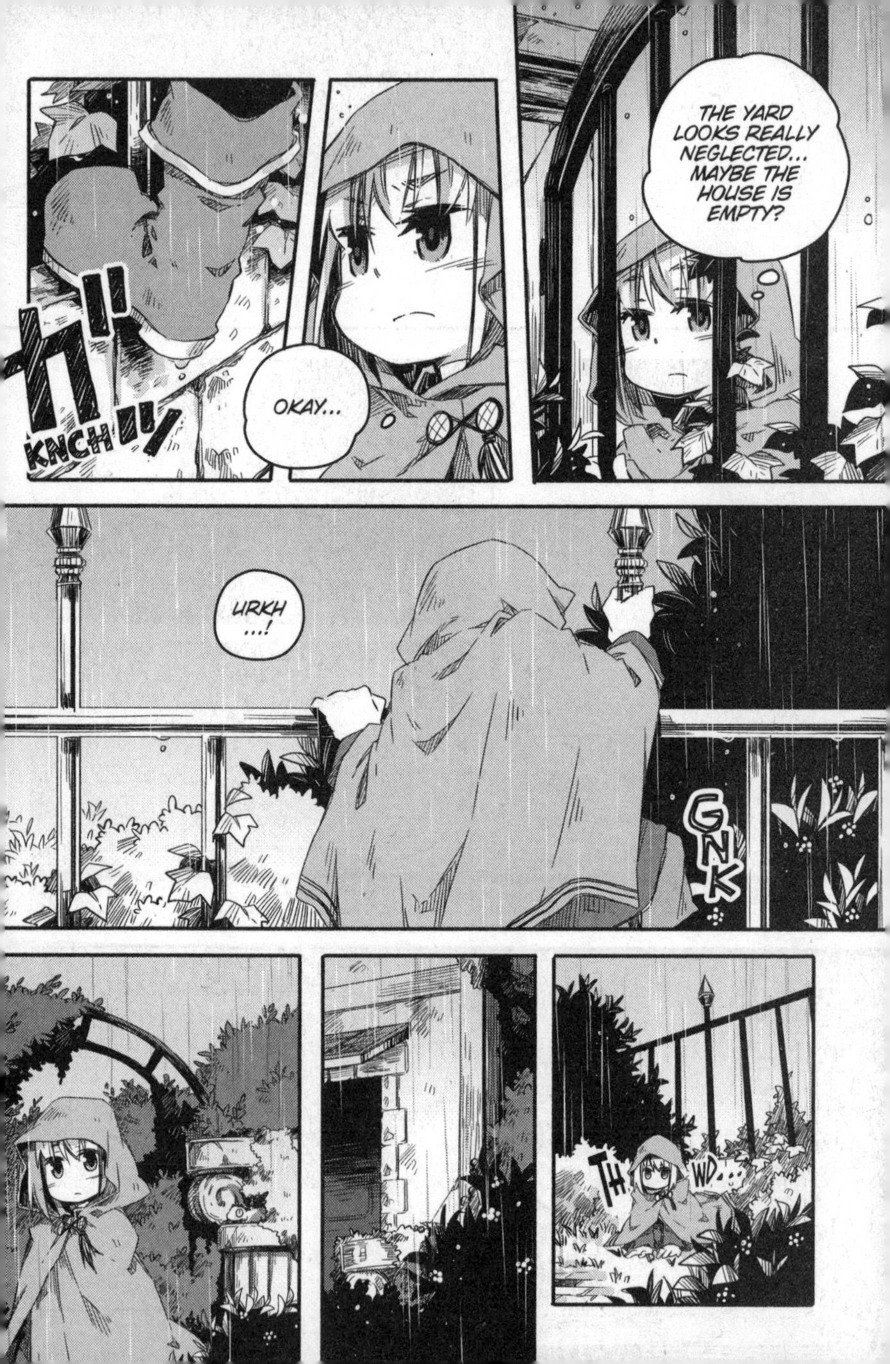
THE YARD LOOKS REALLY NEGLECTED... MAYBE THE HOUSE IS EMPTY?
OKAY...
KNCH
URKH ...!
GNK
THWD...

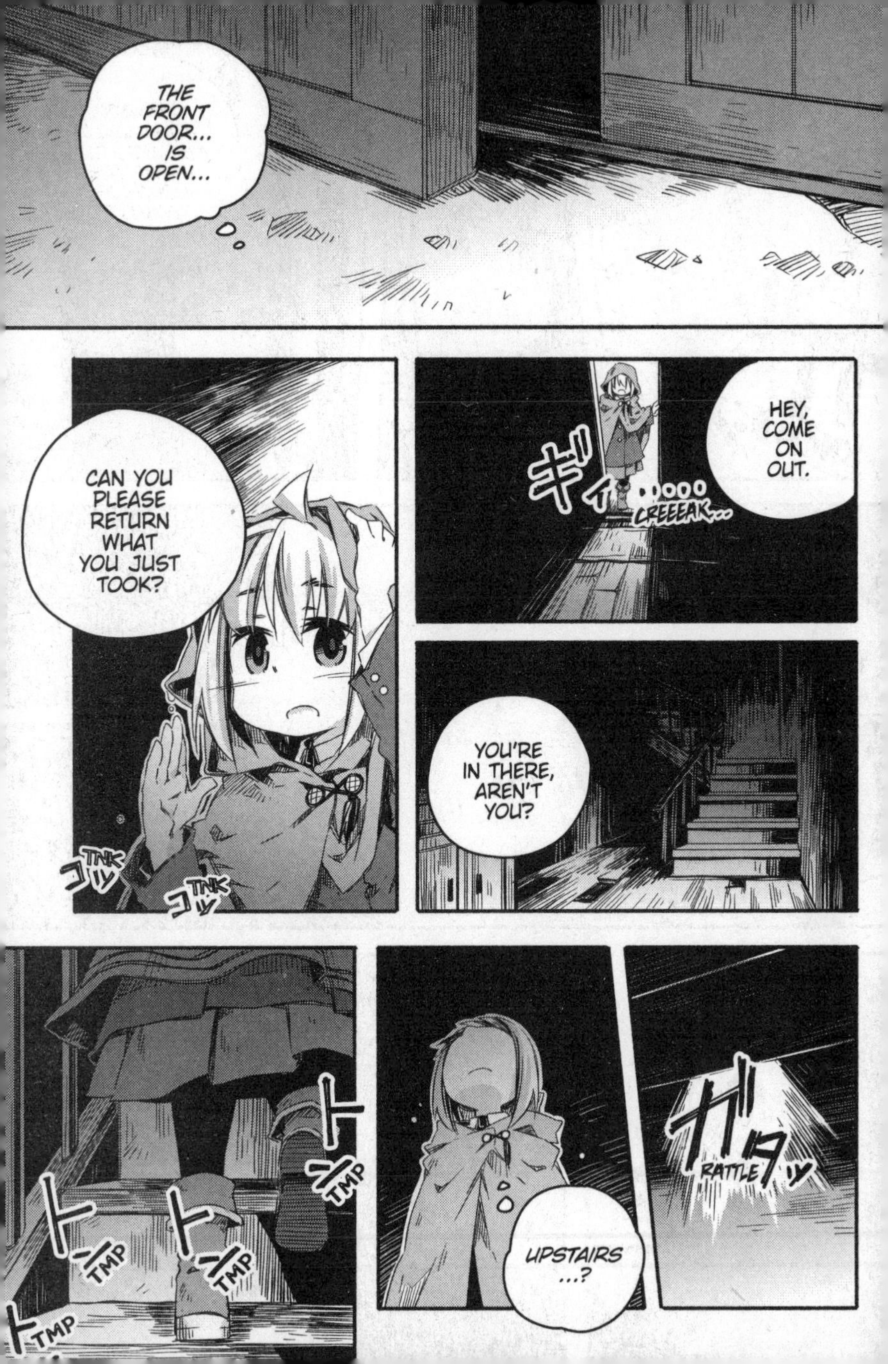
THE FRONT DOOR... IS OPEN...
ギィ
CREEEAK...
HEY, COME ON OUT.
YOU'RE IN THERE, AREN'T YOU?
CAN YOU PLEASE RETURN WHAT YOU JUST TOOK?
コツ
TNK
コツ
TNK
ガタッ
RATTLE
UPSTAIRS ...?
トッ
TMP
トッ
TMP
トッ
TMP
ト
TMP

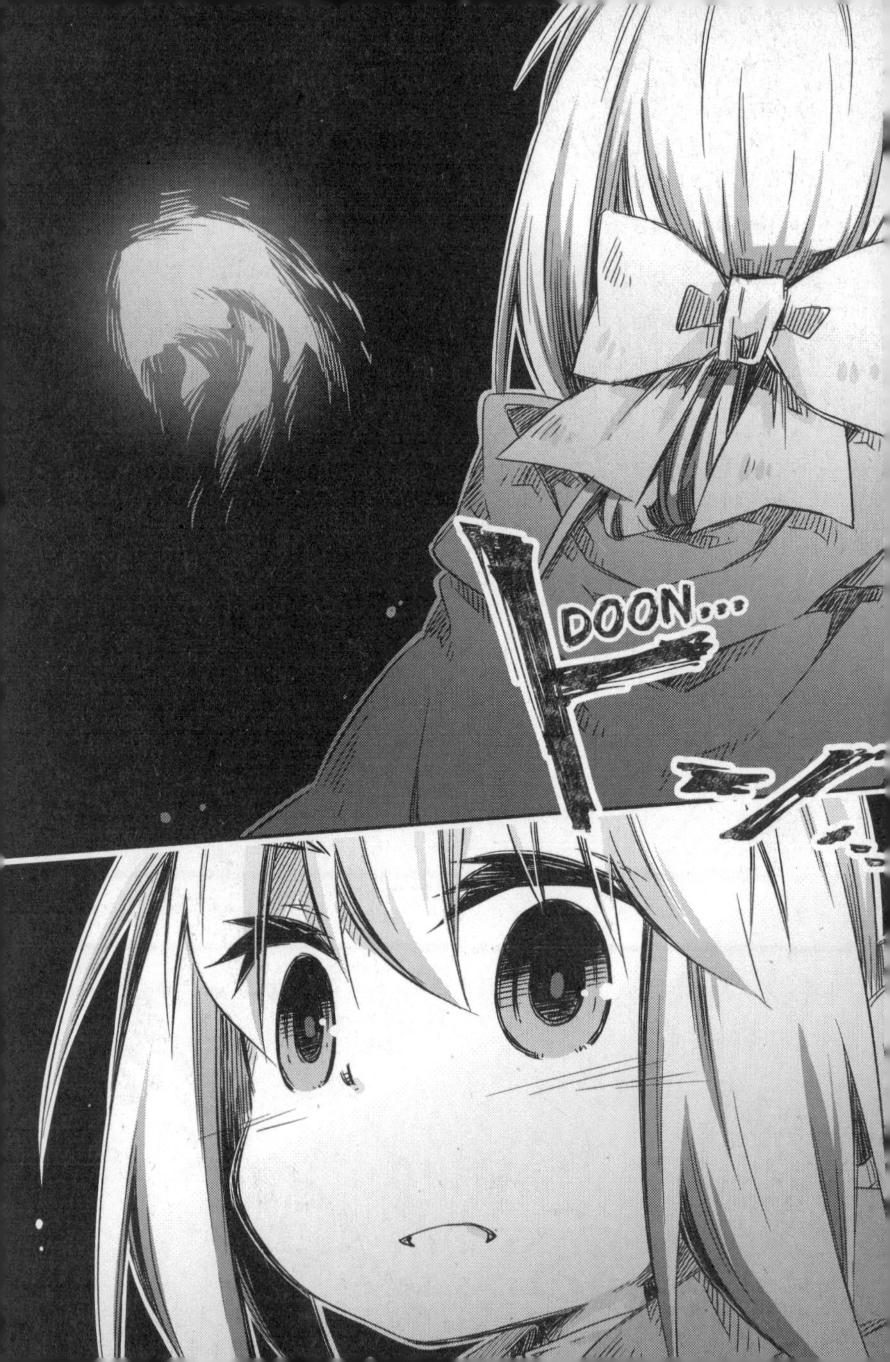
DOON...

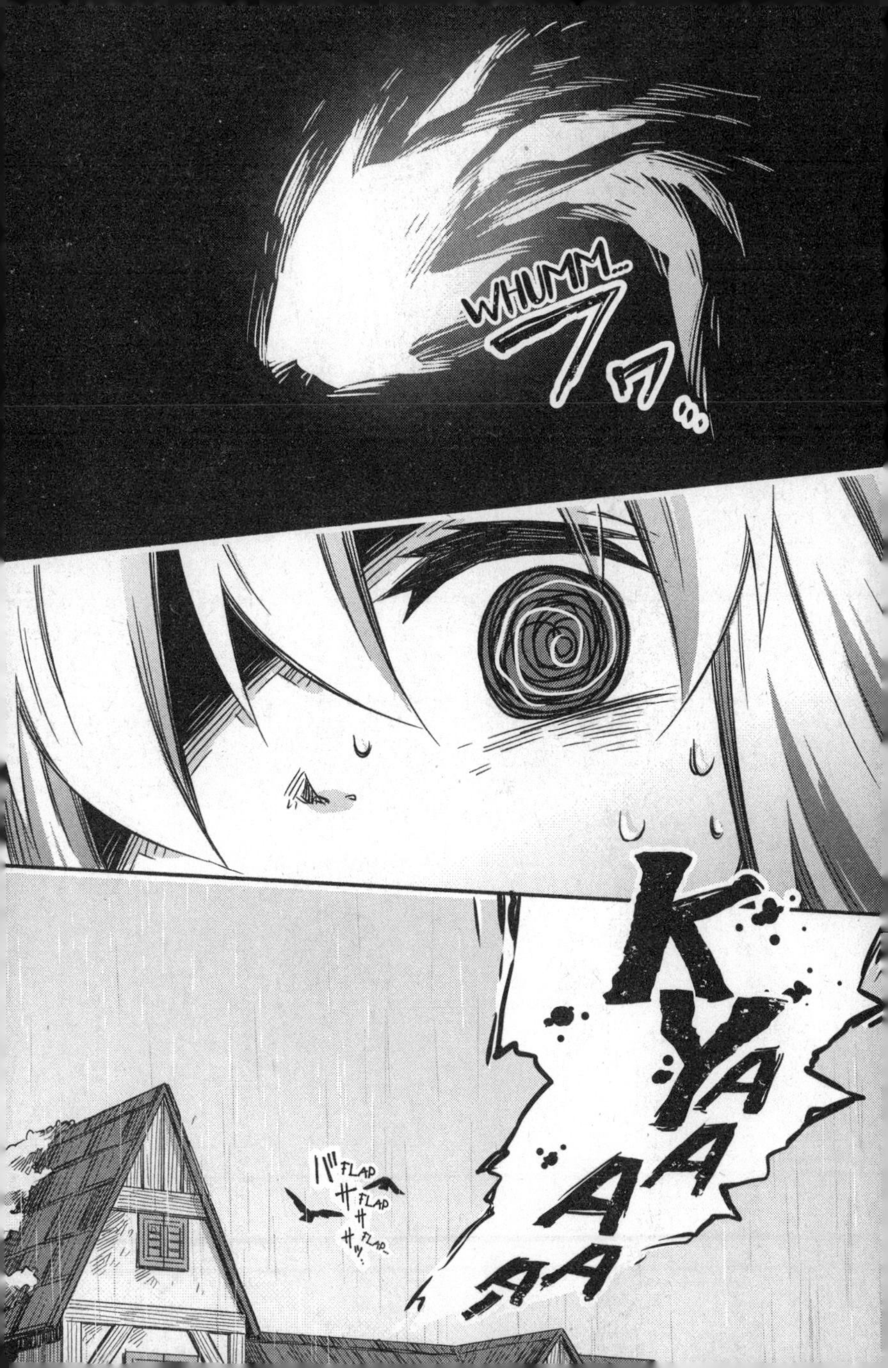
WHUMM...
KYAAAAA
FLAP FLAP FLAP

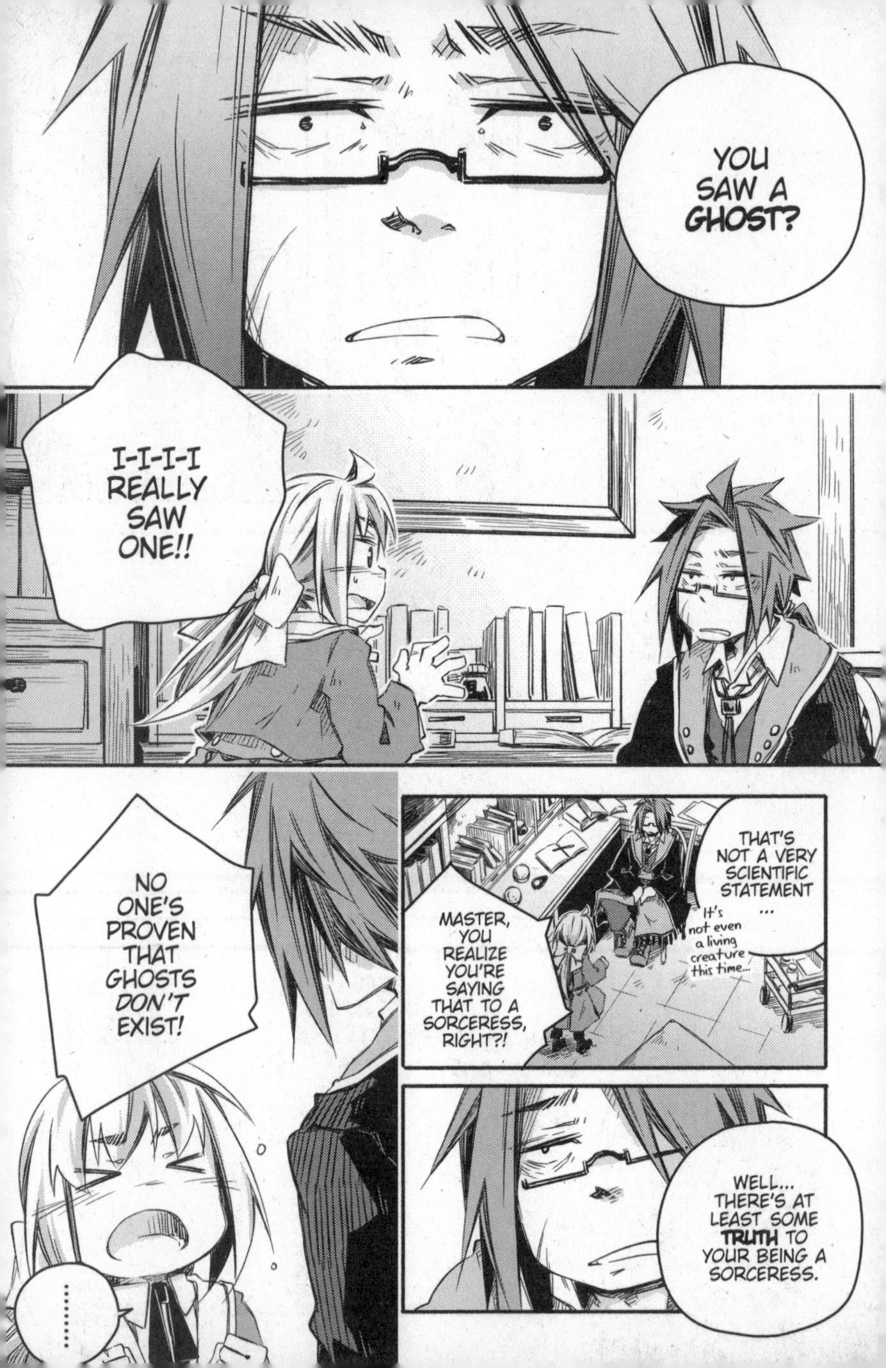
YOU SAW A GHOST?
I-I-I-I REALLY SAW ONE!!
THAT'S NOT A VERY SCIENTIFIC STATEMENT ...
It's not even a living creature this time...
MASTER, YOU REALIZE YOU'RE SAYING THAT TO A SORCERESS, RIGHT?!
WELL... THERE'S AT LEAST SOME TRUTH TO YOUR BEING A SORCERESS.
NO ONE'S PROVEN THAT GHOSTS DON'T EXIST!
......

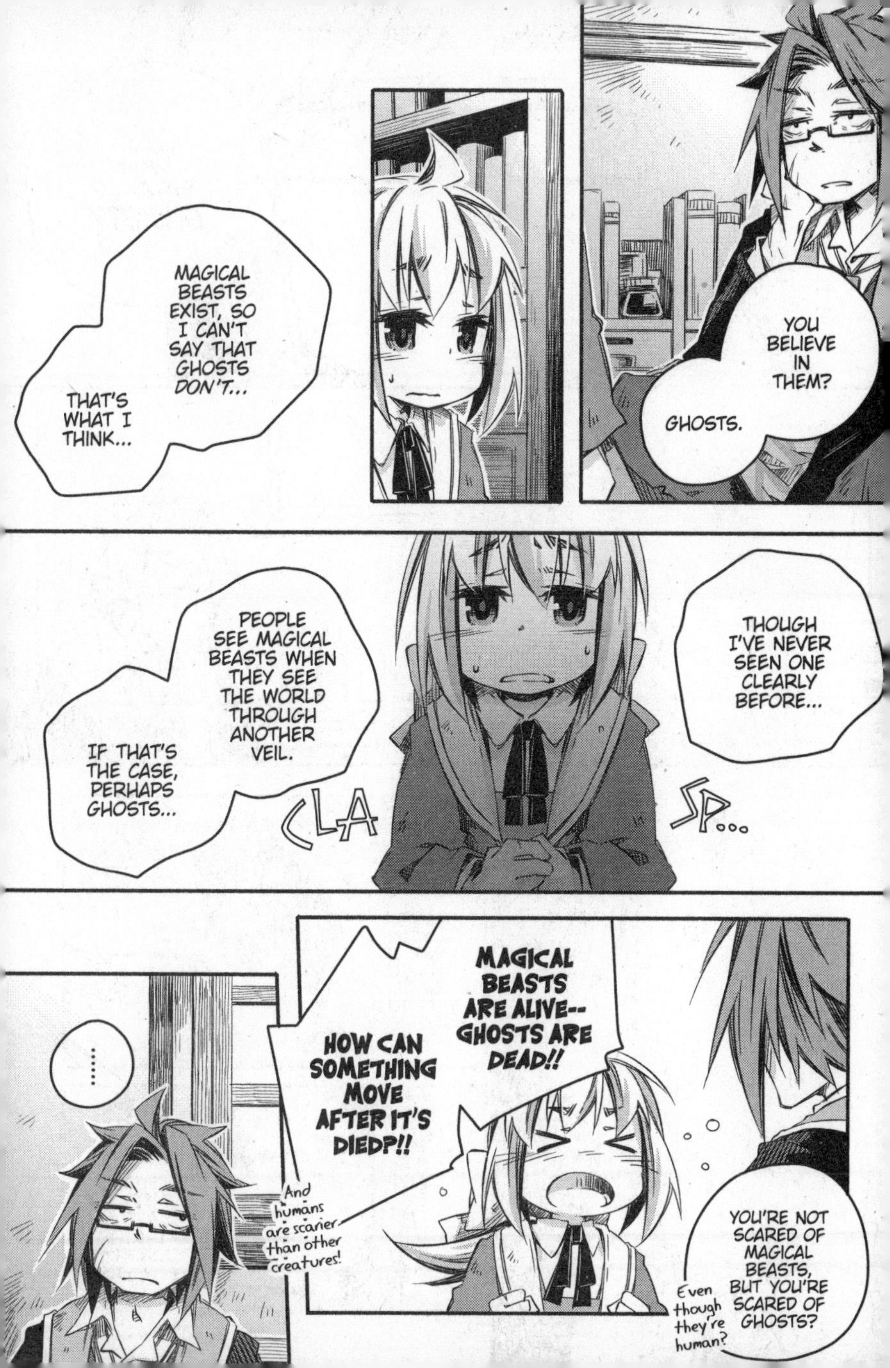
GHOSTS.
YOU BELIEVE IN THEM?
MAGICAL BEASTS EXIST, SO I CAN'T SAY THAT GHOSTS DON'T...
THAT'S WHAT I THINK...
THOUGH I'VE NEVER SEEN ONE CLEARLY BEFORE...
SP...
CLA
PEOPLE SEE MAGICAL BEASTS WHEN THEY SEE THE WORLD THROUGH ANOTHER VEIL.
IF THAT'S THE CASE, PERHAPS GHOSTS...
YOU'RE NOT SCARED OF MAGICAL BEASTS, BUT YOU'RE SCARED OF GHOSTS?
Even though they're human?
MAGICAL BEASTS ARE ALIVE-- GHOSTS ARE DEAD!!
HOW CAN SOMETHING MOVE AFTER IT'S DIED?!!
And humans are scarier than other creatures!
......

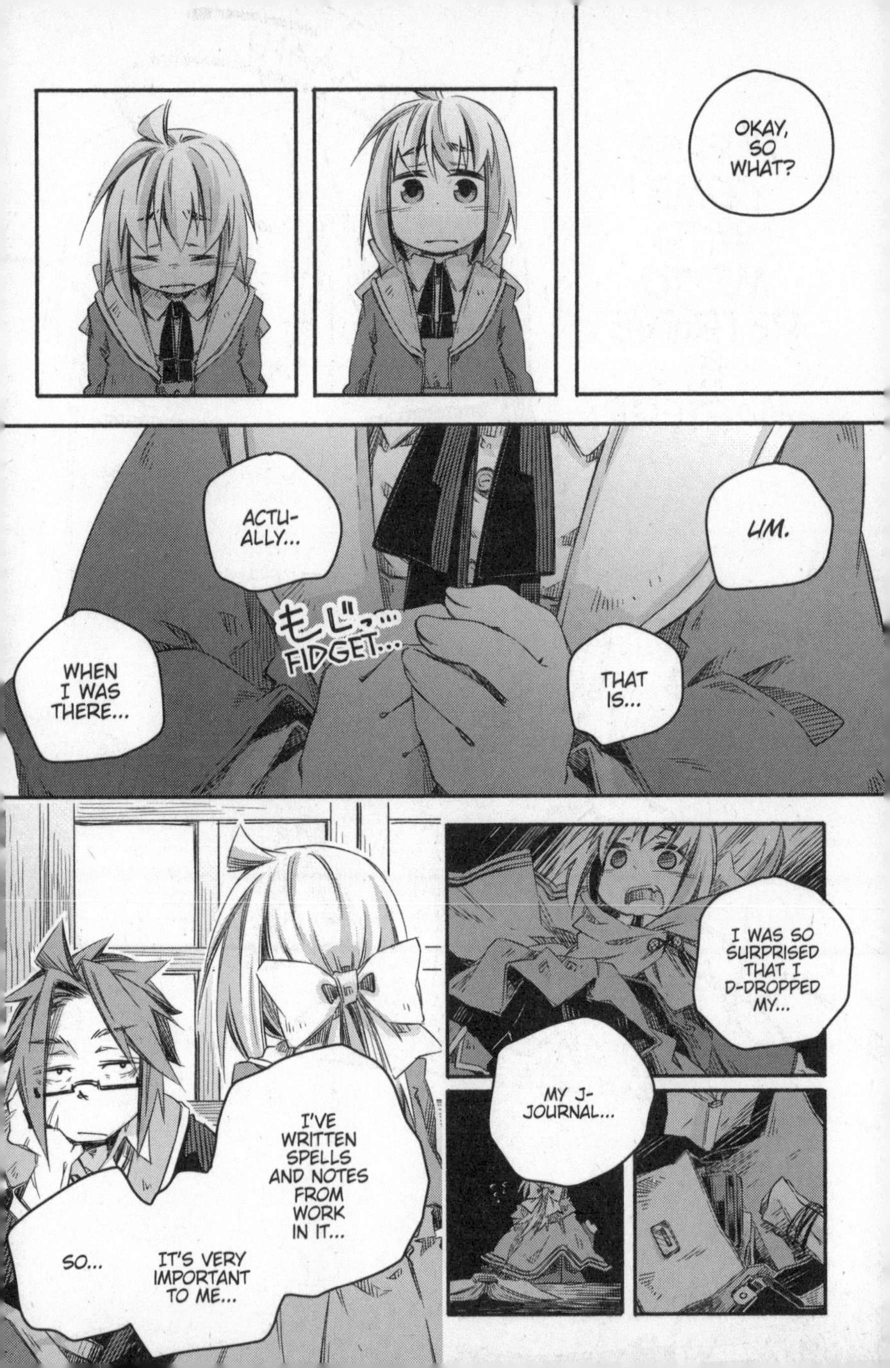
OKAY, SO WHAT?
UM.
ACTU-ALLY...
THAT IS...
もじっ… FIDGET...
WHEN I WAS THERE...
I WAS SO SURPRISED THAT I D-DROPPED MY...
MY J-JOURNAL...
I'VE WRITTEN SPELLS AND NOTES FROM WORK IN IT...
IT'S VERY IMPORTANT TO ME...
SO...

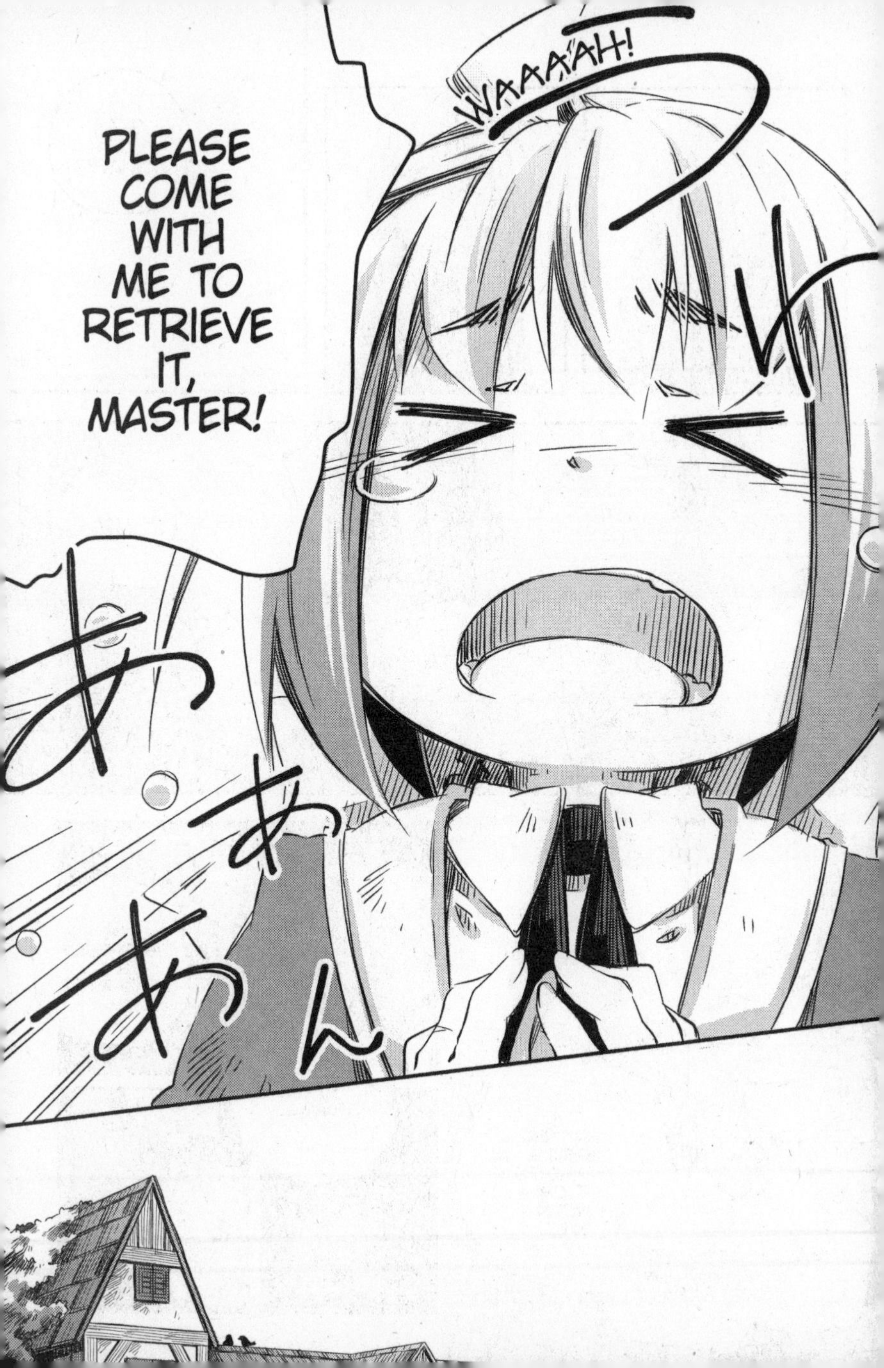
WAAAAH!
PLEASE COME WITH ME TO RETRIEVE IT, MASTER!
あああん

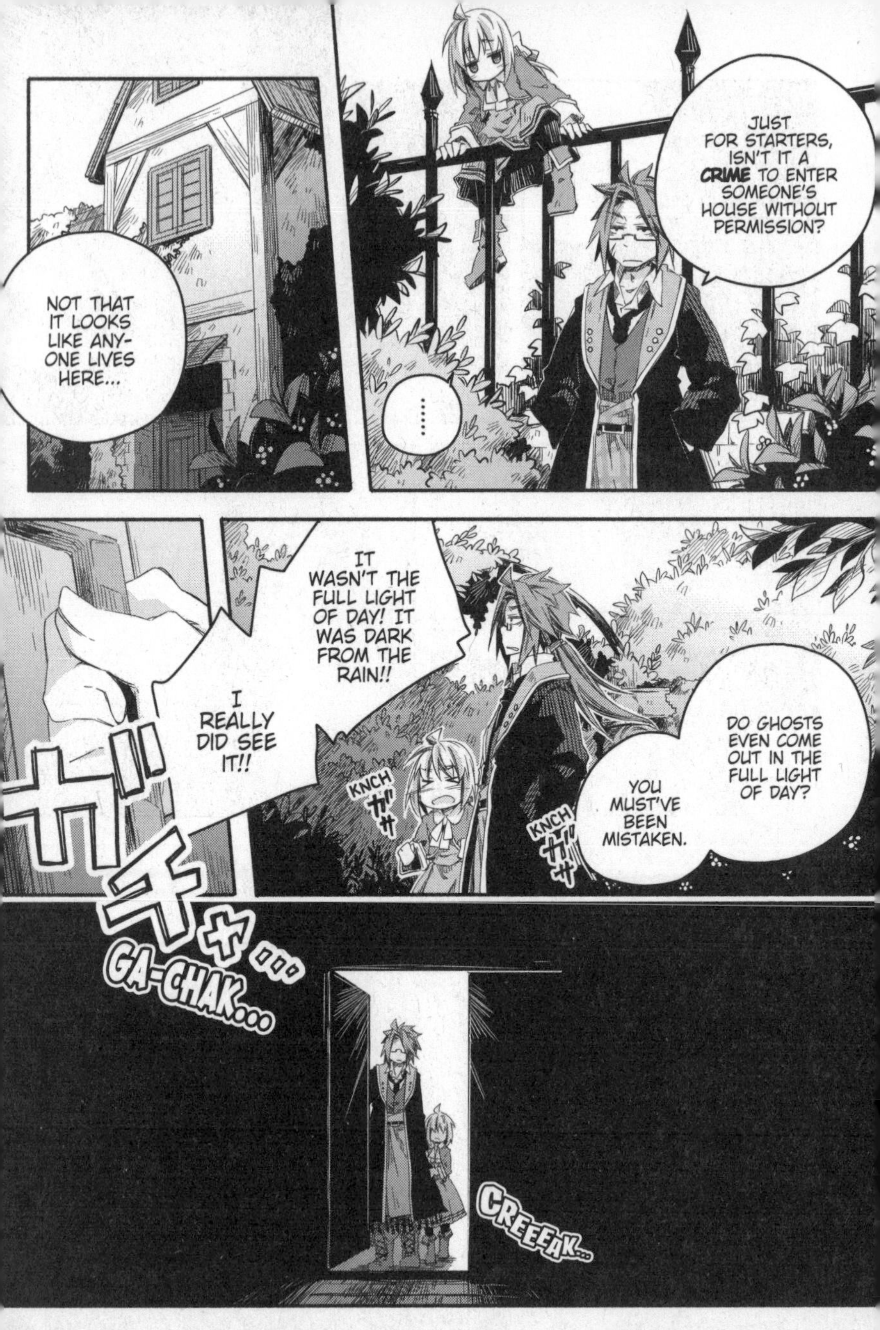
JUST FOR STARTERS, ISN'T IT A **CRIME** TO ENTER SOMEONE'S HOUSE WITHOUT PERMISSION?
......
NOT THAT IT LOOKS LIKE ANY-ONE LIVES HERE...
DO GHOSTS EVEN COME OUT IN THE FULL LIGHT OF DAY?
YOU MUST'VE BEEN MISTAKEN.
KNCH ガサ
IT WASN'T THE FULL LIGHT OF DAY! IT WAS DARK FROM THE RAIN!!
I REALLY DID SEE IT!!
KNCH ガサ
ガチャ...
GA-CHAK...
CREEEAK...

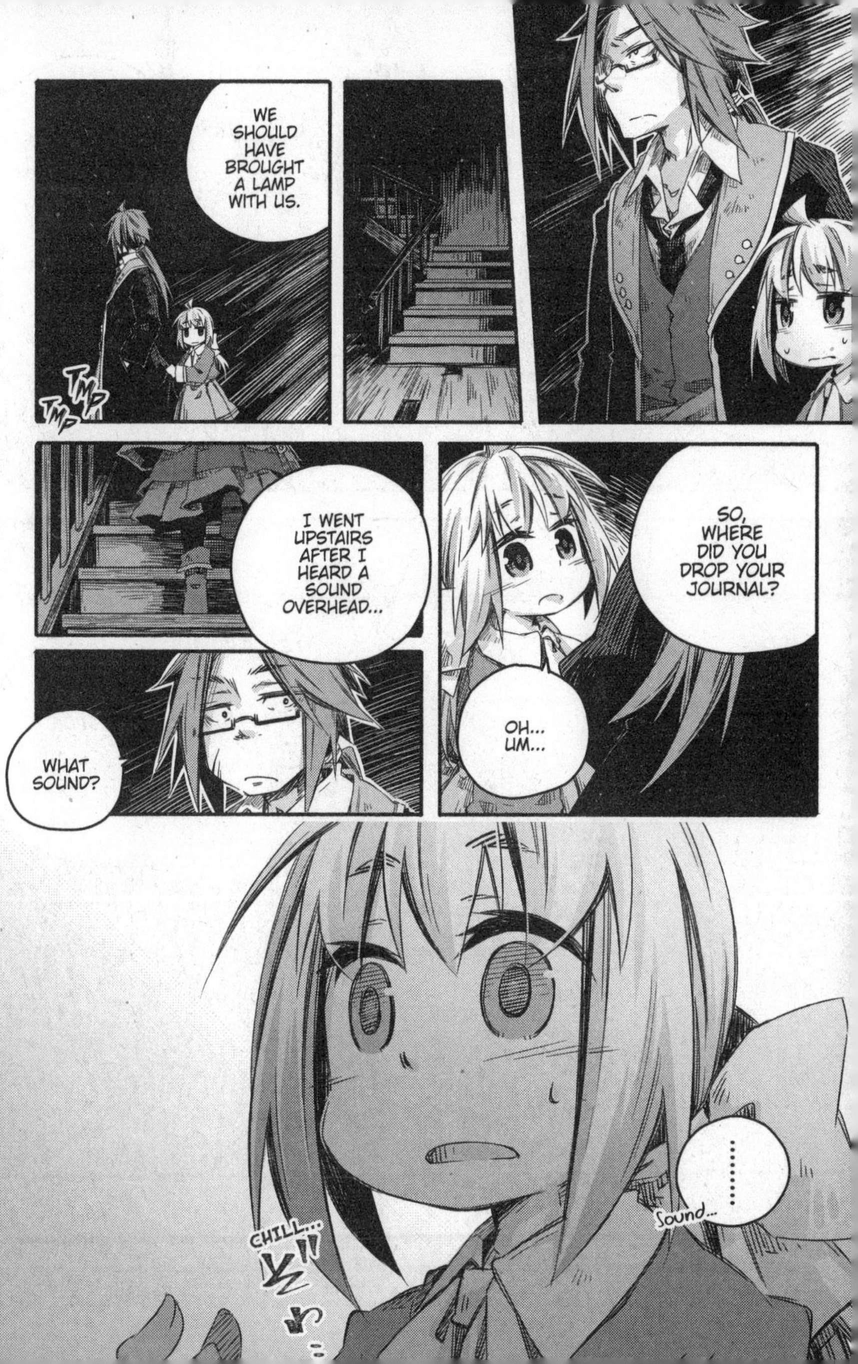
WE SHOULD HAVE BROUGHT A LAMP WITH US.
TMP TMP
SO, WHERE DID YOU DROP YOUR JOURNAL?
OH... UM...
I WENT UPSTAIRS AFTER I HEARD A SOUND OVERHEAD...
WHAT SOUND?
......
Sound...
CHILL...

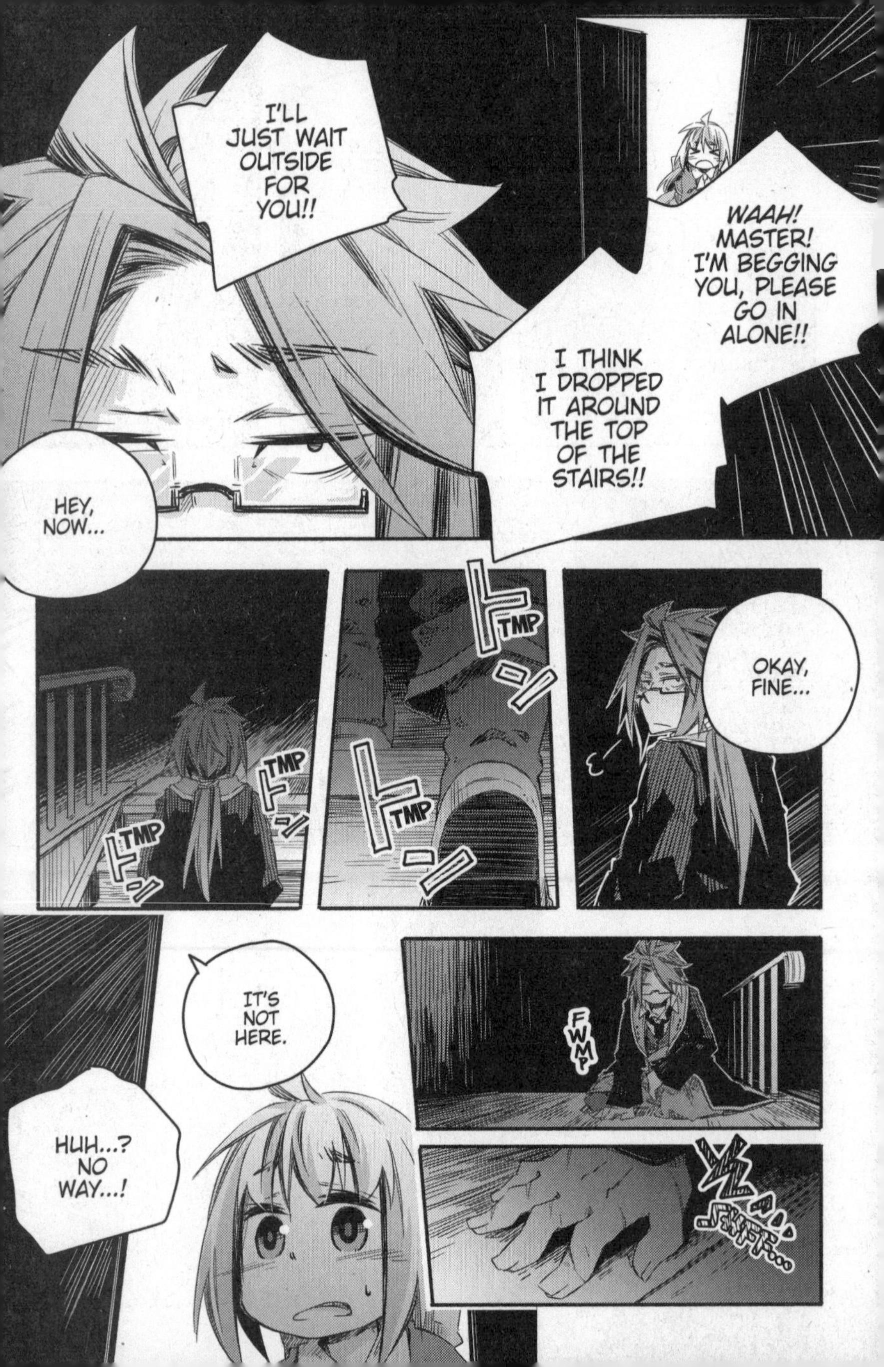
WAAH! MASTER! I'M BEGGING YOU, PLEASE GO IN ALONE!!
I THINK I DROPPED IT AROUND THE TOP OF THE STAIRS!!
I'LL JUST WAIT OUTSIDE FOR YOU!!
HEY, NOW...
OKAY, FINE...
TMP
TMP
TMP
TMP
FWMP
IT'S NOT HERE.
HUH...? NO WAY...!

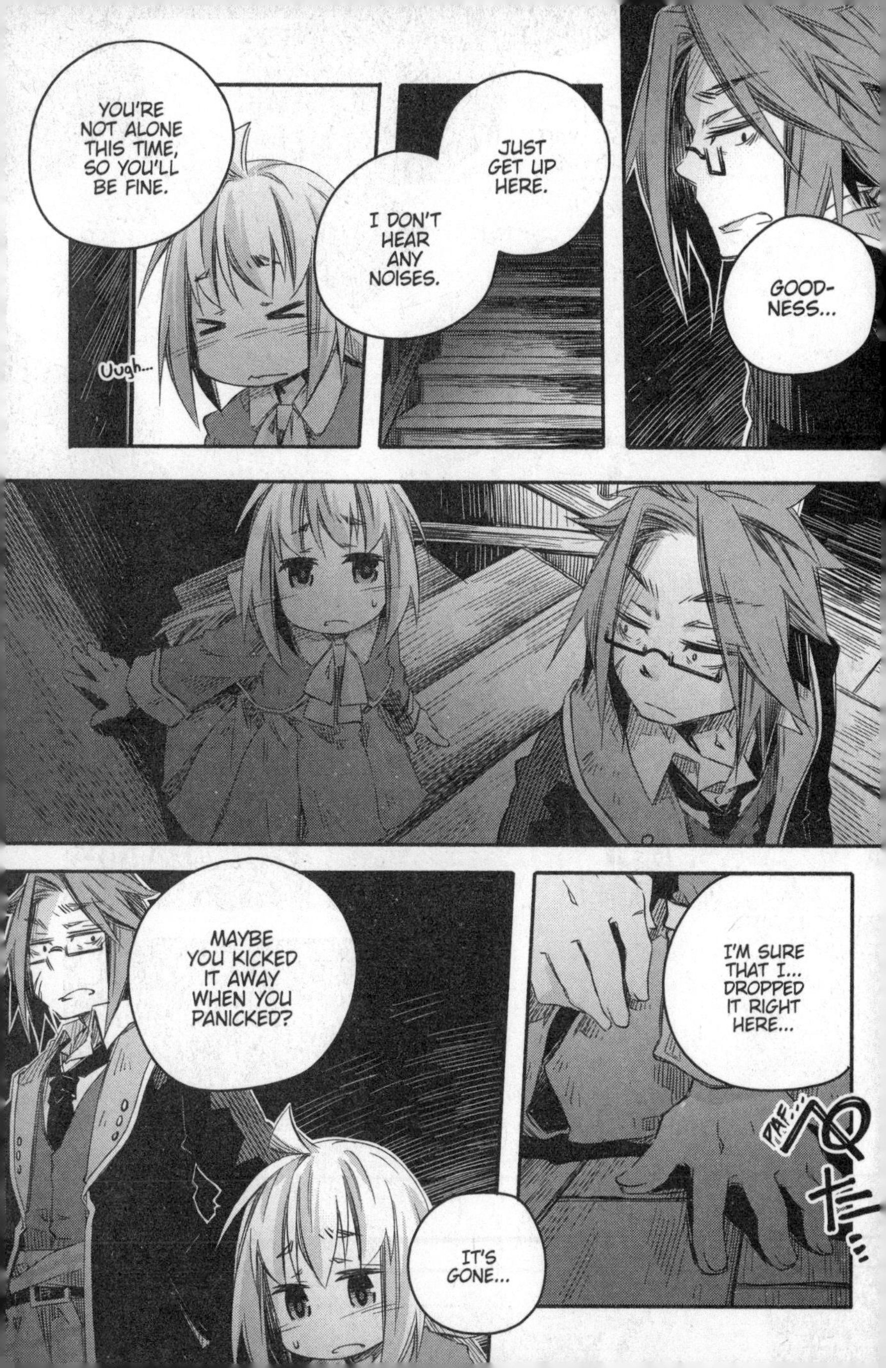
GOODNESS...
JUST GET UP HERE.
I DON'T HEAR ANY NOISES.
YOU'RE NOT ALONE THIS TIME, SO YOU'LL BE FINE.
Uugh...
I'M SURE THAT I... DROPPED IT RIGHT HERE...
PAF...
MAYBE YOU KICKED IT AWAY WHEN YOU PANICKED?
IT'S GONE...

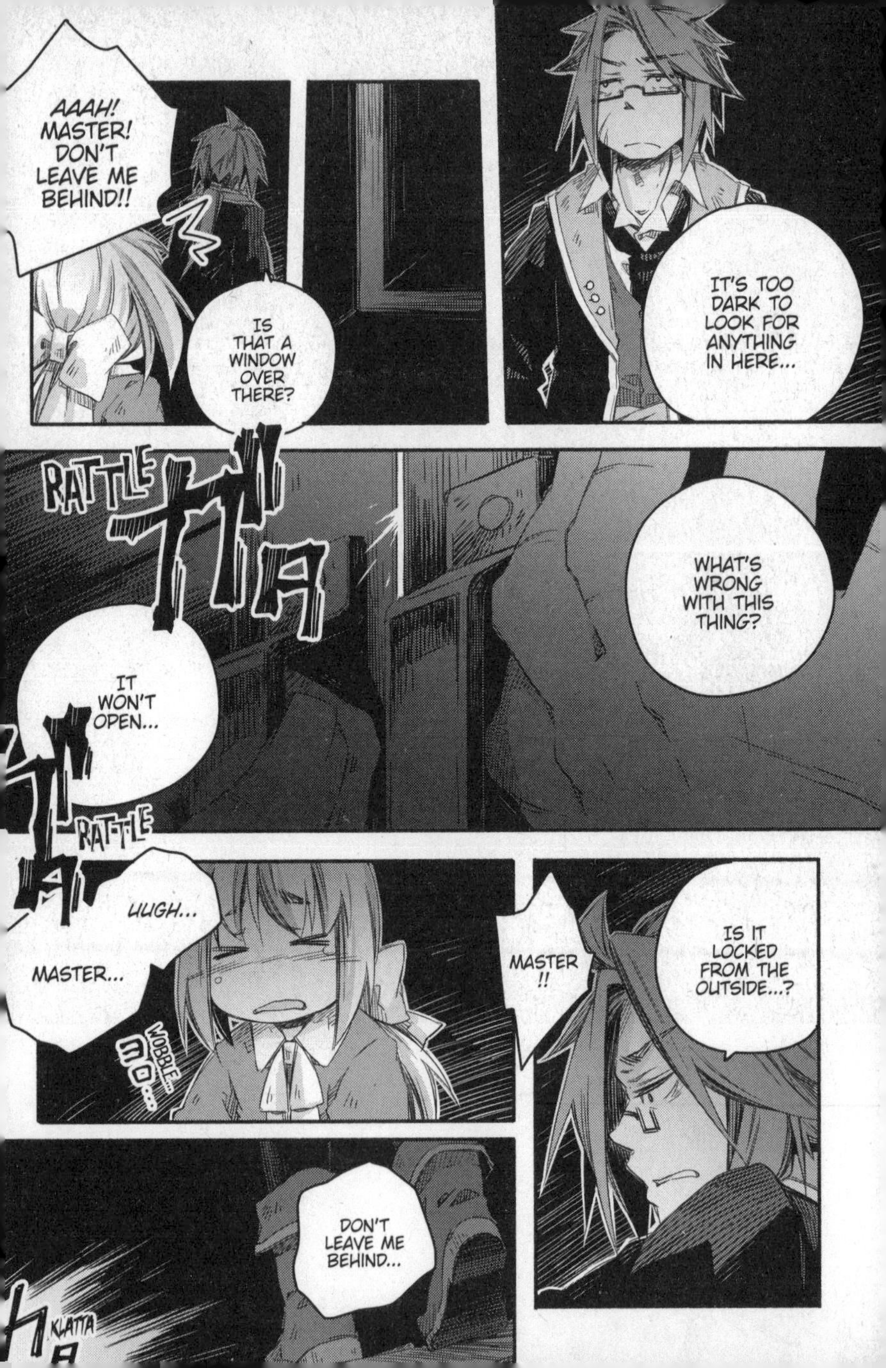

IT'S TOO DARK TO LOOK FOR ANYTHING IN HERE...
IS THAT A WINDOW OVER THERE?
AAAH! MASTER! DON'T LEAVE ME BEHIND!!
RATTLE
WHAT'S WRONG WITH THIS THING?
IT WON'T OPEN...
RATTLE
IS IT LOCKED FROM THE OUTSIDE...?
MASTER !!
UUGH...
MASTER...
WOBBLE...
DON'T LEAVE ME BEHIND...
KLATTA

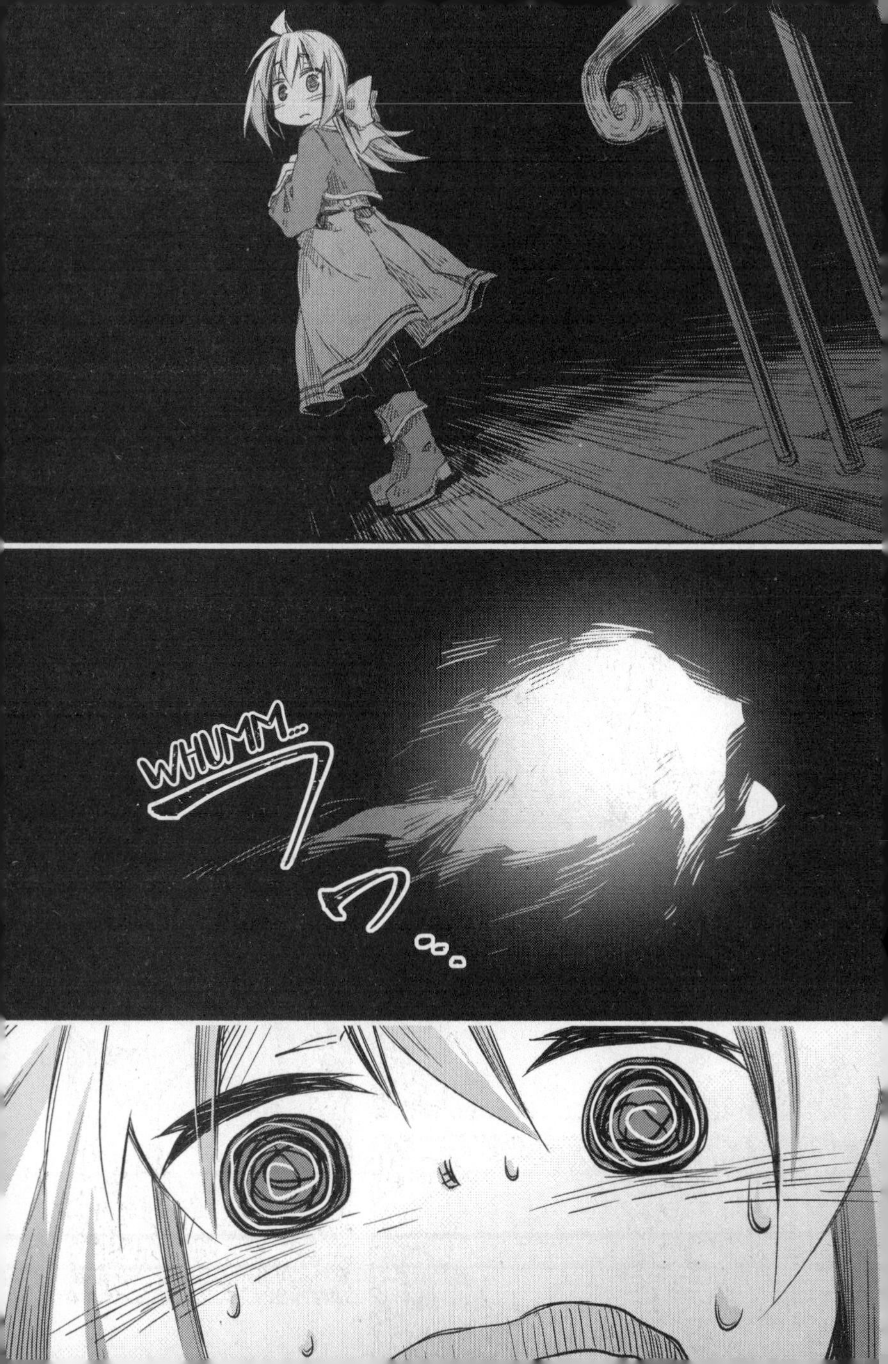
WHUMM...

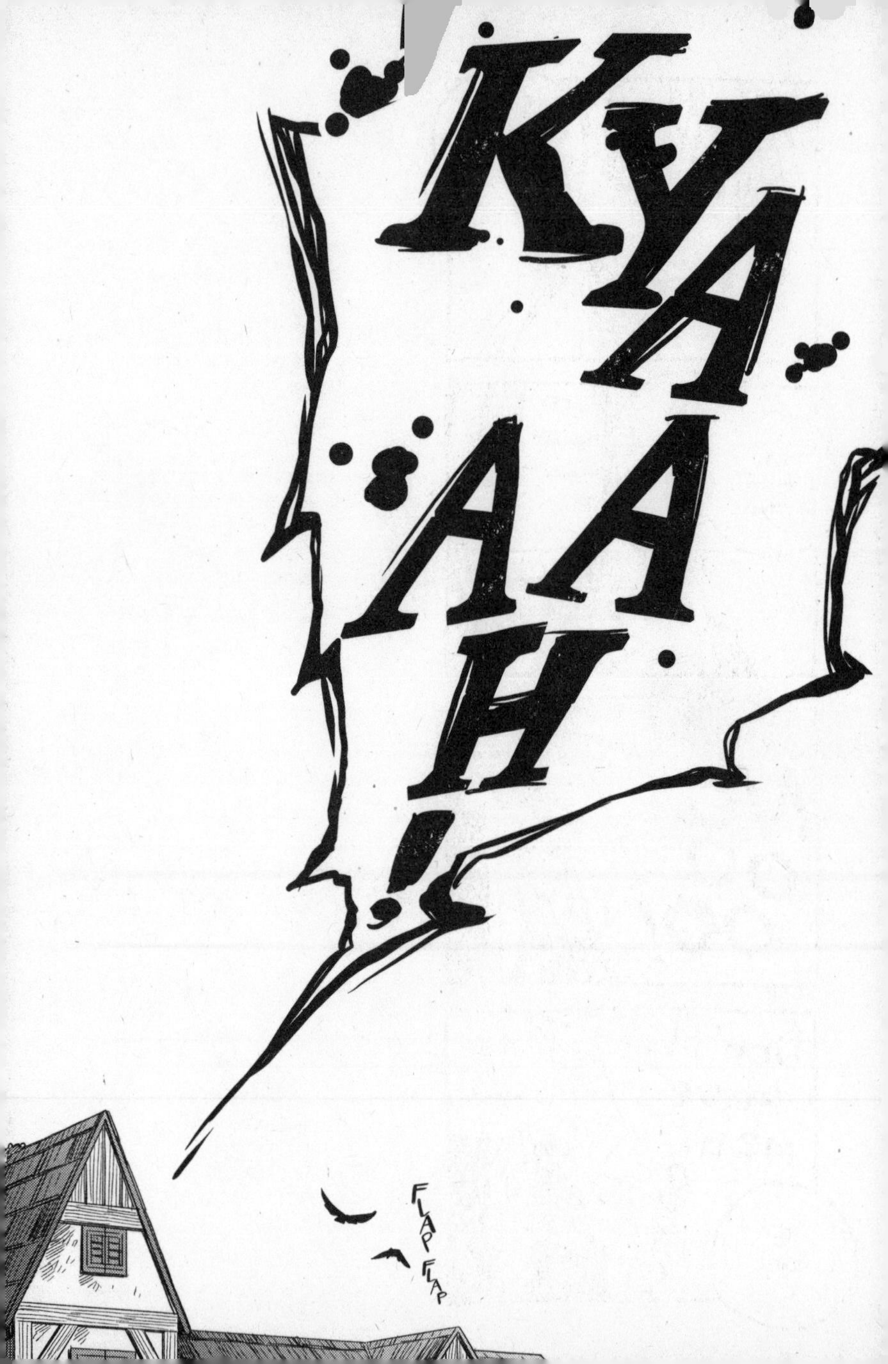
KYAAAAH!!
FLAP FLAP

But... there really was...?
You say that...
but I didn't see anything...
I'll go in again.
NOOOOOO!
I'll go in by myself.
Don't leave me alooooone!
So noisy.

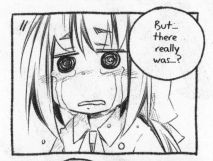

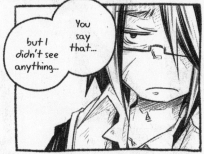

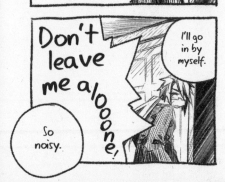

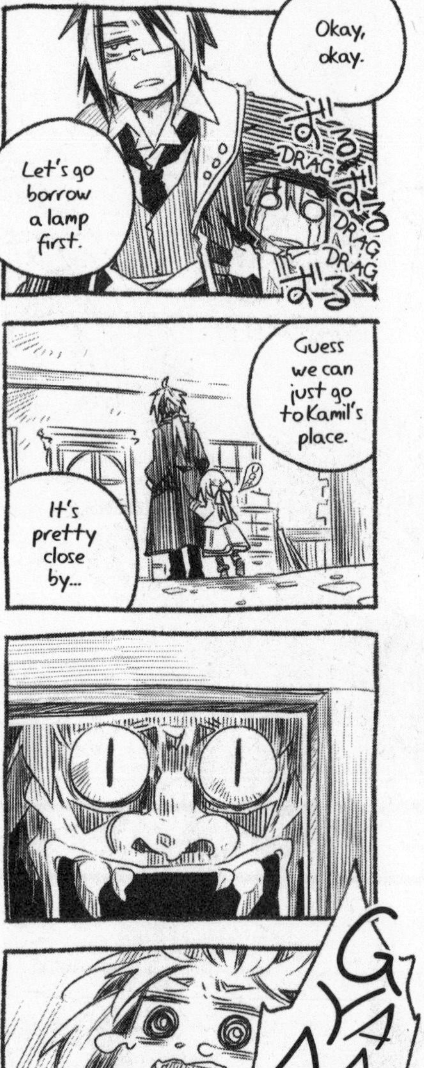

Okay, okay.
ずる DRAG ずる DRAG DRAG ずる
Let's go borrow a lamp first.
Guess we can just go to Kamil's place.
It's pretty close by...
GYAAAAAH!
I told you already. You're being too noisy.

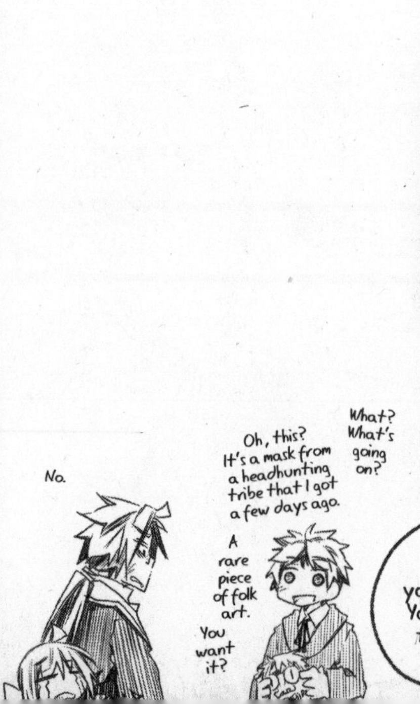

What? What's going on?
Oh, this? It's a mask from a headhunting tribe that I got a few days ago.
A rare piece of folk art.
You want it?
No.

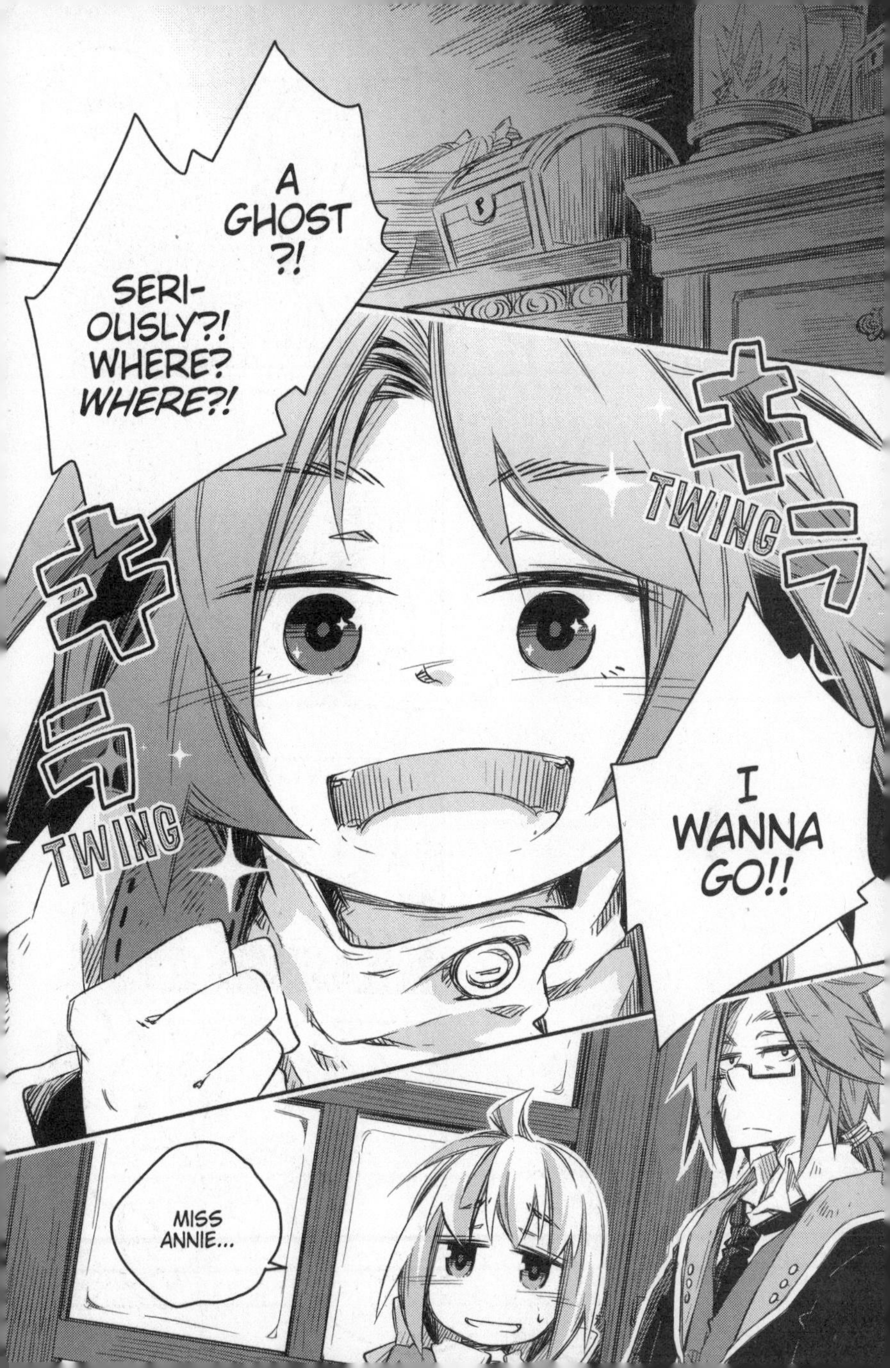
A GHOST ?!
SERI-OUSLY?! WHERE? WHERE?!
TWING
TWING
I WANNA GO!!
MISS ANNIE...

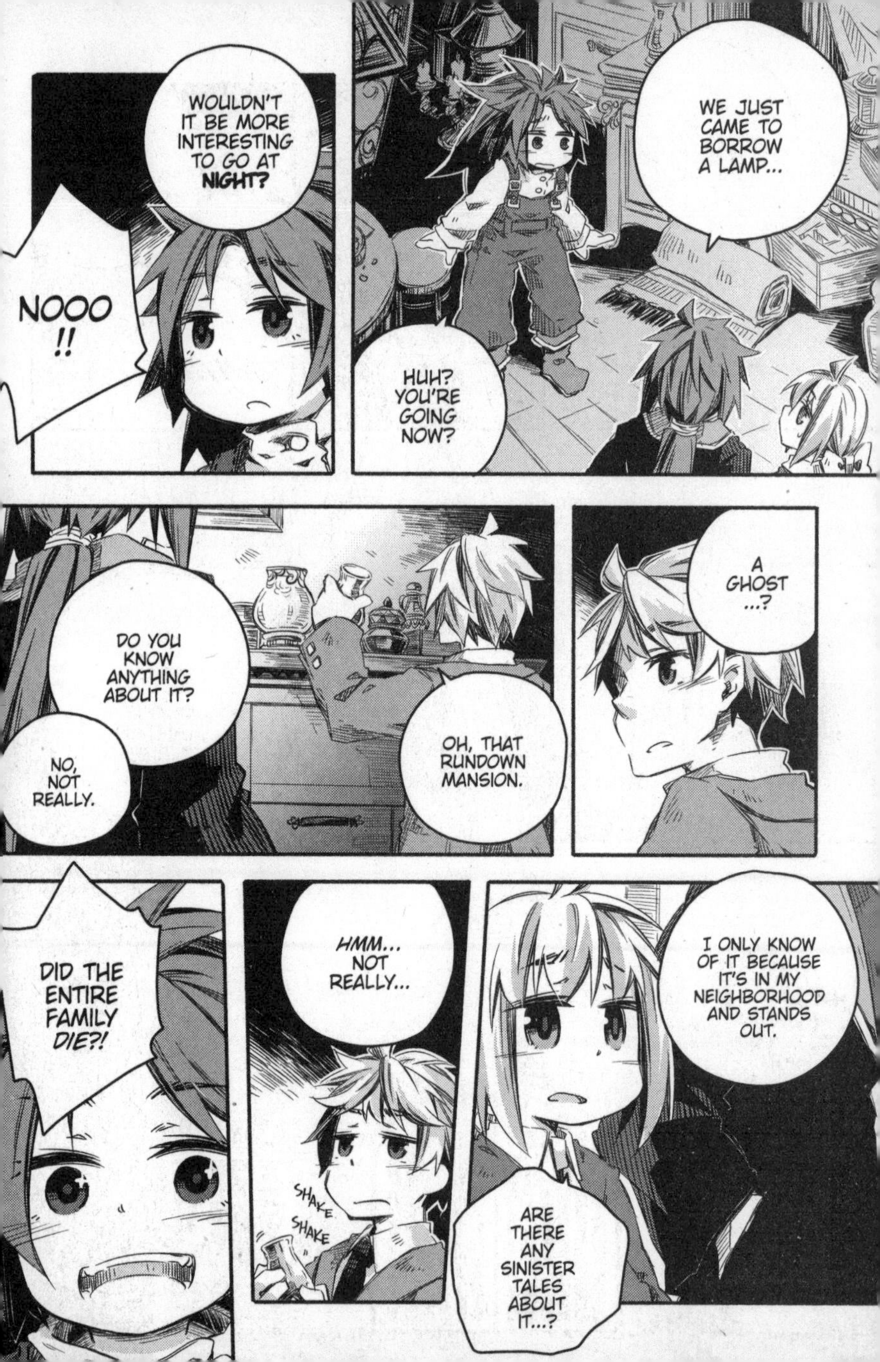
WE JUST CAME TO BORROW A LAMP...
HUH? YOU'RE GOING NOW?
WOULDN'T IT BE MORE INTERESTING TO GO AT **NIGHT?**
NOOO!!
A GHOST ...?
OH, THAT RUNDOWN MANSION.
DO YOU KNOW ANYTHING ABOUT IT?
NO, NOT REALLY.
I ONLY KNOW OF IT BECAUSE IT'S IN MY NEIGHBORHOOD AND STANDS OUT.
ARE THERE ANY SINISTER TALES ABOUT IT...?
HMM... NOT REALLY...
SHAKE
SHAKE
DID THE ENTIRE FAMILY *DIE?!*

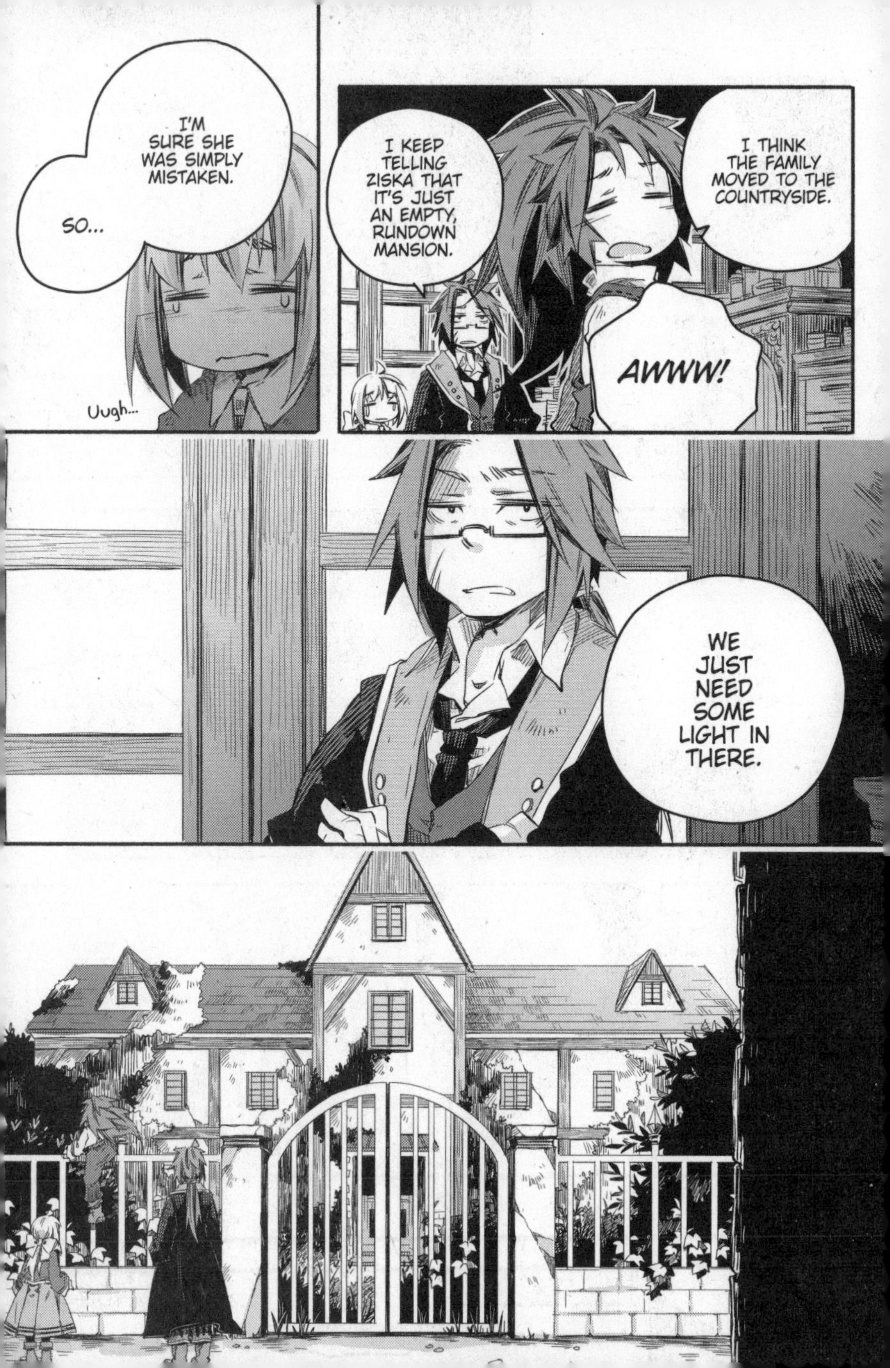
I THINK THE FAMILY MOVED TO THE COUNTRYSIDE.
I KEEP TELLING ZISKA THAT IT'S JUST AN EMPTY, RUNDOWN MANSION.
AWWW!
I'M SURE SHE WAS SIMPLY MISTAKEN.
SO...
Uugh...
WE JUST NEED SOME LIGHT IN THERE.

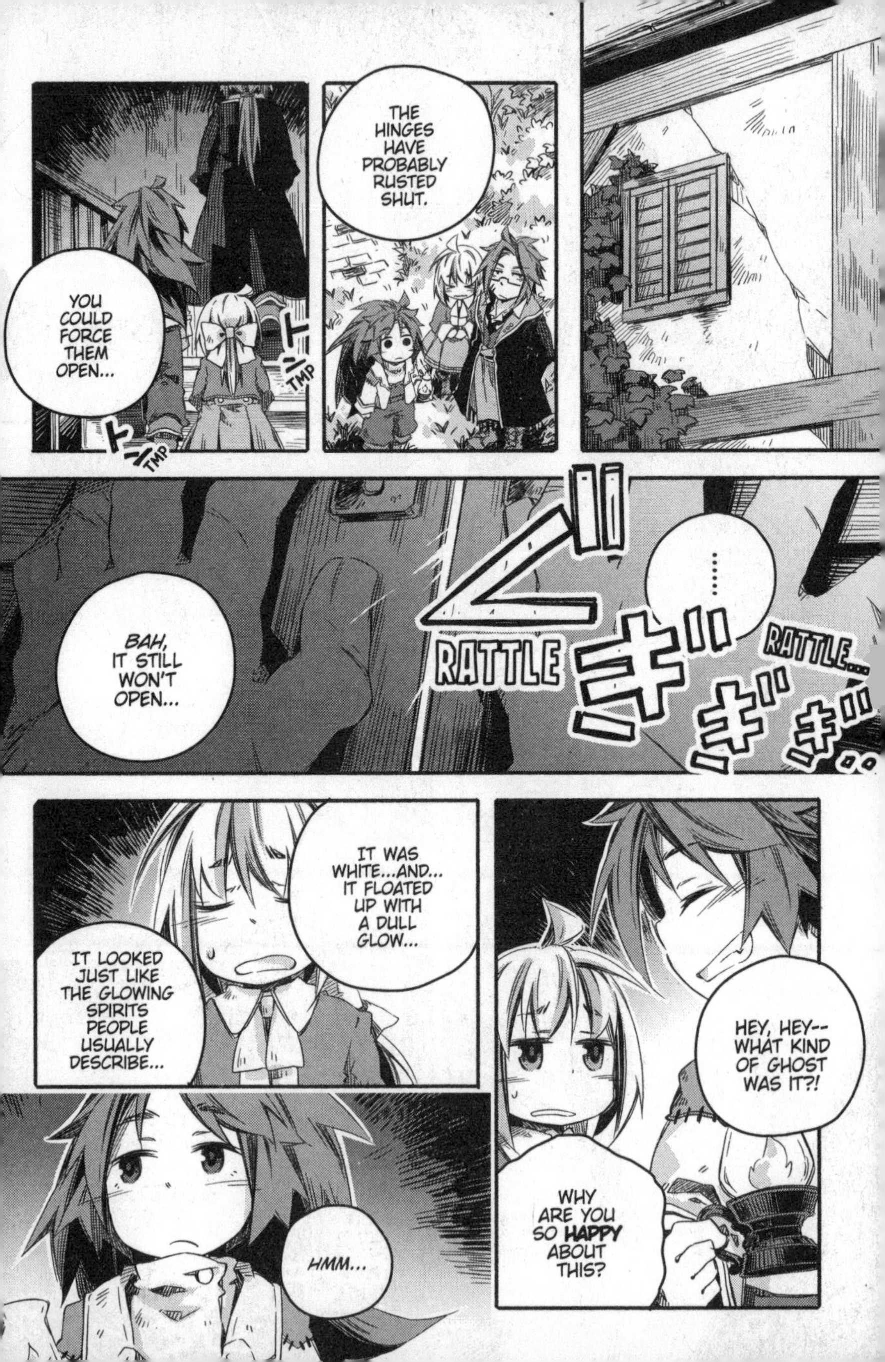
THE HINGES HAVE PROBABLY RUSTED SHUT.
YOU COULD FORCE THEM OPEN...
TMP
TMP
......
RATTLE...
RATTLE
BAH, IT STILL WON'T OPEN...
HEY, HEY--WHAT KIND OF GHOST WAS IT?!
WHY ARE YOU SO **HAPPY** ABOUT THIS?
IT WAS WHITE...AND... IT FLOATED UP WITH A DULL GLOW...
IT LOOKED JUST LIKE THE GLOWING SPIRITS PEOPLE USUALLY DESCRIBE...
HMM...

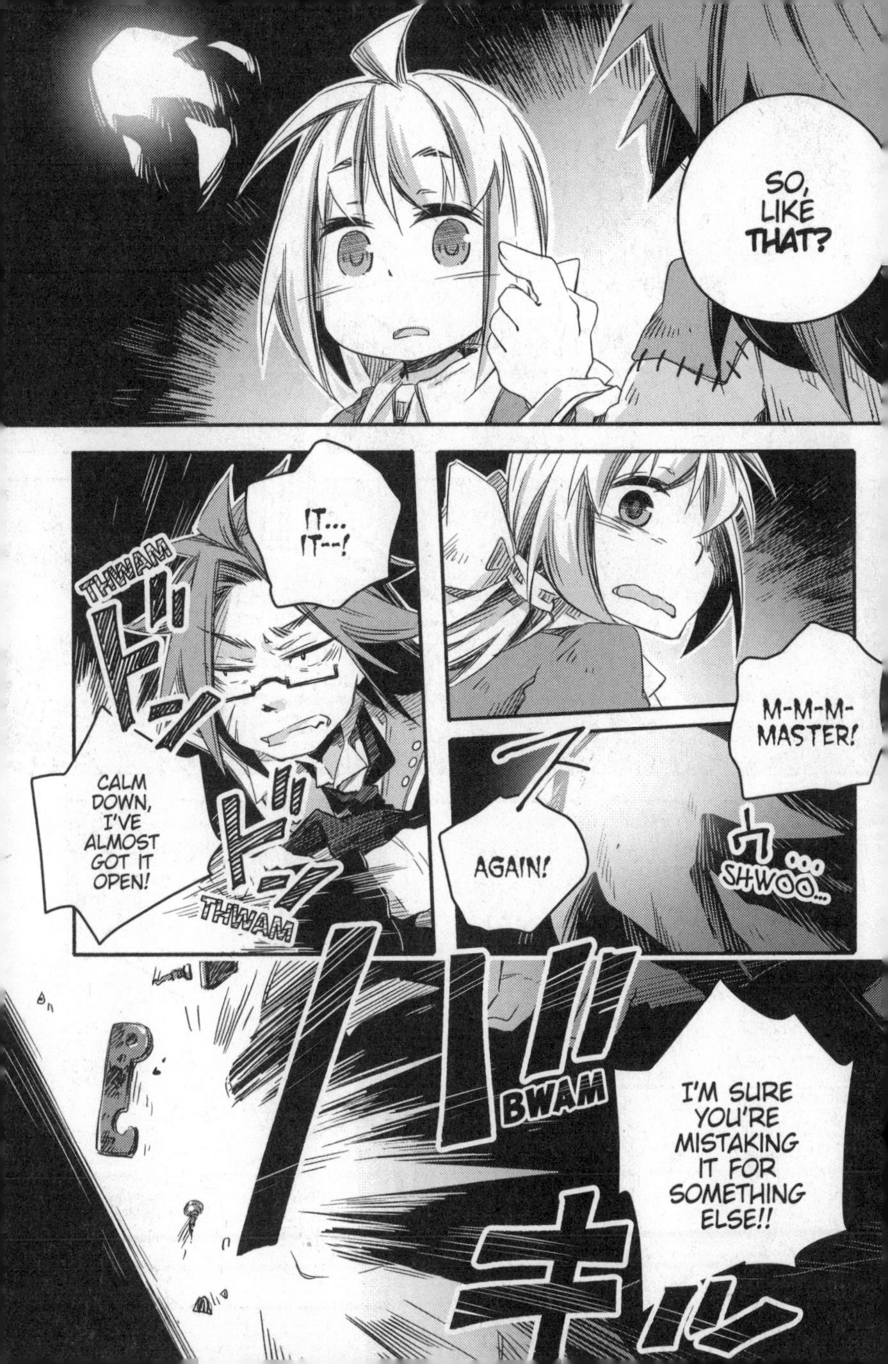
SO, LIKE THAT?
M-M-M-MASTER!
SHWOO...
AGAIN!
IT... IT--!
THWAM
CALM DOWN, I'VE ALMOST GOT IT OPEN!
THWAM
BWAM
I'M SURE YOU'RE MISTAKING IT FOR SOMETHING ELSE!!

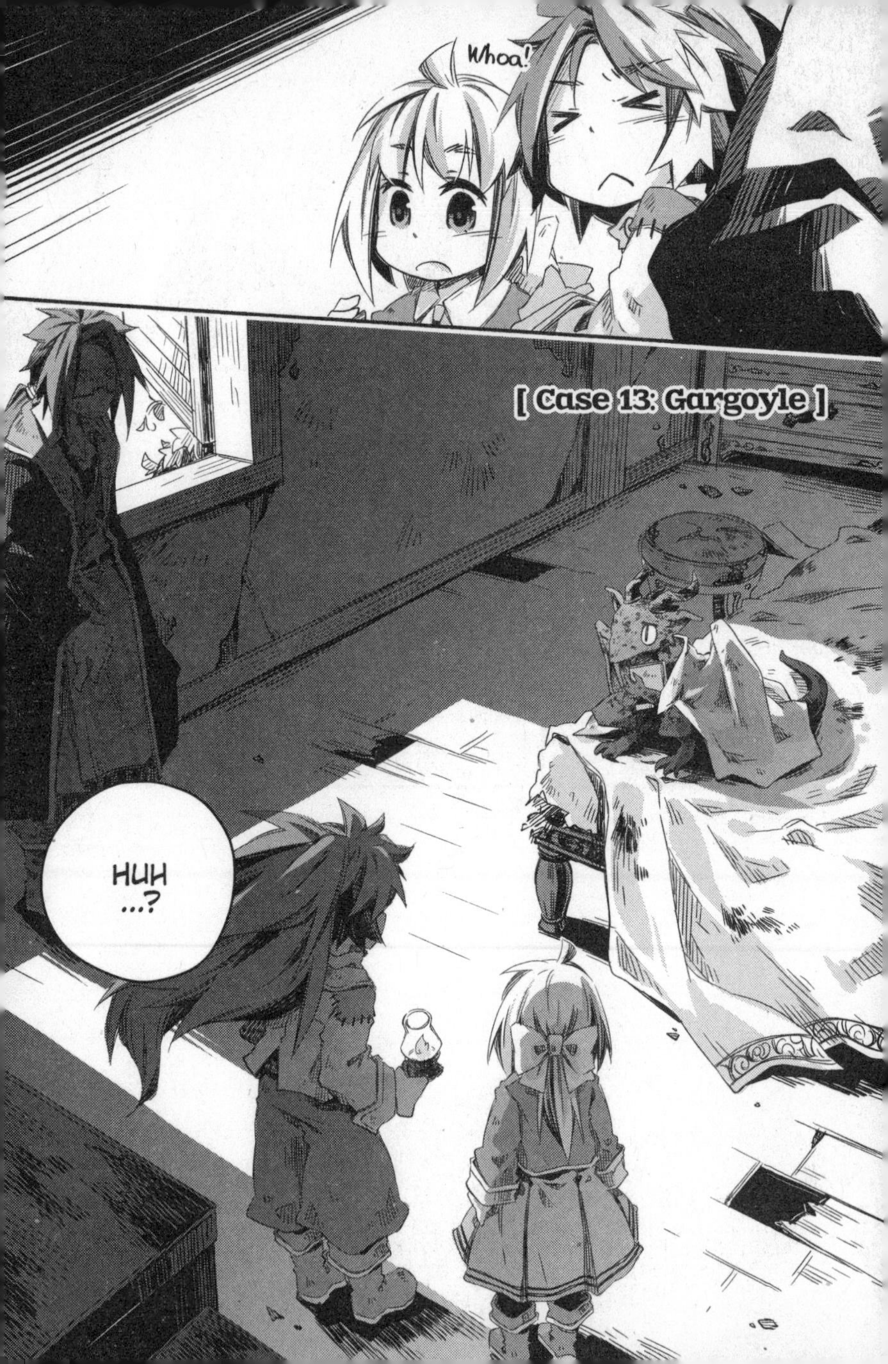
Whoa!
[Case 13: Gargoyle]
HUH ...?

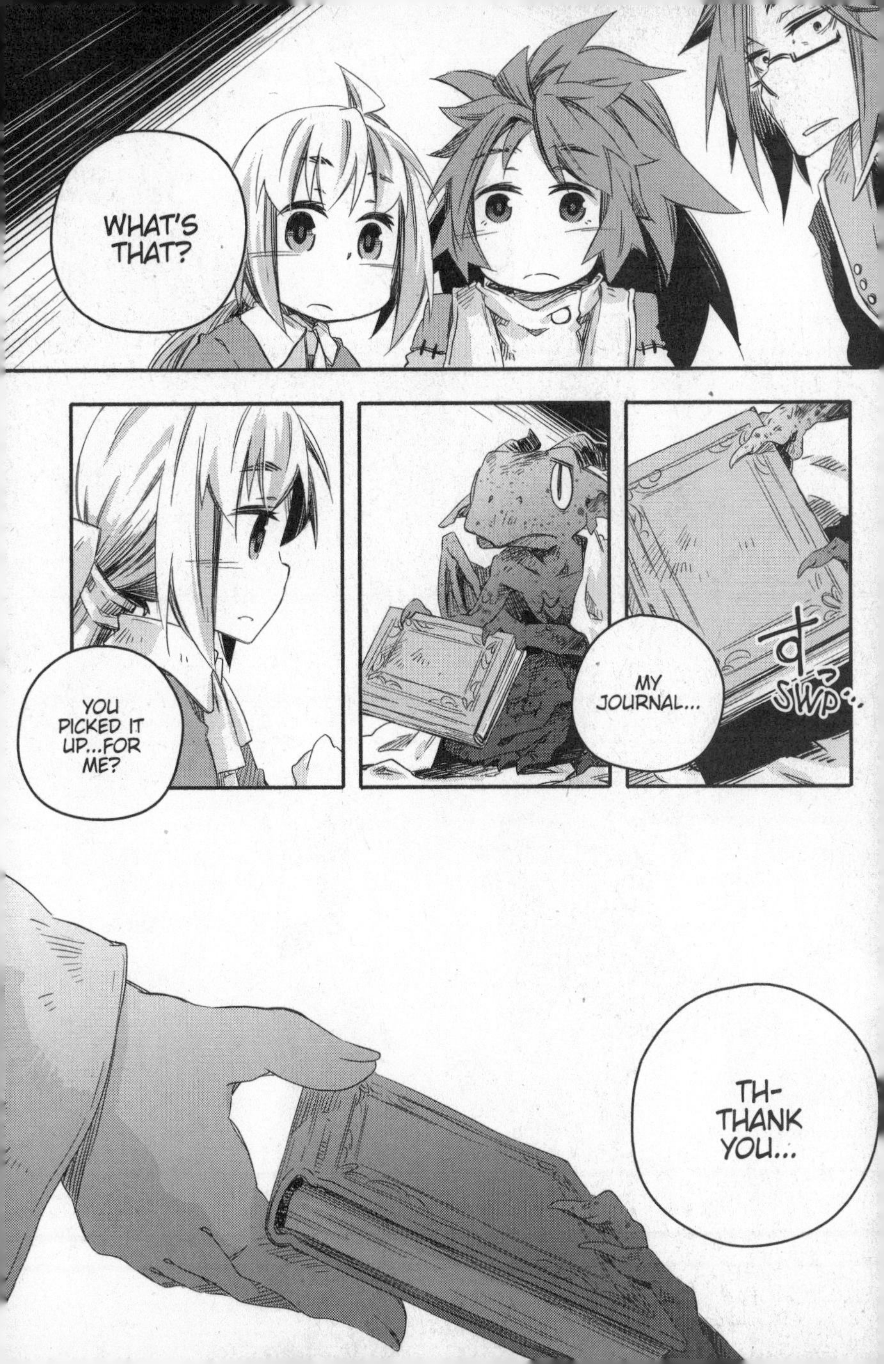
WHAT'S THAT?
す
SWP...
MY JOURNAL...
YOU PICKED IT UP...FOR ME?
TH-THANK YOU...

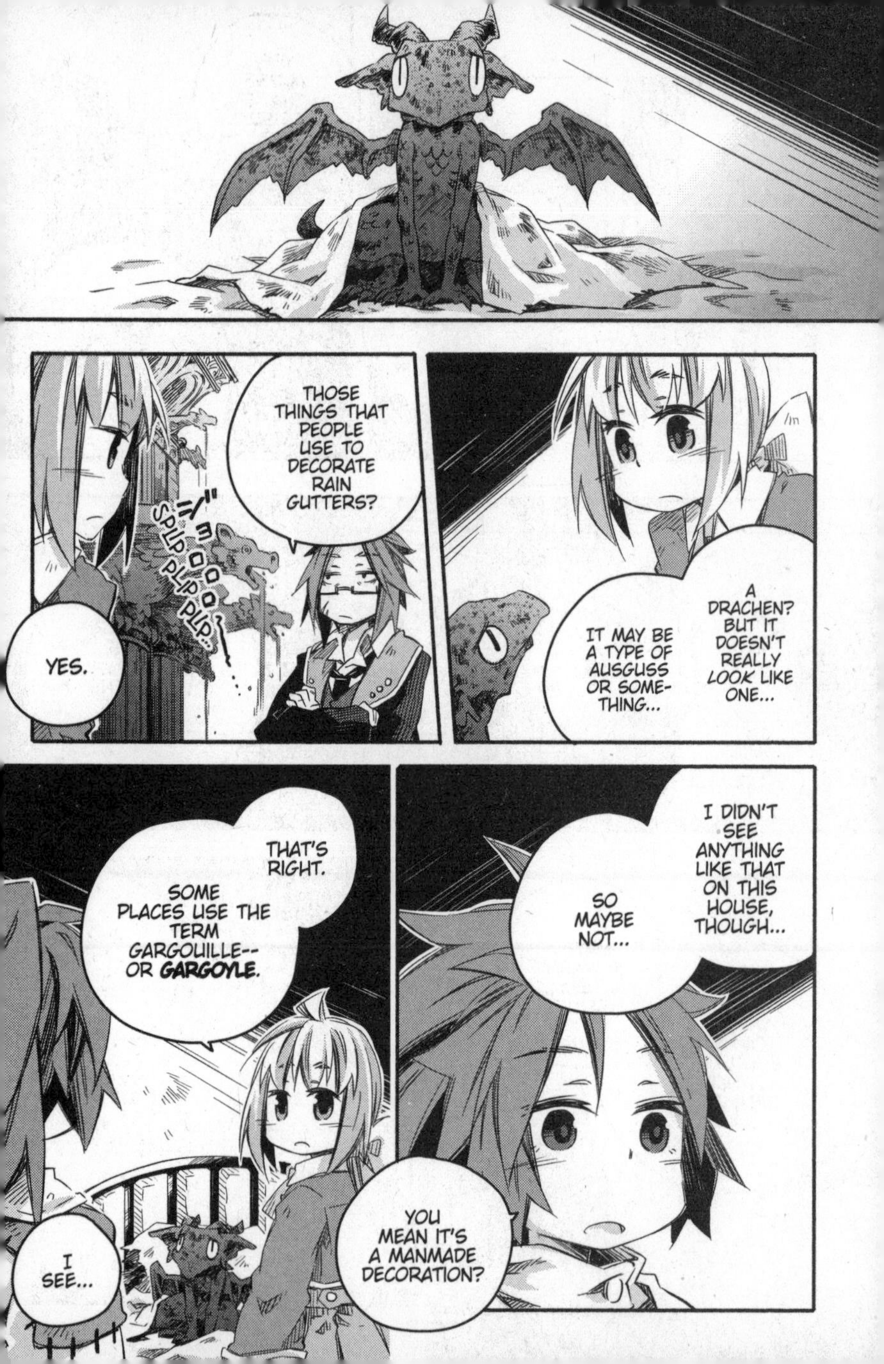
A DRACHEN? BUT IT DOESN'T REALLY *LOOK* LIKE ONE...
IT MAY BE A TYPE OF AUSGUSS OR SOME-THING...
THOSE THINGS THAT PEOPLE USE TO DECORATE RAIN GUTTERS?
SPLIP PLIP PLIP...
YES.
I DIDN'T SEE ANYTHING LIKE THAT ON THIS HOUSE, THOUGH...
SO MAYBE NOT...
YOU MEAN IT'S A MANMADE DECORATION?
THAT'S RIGHT.
SOME PLACES USE THE TERM GARGOUILLE-- OR **GARGOYLE**.
I SEE...

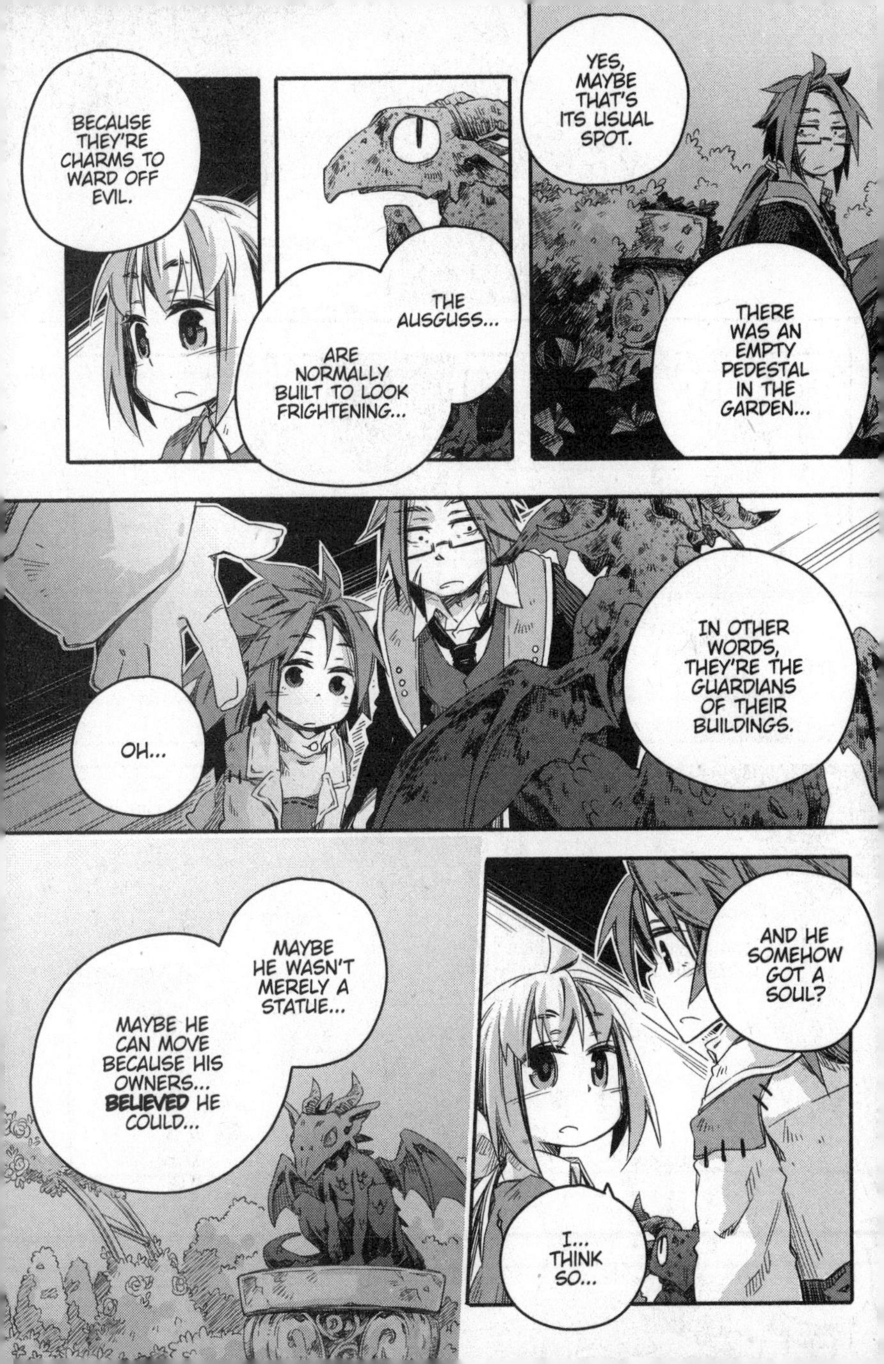
YES, MAYBE THAT'S ITS USUAL SPOT.
THERE WAS AN EMPTY PEDESTAL IN THE GARDEN...
THE AUSGUSS...
ARE NORMALLY BUILT TO LOOK FRIGHTENING...
BECAUSE THEY'RE CHARMS TO WARD OFF EVIL.
IN OTHER WORDS, THEY'RE THE GUARDIANS OF THEIR BUILDINGS.
OH...
AND HE SOMEHOW GOT A SOUL?
I... THINK SO...
MAYBE HE WASN'T MERELY A STATUE...
MAYBE HE CAN MOVE BECAUSE HIS OWNERS... **BELIEVED** HE COULD...

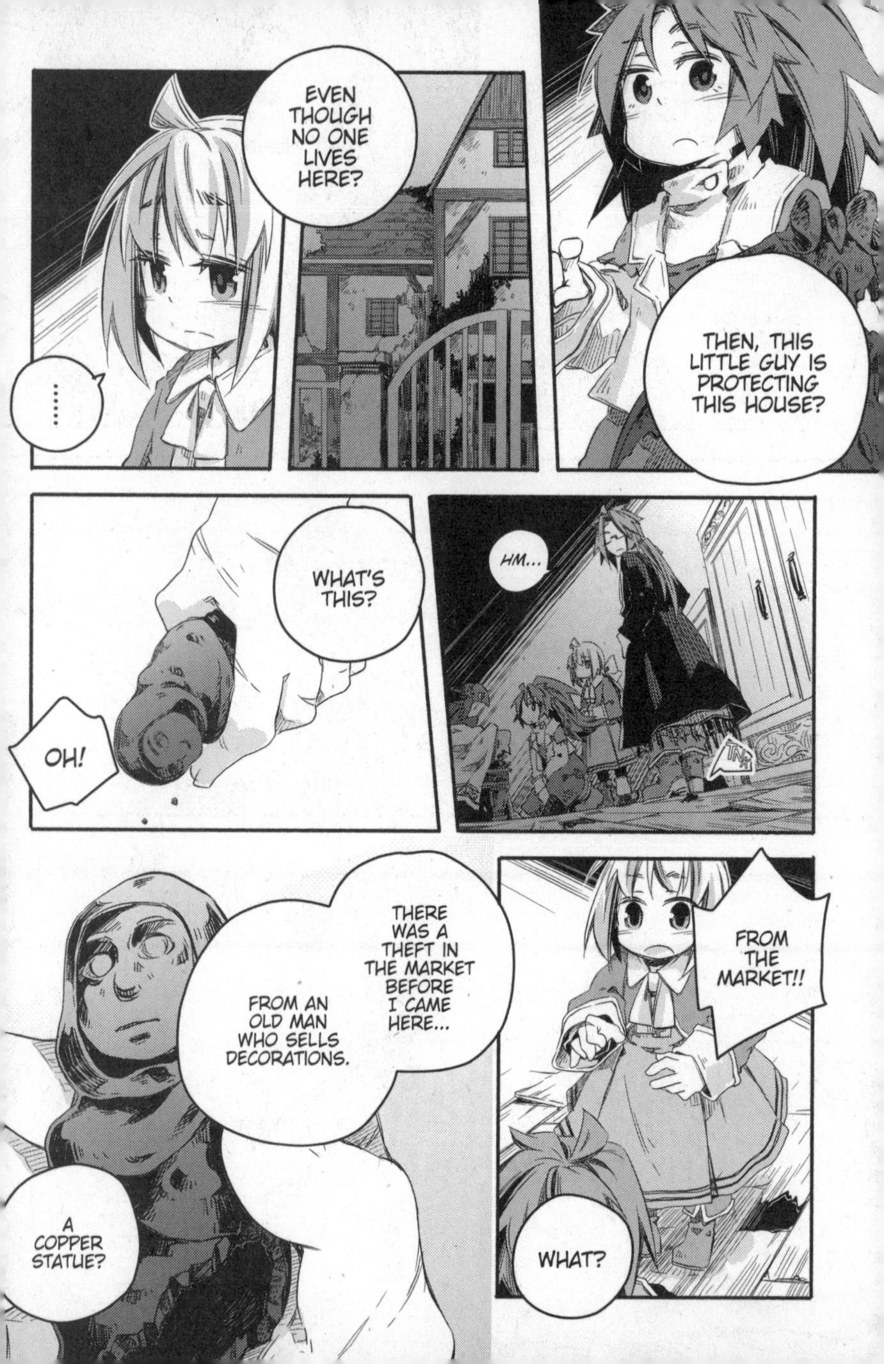
THEN, THIS LITTLE GUY IS PROTECTING THIS HOUSE?
EVEN THOUGH NO ONE LIVES HERE?
......
HM...
TNK
WHAT'S THIS?
OH!
FROM THE MARKET!!
WHAT?
THERE WAS A THEFT IN THE MARKET BEFORE I CAME HERE...
FROM AN OLD MAN WHO SELLS DECORATIONS.
A COPPER STATUE?

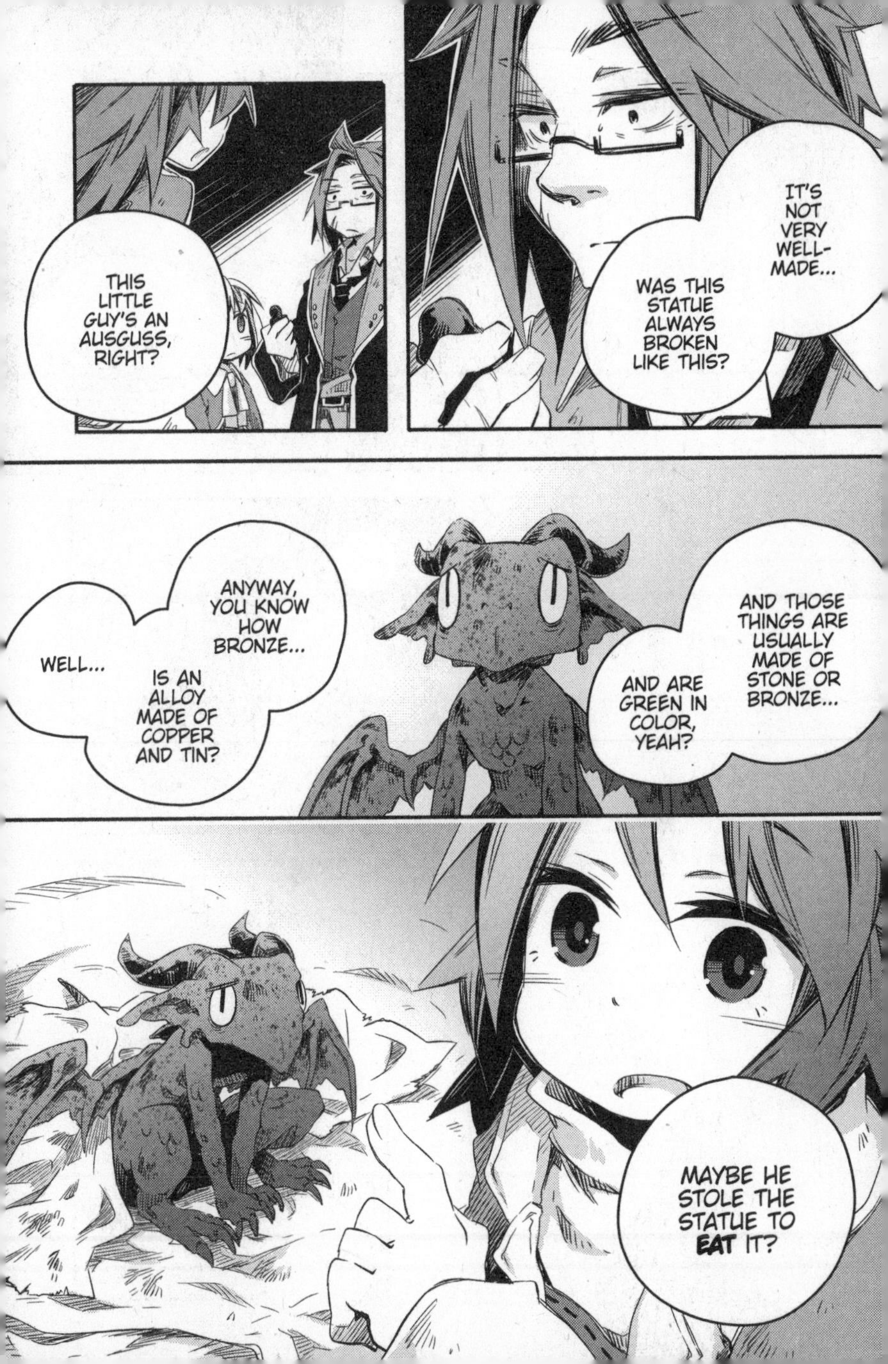
IT'S NOT VERY WELL-MADE...
WAS THIS STATUE ALWAYS BROKEN LIKE THIS?
THIS LITTLE GUY'S AN AUSGUSS, RIGHT?
AND THOSE THINGS ARE USUALLY MADE OF STONE OR BRONZE...
AND ARE GREEN IN COLOR, YEAH?
ANYWAY, YOU KNOW HOW BRONZE...
IS AN ALLOY MADE OF COPPER AND TIN?
WELL...
MAYBE HE STOLE THE STATUE TO **EAT** IT?

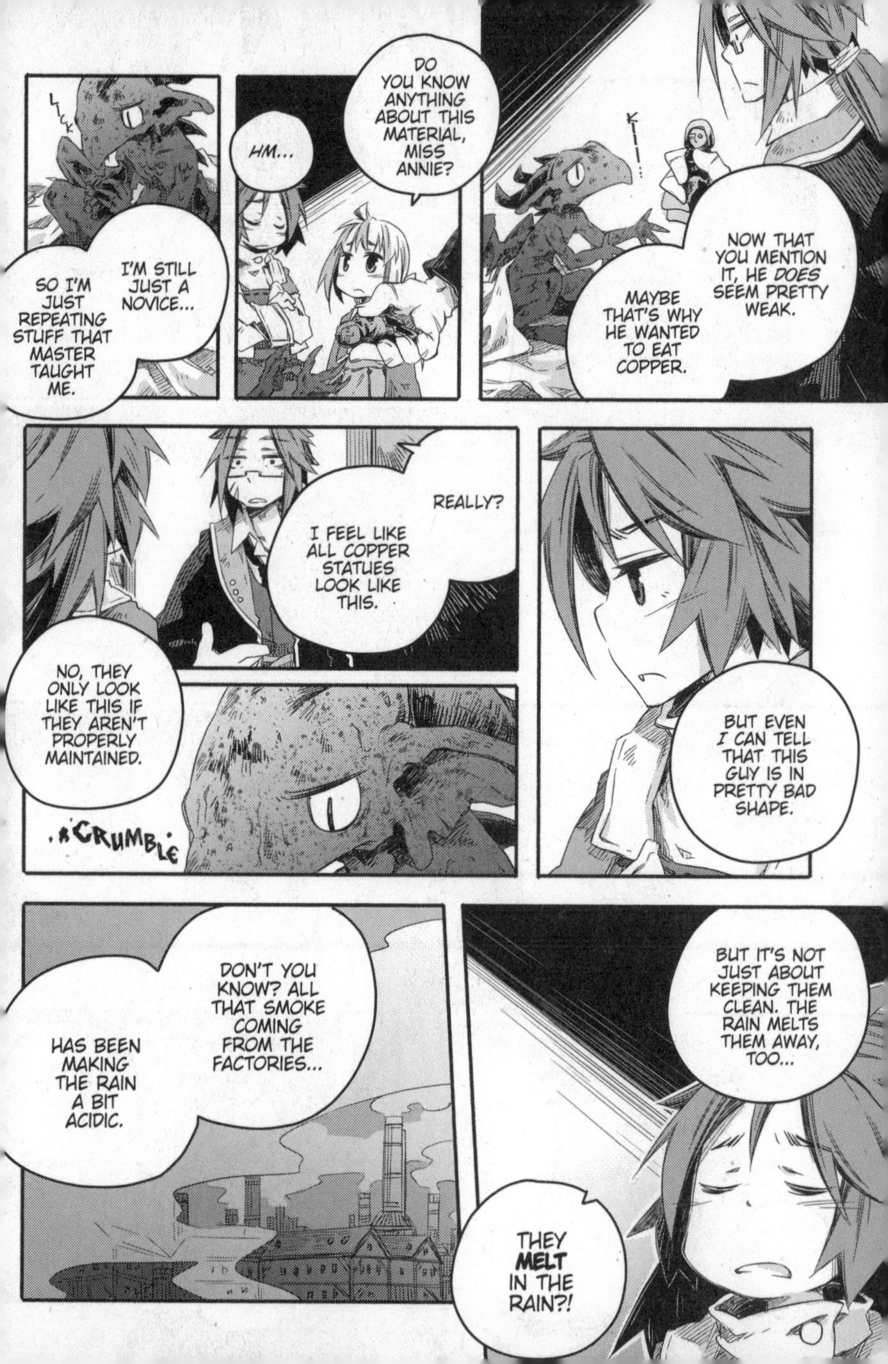
NOW THAT YOU MENTION IT, HE *DOES* SEEM PRETTY WEAK.
MAYBE THAT'S WHY HE WANTED TO EAT COPPER.
DO YOU KNOW ANYTHING ABOUT THIS MATERIAL, MISS ANNIE?
HM...
LICK
I'M STILL JUST A NOVICE...
SO I'M JUST REPEATING STUFF THAT MASTER TAUGHT ME.
BUT EVEN *I* CAN TELL THAT THIS GUY IS IN PRETTY BAD SHAPE.
REALLY?
I FEEL LIKE ALL COPPER STATUES LOOK LIKE THIS.
NO, THEY ONLY LOOK LIKE THIS IF THEY AREN'T PROPERLY MAINTAINED.
CRUMBLE
BUT IT'S NOT JUST ABOUT KEEPING THEM CLEAN. THE RAIN MELTS THEM AWAY, TOO...
THEY **MELT** IN THE RAIN?!
DON'T YOU KNOW? ALL THAT SMOKE COMING FROM THE FACTORIES...
HAS BEEN MAKING THE RAIN A BIT ACIDIC.

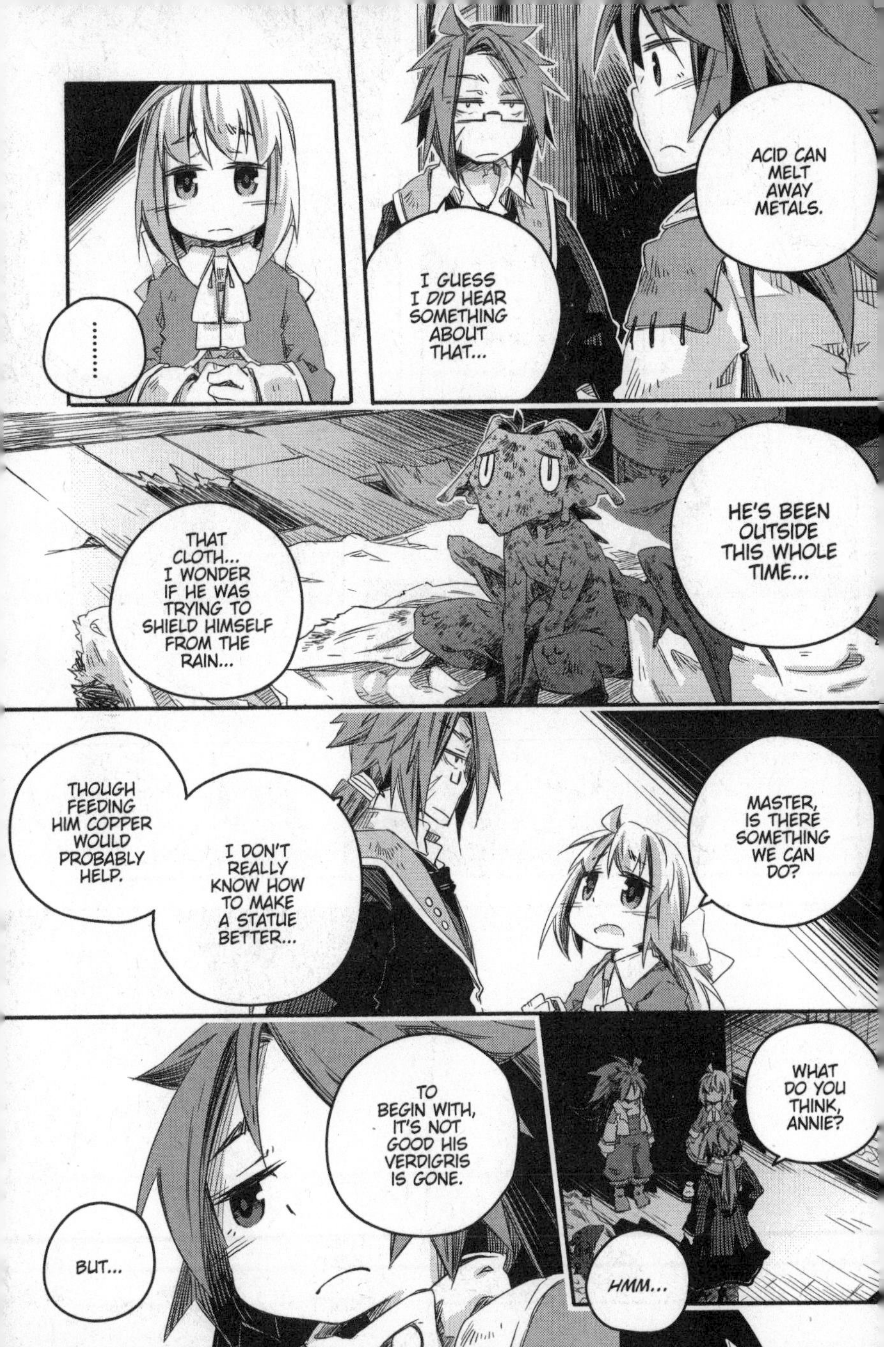
ACID CAN MELT AWAY METALS.
I GUESS I *DID* HEAR SOMETHING ABOUT THAT...
......
HE'S BEEN OUTSIDE THIS WHOLE TIME...
THAT CLOTH... I WONDER IF HE WAS TRYING TO SHIELD HIMSELF FROM THE RAIN...
MASTER, IS THERE SOMETHING WE CAN DO?
I DON'T REALLY KNOW HOW TO MAKE A STATUE BETTER...
THOUGH FEEDING HIM COPPER WOULD PROBABLY HELP.
WHAT DO YOU THINK, ANNIE?
HMM...
TO BEGIN WITH, IT'S NOT GOOD HIS VERDIGRIS IS GONE.
BUT...

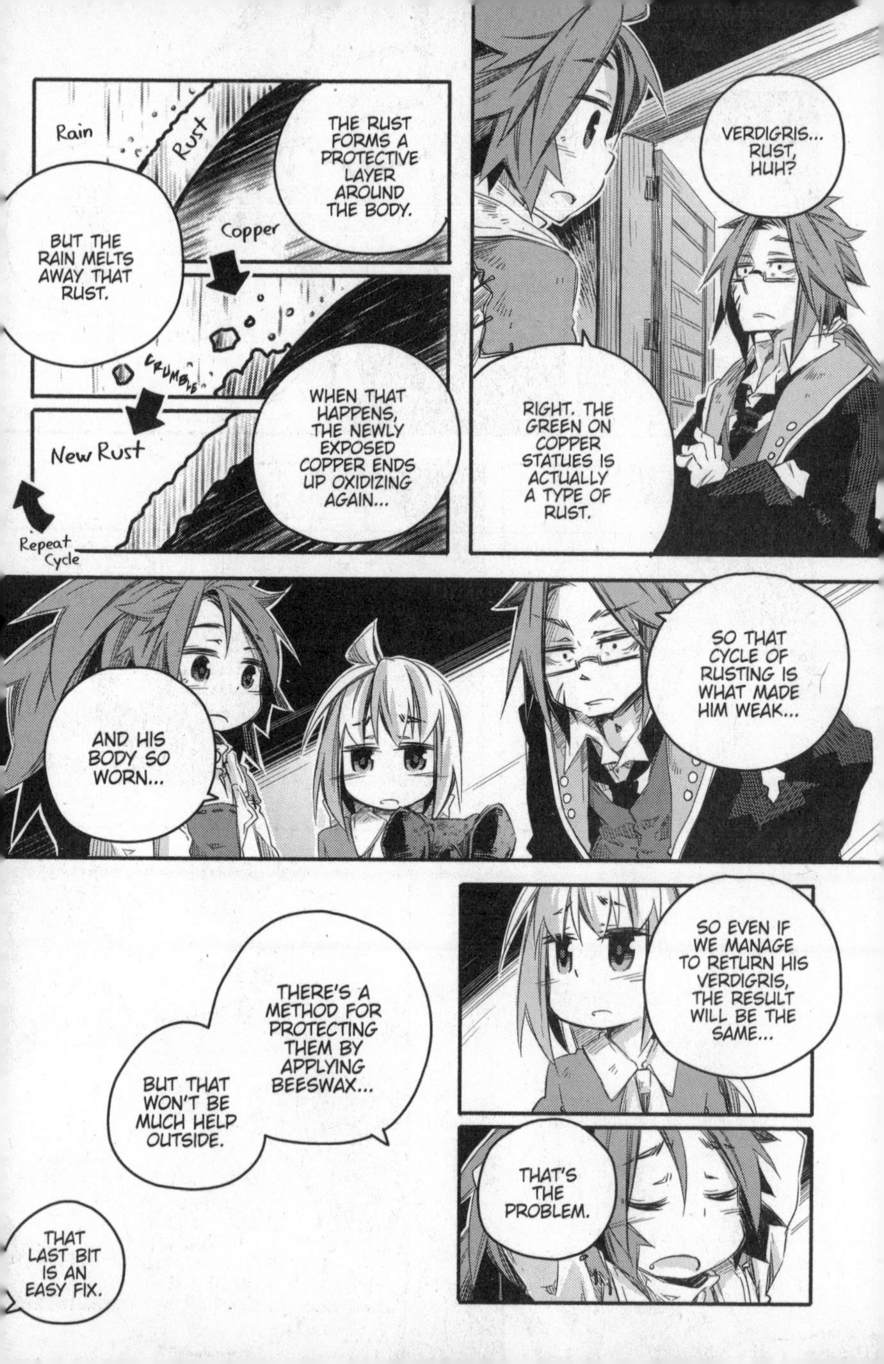
VERDIGRIS... RUST, HUH?
RIGHT. THE GREEN ON COPPER STATUES IS ACTUALLY A TYPE OF RUST.
THE RUST FORMS A PROTECTIVE LAYER AROUND THE BODY.
Rain
Rust
Copper
BUT THE RAIN MELTS AWAY THAT RUST.
CRUMBLE
WHEN THAT HAPPENS, THE NEWLY EXPOSED COPPER ENDS UP OXIDIZING AGAIN...
New Rust
Repeat Cycle
SO THAT CYCLE OF RUSTING IS WHAT MADE HIM WEAK...
AND HIS BODY SO WORN...
SO EVEN IF WE MANAGE TO RETURN HIS VERDIGRIS, THE RESULT WILL BE THE SAME...
THAT'S THE PROBLEM.
THERE'S A METHOD FOR PROTECTING THEM BY APPLYING BEESWAX...
BUT THAT WON'T BE MUCH HELP OUTSIDE.
THAT LAST BIT IS AN EASY FIX.

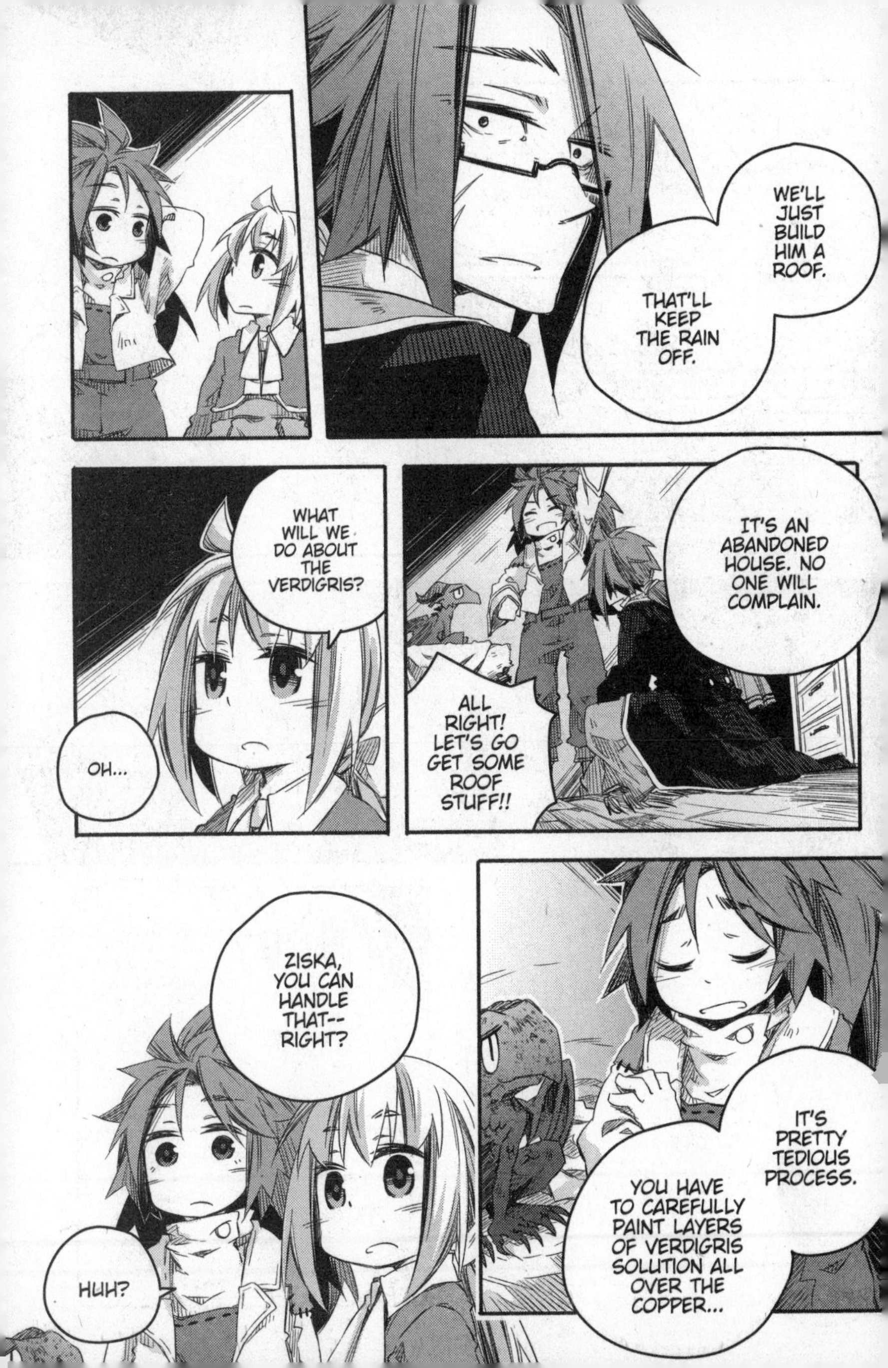
WE'LL JUST BUILD HIM A ROOF.
THAT'LL KEEP THE RAIN OFF.
IT'S AN ABANDONED HOUSE. NO ONE WILL COMPLAIN.
ALL RIGHT! LET'S GO GET SOME ROOF STUFF!!
WHAT WILL WE DO ABOUT THE VERDIGRIS?
OH...
IT'S PRETTY TEDIOUS PROCESS.
YOU HAVE TO CAREFULLY PAINT LAYERS OF VERDIGRIS SOLUTION ALL OVER THE COPPER...
ZISKA, YOU CAN HANDLE THAT-- RIGHT?
HUH?

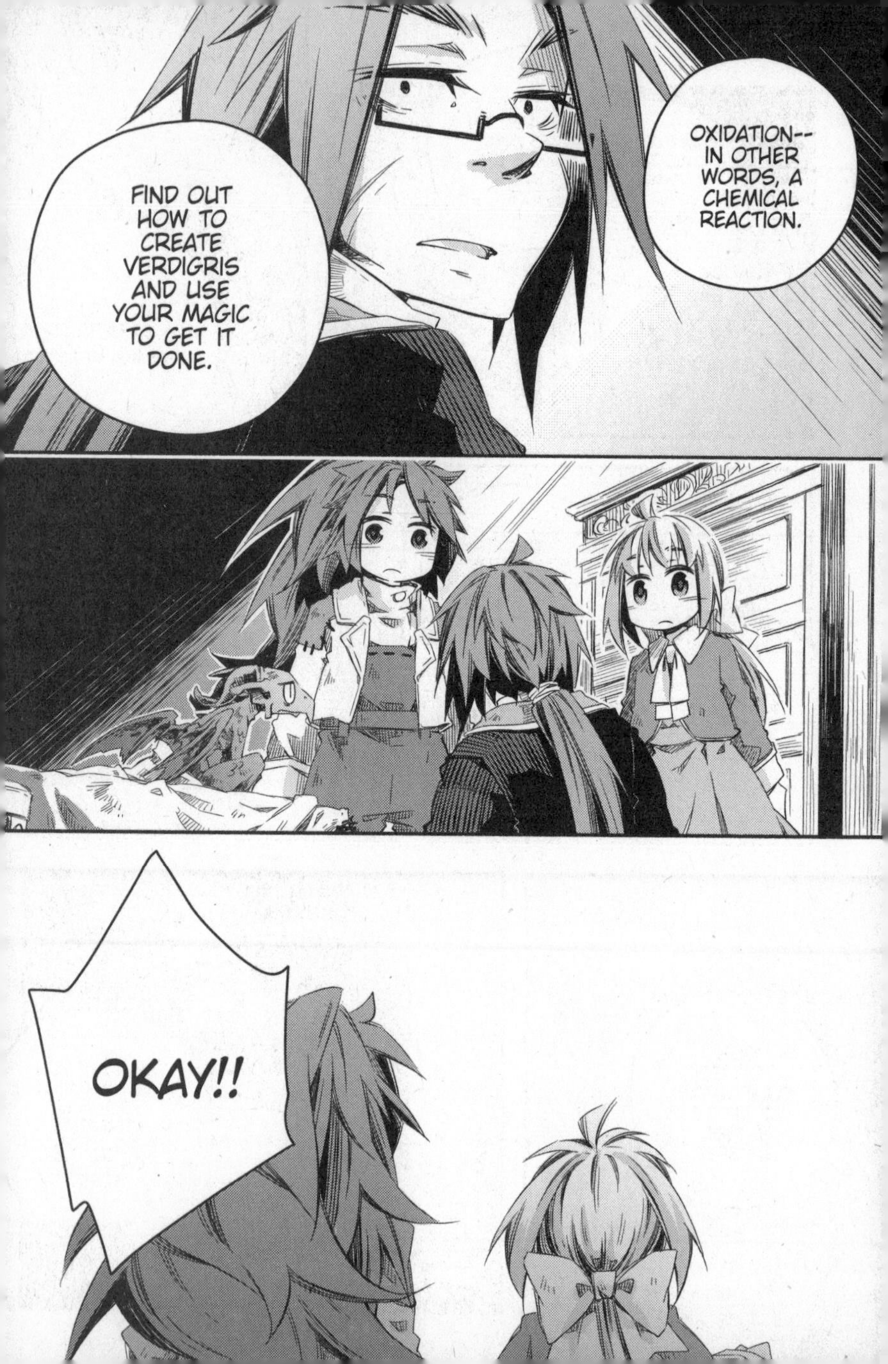
OXIDATION-- IN OTHER WORDS, A CHEMICAL REACTION.
FIND OUT HOW TO CREATE VERDIGRIS AND USE YOUR MAGIC TO GET IT DONE.
OKAY!!

Collaboration: Otsuka Art (http://ww81.tiki.ne.jp/~bronzeotsuka/)

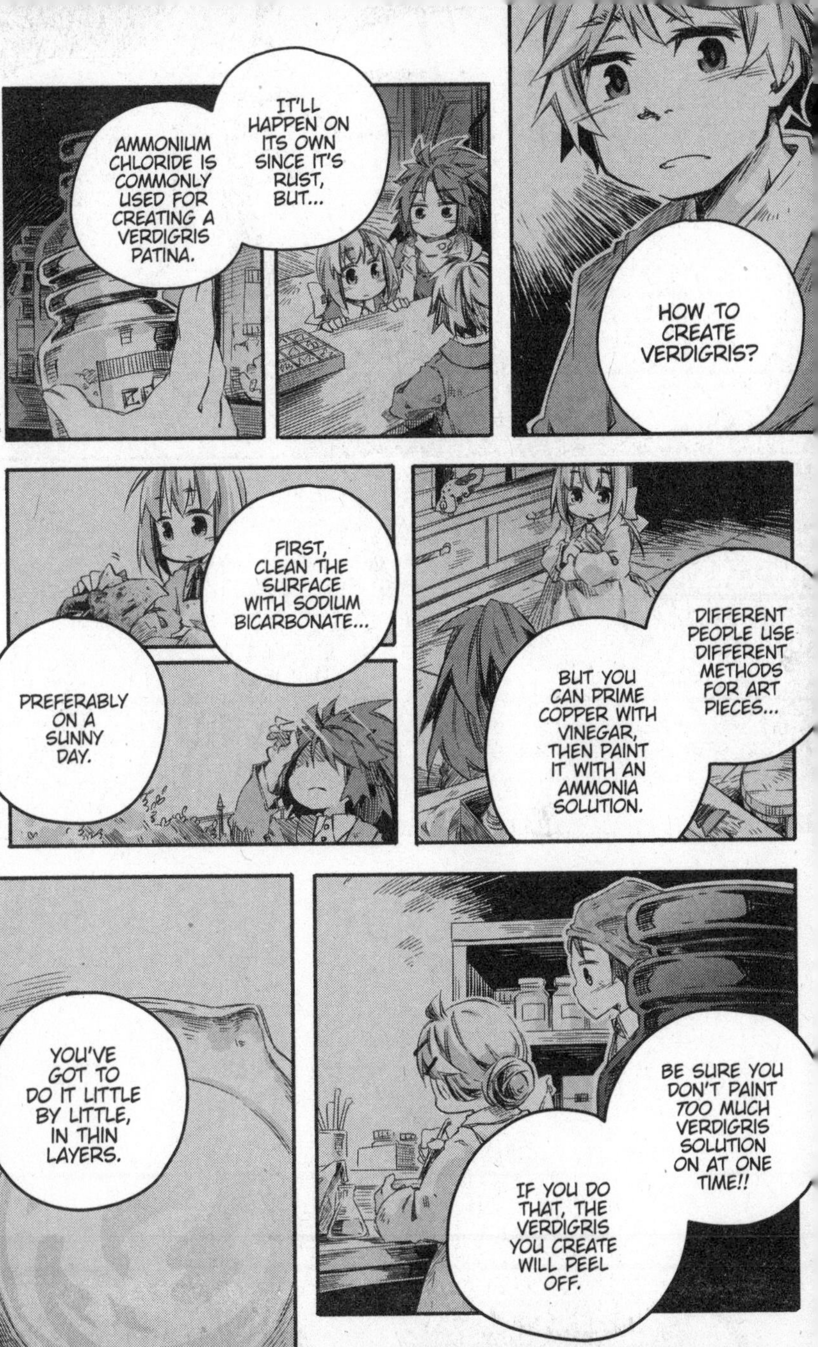
HOW TO CREATE VERDIGRIS?
IT'LL HAPPEN ON ITS OWN SINCE IT'S RUST, BUT...
AMMONIUM CHLORIDE IS COMMONLY USED FOR CREATING A VERDIGRIS PATINA.
DIFFERENT PEOPLE USE DIFFERENT METHODS FOR ART PIECES...
BUT YOU CAN PRIME COPPER WITH VINEGAR, THEN PAINT IT WITH AN AMMONIA SOLUTION.
FIRST, CLEAN THE SURFACE WITH SODIUM BICARBONATE...
PREFERABLY ON A SUNNY DAY.
BE SURE YOU DON'T PAINT *TOO MUCH* VERDIGRIS SOLUTION ON AT ONE TIME!!
IF YOU DO THAT, THE VERDIGRIS YOU CREATE WILL PEEL OFF.
YOU'VE GOT TO DO IT LITTLE BY LITTLE, IN THIN LAYERS.

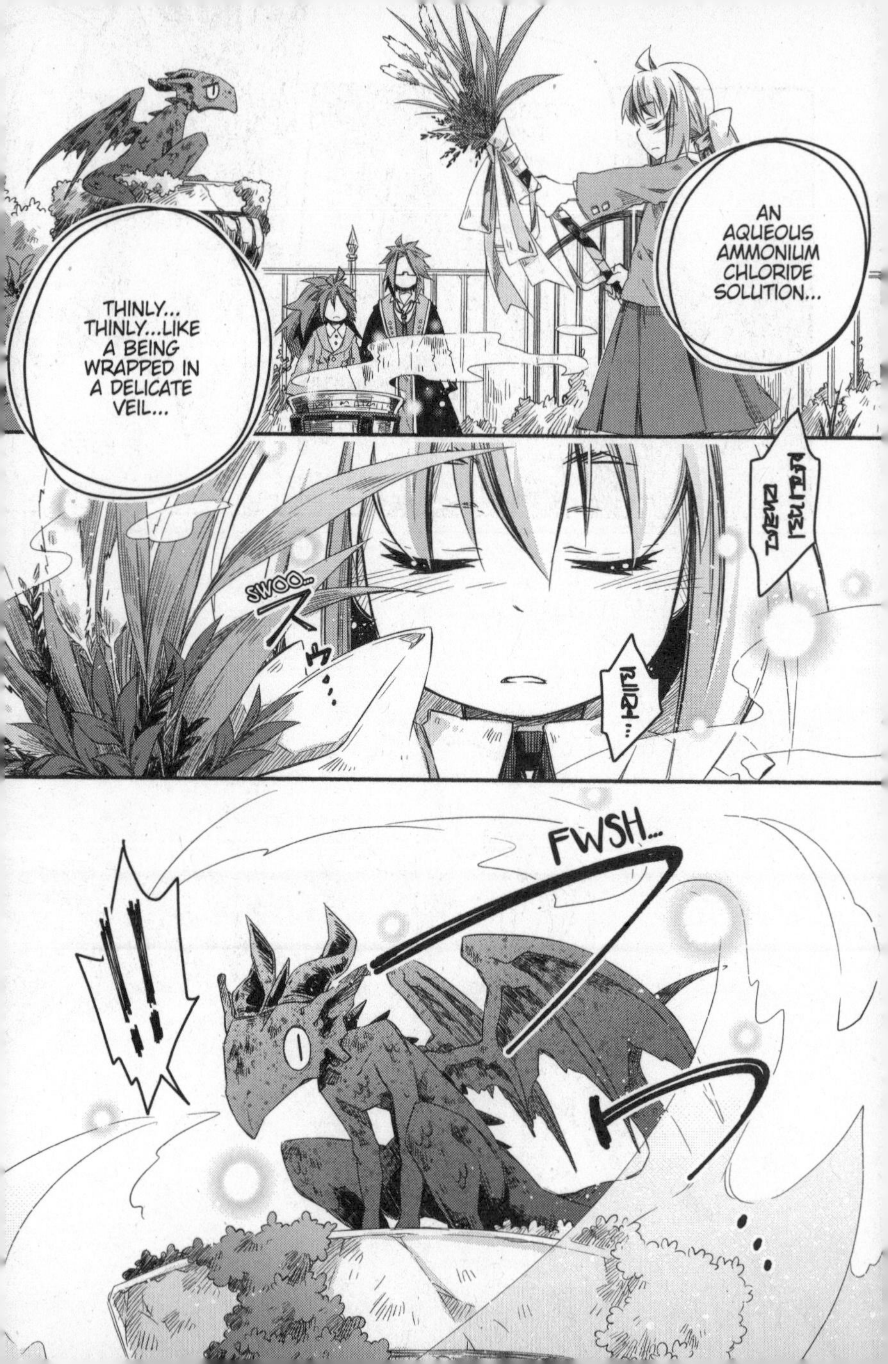

AN AQUEOUS AMMONIUM CHLORIDE SOLUTION...
THINLY... THINLY...LIKE A BEING WRAPPED IN A DELICATE VEIL...
RUSTLE RUSTLE
RUSTLE...
SWOO...
FWSH...
!!
...

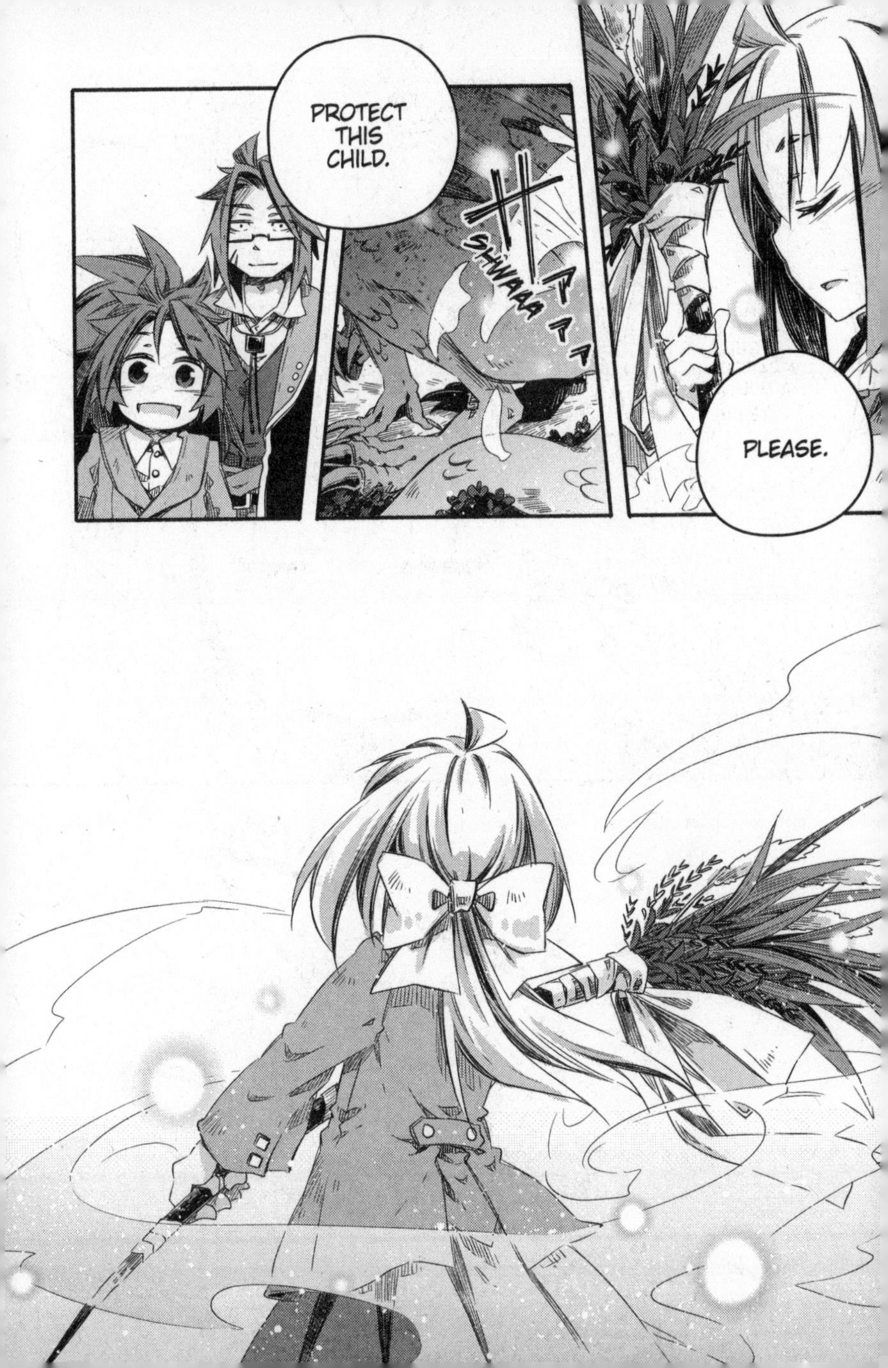
PROTECT THIS CHILD.
SHWAAA
PLEASE.

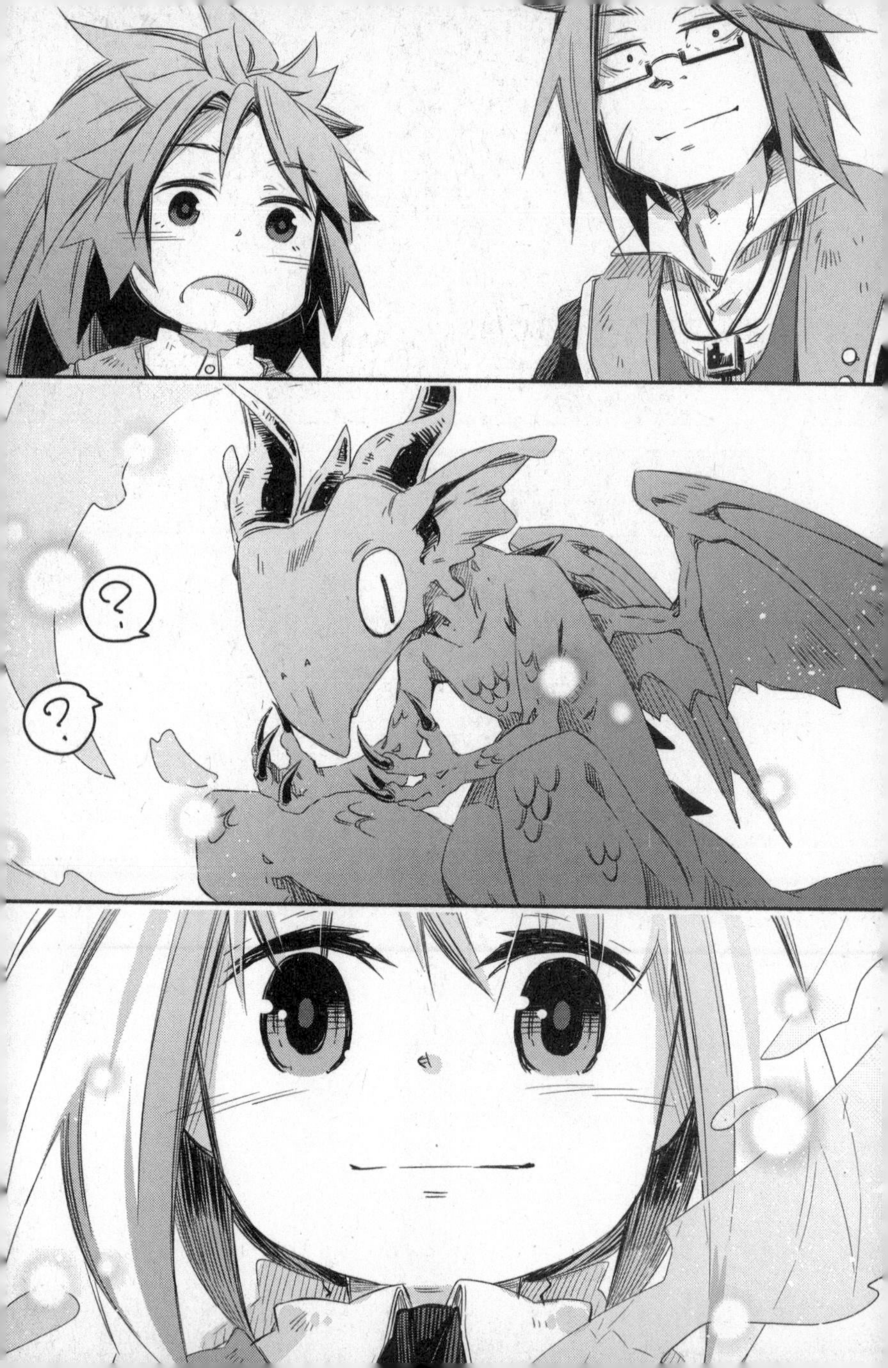
?
?

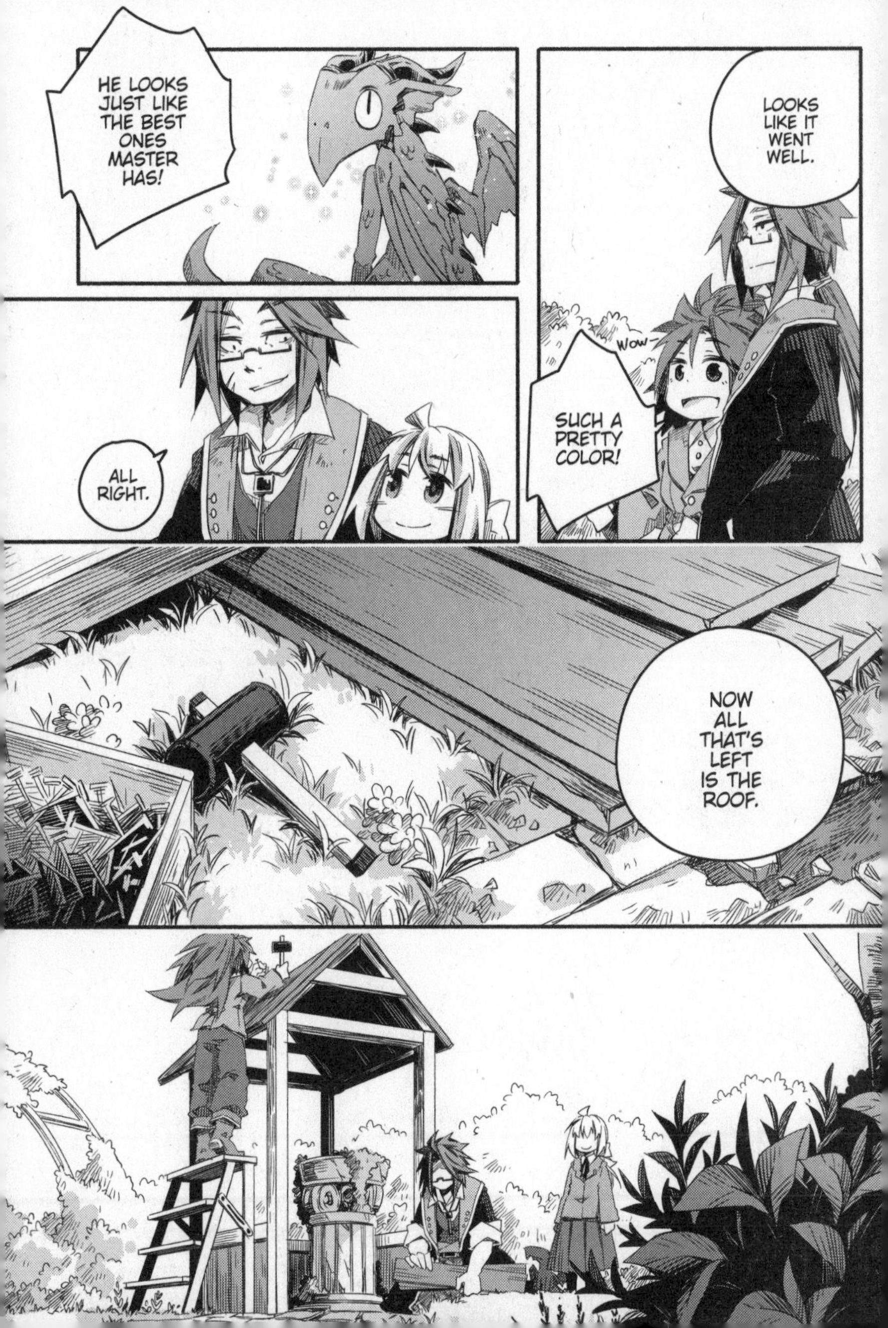
LOOKS LIKE IT WENT WELL.
WOW
SUCH A PRETTY COLOR!
HE LOOKS JUST LIKE THE BEST ONES MASTER HAS!
ALL RIGHT.
NOW ALL THAT'S LEFT IS THE ROOF.

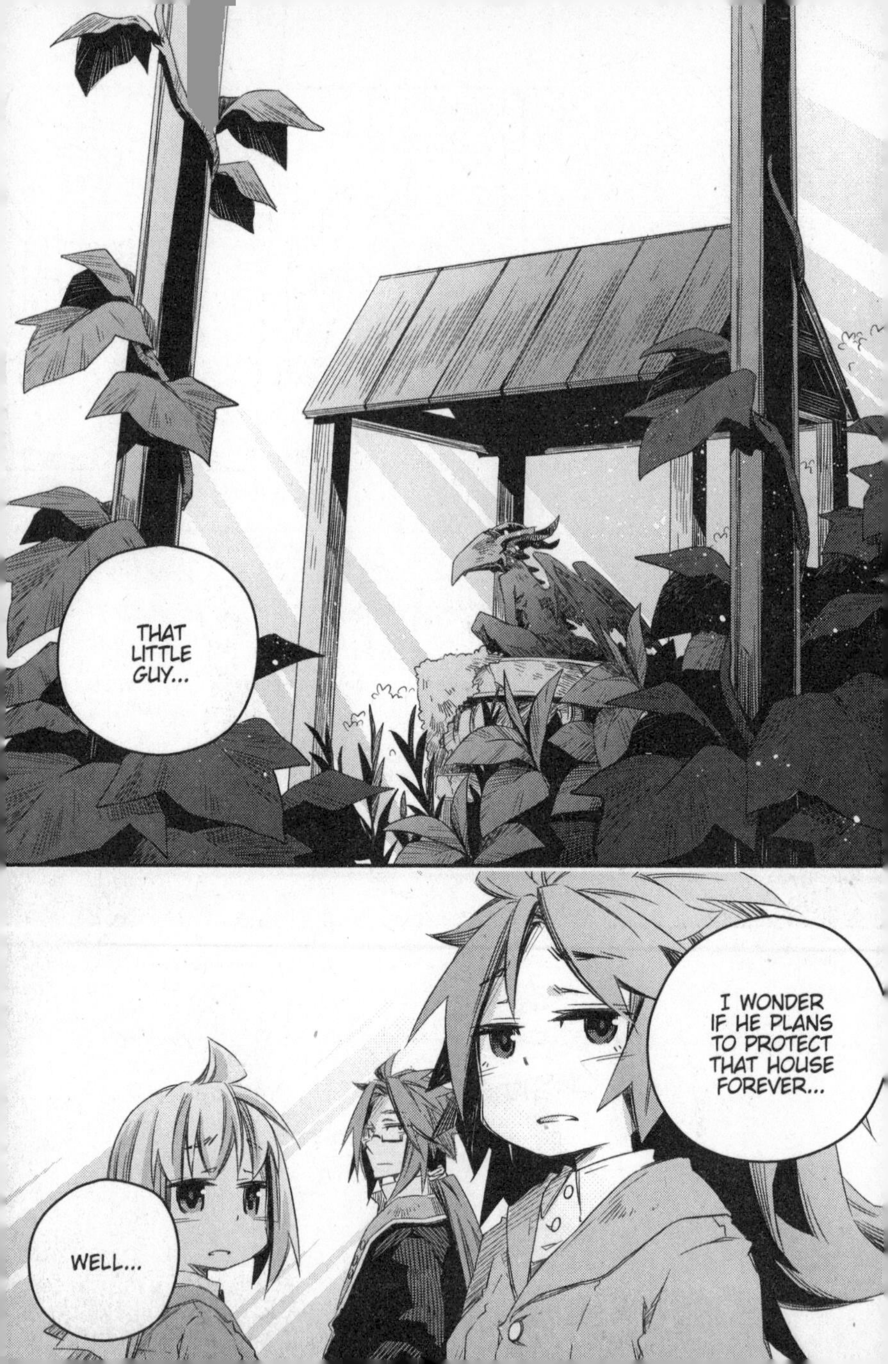
THAT LITTLE GUY...
I WONDER IF HE PLANS TO PROTECT THAT HOUSE FOREVER...
WELL...

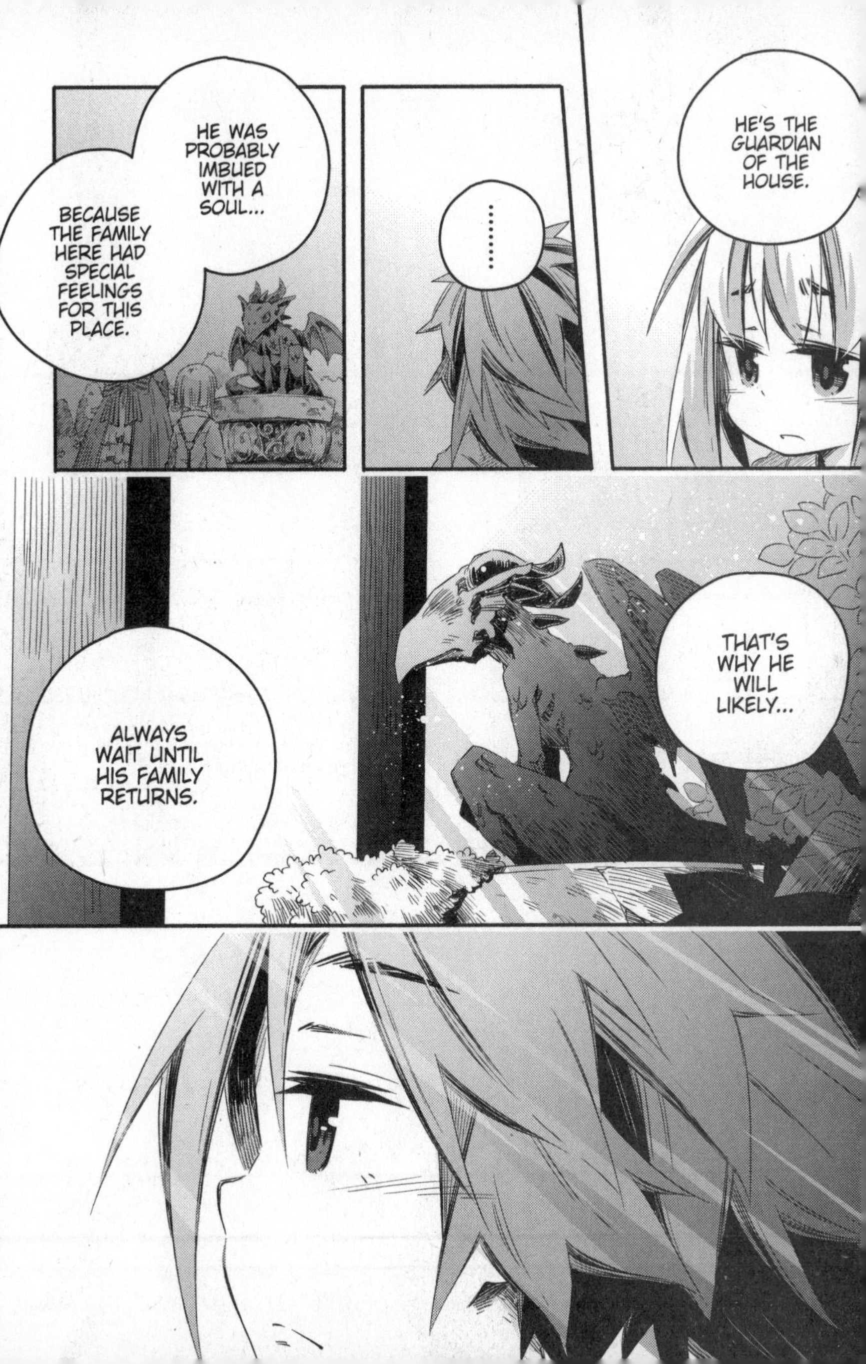
HE'S THE GUARDIAN OF THE HOUSE.
......
HE WAS PROBABLY IMBUED WITH A SOUL...
BECAUSE THE FAMILY HERE HAD SPECIAL FEELINGS FOR THIS PLACE.
THAT'S WHY HE WILL LIKELY...
ALWAYS WAIT UNTIL HIS FAMILY RETURNS.

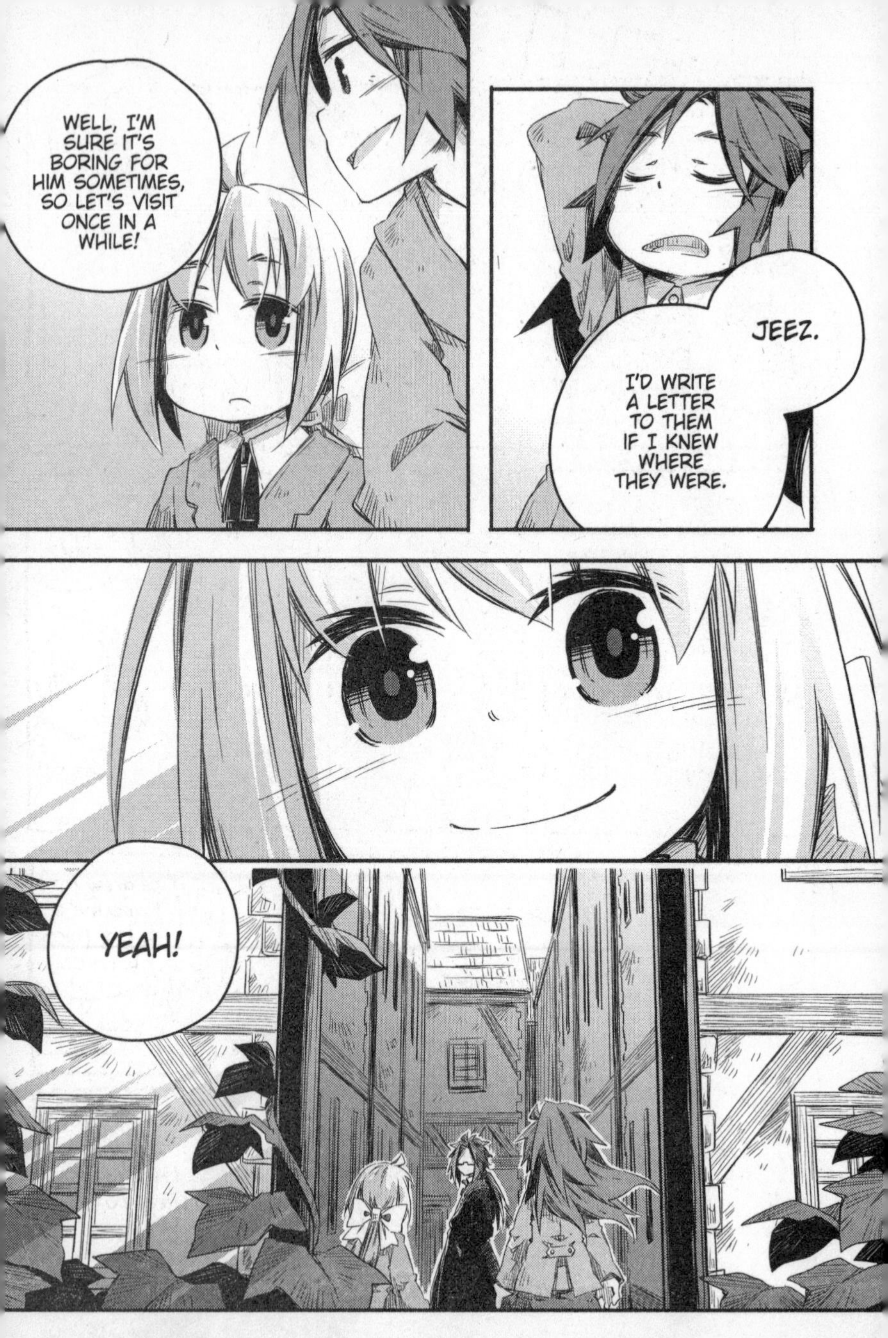
JEEZ.
I'D WRITE A LETTER TO THEM IF I KNEW WHERE THEY WERE.
WELL, I'M SURE IT'S BORING FOR HIM SOMETIMES, SO LET'S VISIT ONCE IN A WHILE!
YEAH!

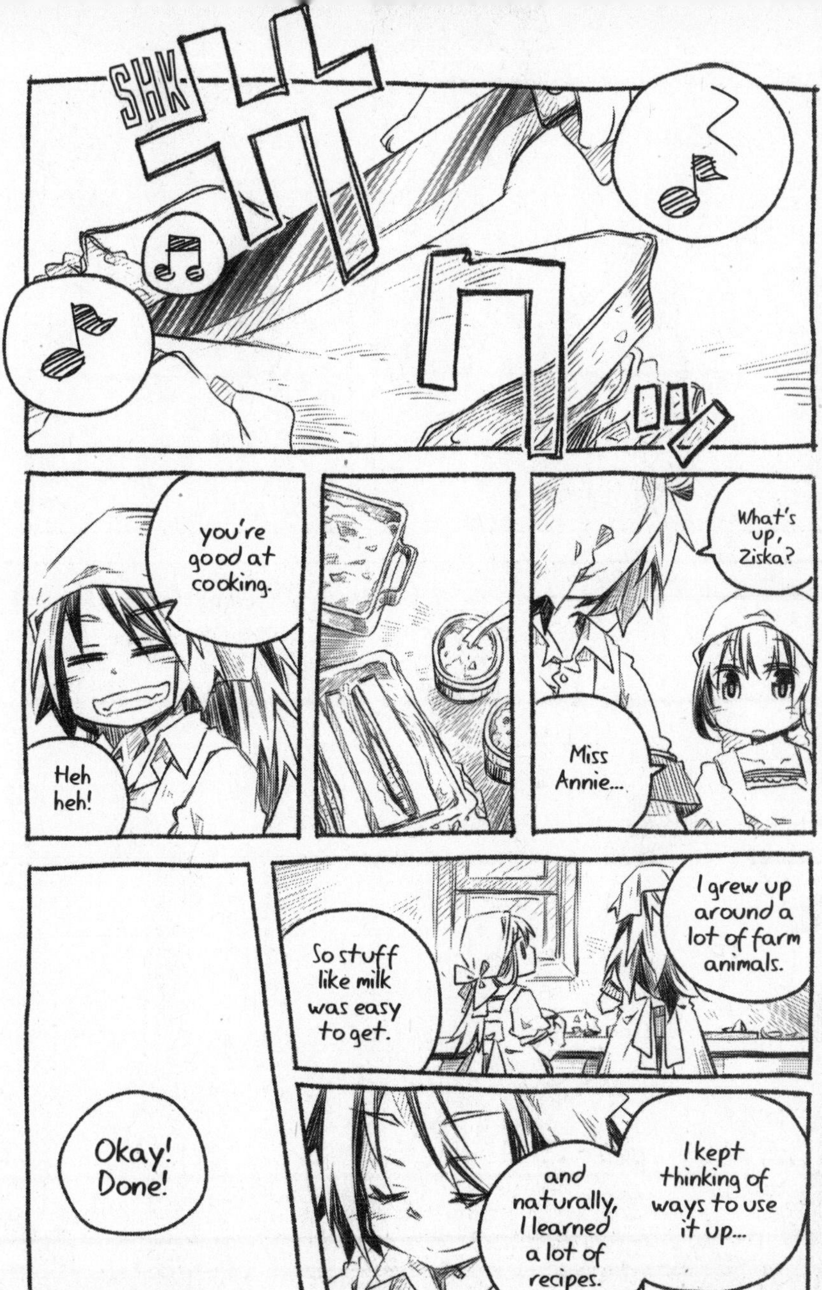
SHK
What's up, Ziska?
Miss Annie...
you're good at cooking.
Heh heh!
I grew up around a lot of farm animals.
So stuff like milk was easy to get.
I kept thinking of ways to use it up...
and naturally, I learned a lot of recipes.
Okay! Done!

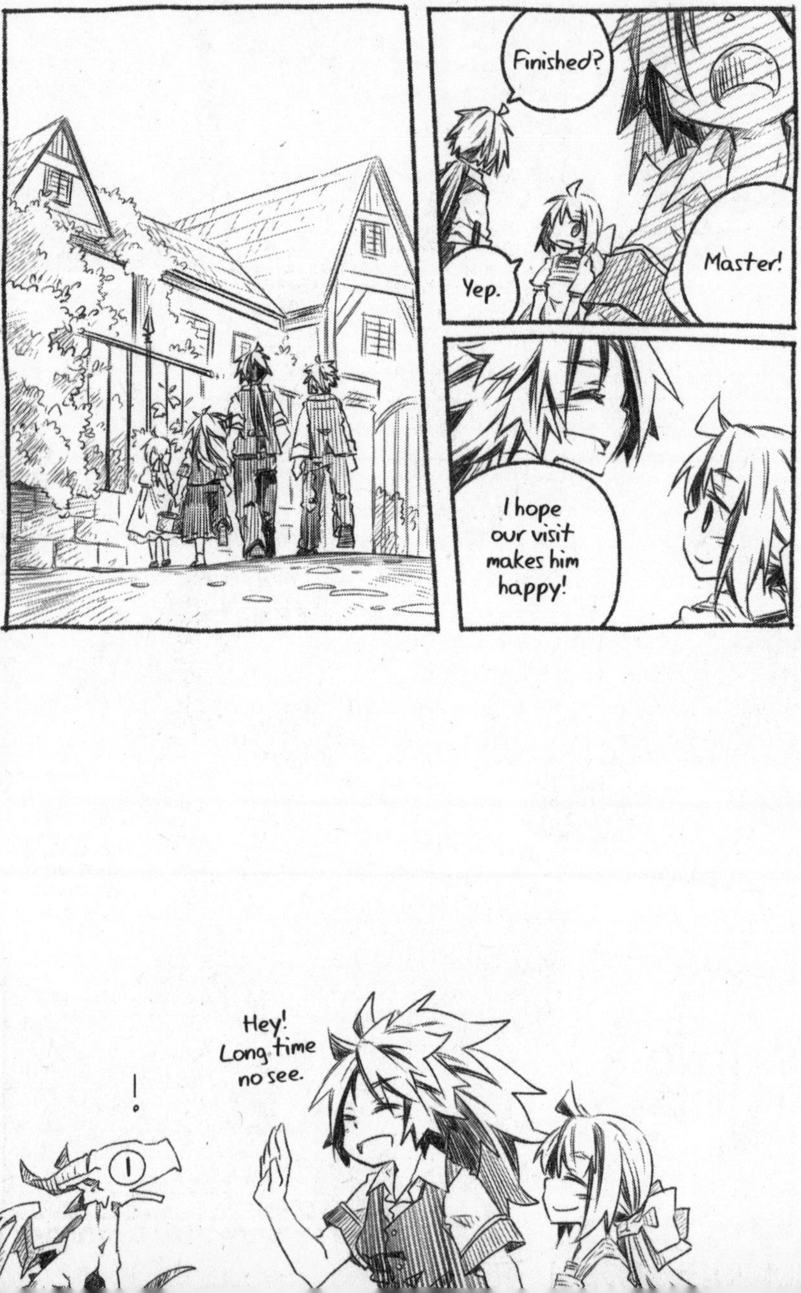
Master!
Finished?
Yep.
I hope our visit makes him happy!
Hey! Long time no see.
!

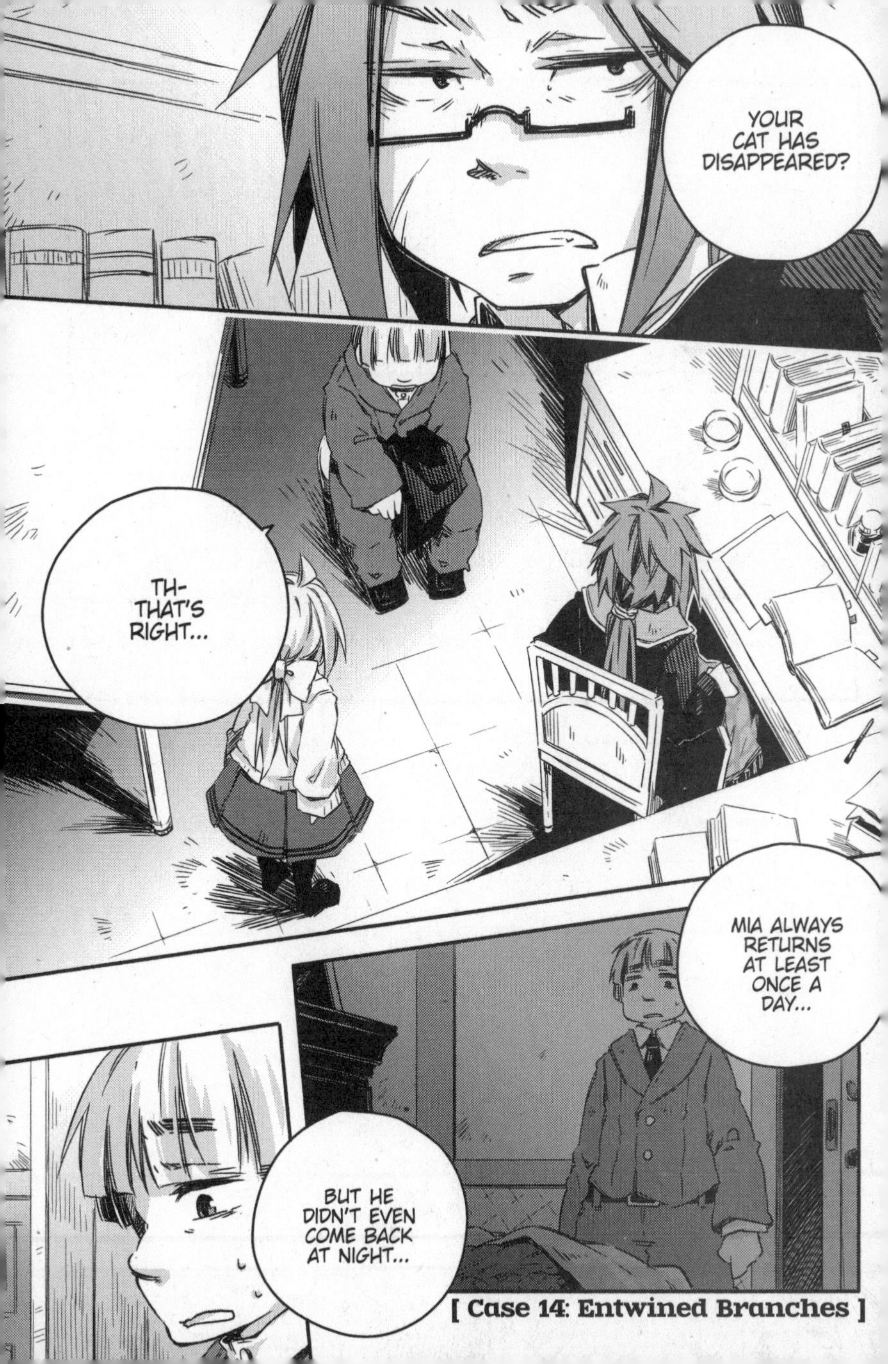
YOUR CAT HAS DISAPPEARED?
TH- THAT'S RIGHT...
MIA ALWAYS RETURNS AT LEAST ONCE A DAY...
BUT HE DIDN'T EVEN COME BACK AT NIGHT...
[Case 14: Entwined Branches]

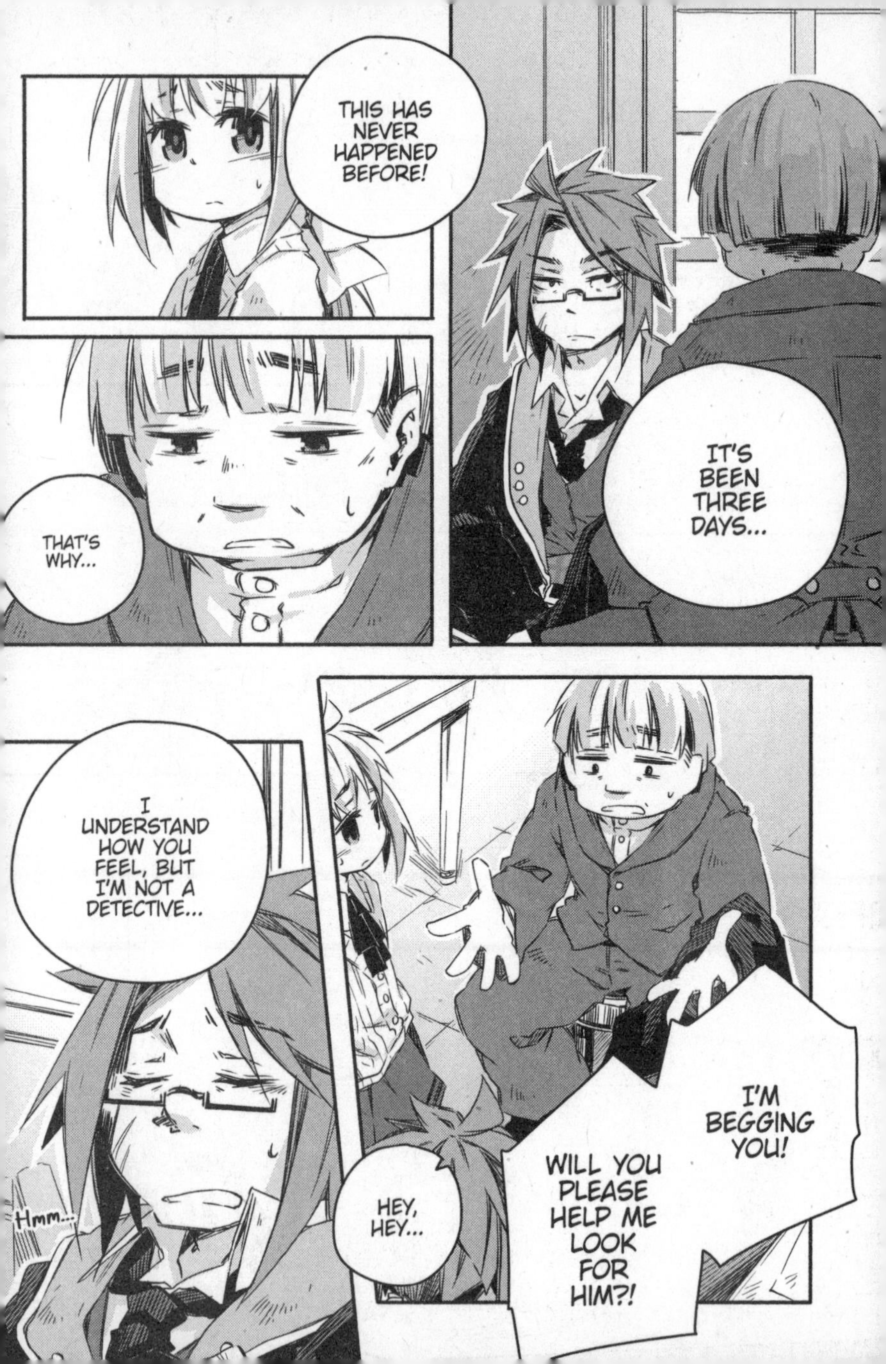
IT'S BEEN THREE DAYS...
THIS HAS NEVER HAPPENED BEFORE!
THAT'S WHY...
I'M BEGGING YOU!
WILL YOU PLEASE HELP ME LOOK FOR HIM?!
HEY, HEY...
I UNDERSTAND HOW YOU FEEL, BUT I'M NOT A DETECTIVE...
Hmm...

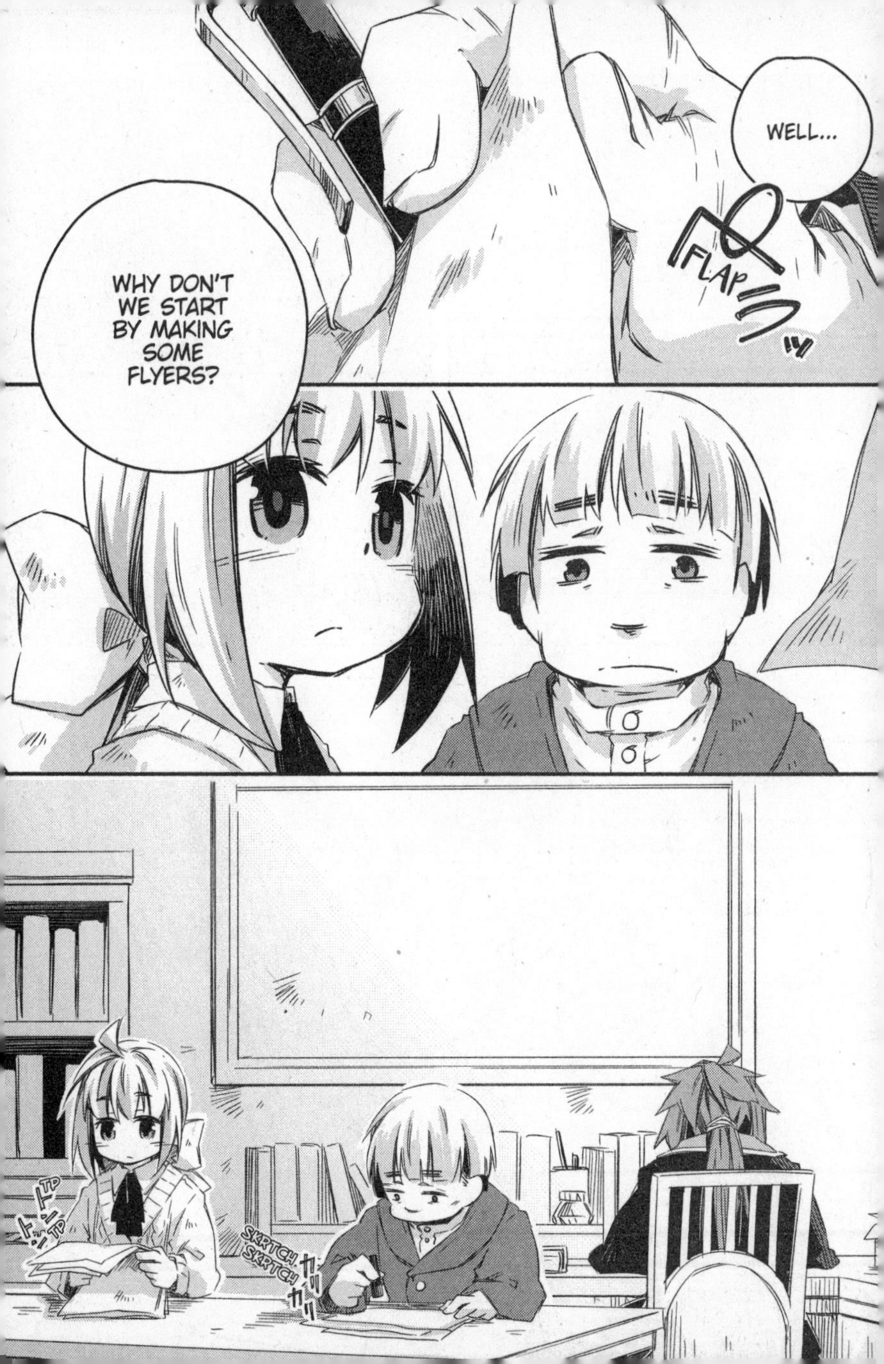
WELL...
FLAP
WHY DON'T WE START BY MAKING SOME FLYERS?
SKRTCH SKRTCH
TP TP

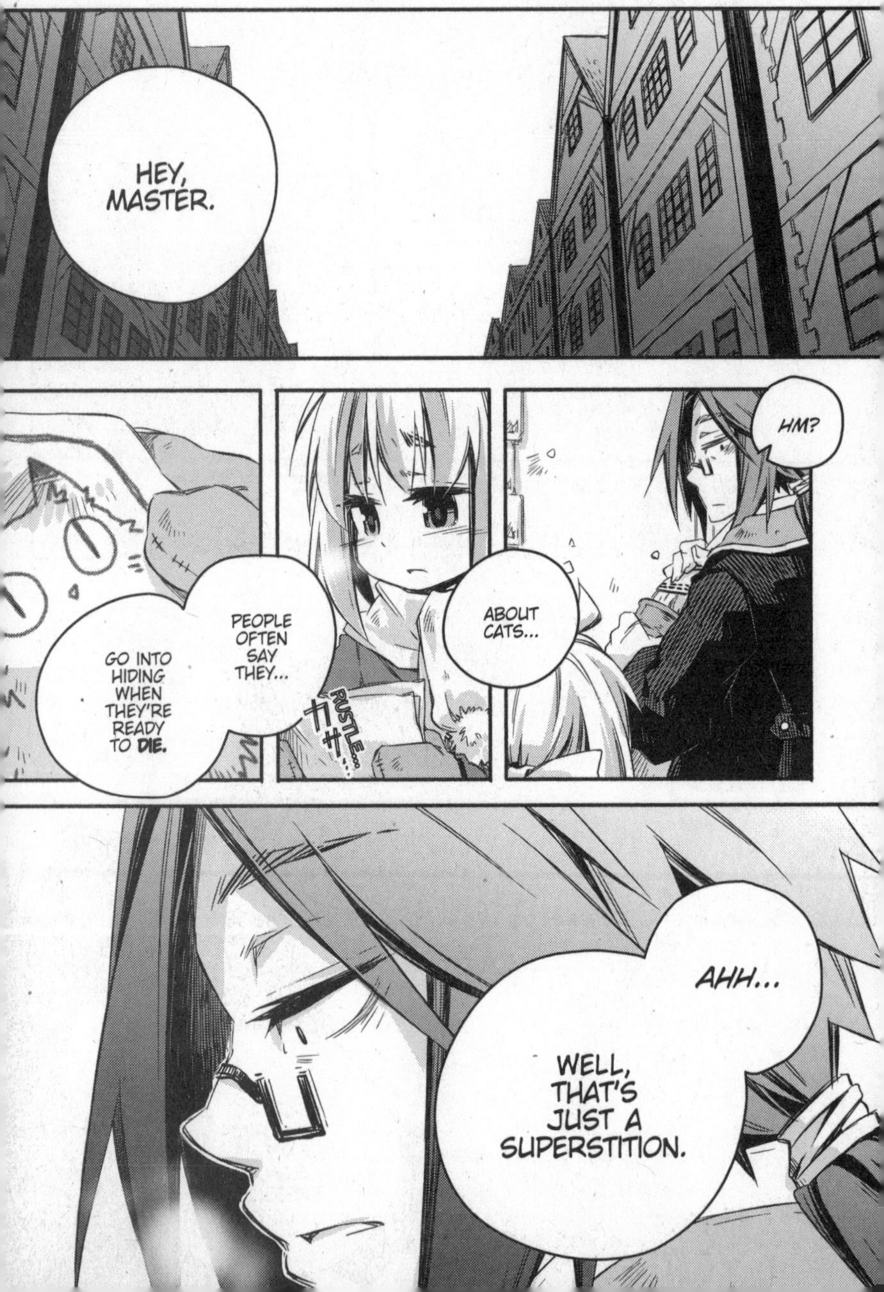
HEY, MASTER.
HM?
ABOUT CATS...
PEOPLE OFTEN SAY THEY...
RUSTLE...
GO INTO HIDING WHEN THEY'RE READY TO DIE.
AHH...
WELL, THAT'S JUST A SUPERSTITION.

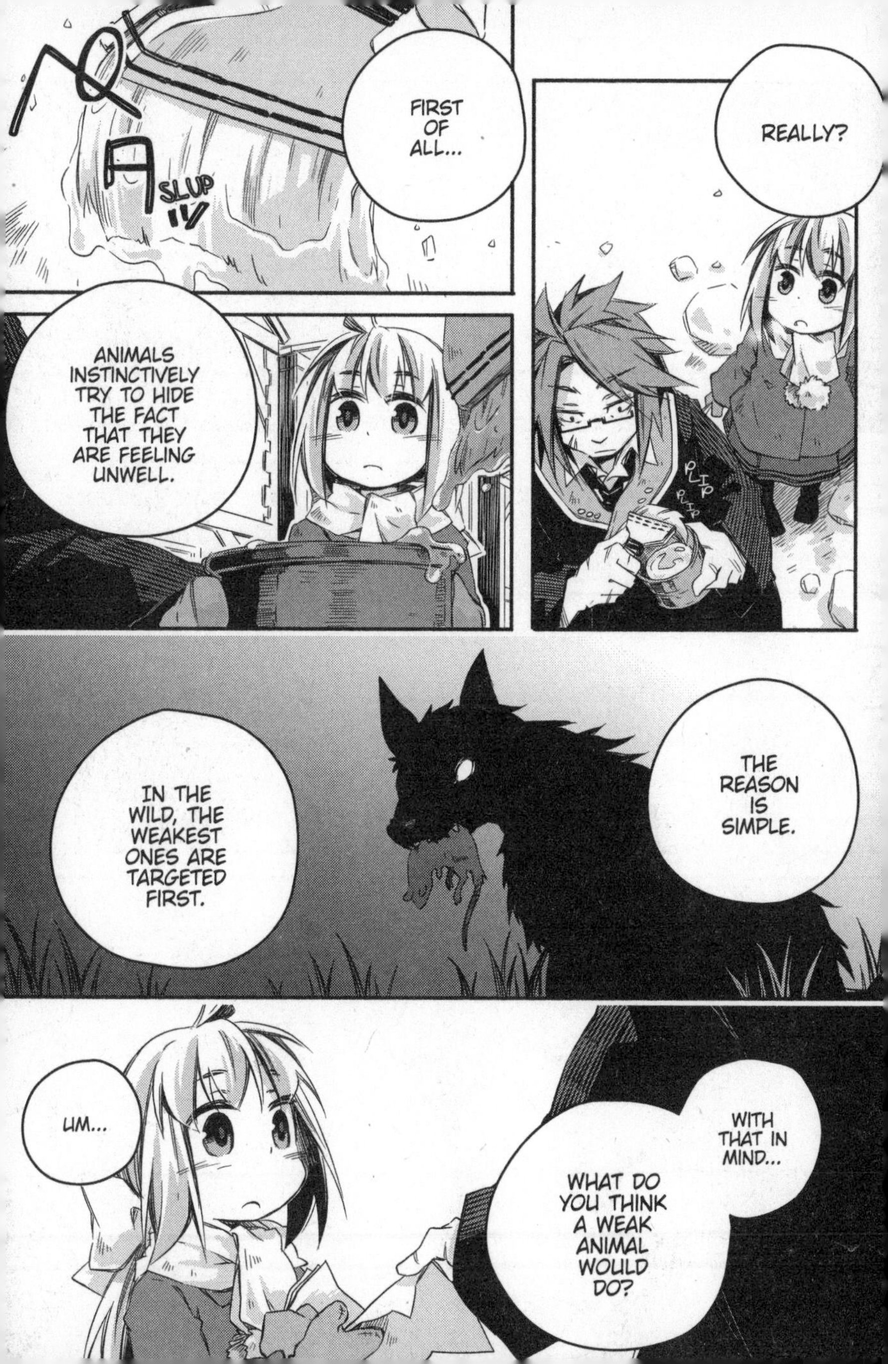
REALLY?
PLIP PLIP
FIRST OF ALL...
SLUP
ANIMALS INSTINCTIVELY TRY TO HIDE THE FACT THAT THEY ARE FEELING UNWELL.
THE REASON IS SIMPLE.
IN THE WILD, THE WEAKEST ONES ARE TARGETED FIRST.
WITH THAT IN MIND...
WHAT DO YOU THINK A WEAK ANIMAL WOULD DO?
UM...

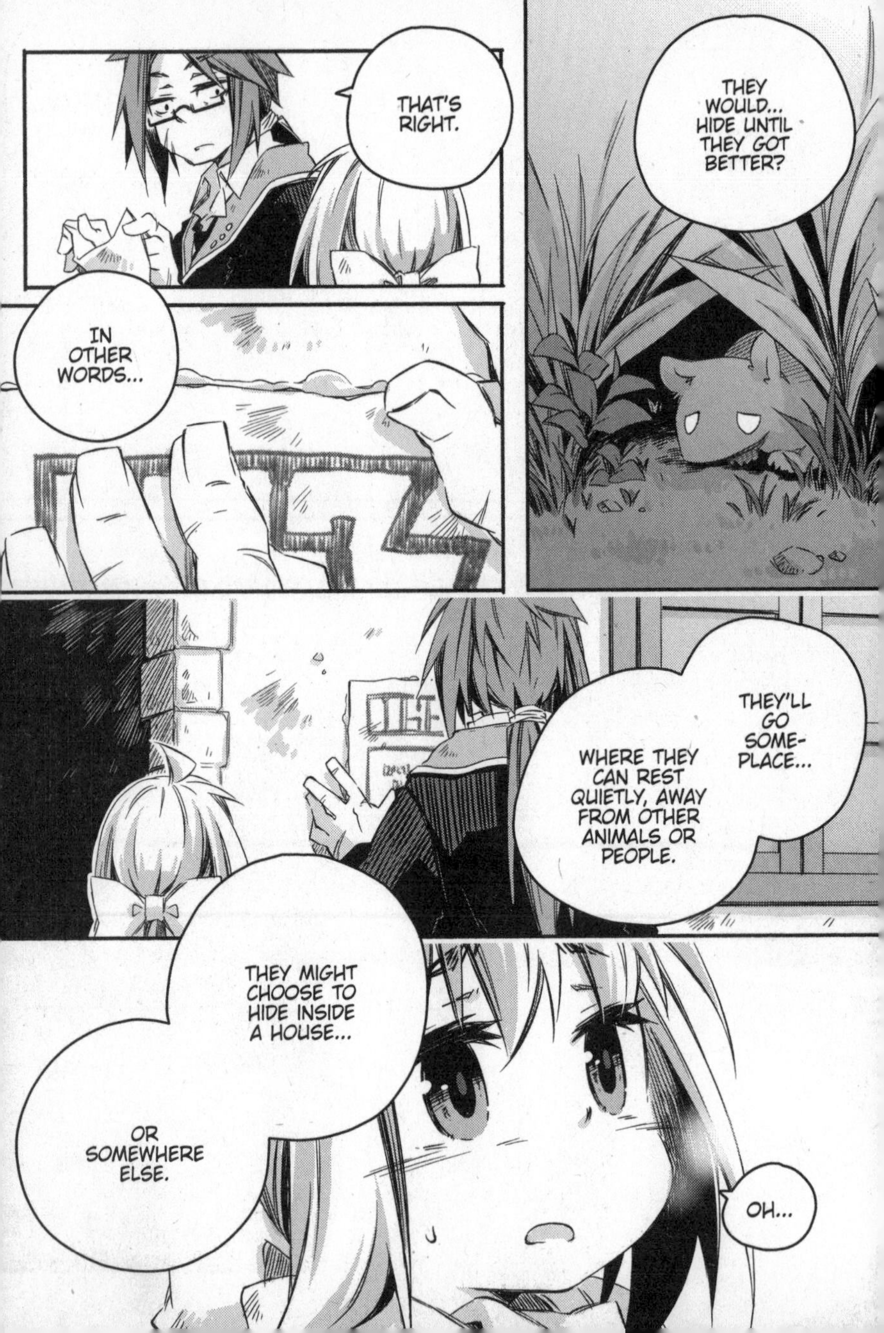
THEY WOULD... HIDE UNTIL THEY GOT BETTER?
THAT'S RIGHT.
IN OTHER WORDS...
THEY'LL GO SOME-PLACE...
WHERE THEY CAN REST QUIETLY, AWAY FROM OTHER ANIMALS OR PEOPLE.
THEY MIGHT CHOOSE TO HIDE INSIDE A HOUSE...
OR SOMEWHERE ELSE.
OH...

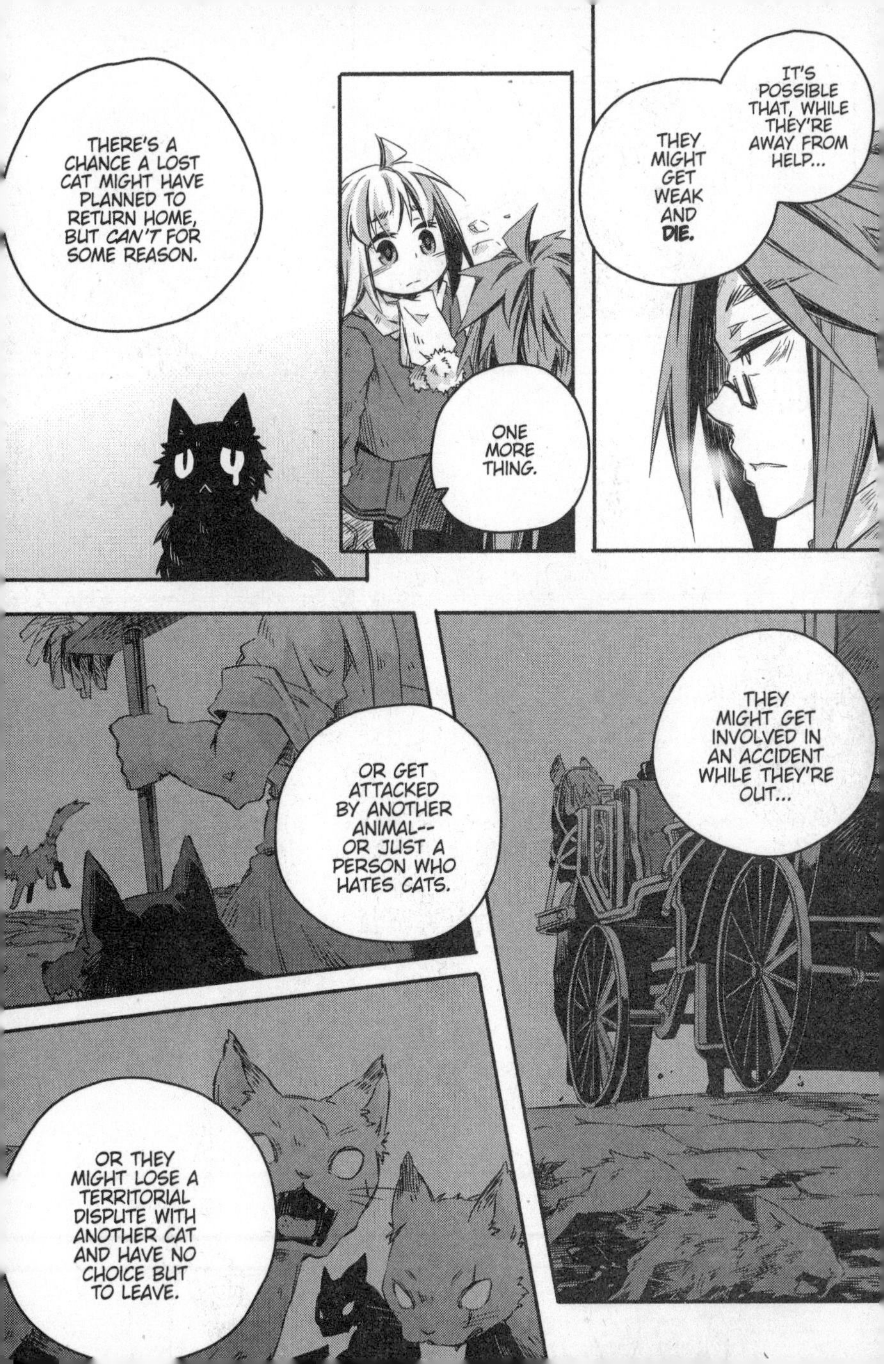
IT'S POSSIBLE THAT, WHILE THEY'RE AWAY FROM HELP...
THEY MIGHT GET WEAK AND **DIE.**
ONE MORE THING.
THERE'S A CHANCE A LOST CAT MIGHT HAVE PLANNED TO RETURN HOME, BUT *CAN'T* FOR SOME REASON.
THEY MIGHT GET INVOLVED IN AN ACCIDENT WHILE THEY'RE OUT...
OR GET ATTACKED BY ANOTHER ANIMAL-- OR JUST A PERSON WHO HATES CATS.
OR THEY MIGHT LOSE A TERRITORIAL DISPUTE WITH ANOTHER CAT AND HAVE NO CHOICE BUT TO LEAVE.

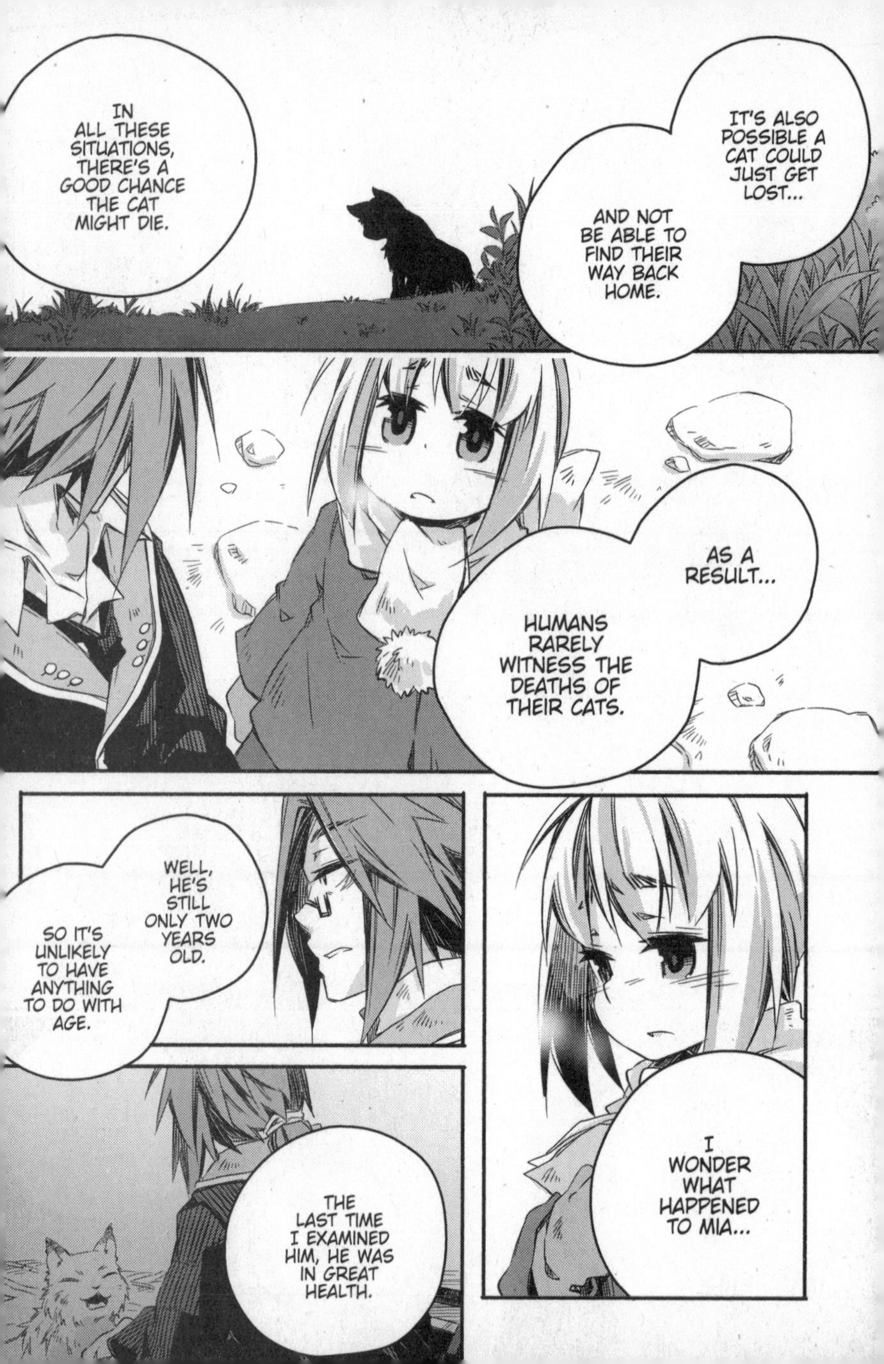
IN ALL THESE SITUATIONS, THERE'S A GOOD CHANCE THE CAT MIGHT DIE.
IT'S ALSO POSSIBLE A CAT COULD JUST GET LOST...
AND NOT BE ABLE TO FIND THEIR WAY BACK HOME.
AS A RESULT...
HUMANS RARELY WITNESS THE DEATHS OF THEIR CATS.
I WONDER WHAT HAPPENED TO MIA...
WELL, HE'S STILL ONLY TWO YEARS OLD.
SO IT'S UNLIKELY TO HAVE ANYTHING TO DO WITH AGE.
THE LAST TIME I EXAMINED HIM, HE WAS IN GREAT HEALTH.

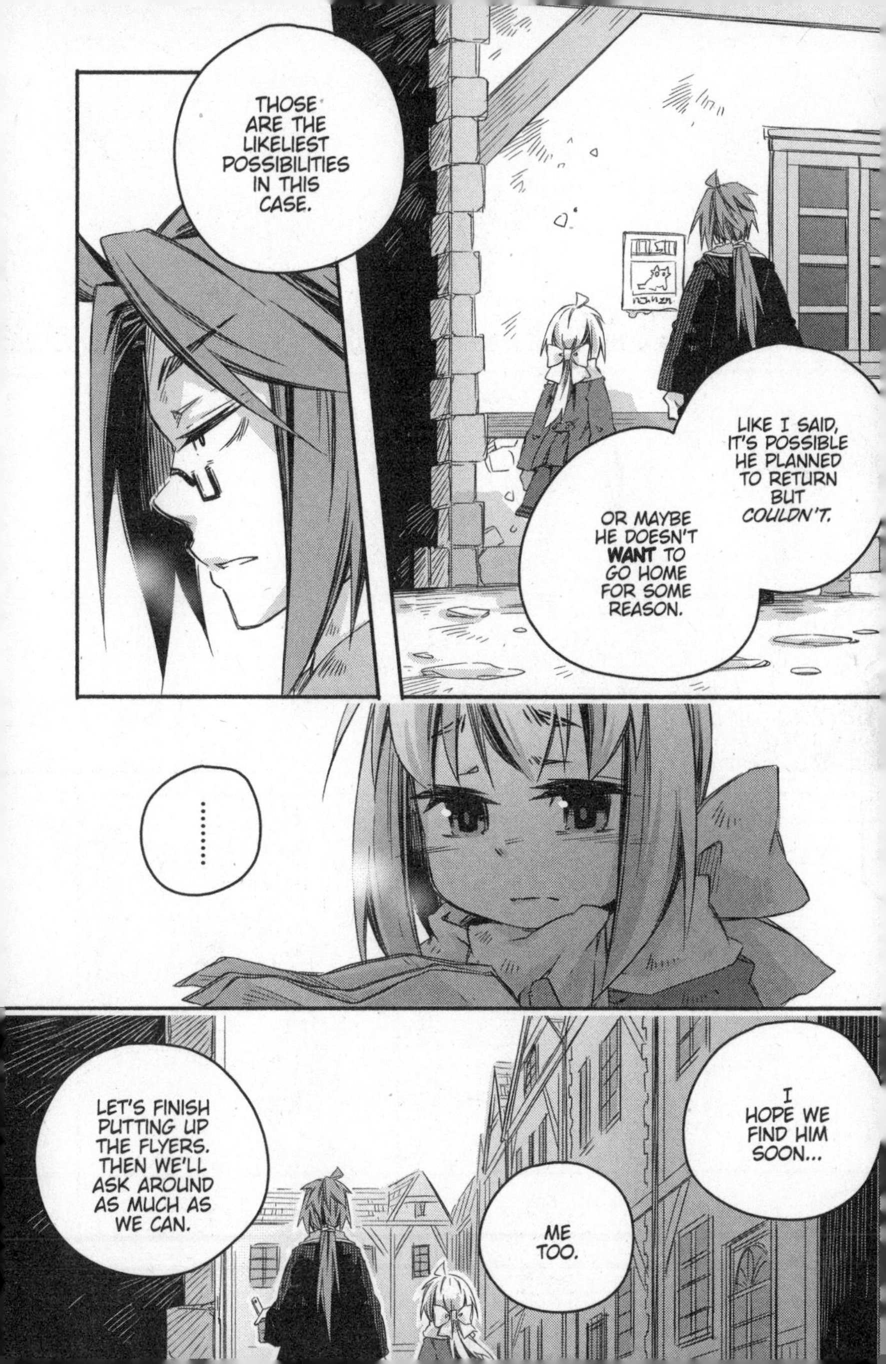
LIKE I SAID, IT'S POSSIBLE HE PLANNED TO RETURN BUT *COULDN'T.*
OR MAYBE HE DOESN'T **WANT** TO GO HOME FOR SOME REASON.
THOSE ARE THE LIKELIEST POSSIBILITIES IN THIS CASE.
....
I HOPE WE FIND HIM SOON...
ME TOO.
LET'S FINISH PUTTING UP THE FLYERS. THEN WE'LL ASK AROUND AS MUCH AS WE CAN.

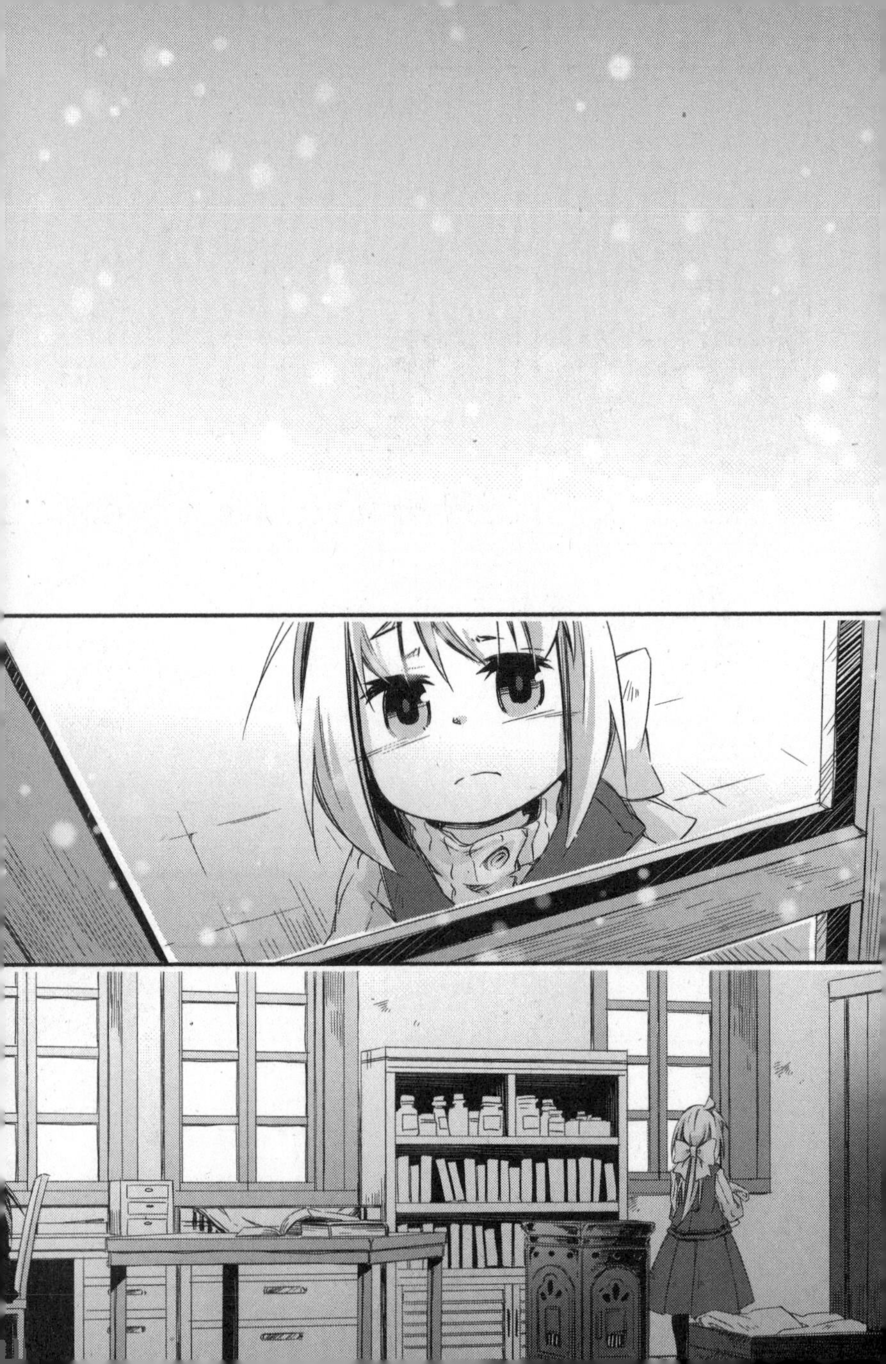

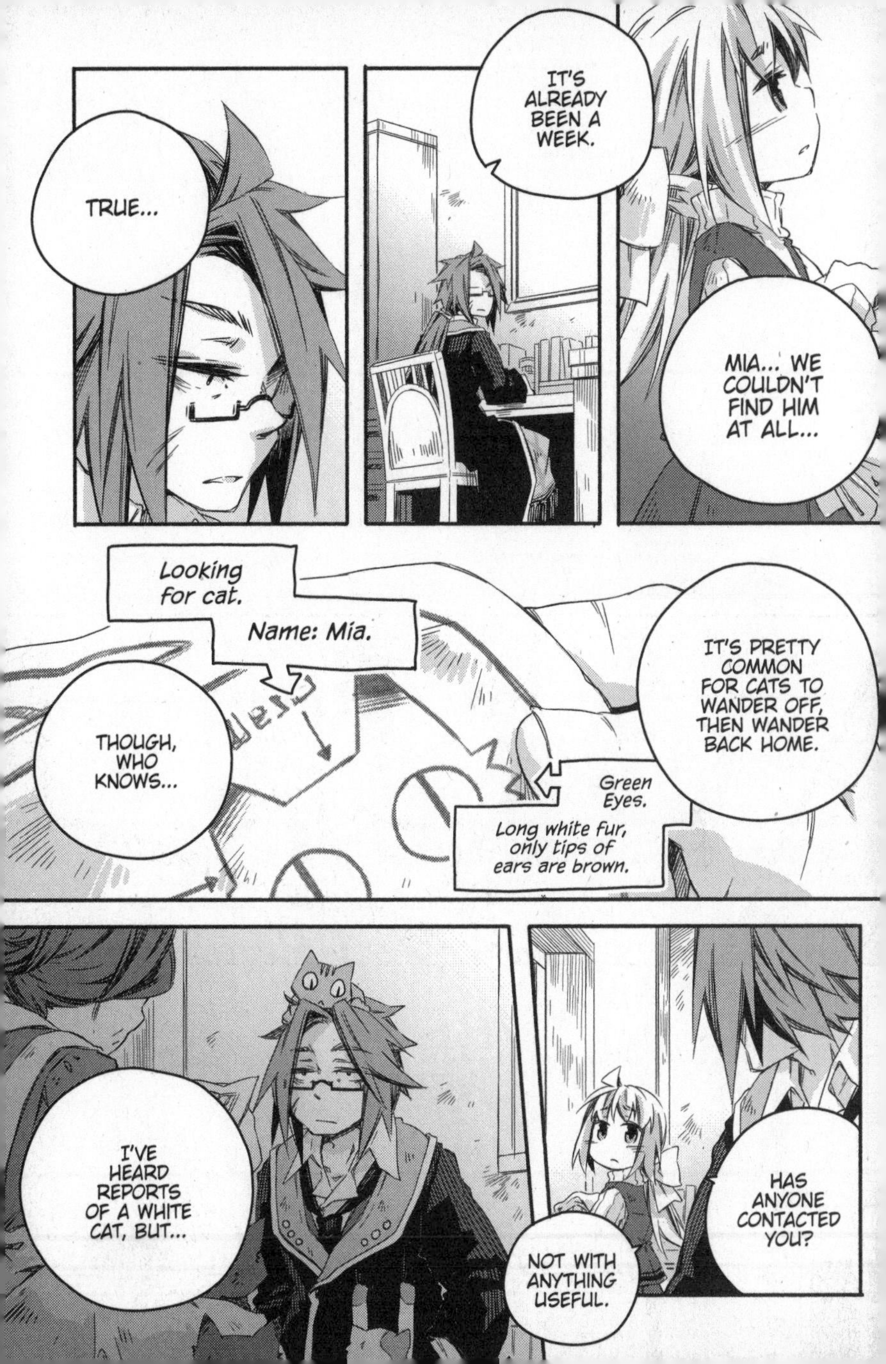
IT'S ALREADY BEEN A WEEK.
MIA... WE COULDN'T FIND HIM AT ALL...
TRUE...
IT'S PRETTY COMMON FOR CATS TO WANDER OFF, THEN WANDER BACK HOME.
Looking for cat.
Name: Mia.
Green Eyes.
Long white fur, only tips of ears are brown.
THOUGH, WHO KNOWS...
HAS ANYONE CONTACTED YOU?
NOT WITH ANYTHING USEFUL.
I'VE HEARD REPORTS OF A WHITE CAT, BUT...

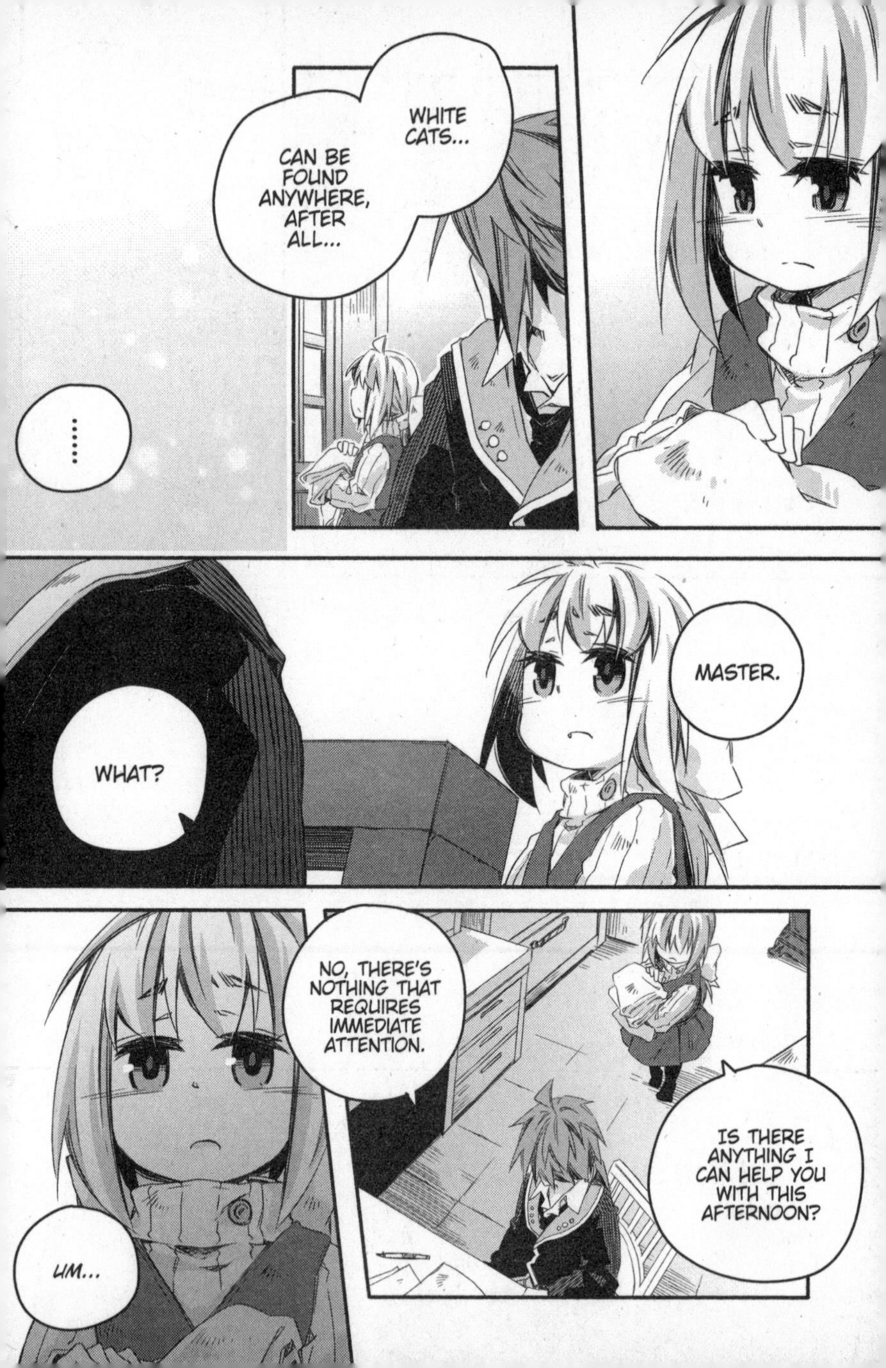
WHITE CATS...
CAN BE FOUND ANYWHERE, AFTER ALL...
......
MASTER.
WHAT?
IS THERE ANYTHING I CAN HELP YOU WITH THIS AFTERNOON?
NO, THERE'S NOTHING THAT REQUIRES IMMEDIATE ATTENTION.
UM...

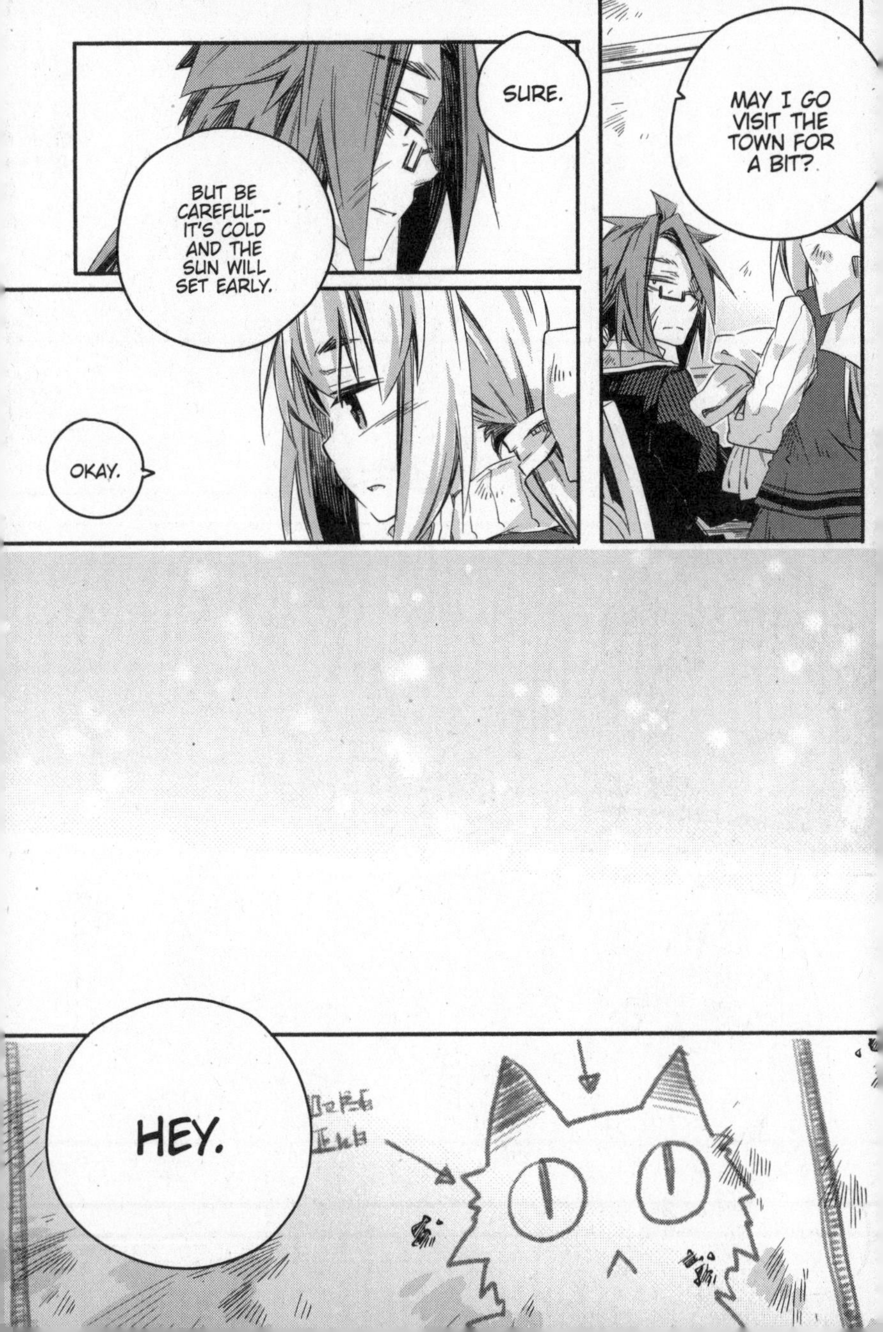
MAY I GO VISIT THE TOWN FOR A BIT?
SURE.
BUT BE CAREFUL-- IT'S COLD AND THE SUN WILL SET EARLY.
OKAY.
HEY.

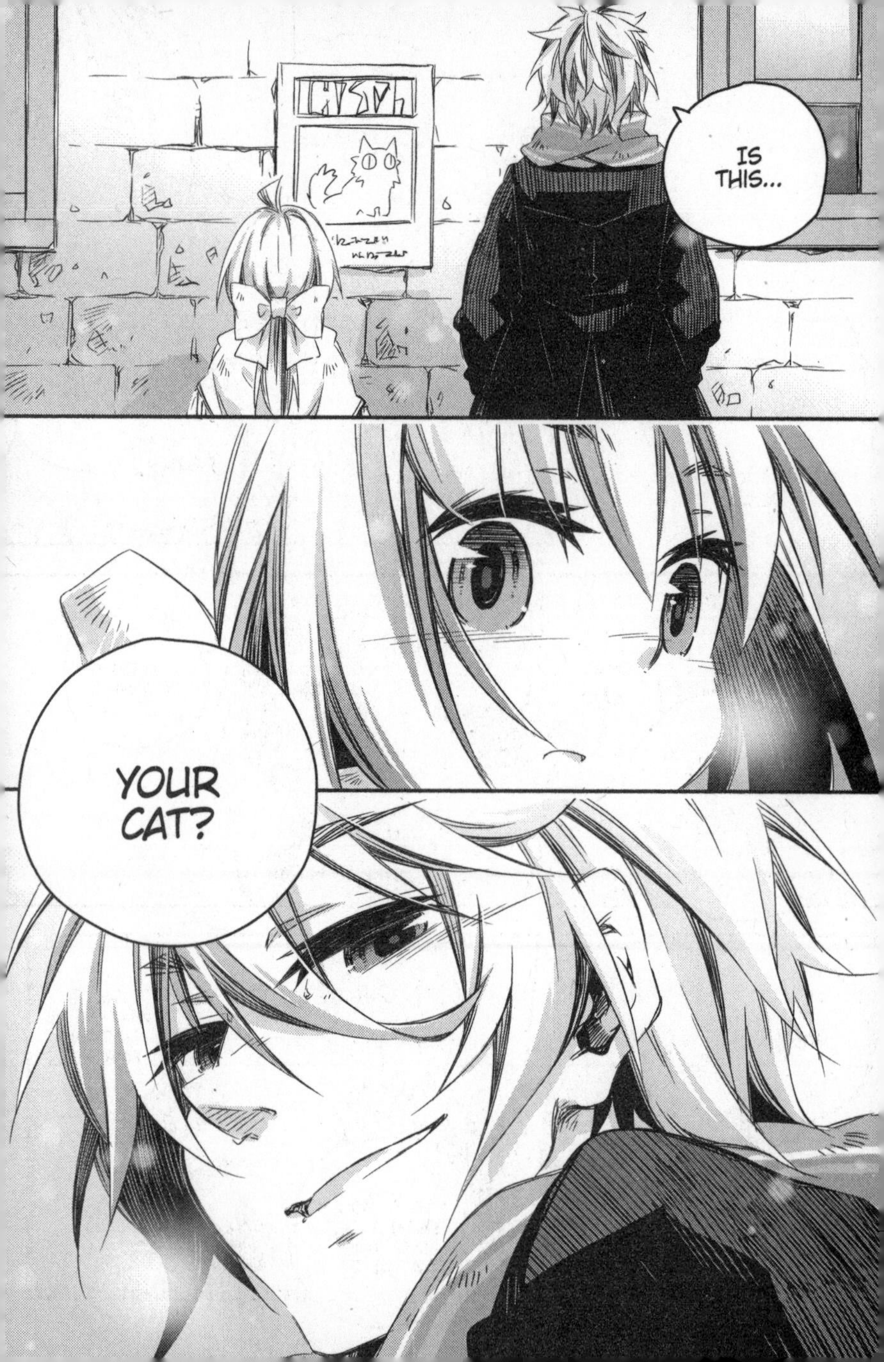
IS THIS...
YOUR CAT?

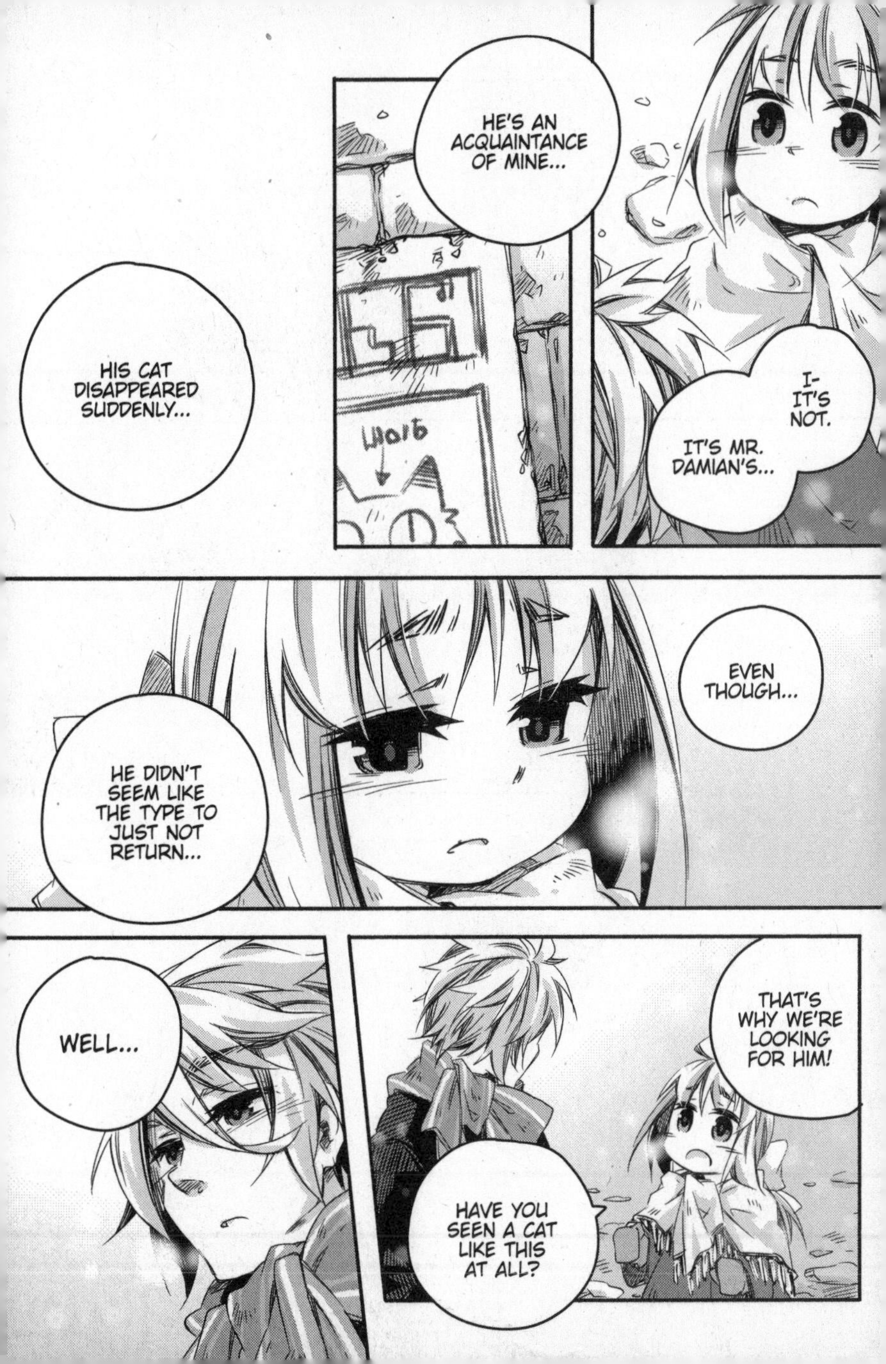
I- IT'S NOT.
IT'S MR. DAMIAN'S...
HE'S AN ACQUAINTANCE OF MINE...
HIS CAT DISAPPEARED SUDDENLY...
EVEN THOUGH...
HE DIDN'T SEEM LIKE THE TYPE TO JUST NOT RETURN...
THAT'S WHY WE'RE LOOKING FOR HIM!
HAVE YOU SEEN A CAT LIKE THIS AT ALL?
WELL...

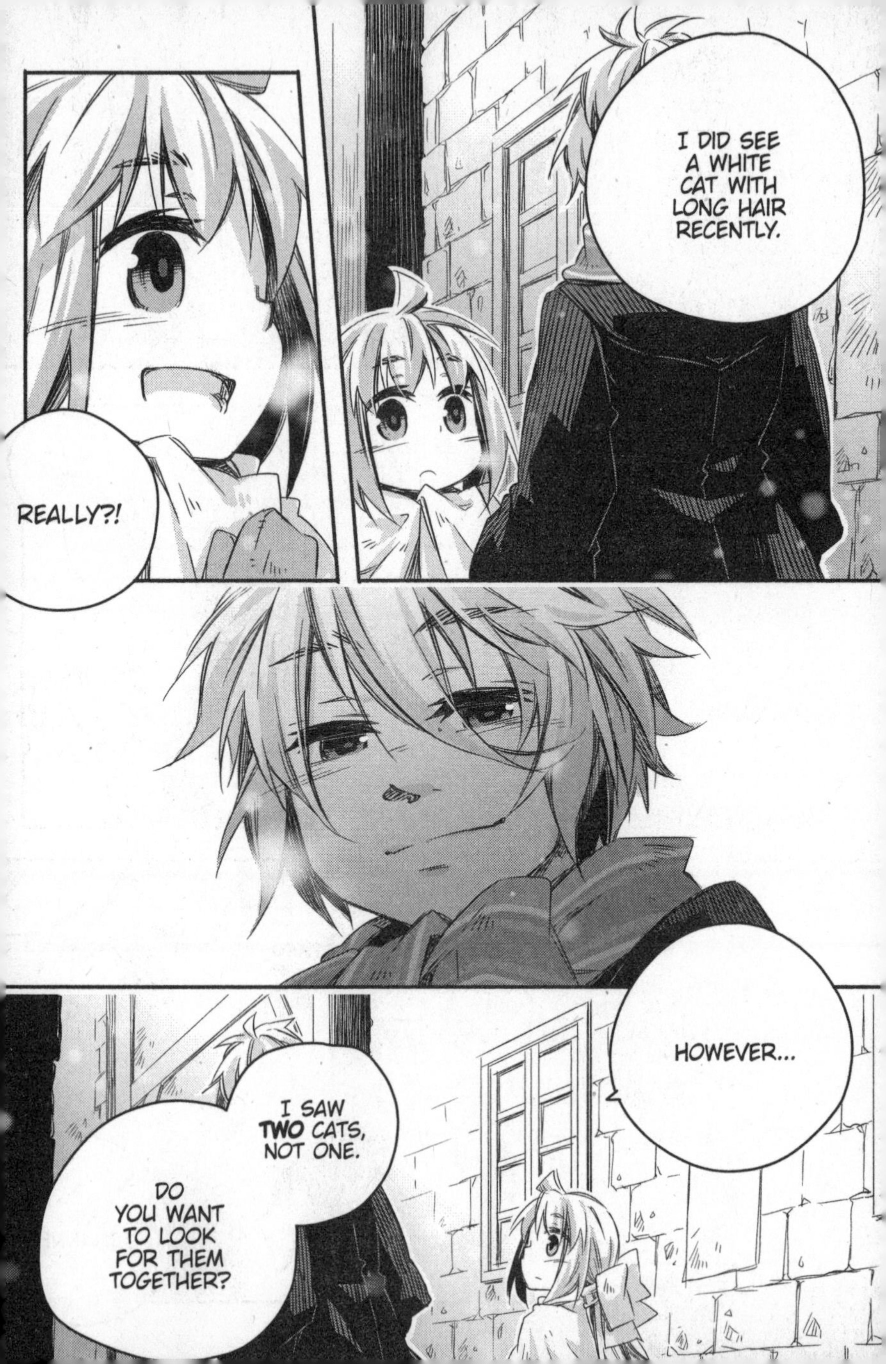
I DID SEE A WHITE CAT WITH LONG HAIR RECENTLY.
REALLY?!
HOWEVER...
I SAW **TWO** CATS, NOT ONE.
DO YOU WANT TO LOOK FOR THEM TOGETHER?

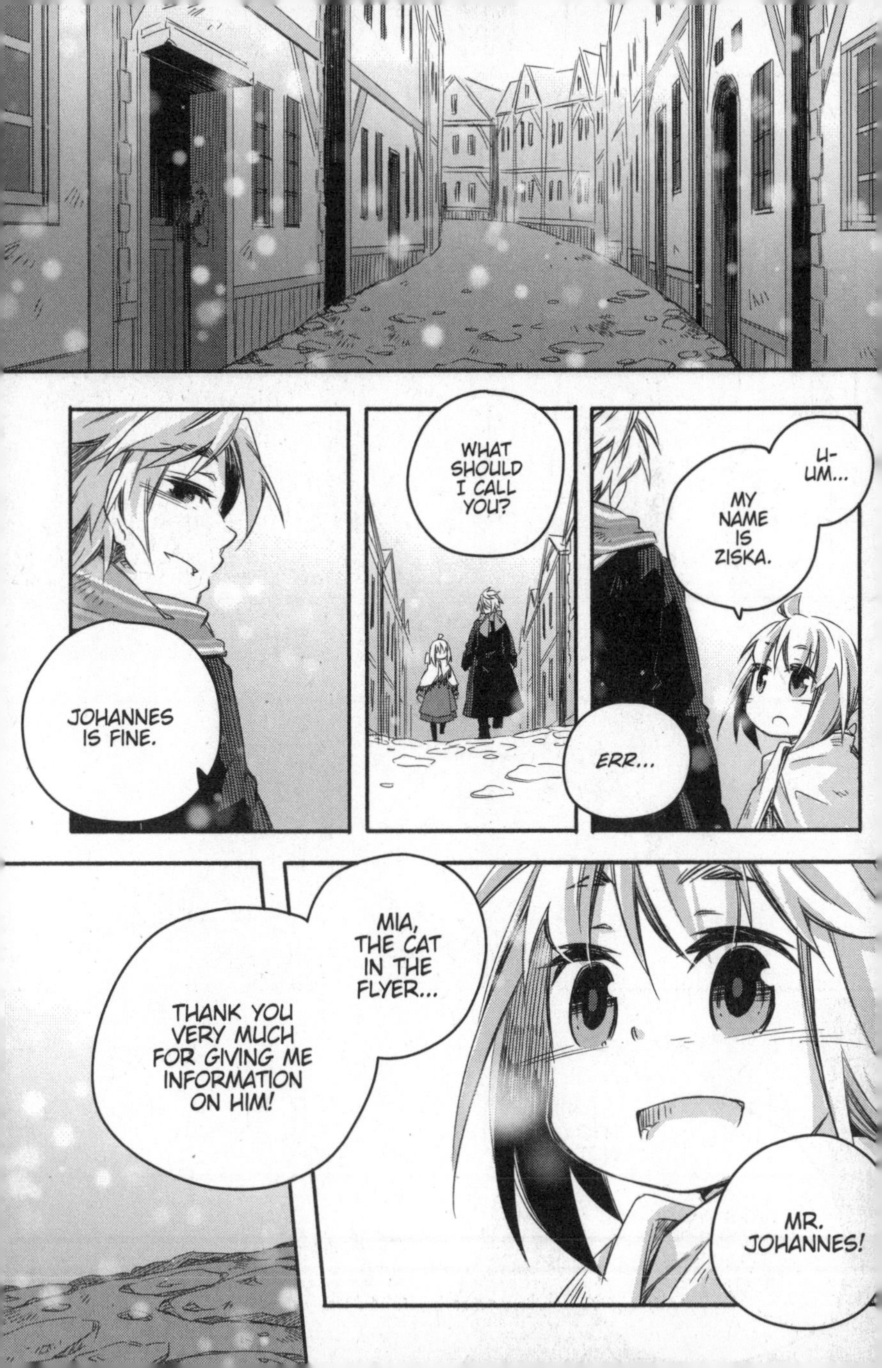
U-UM...
MY NAME IS ZISKA.
ERR...
WHAT SHOULD I CALL YOU?
JOHANNES IS FINE.
MIA, THE CAT IN THE FLYER...
THANK YOU VERY MUCH FOR GIVING ME INFORMATION ON HIM!
MR. JOHANNES!

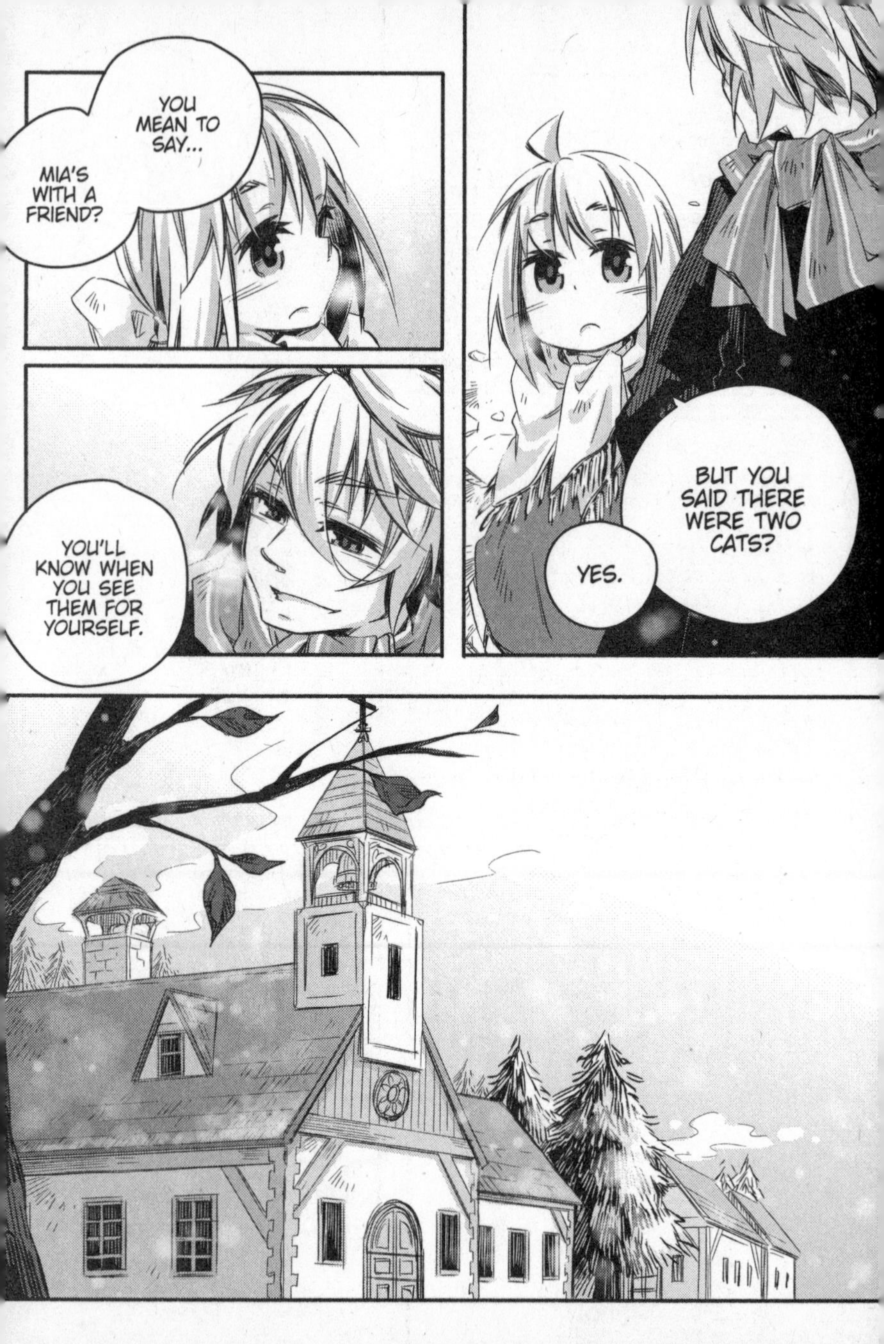
BUT YOU SAID THERE WERE TWO CATS?
YES.
YOU MEAN TO SAY...
MIA'S WITH A FRIEND?
YOU'LL KNOW WHEN YOU SEE THEM FOR YOURSELF.

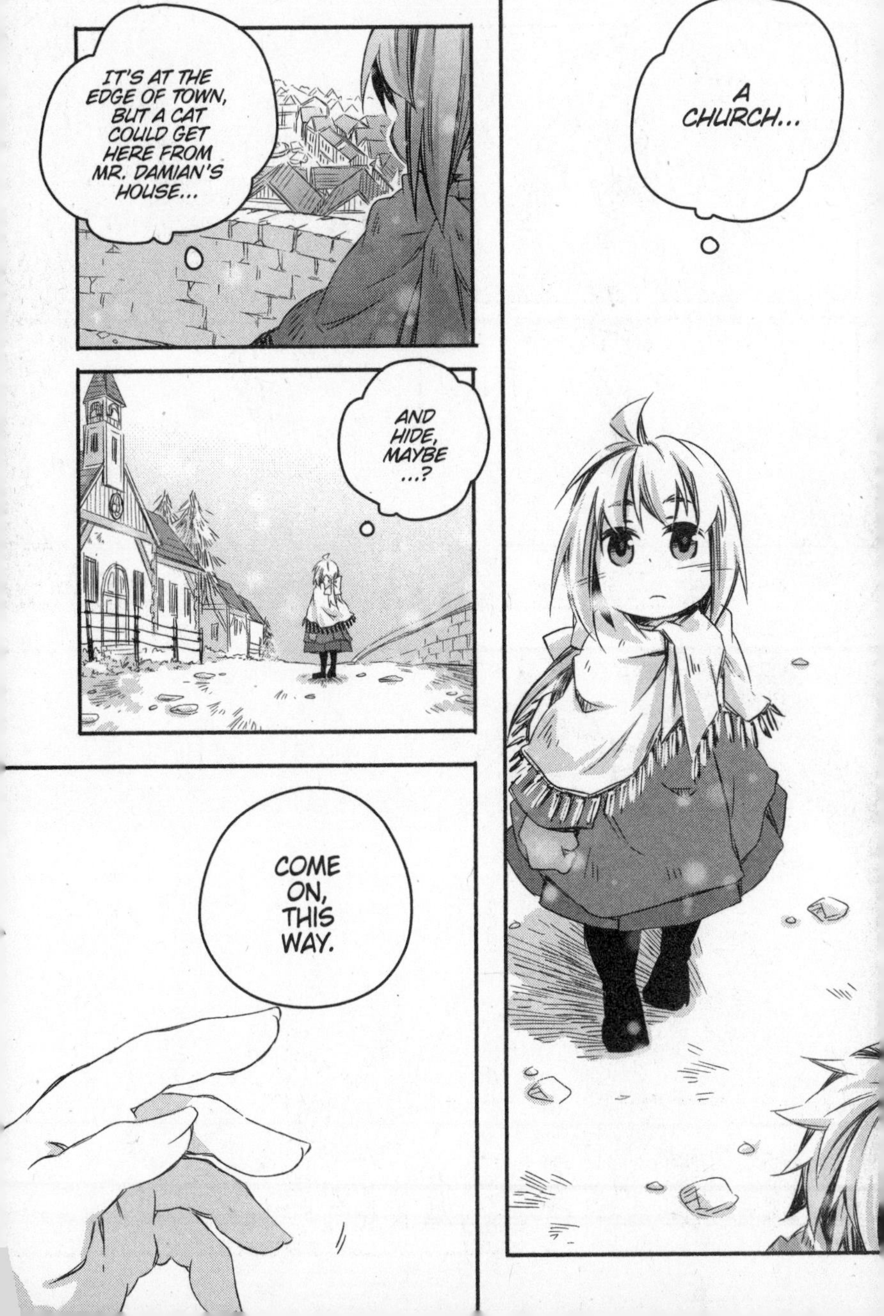
A CHURCH...
IT'S AT THE EDGE OF TOWN, BUT A CAT COULD GET HERE FROM MR. DAMIAN'S HOUSE...
AND HIDE, MAYBE ...?
COME ON, THIS WAY.

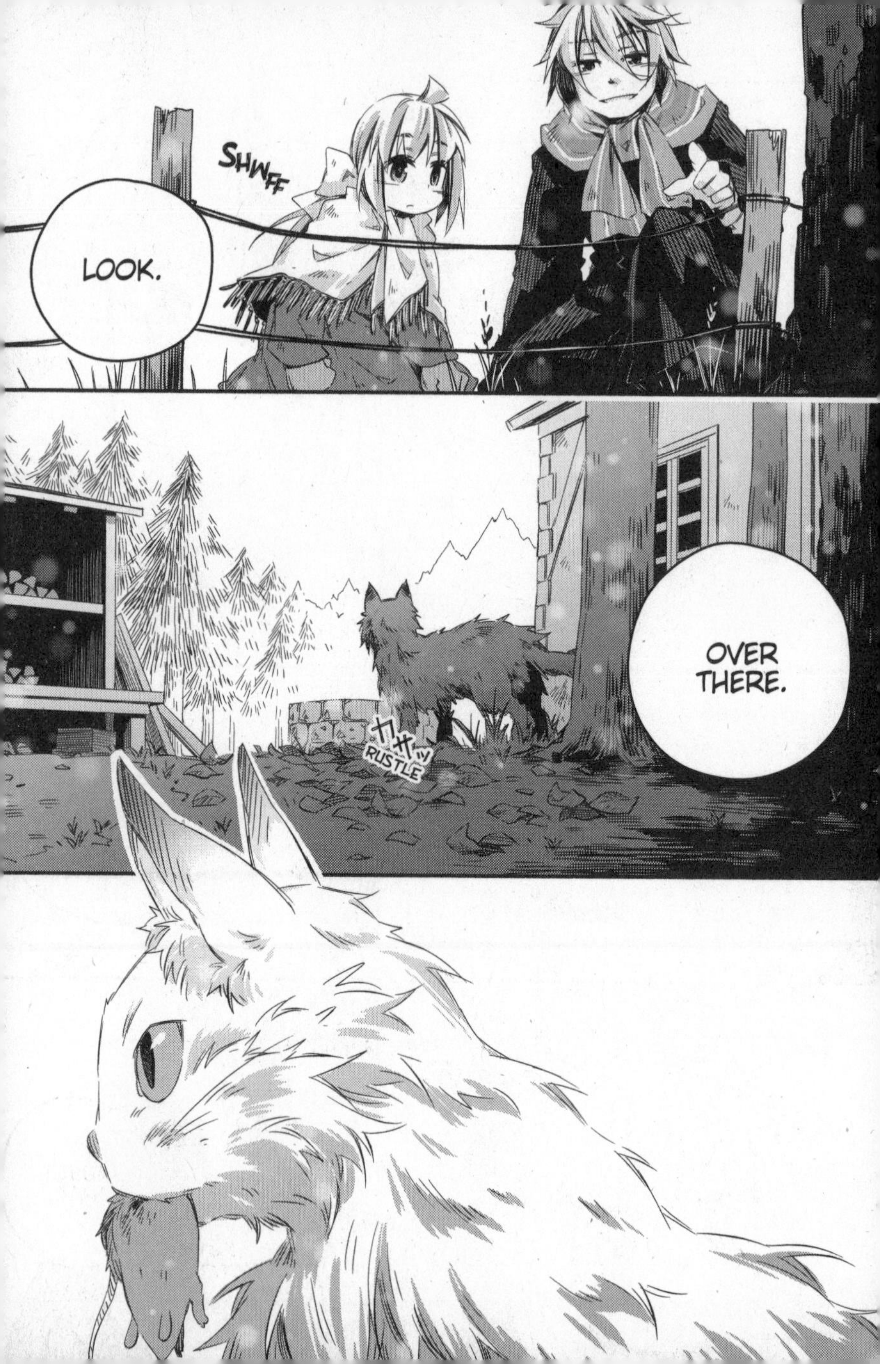
SHWFF
LOOK.
OVER THERE.
RUSTLE

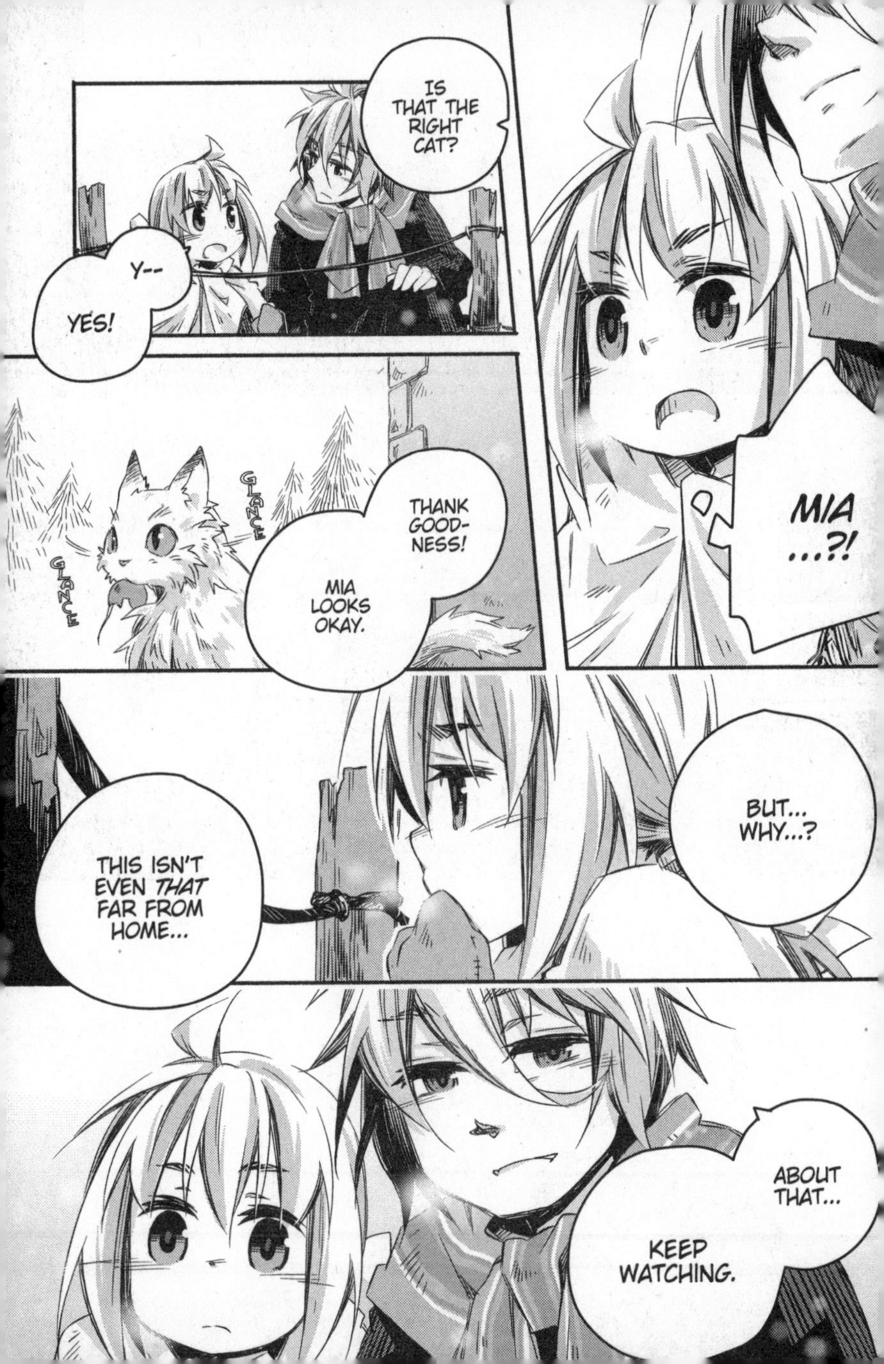
MIA ...?!
IS THAT THE RIGHT CAT?
Y-- YES!
GLANCE
GLANCE
THANK GOODNESS! MIA LOOKS OKAY.
BUT... WHY...?
THIS ISN'T EVEN *THAT* FAR FROM HOME...
ABOUT THAT... KEEP WATCHING.

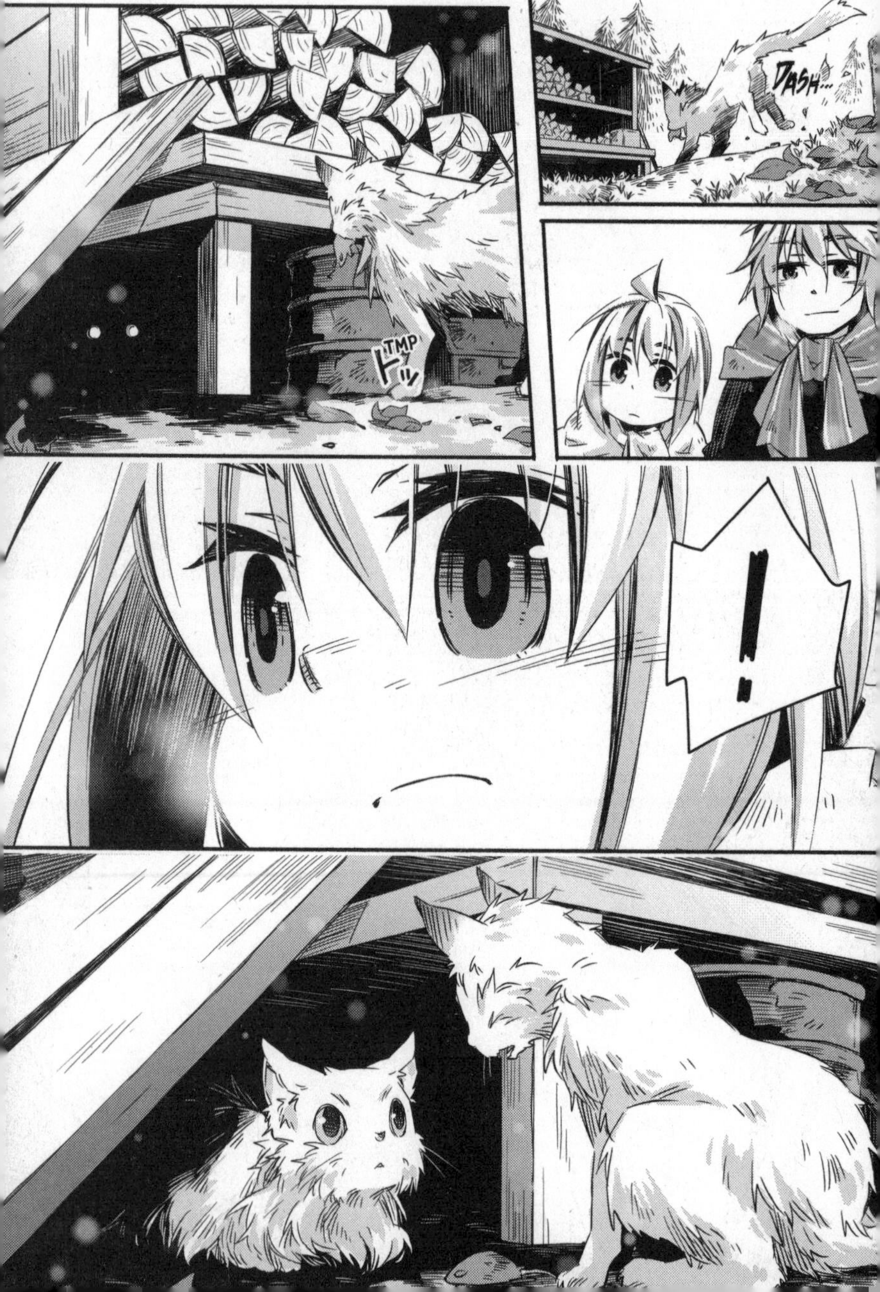
DASH...
TMP ドッ
!

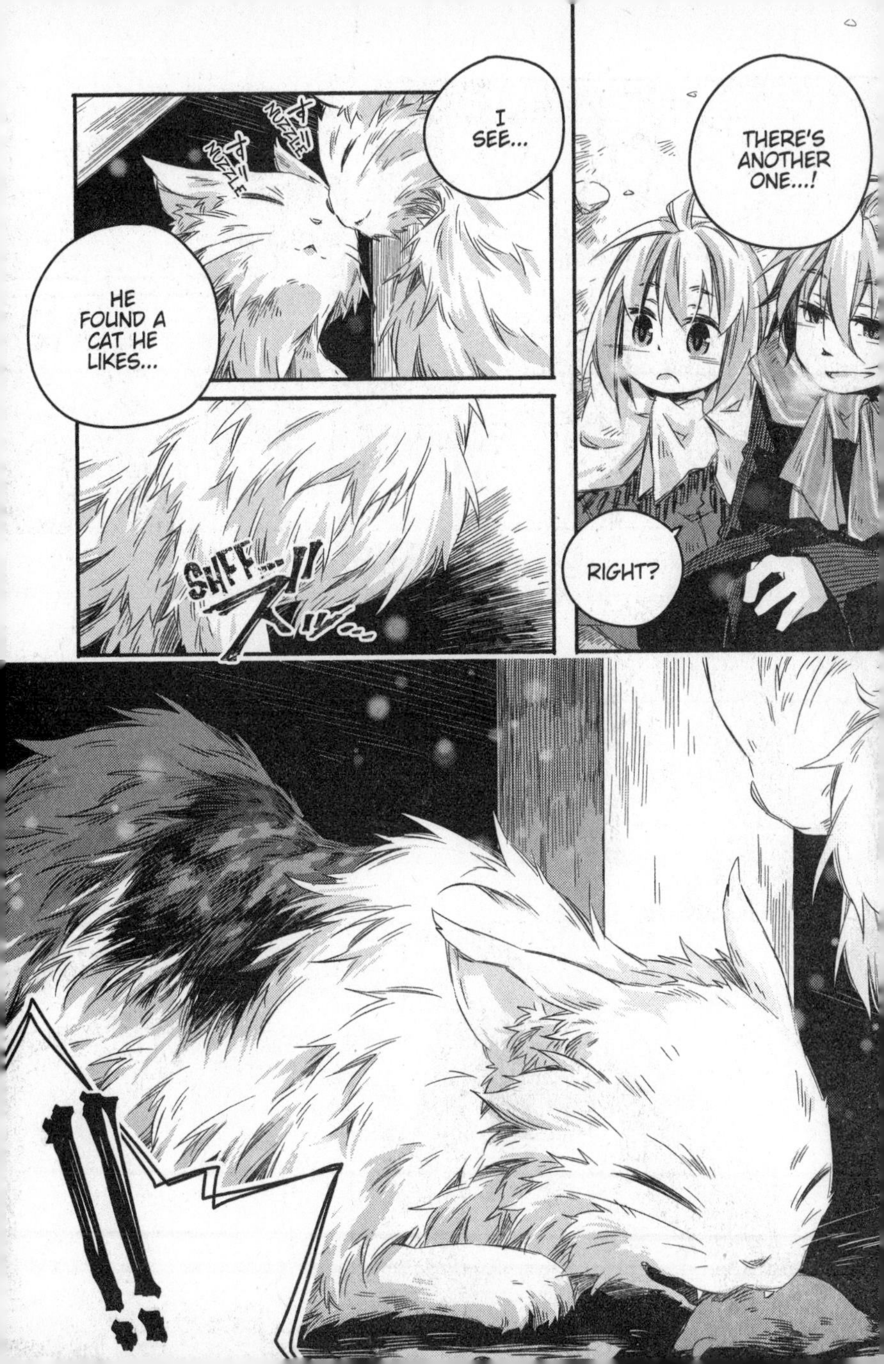
THERE'S ANOTHER ONE...!
RIGHT?
I SEE...
NUZZLE
NUZZLE
HE FOUND A CAT HE LIKES...
SHFF...
!!

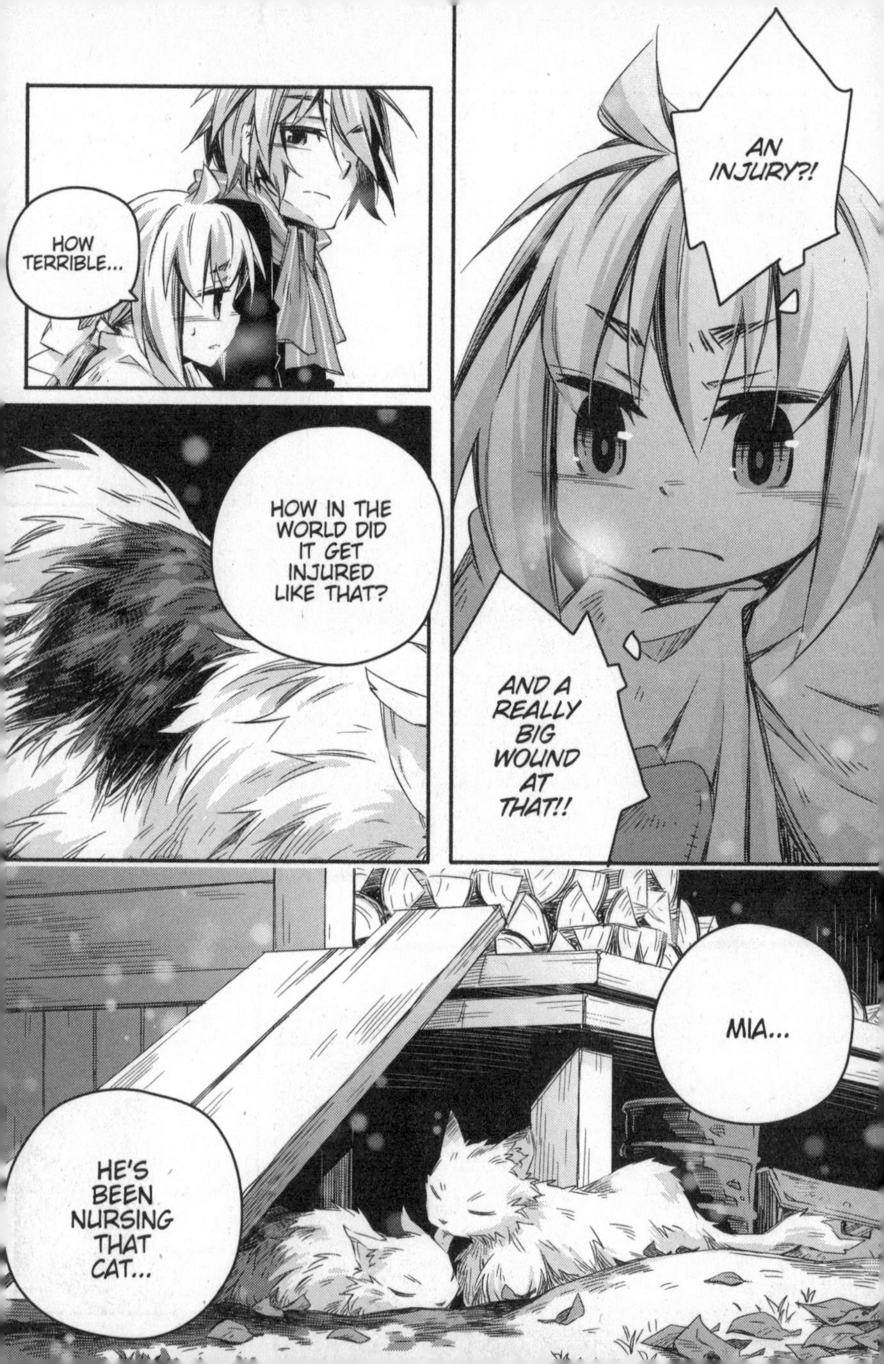
AN INJURY?!
AND A REALLY BIG WOUND AT THAT!!
HOW TERRIBLE...
HOW IN THE WORLD DID IT GET INJURED LIKE THAT?
MIA...
HE'S BEEN NURSING THAT CAT...

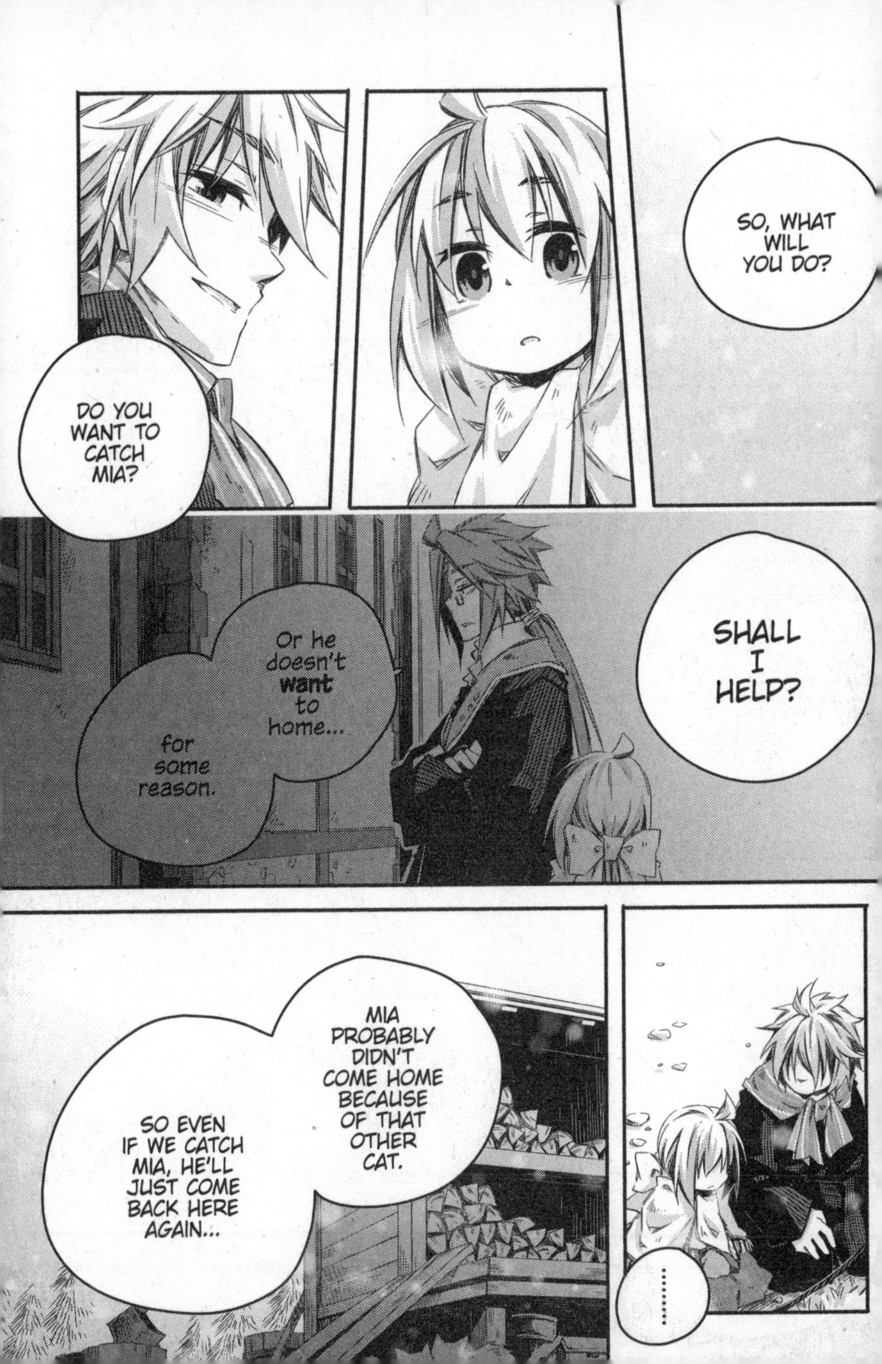
SO, WHAT WILL YOU DO?
DO YOU WANT TO CATCH MIA?
SHALL I HELP?
Or he doesn't **want** to home...
for some reason.
......
MIA PROBABLY DIDN'T COME HOME BECAUSE OF THAT OTHER CAT.
SO EVEN IF WE CATCH MIA, HE'LL JUST COME BACK HERE AGAIN...

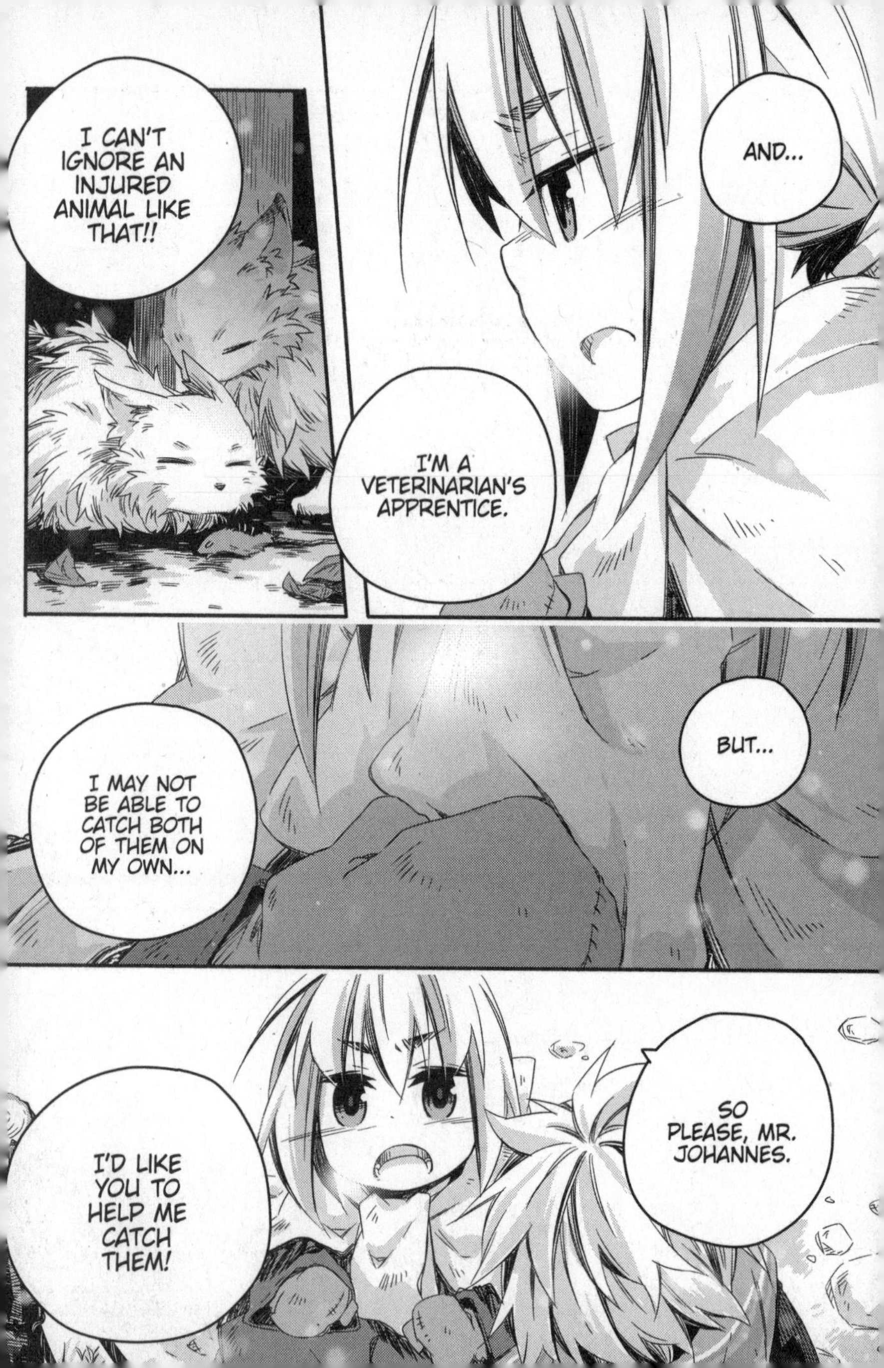
AND...
I'M A VETERINARIAN'S APPRENTICE.
I CAN'T IGNORE AN INJURED ANIMAL LIKE THAT!!
BUT...
I MAY NOT BE ABLE TO CATCH BOTH OF THEM ON MY OWN...
SO PLEASE, MR. JOHANNES.
I'D LIKE YOU TO HELP ME CATCH THEM!

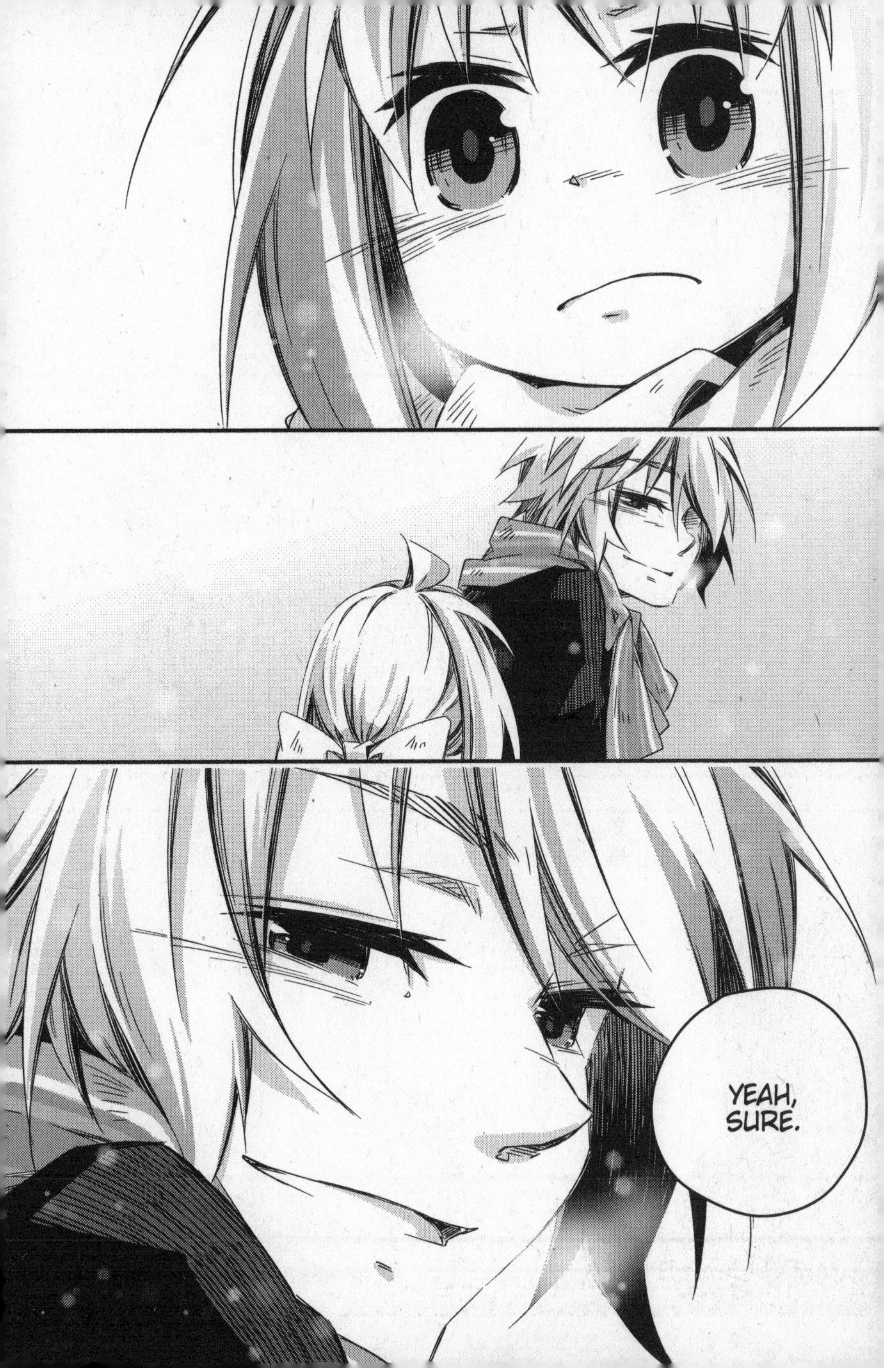
YEAH, SURE.

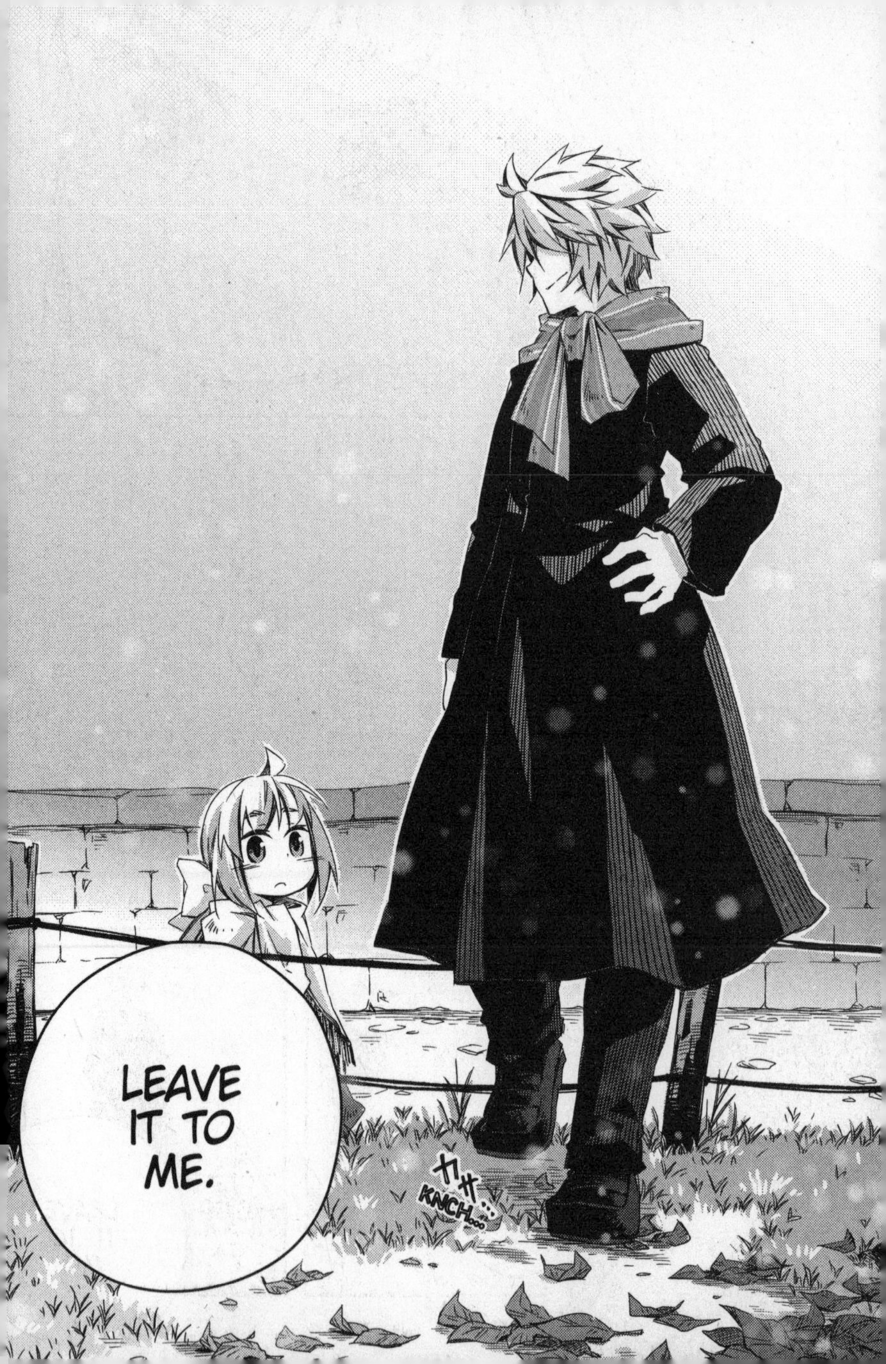
LEAVE IT TO ME.
KNCH...

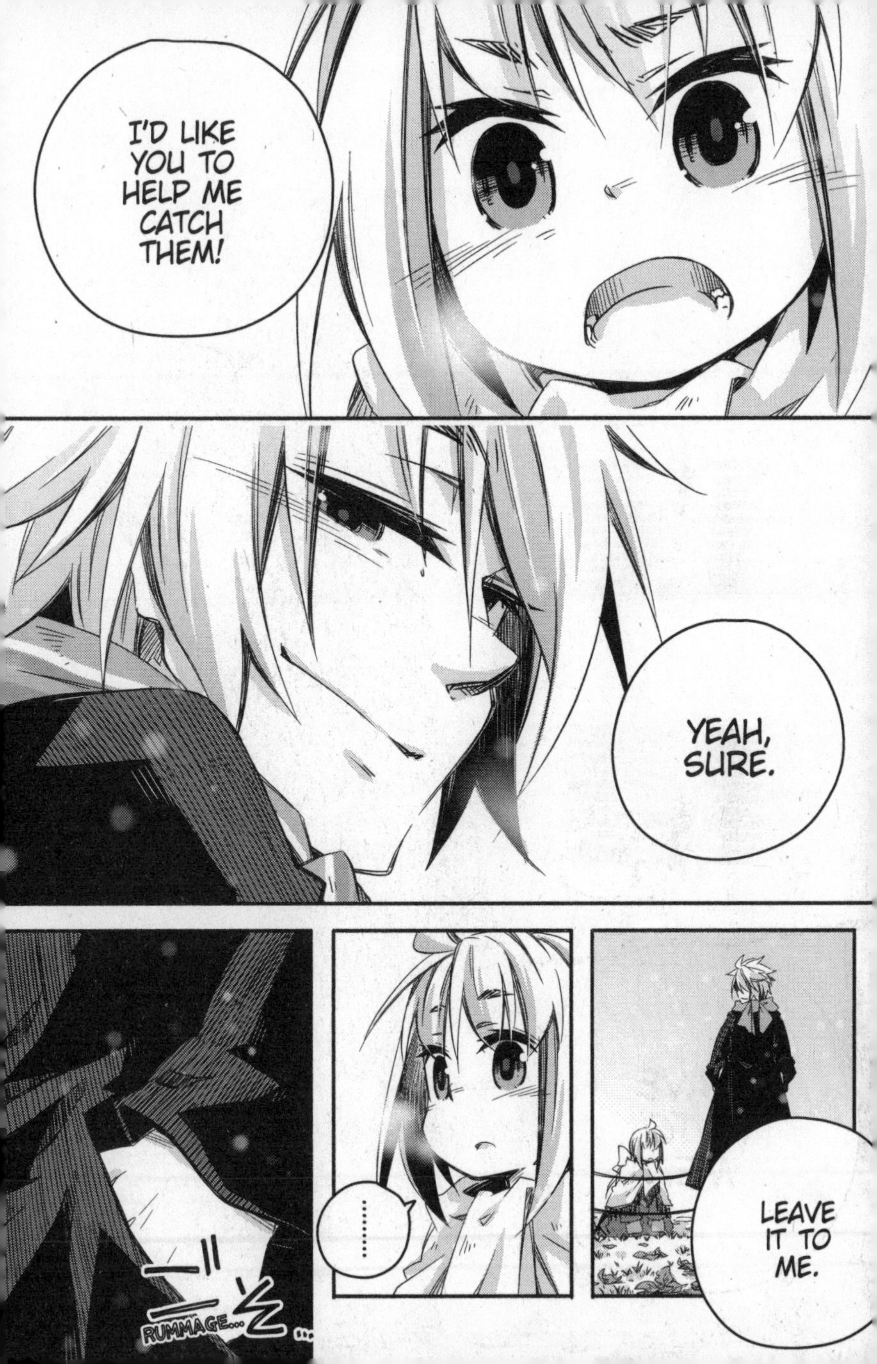
I'D LIKE YOU TO HELP ME CATCH THEM!
YEAH, SURE.
LEAVE IT TO ME.
......
RUMMAGE...

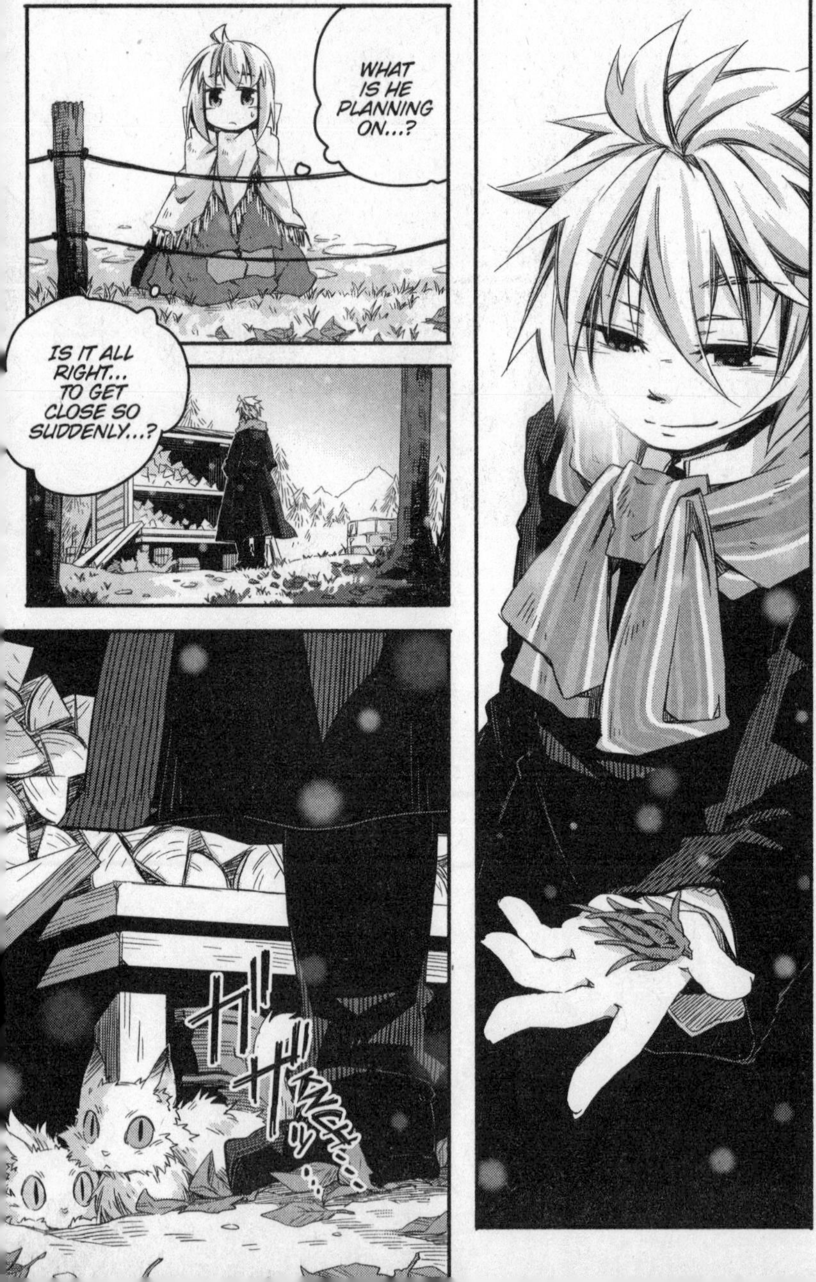
WHAT IS HE PLANNING ON...?
IS IT ALL RIGHT... TO GET CLOSE SO SUDDENLY...?
ガ ガ
TWITCH...

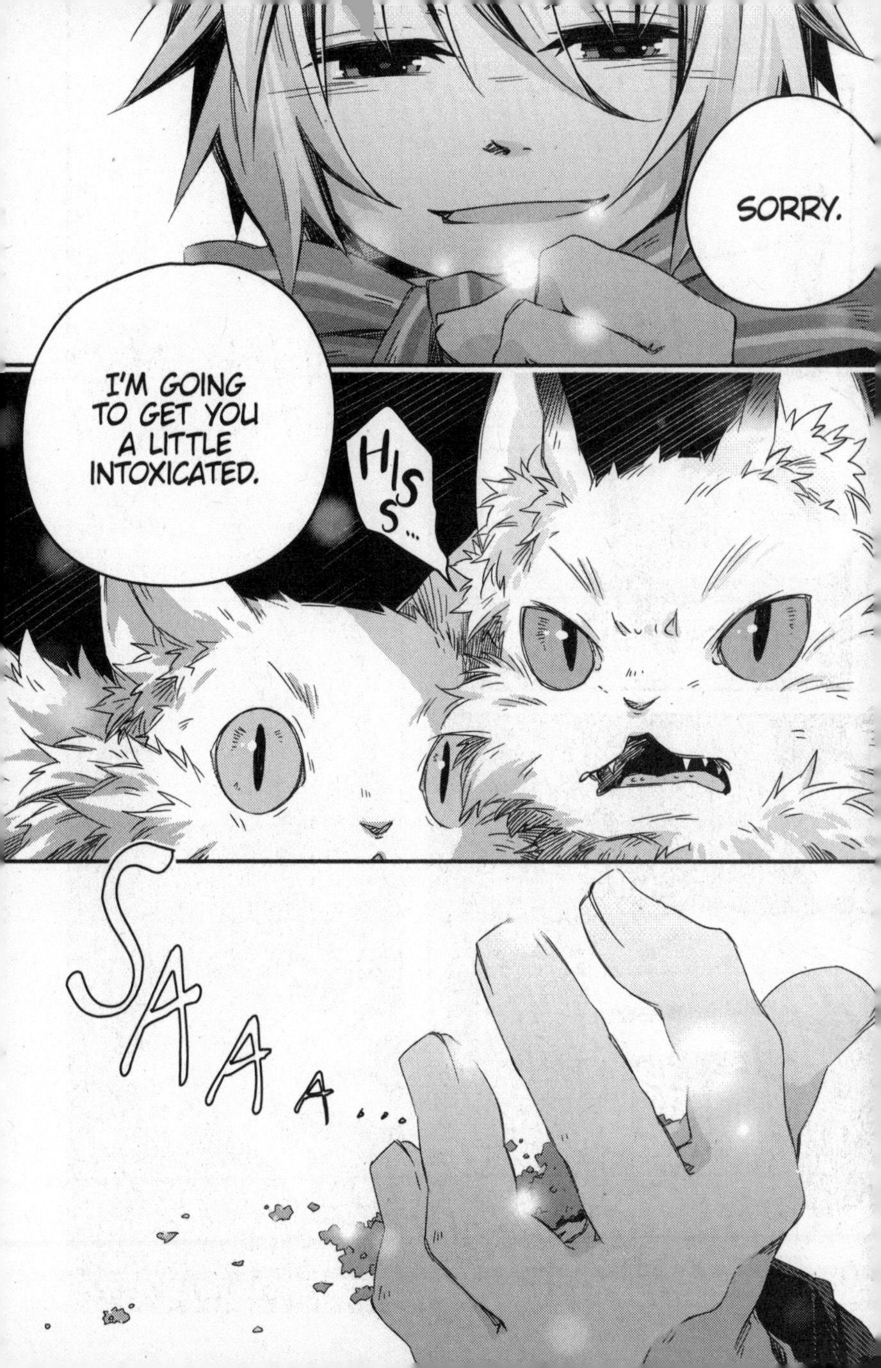
SORRY.
I'M GOING TO GET YOU A LITTLE INTOXICATED.
HISS...
SAAA...

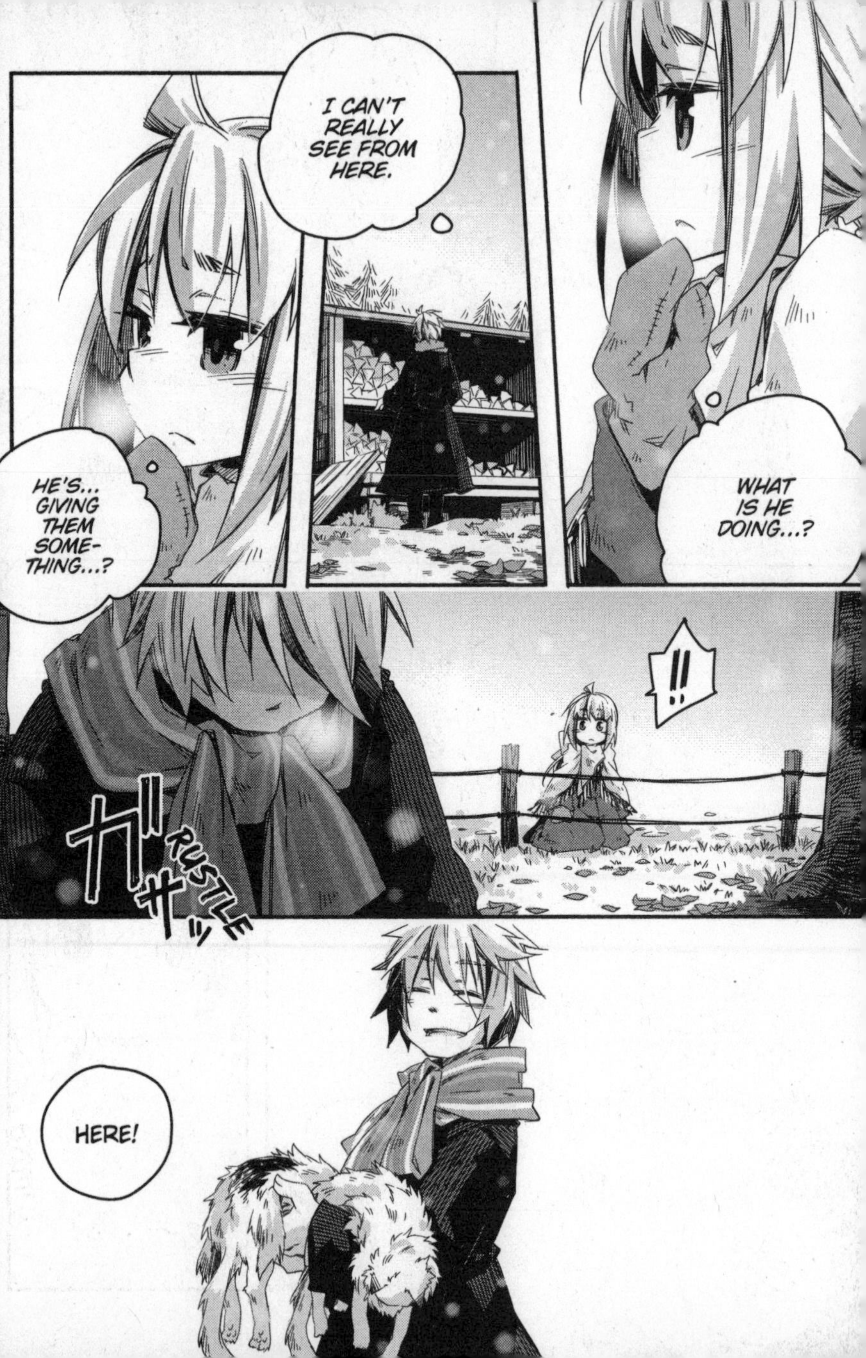
WHAT IS HE DOING...?
I CAN'T REALLY SEE FROM HERE.
HE'S... GIVING THEM SOME-THING...?
!!
RUSTLE
HERE!

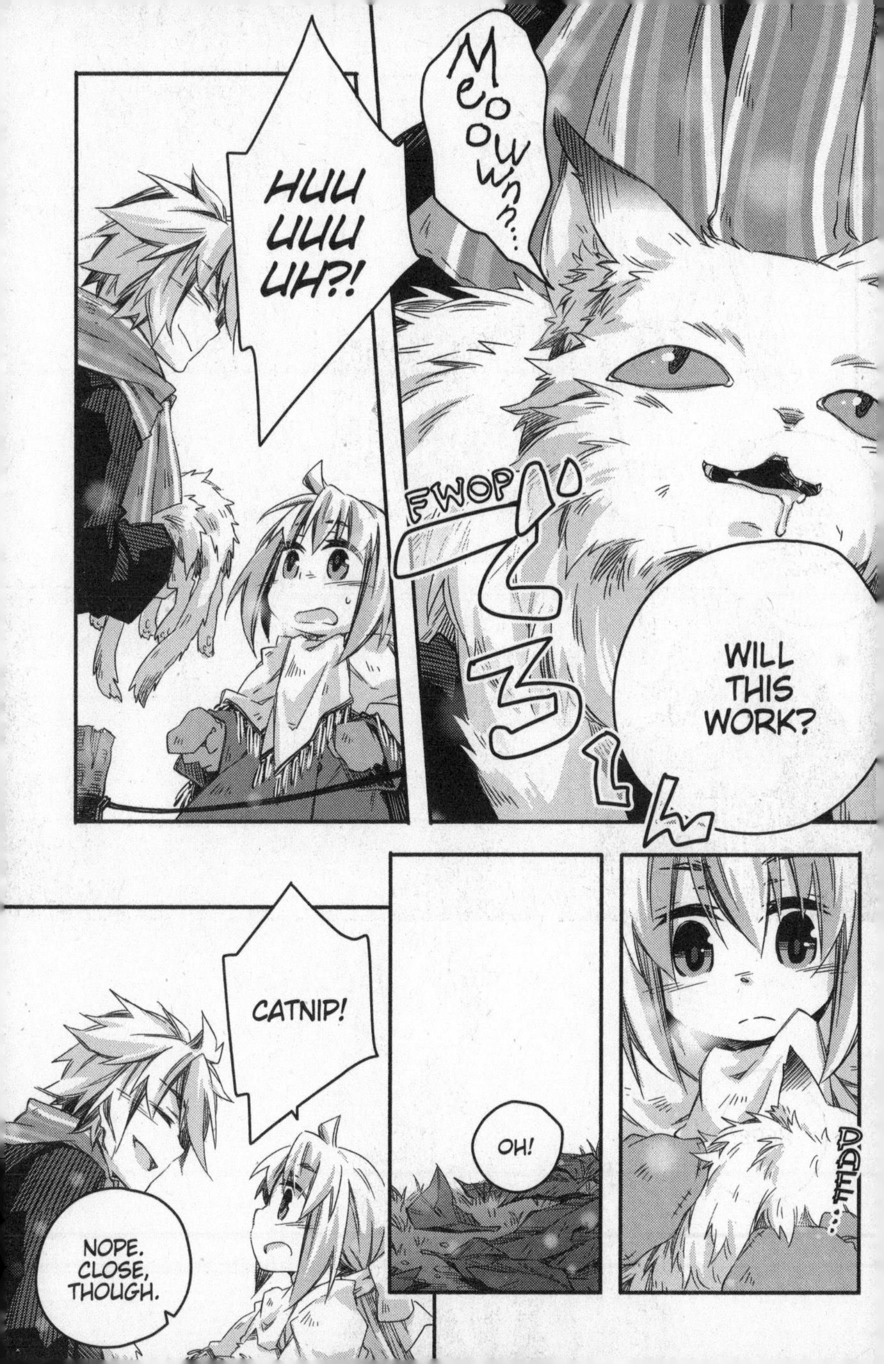
Meoownn...
FWOP
ごろん
WILL THIS WORK?
HUUUUUUH?!
PAFF...
OH!
CATNIP!
NOPE. CLOSE, THOUGH.

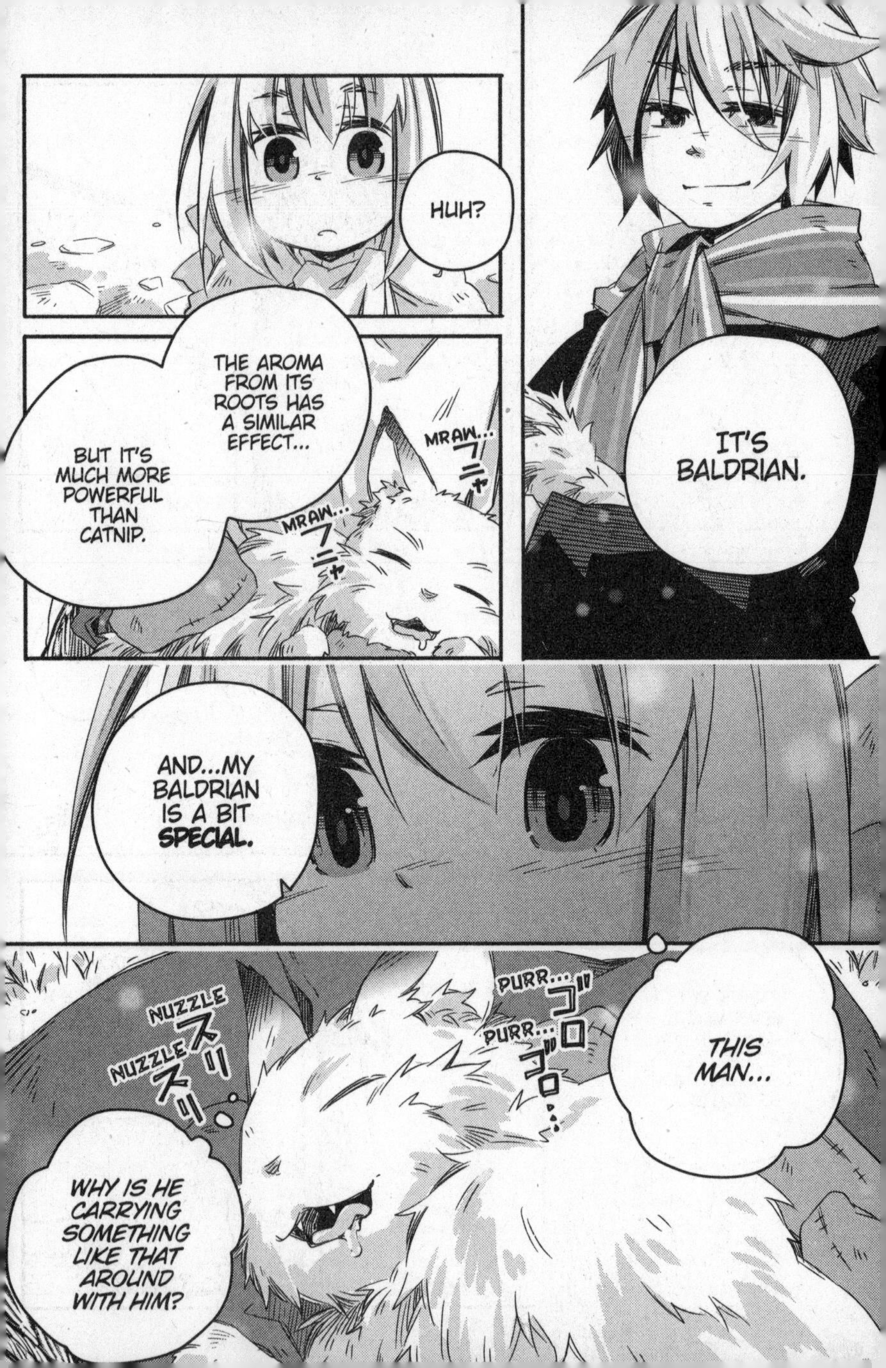
IT'S BALDRIAN.
HUH?
MRAW... フニャ
THE AROMA FROM ITS ROOTS HAS A SIMILAR EFFECT...
MRAW... フニャ
BUT IT'S MUCH MORE POWERFUL THAN CATNIP.
AND...MY BALDRIAN IS A BIT **SPECIAL.**
THIS MAN...
PURR... ゴロ
PURR... ゴロ...
NUZZLE スリ
NUZZLE スリ
WHY IS HE CARRYING SOMETHING LIKE THAT AROUND WITH HIM?

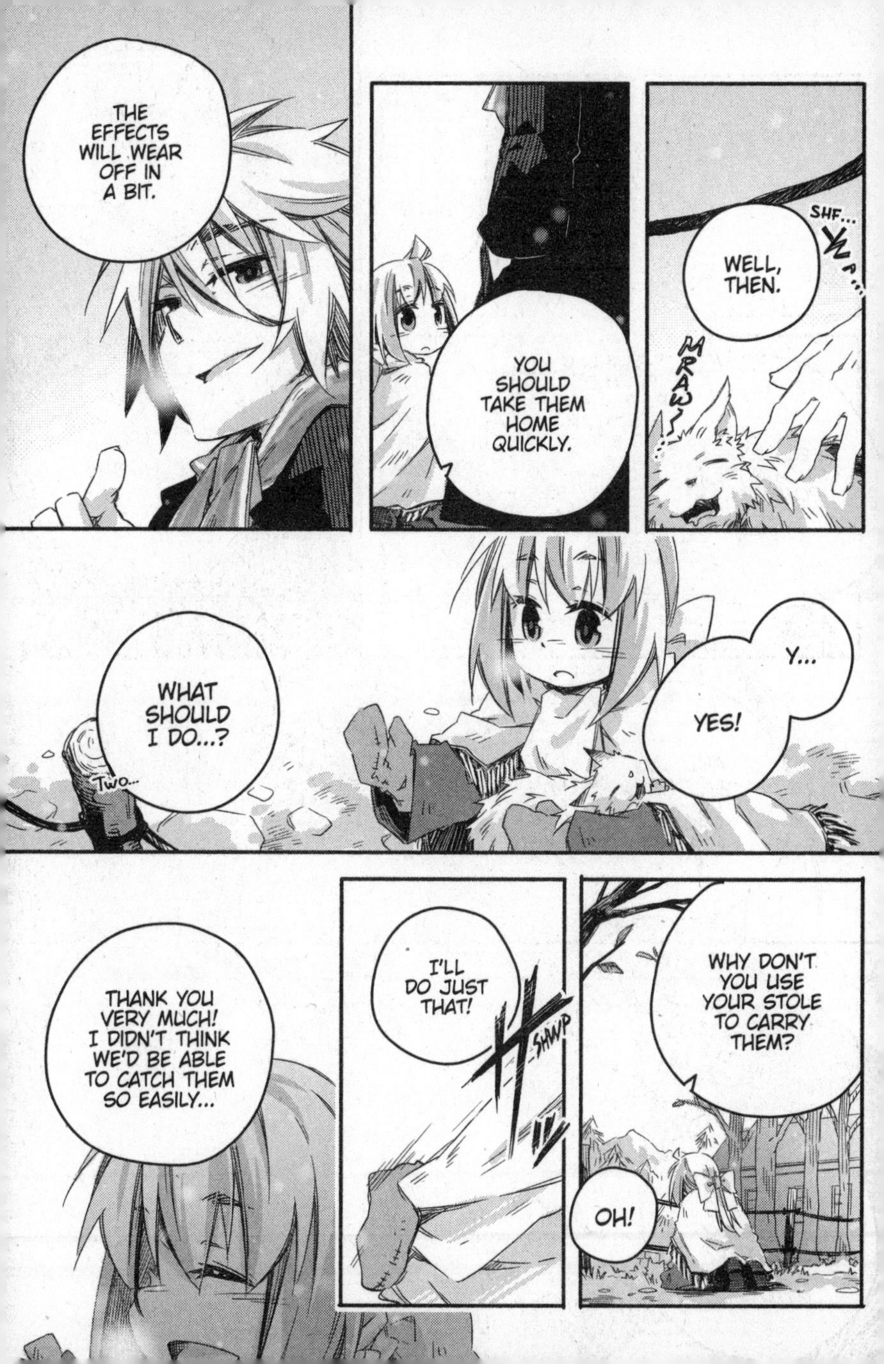
SHF...
WELL, THEN.
MRAW
YOU SHOULD TAKE THEM HOME QUICKLY.
THE EFFECTS WILL WEAR OFF IN A BIT.
Y...
YES!
WHAT SHOULD I DO...?
Two...
WHY DON'T YOU USE YOUR STOLE TO CARRY THEM?
OH!
I'LL DO JUST THAT!
SHWP
THANK YOU VERY MUCH! I DIDN'T THINK WE'D BE ABLE TO CATCH THEM SO EASILY...

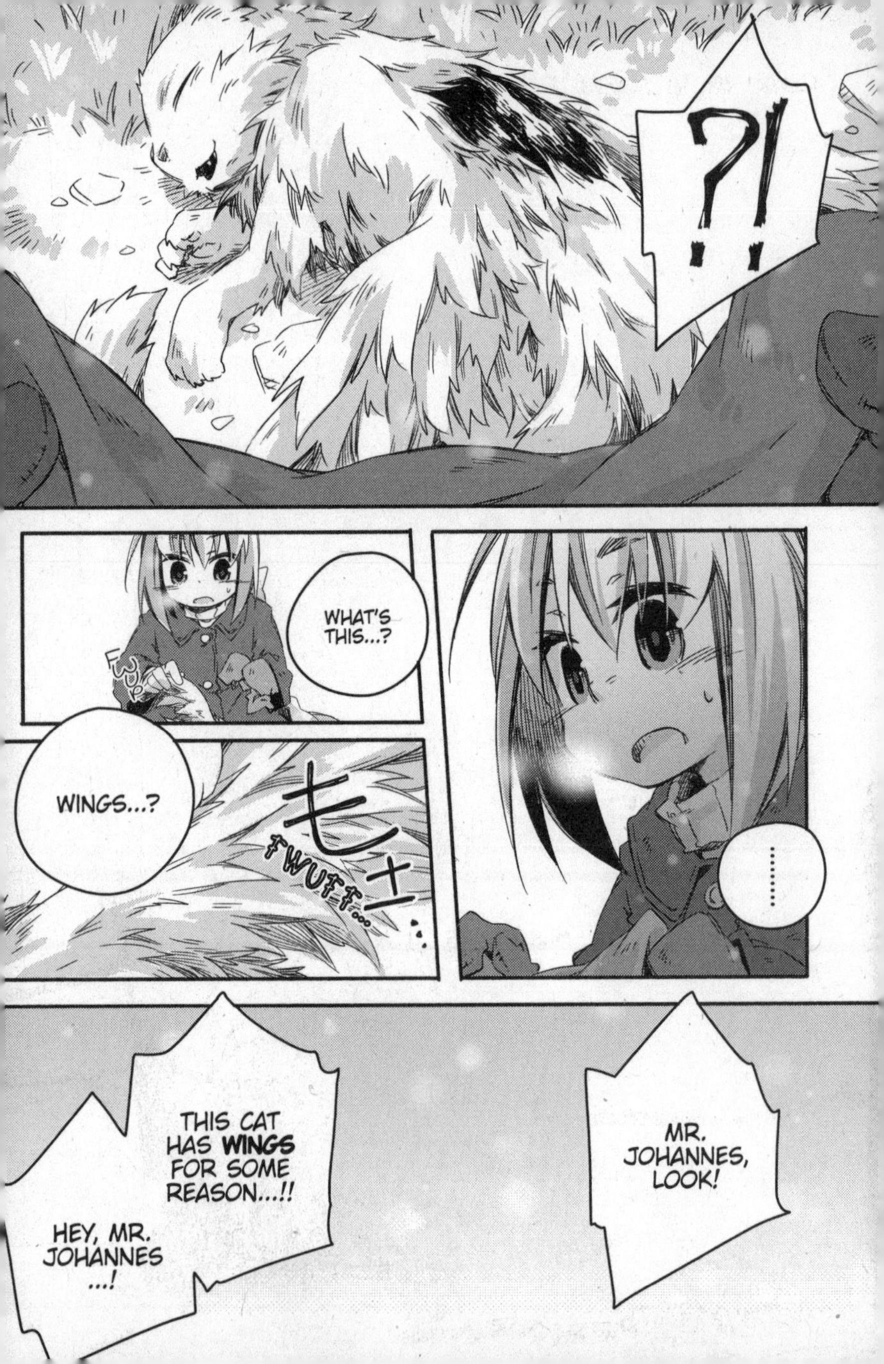
?!
......
WHAT'S THIS...?
FWUP
WINGS...?
FWUFF...
MR. JOHANNES, LOOK!
THIS CAT HAS **WINGS** FOR SOME REASON...!!
HEY, MR. JOHANNES ...!

[Case 15: Winged Cat]

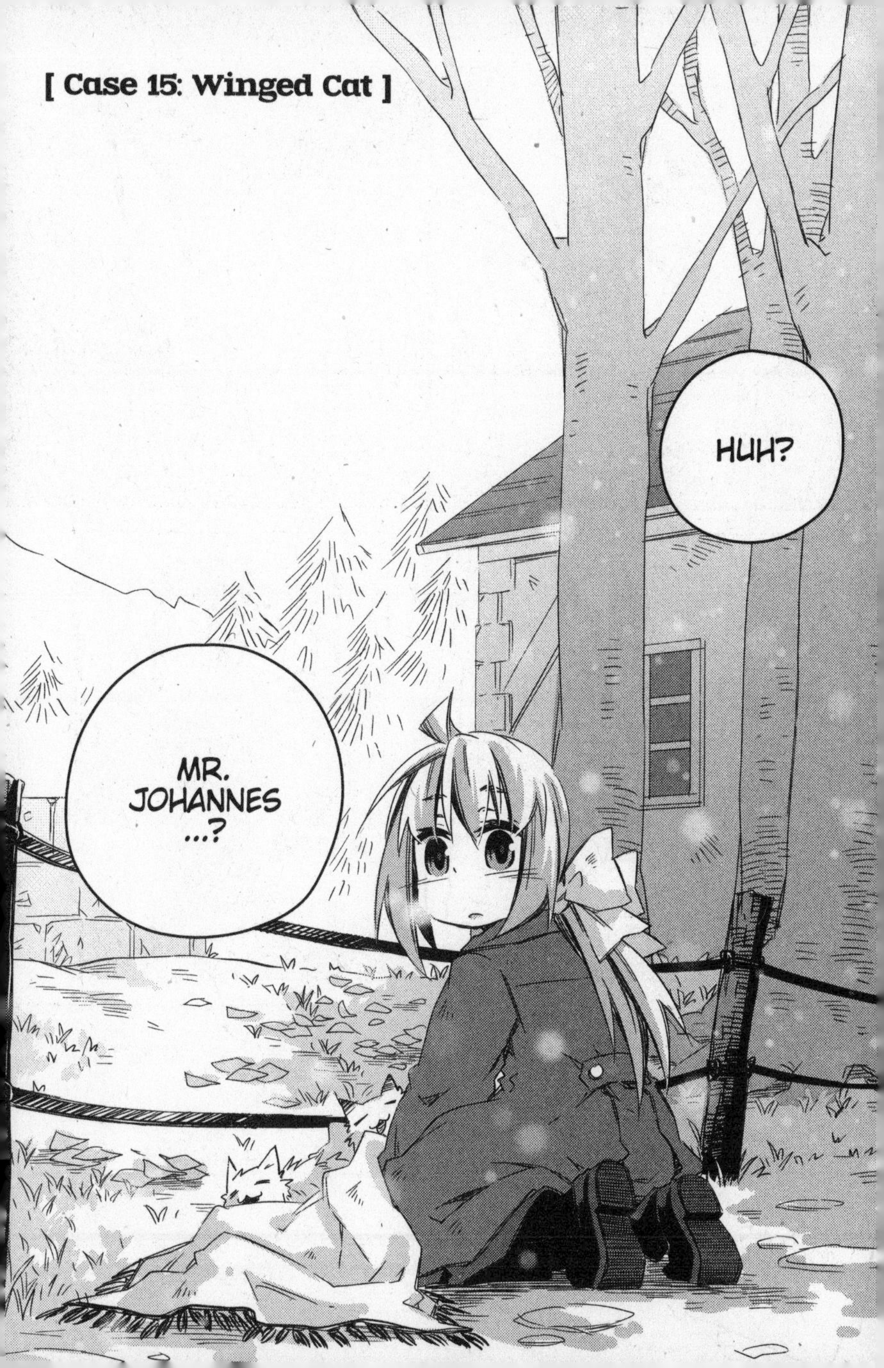
HUH?
MR. JOHANNES ...?

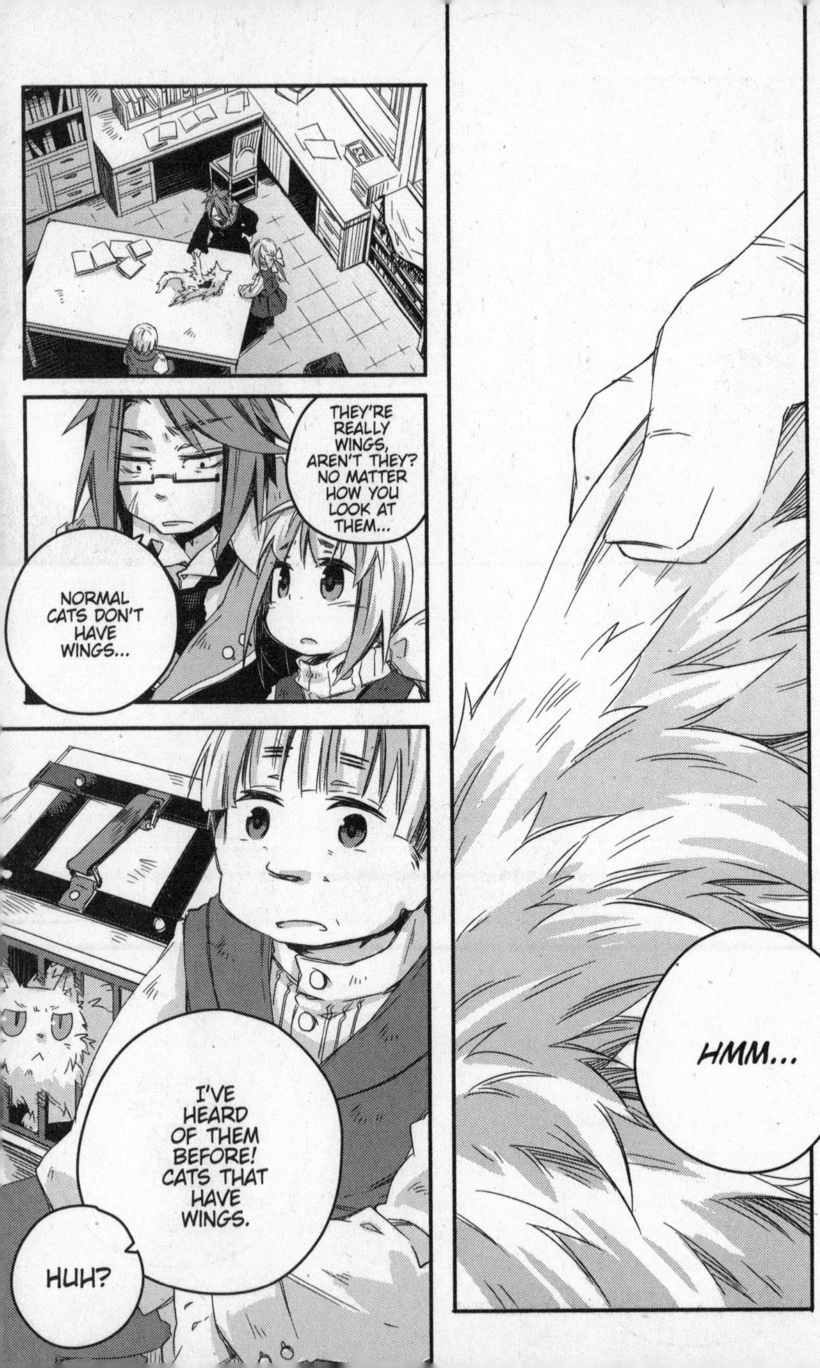
HMM...
THEY'RE REALLY WINGS, AREN'T THEY? NO MATTER HOW YOU LOOK AT THEM...
NORMAL CATS DON'T HAVE WINGS...
I'VE HEARD OF THEM BEFORE! CATS THAT HAVE WINGS.
HUH?

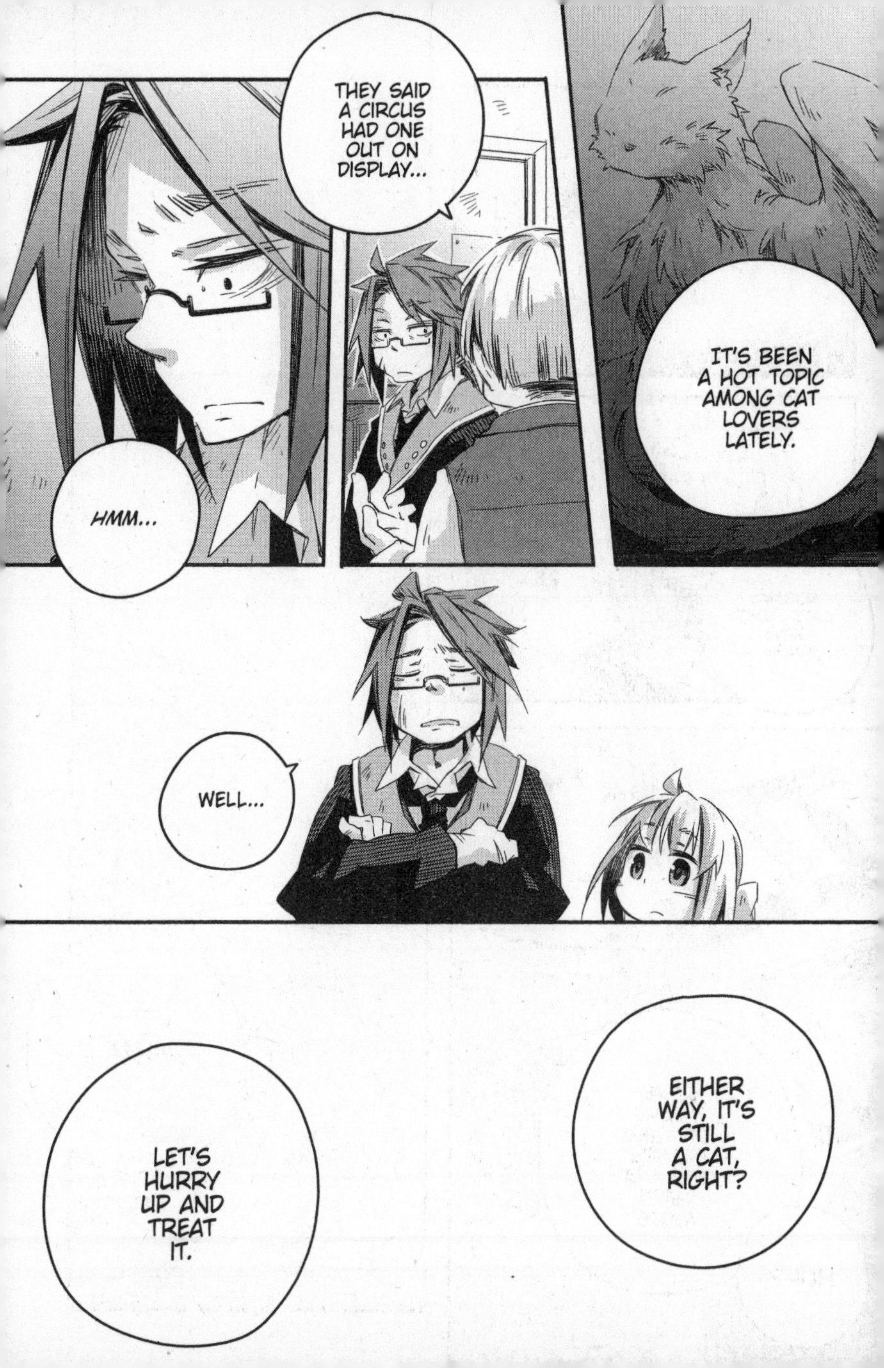
IT'S BEEN A HOT TOPIC AMONG CAT LOVERS LATELY.
THEY SAID A CIRCUS HAD ONE OUT ON DISPLAY...
HMM...
WELL...
EITHER WAY, IT'S STILL A CAT, RIGHT?
LET'S HURRY UP AND TREAT IT.

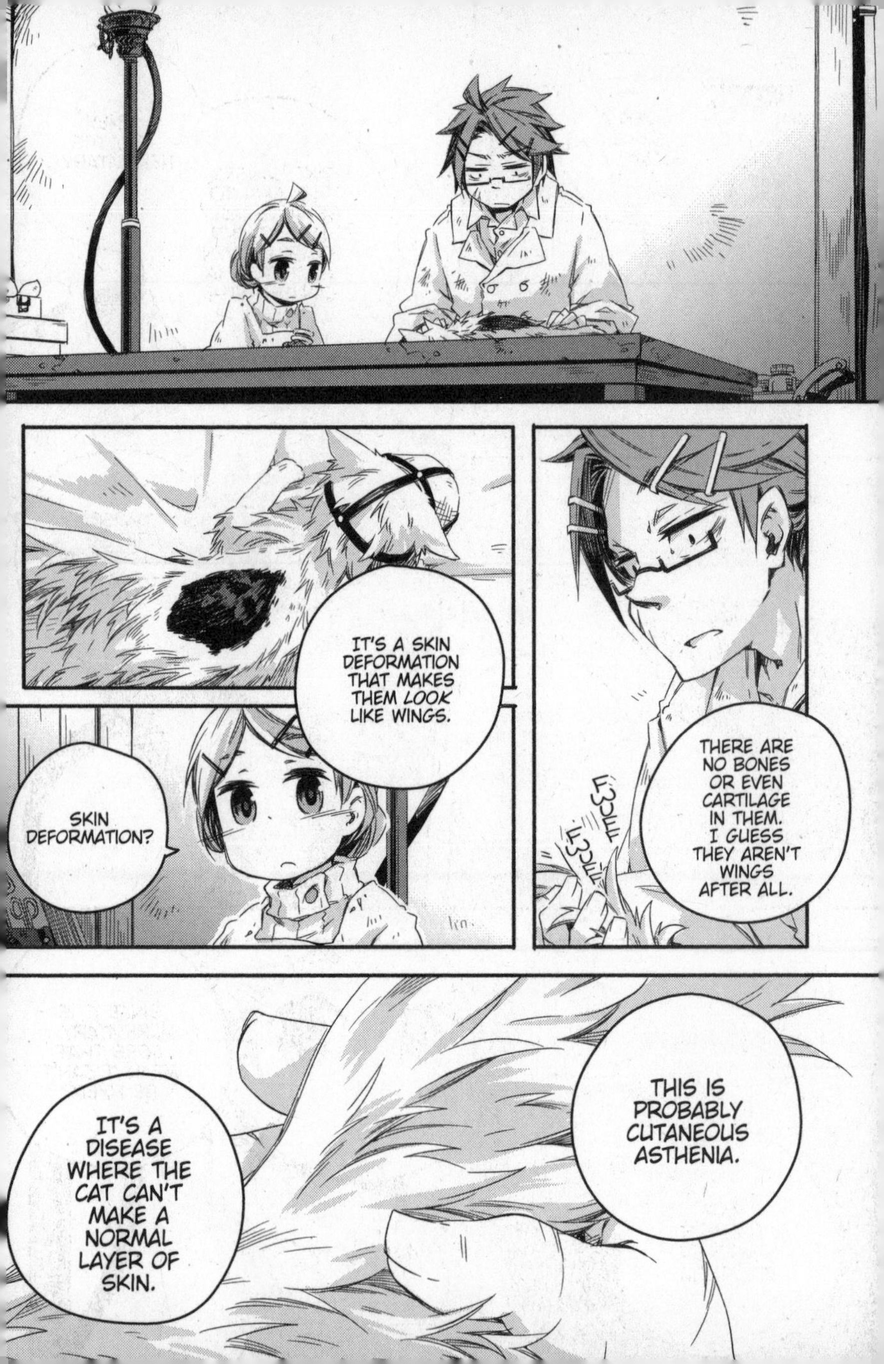
THERE ARE NO BONES OR EVEN CARTILAGE IN THEM. I GUESS THEY AREN'T WINGS AFTER ALL.
IT'S A SKIN DEFORMATION THAT MAKES THEM *LOOK* LIKE WINGS.
SKIN DEFORMATION?
THIS IS PROBABLY CUTANEOUS ASTHENIA.
IT'S A DISEASE WHERE THE CAT CAN'T MAKE A NORMAL LAYER OF SKIN.

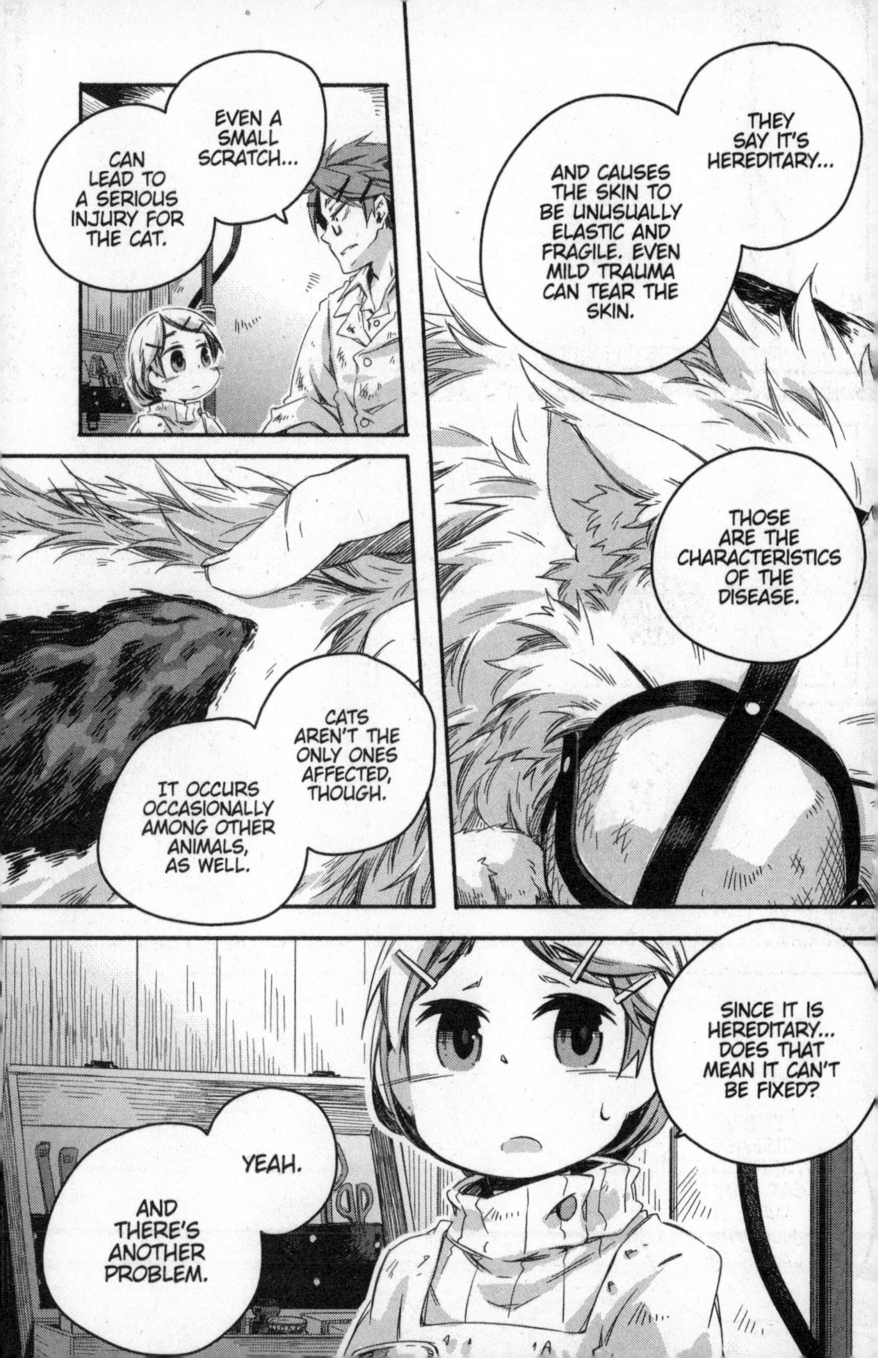
THEY SAY IT'S HEREDITARY...
AND CAUSES THE SKIN TO BE UNUSUALLY ELASTIC AND FRAGILE. EVEN MILD TRAUMA CAN TEAR THE SKIN.
THOSE ARE THE CHARACTERISTICS OF THE DISEASE.
EVEN A SMALL SCRATCH...
CAN LEAD TO A SERIOUS INJURY FOR THE CAT.
CATS AREN'T THE ONLY ONES AFFECTED, THOUGH.
IT OCCURS OCCASIONALLY AMONG OTHER ANIMALS, AS WELL.
SINCE IT IS HEREDITARY... DOES THAT MEAN IT CAN'T BE FIXED?
YEAH.
AND THERE'S ANOTHER PROBLEM.

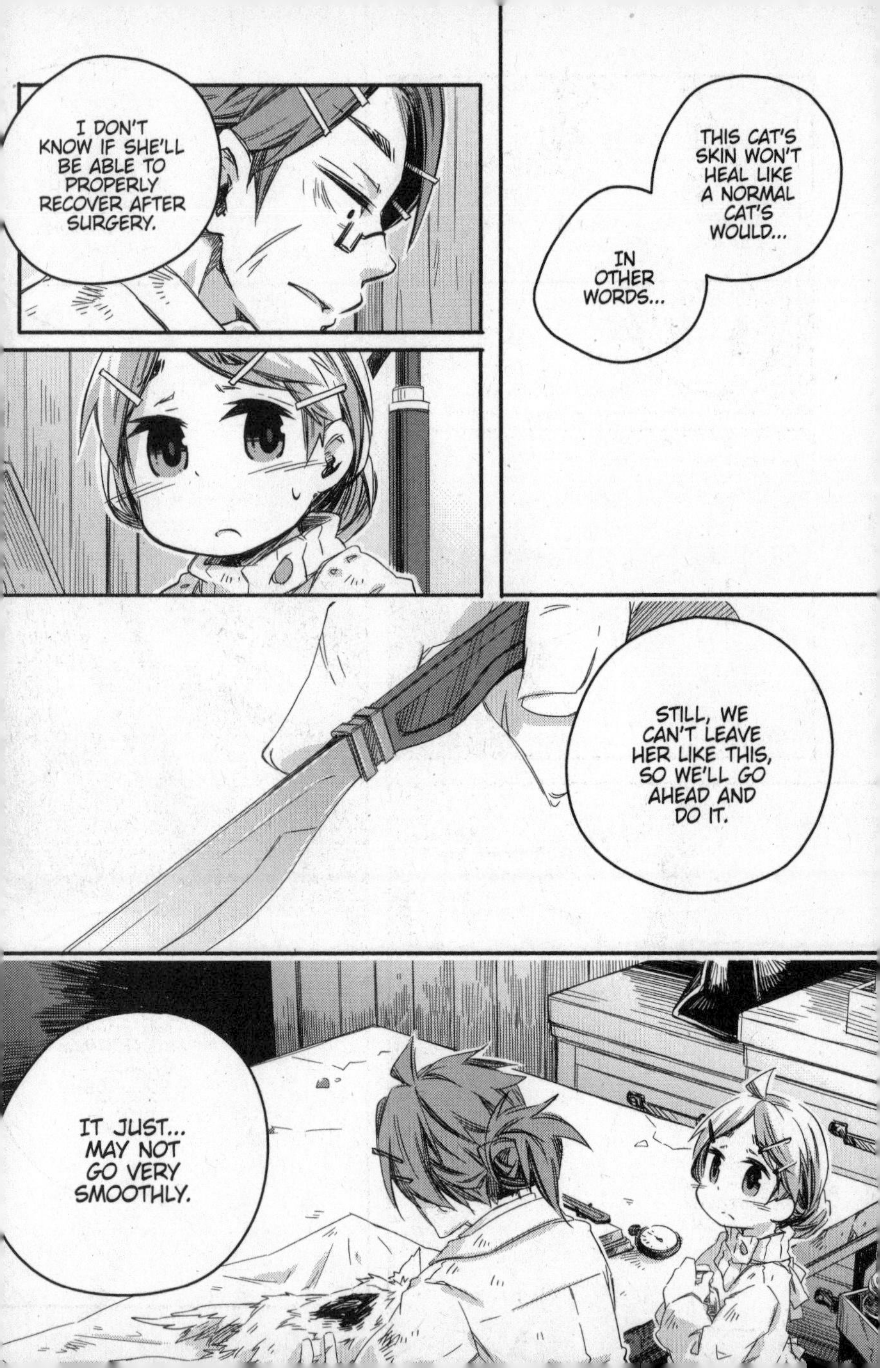
THIS CAT'S SKIN WON'T HEAL LIKE A NORMAL CAT'S WOULD...
IN OTHER WORDS...
I DON'T KNOW IF SHE'LL BE ABLE TO PROPERLY RECOVER AFTER SURGERY.
STILL, WE CAN'T LEAVE HER LIKE THIS, SO WE'LL GO AHEAD AND DO IT.
IT JUST... MAY NOT GO VERY SMOOTHLY.

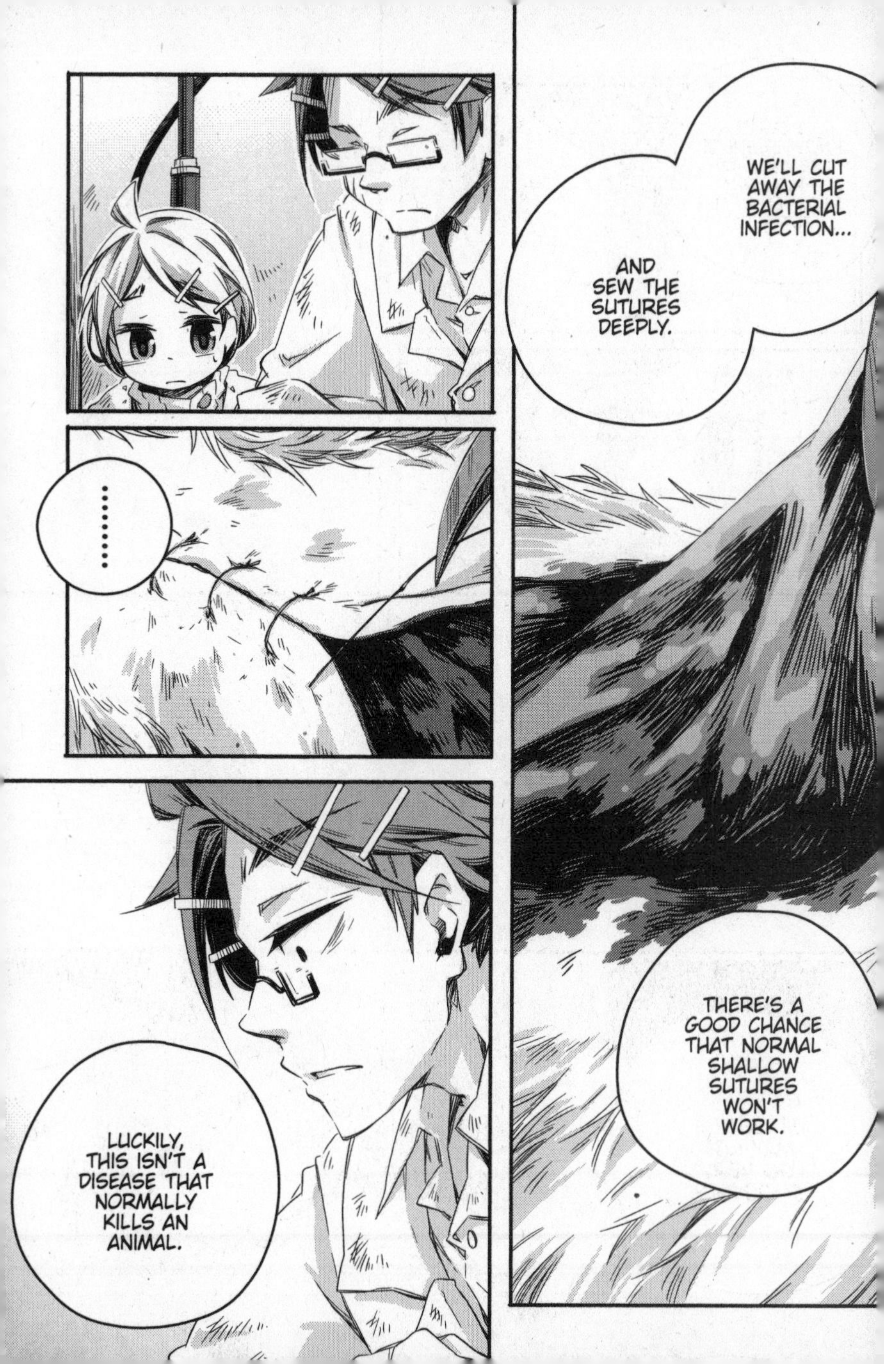
WE'LL CUT AWAY THE BACTERIAL INFECTION...
AND SEW THE SUTURES DEEPLY.
THERE'S A GOOD CHANCE THAT NORMAL SHALLOW SUTURES WON'T WORK.
....
LUCKILY, THIS ISN'T A DISEASE THAT NORMALLY KILLS AN ANIMAL.

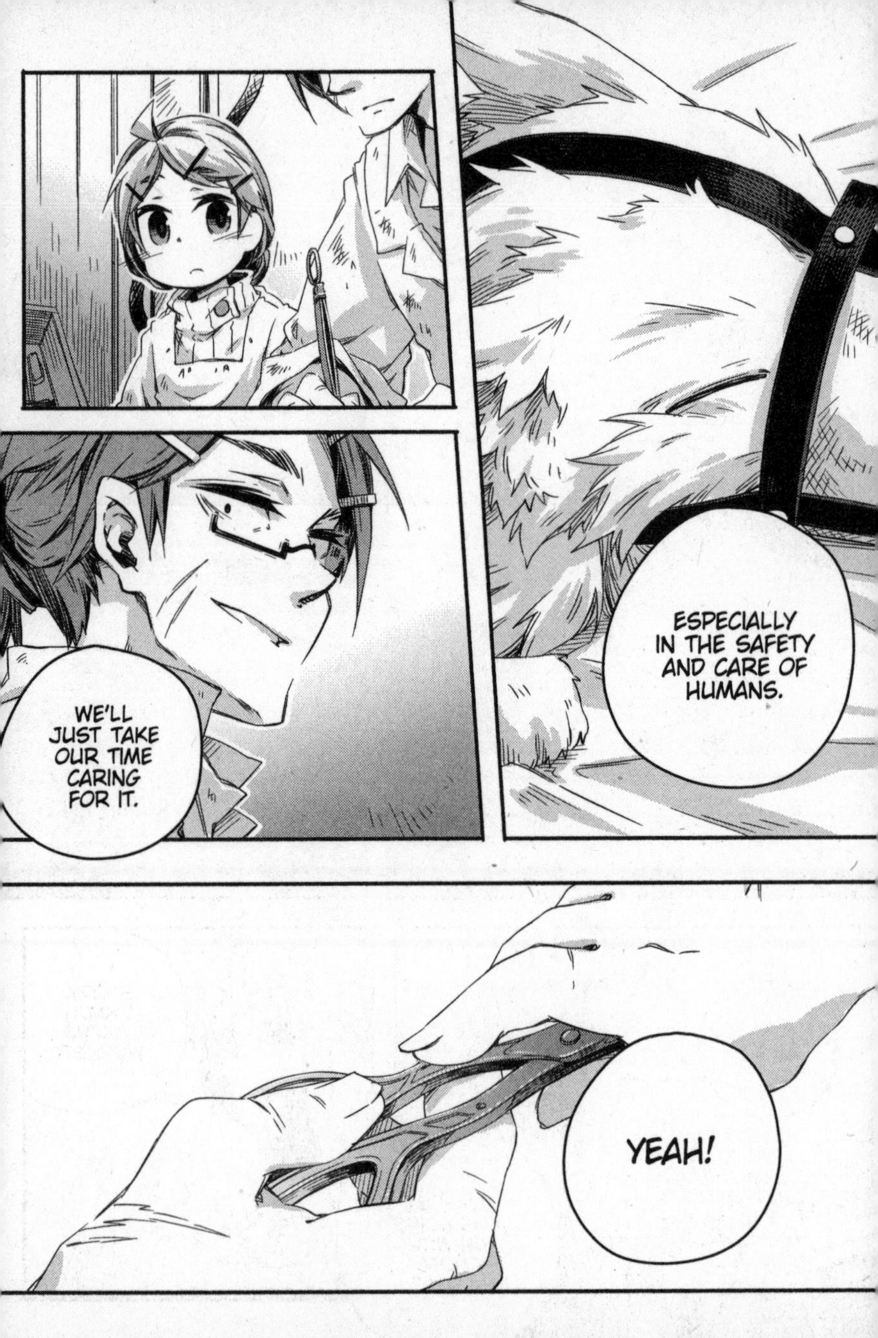
ESPECIALLY IN THE SAFETY AND CARE OF HUMANS.
WE'LL JUST TAKE OUR TIME CARING FOR IT.
YEAH!

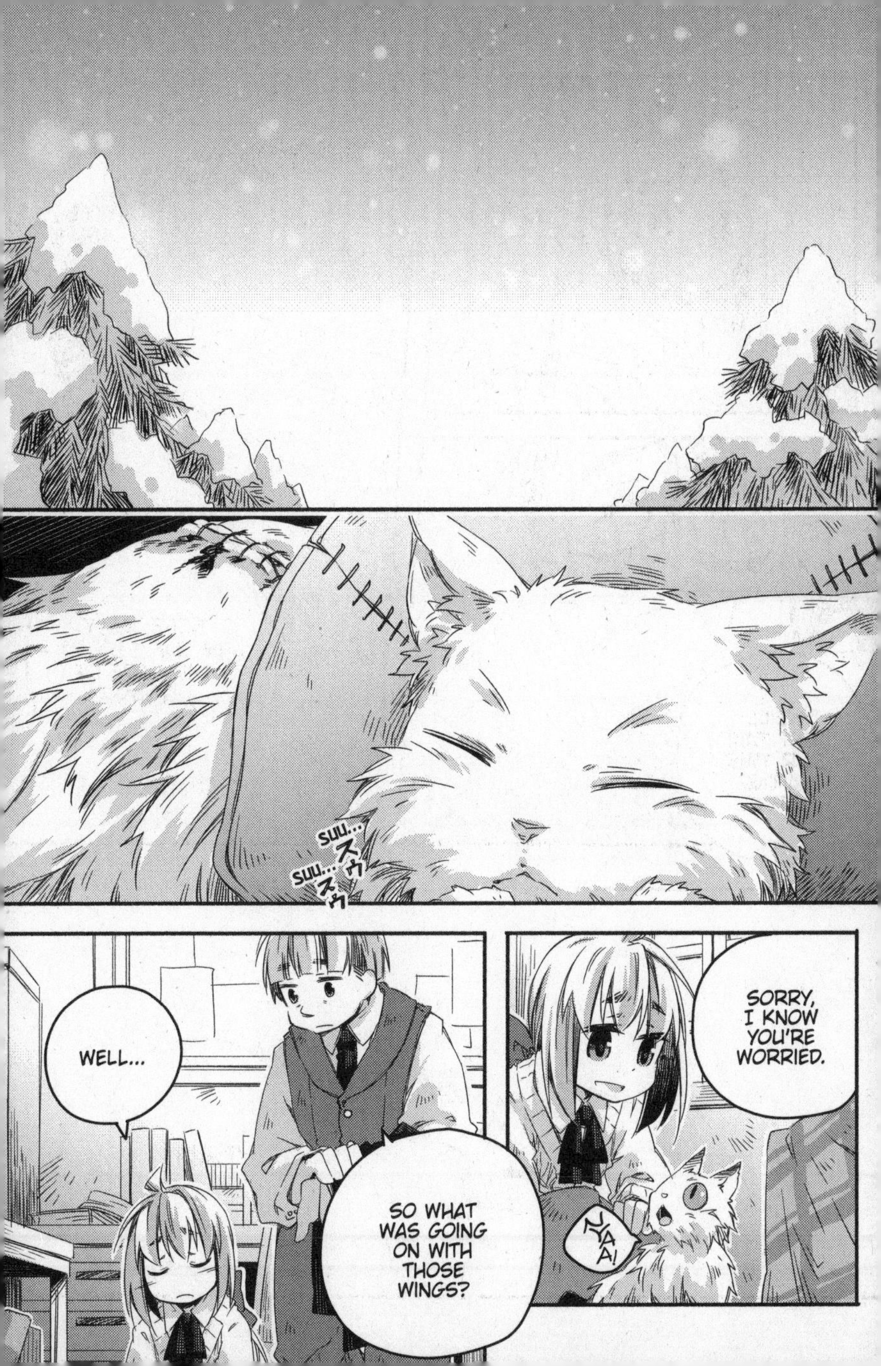
suu... スゥ
suu... スゥ
SORRY, I KNOW YOU'RE WORRIED.
NYAA!
WELL...
SO WHAT WAS GOING ON WITH THOSE WINGS?

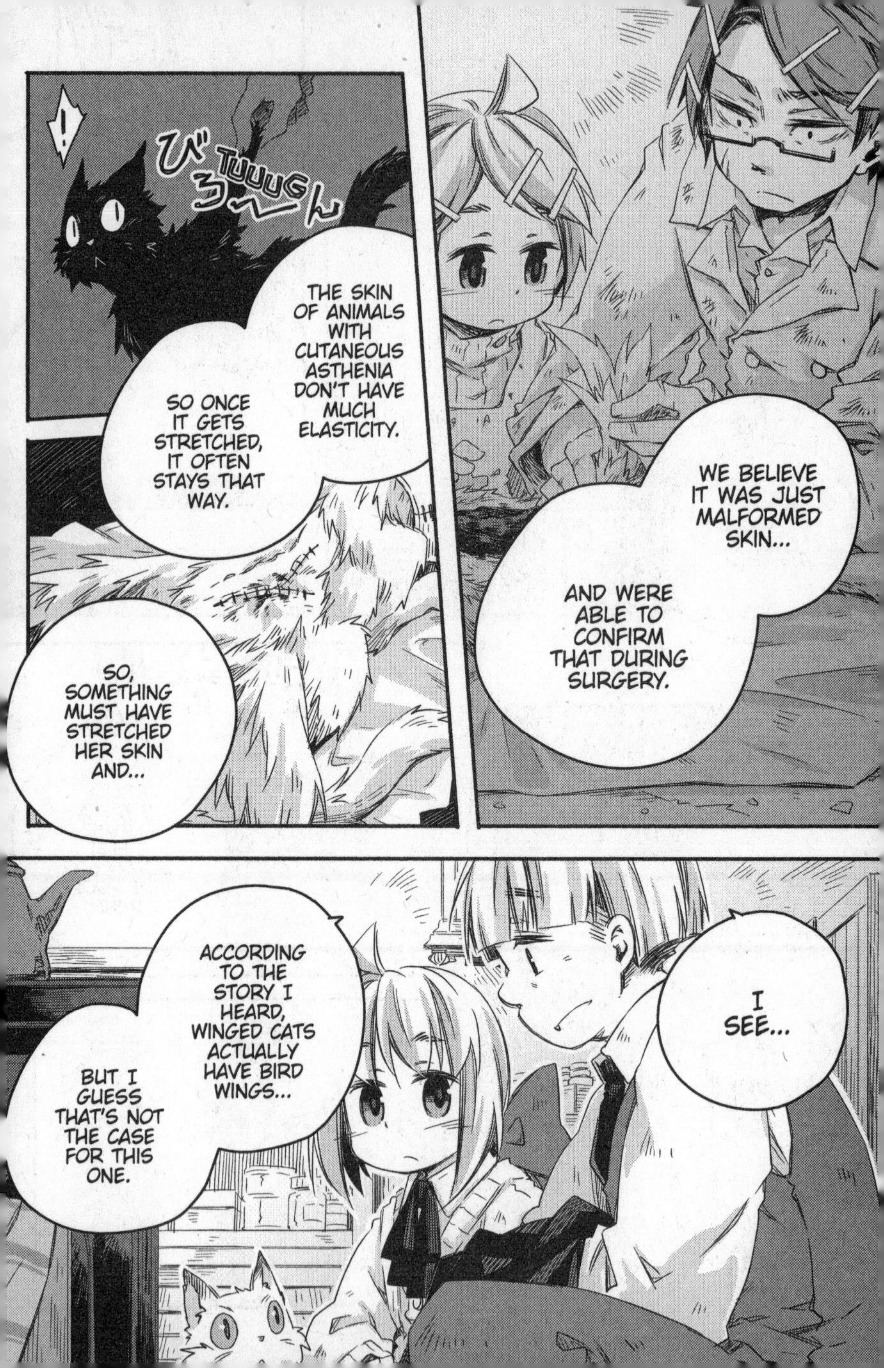
WE BELIEVE IT WAS JUST MALFORMED SKIN...
AND WERE ABLE TO CONFIRM THAT DURING SURGERY.
!
びろ〜ん
TUUUG
THE SKIN OF ANIMALS WITH CUTANEOUS ASTHENIA DON'T HAVE MUCH ELASTICITY.
SO ONCE IT GETS STRETCHED, IT OFTEN STAYS THAT WAY.
SO, SOMETHING MUST HAVE STRETCHED HER SKIN AND...
I SEE...
ACCORDING TO THE STORY I HEARD, WINGED CATS ACTUALLY HAVE BIRD WINGS...
BUT I GUESS THAT'S NOT THE CASE FOR THIS ONE.

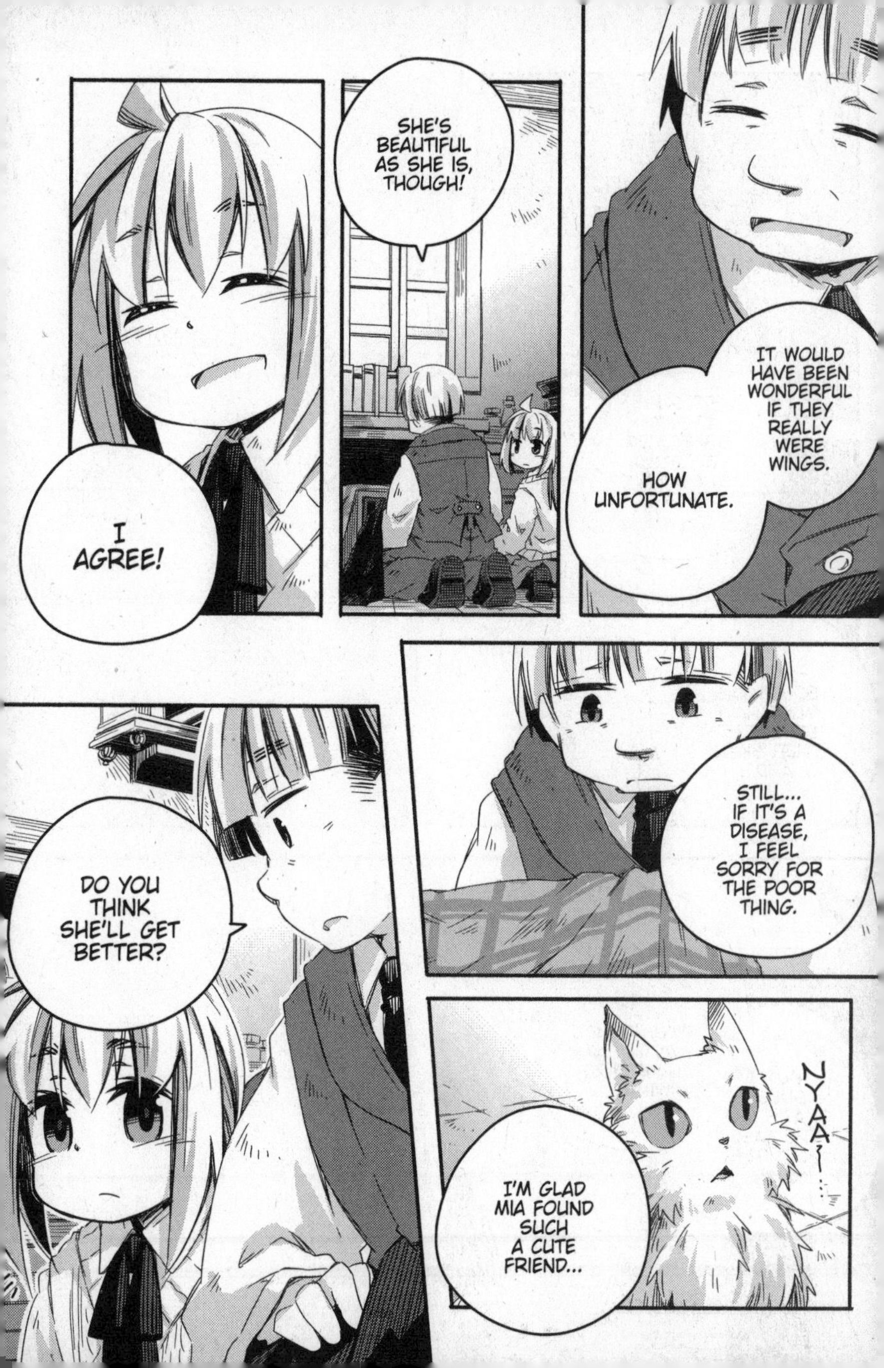
IT WOULD HAVE BEEN WONDERFUL IF THEY REALLY WERE WINGS.
HOW UNFORTUNATE.
SHE'S BEAUTIFUL AS SHE IS, THOUGH!
I AGREE!
STILL... IF IT'S A DISEASE, I FEEL SORRY FOR THE POOR THING.
NYAA~...
I'M GLAD MIA FOUND SUCH A CUTE FRIEND...
DO YOU THINK SHE'LL GET BETTER?

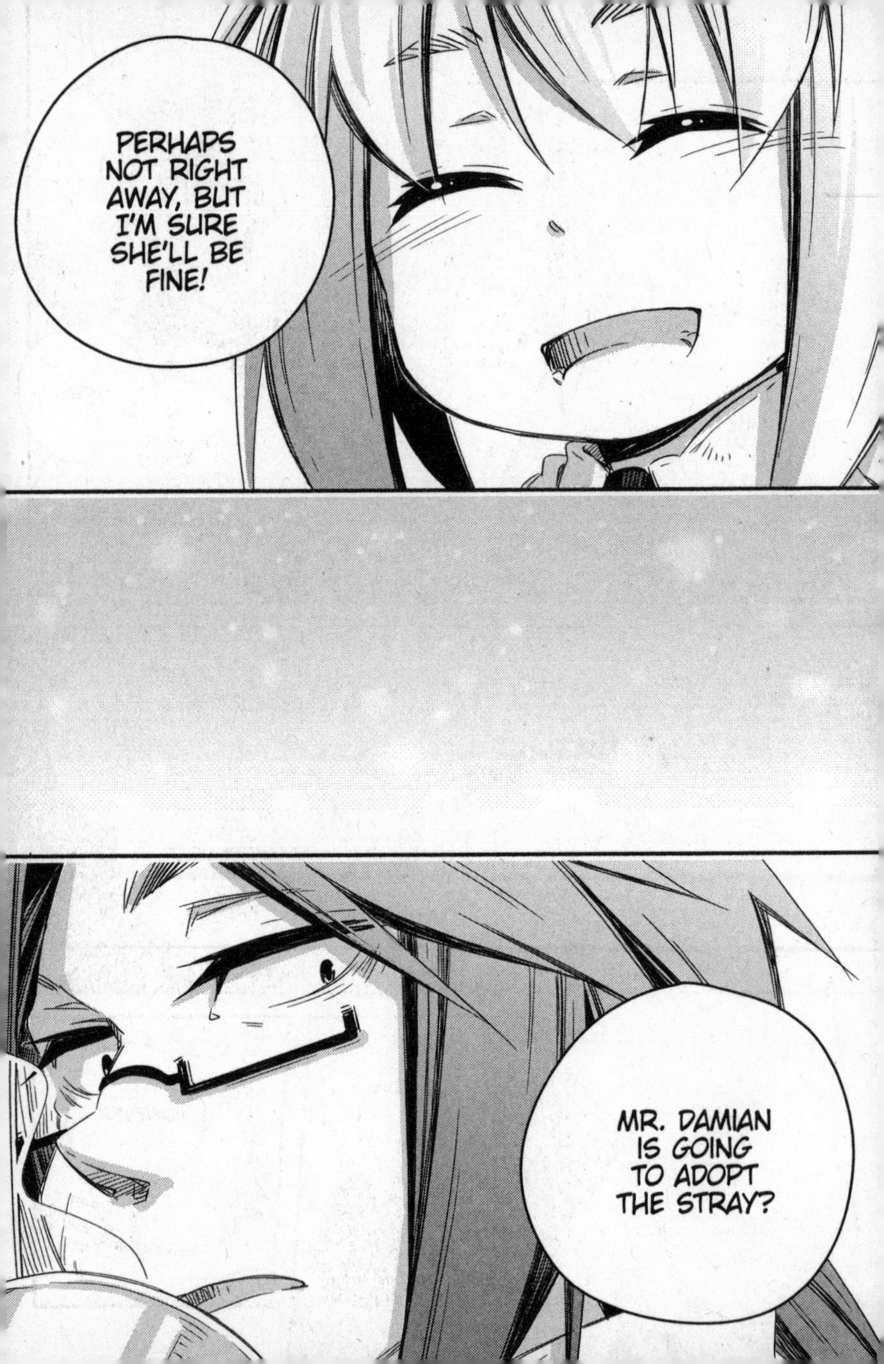
PERHAPS NOT RIGHT AWAY, BUT I'M SURE SHE'LL BE FINE!
MR. DAMIAN IS GOING TO ADOPT THE STRAY?

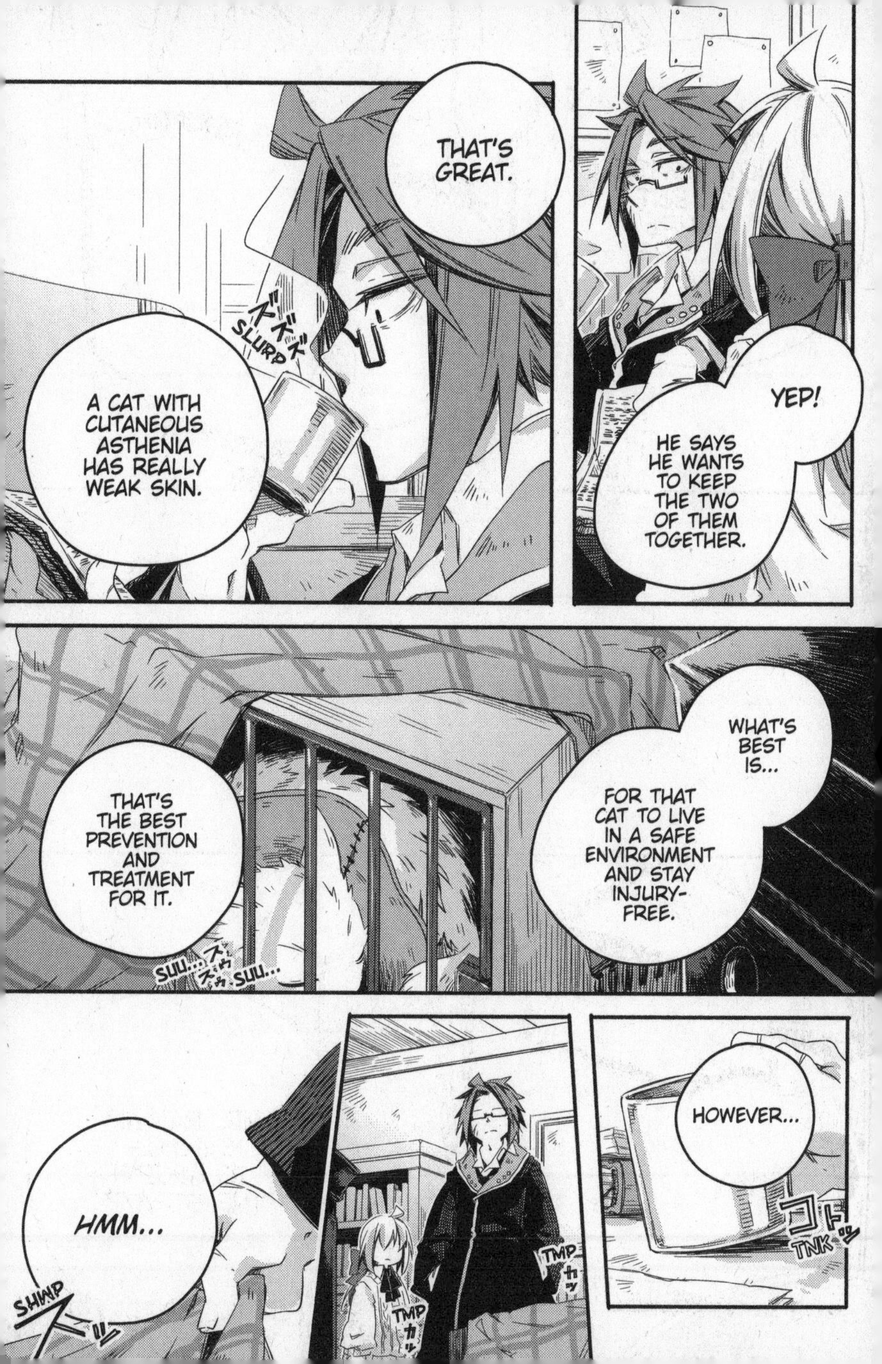
YEP!
HE SAYS HE WANTS TO KEEP THE TWO OF THEM TOGETHER.
THAT'S GREAT.
SLURP
A CAT WITH CUTANEOUS ASTHENIA HAS REALLY WEAK SKIN.
WHAT'S BEST IS...
FOR THAT CAT TO LIVE IN A SAFE ENVIRONMENT AND STAY INJURY-FREE.
THAT'S THE BEST PREVENTION AND TREATMENT FOR IT.
SUU... SUU...
HOWEVER...
TNK
TMP
TMP
HMM...
SHWP

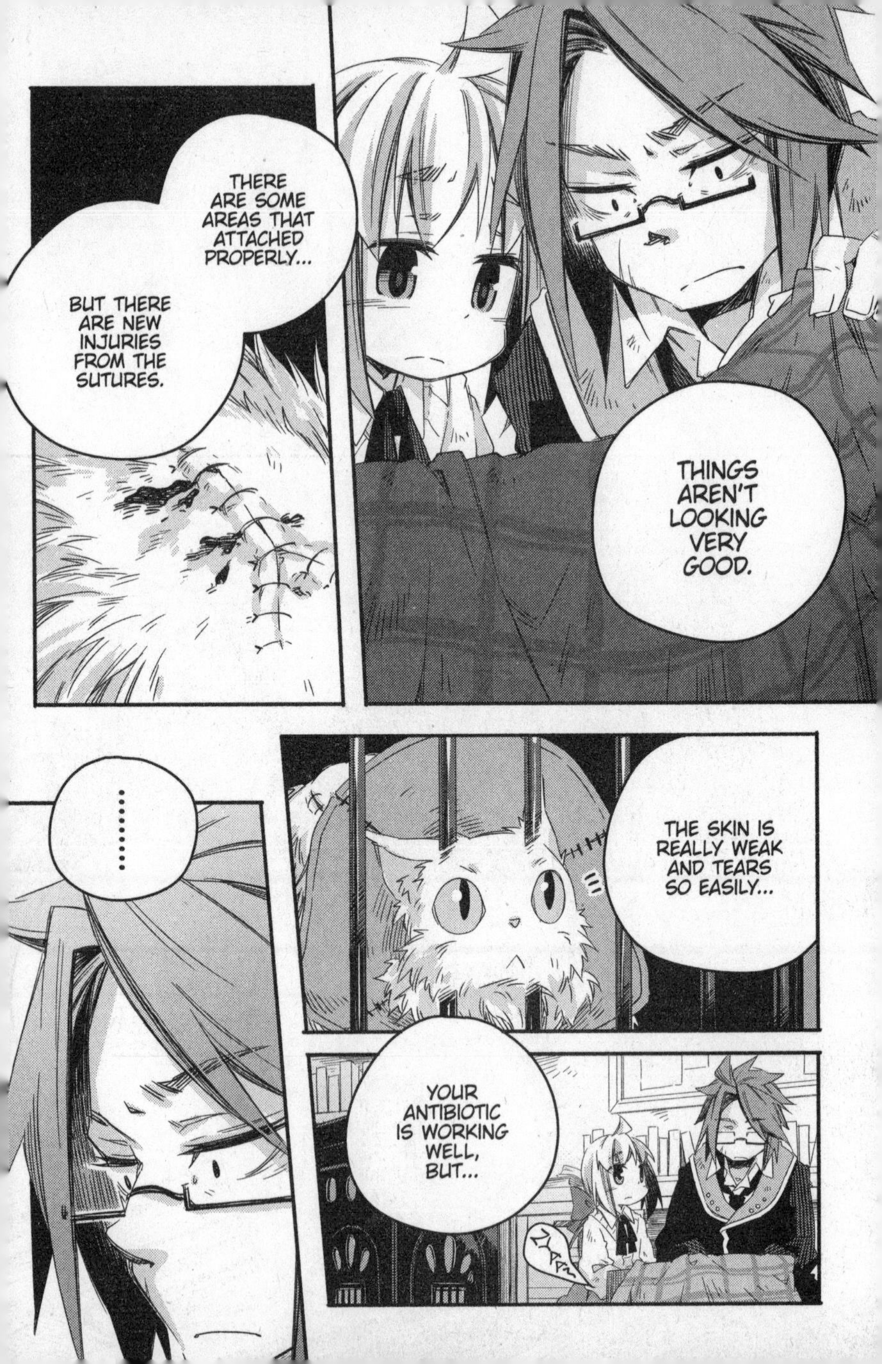
THINGS AREN'T LOOKING VERY GOOD.
THERE ARE SOME AREAS THAT ATTACHED PROPERLY...
BUT THERE ARE NEW INJURIES FROM THE SUTURES.
THE SKIN IS REALLY WEAK AND TEARS SO EASILY...
YOUR ANTIBIOTIC IS WORKING WELL, BUT...
....

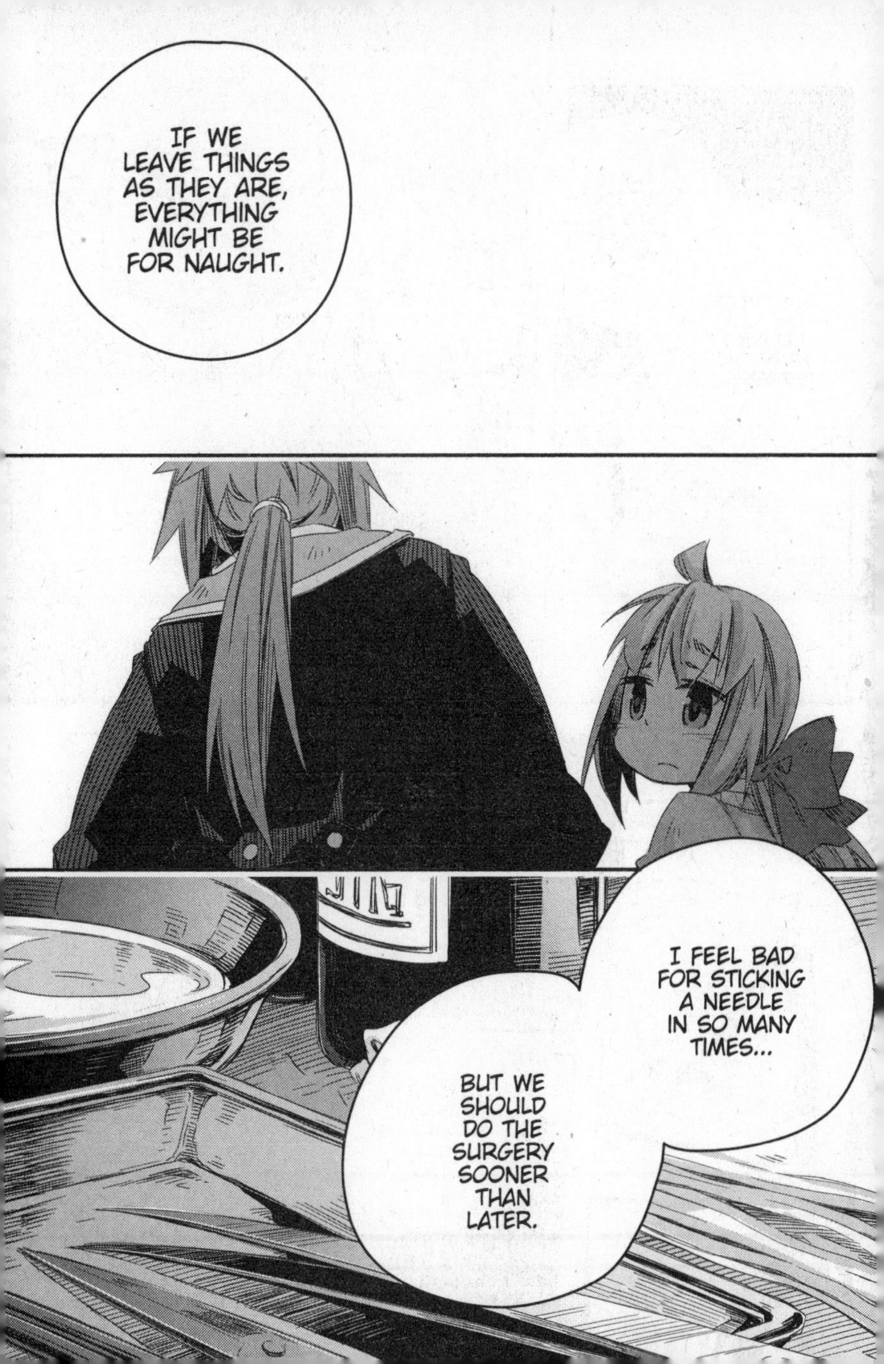
IF WE LEAVE THINGS AS THEY ARE, EVERYTHING MIGHT BE FOR NAUGHT.
I FEEL BAD FOR STICKING A NEEDLE IN SO MANY TIMES...
BUT WE SHOULD DO THE SURGERY SOONER THAN LATER.

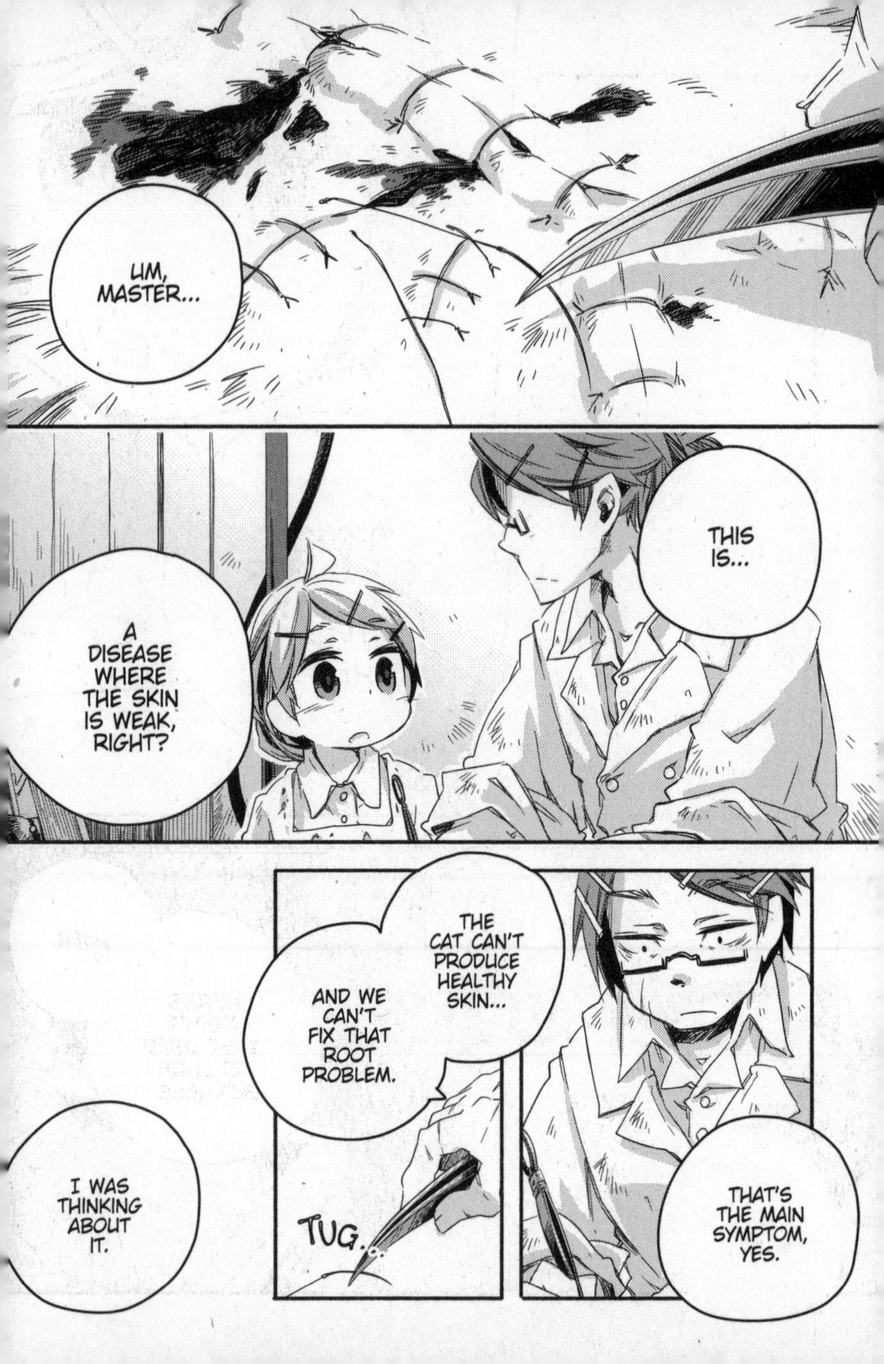
UM, MASTER...
THIS IS...
A DISEASE WHERE THE SKIN IS WEAK, RIGHT?
THAT'S THE MAIN SYMPTOM, YES.
THE CAT CAN'T PRODUCE HEALTHY SKIN...
AND WE CAN'T FIX THAT ROOT PROBLEM.
TUG.
I WAS THINKING ABOUT IT.

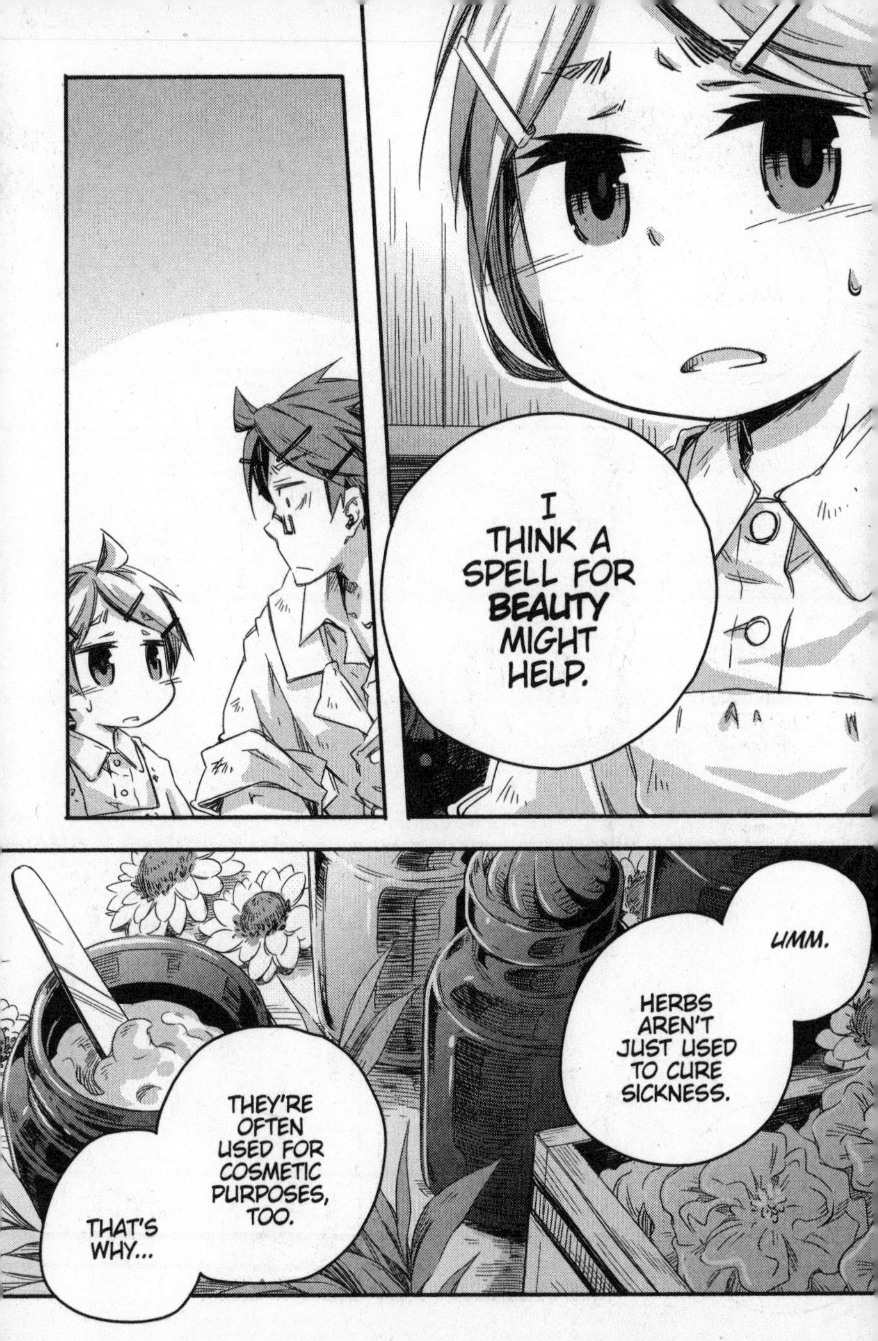
I THINK A SPELL FOR BEAUTY MIGHT HELP.
UMM.
HERBS AREN'T JUST USED TO CURE SICKNESS.
THEY'RE OFTEN USED FOR COSMETIC PURPOSES, TOO.
THAT'S WHY...

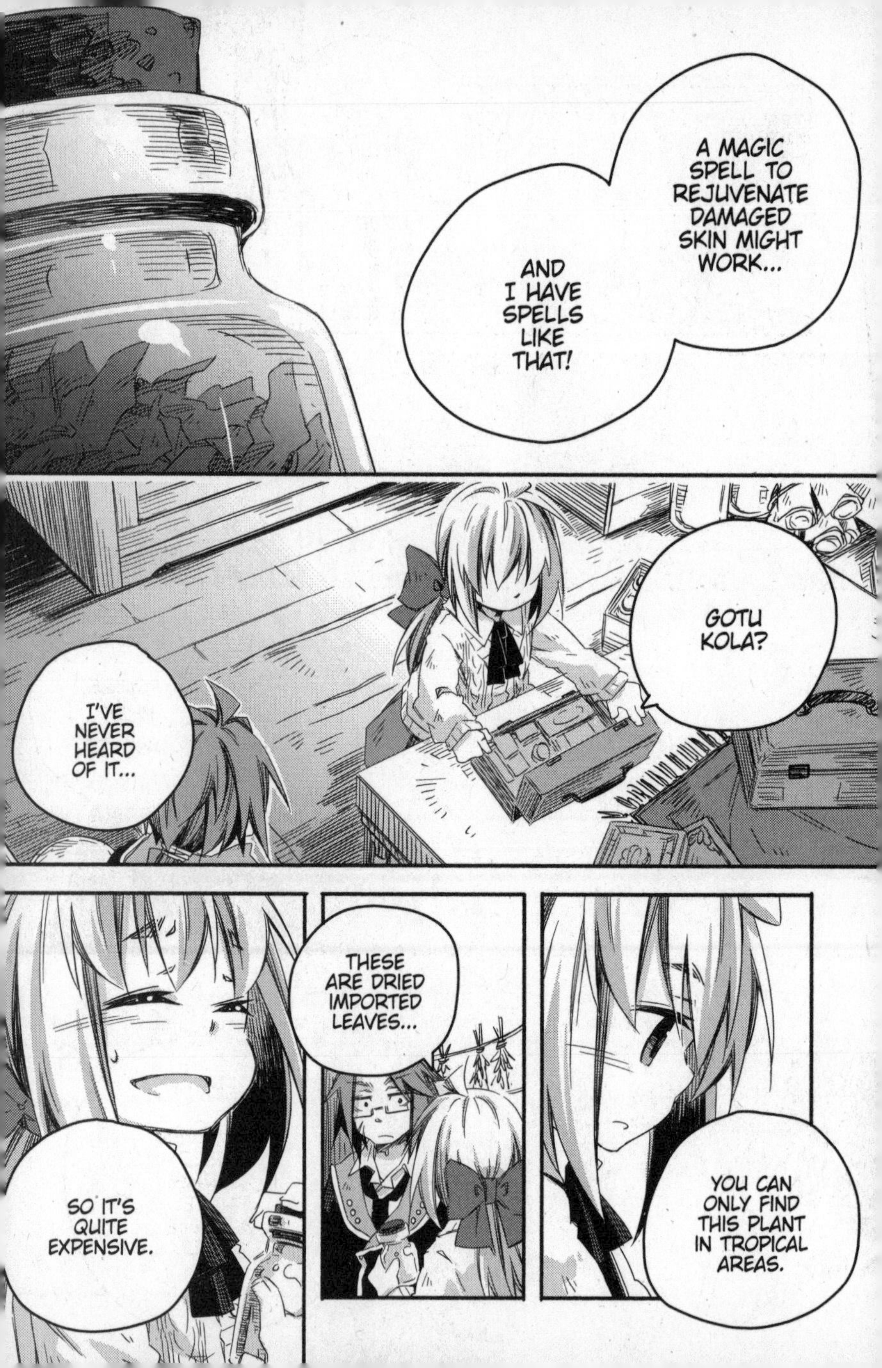
A MAGIC SPELL TO REJUVENATE DAMAGED SKIN MIGHT WORK...
AND I HAVE SPELLS LIKE THAT!
GOTU KOLA?
I'VE NEVER HEARD OF IT...
YOU CAN ONLY FIND THIS PLANT IN TROPICAL AREAS.
THESE ARE DRIED IMPORTED LEAVES...
SO IT'S QUITE EXPENSIVE.

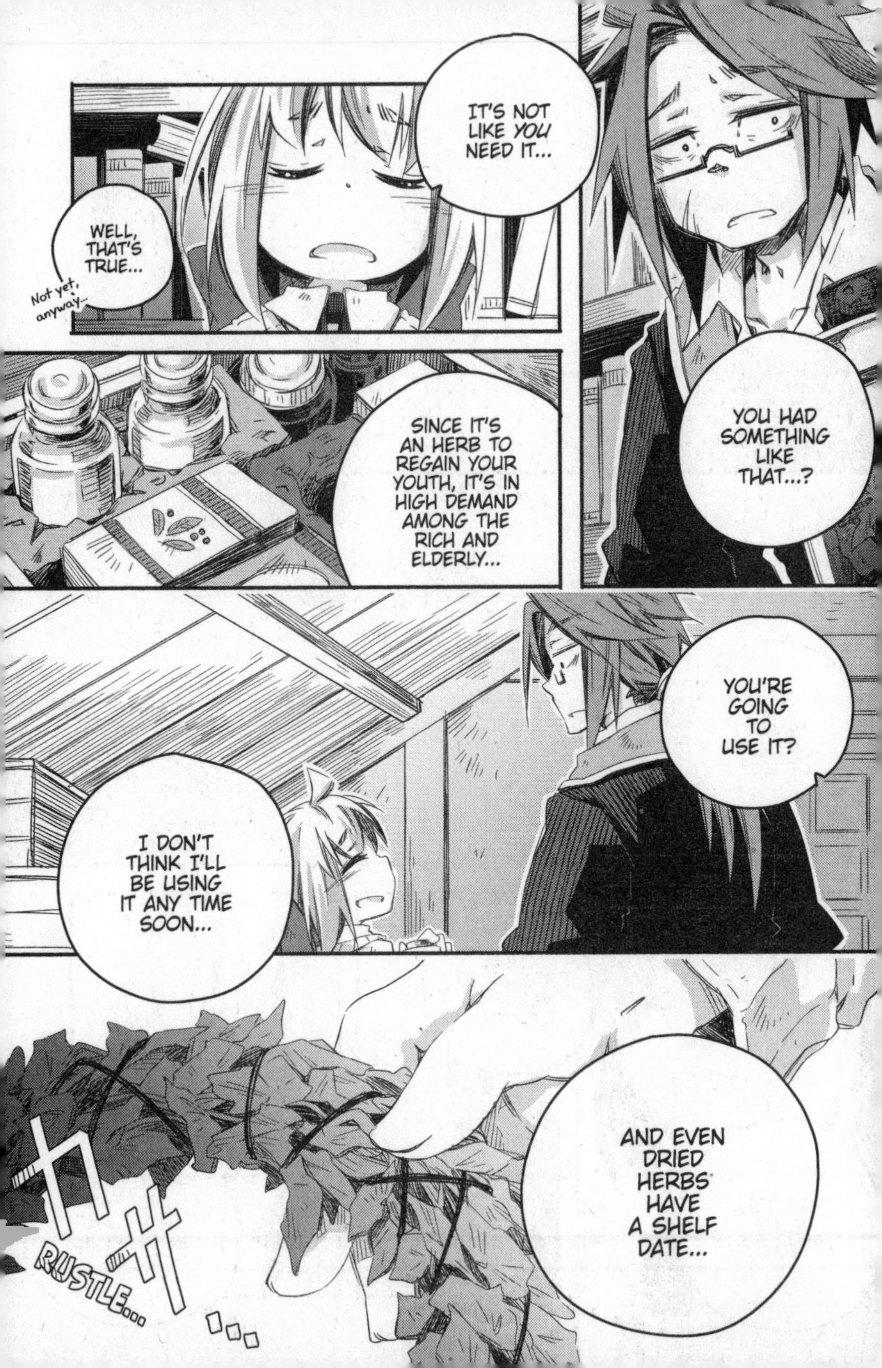
IT'S NOT LIKE *YOU* NEED IT...
WELL, THAT'S TRUE...
Not yet, anyway...
YOU HAD SOMETHING LIKE THAT...?
SINCE IT'S AN HERB TO REGAIN YOUR YOUTH, IT'S IN HIGH DEMAND AMONG THE RICH AND ELDERLY...
YOU'RE GOING TO USE IT?
I DON'T THINK I'LL BE USING IT ANY TIME SOON...
AND EVEN DRIED HERBS HAVE A SHELF DATE...
RUSTLE...
...

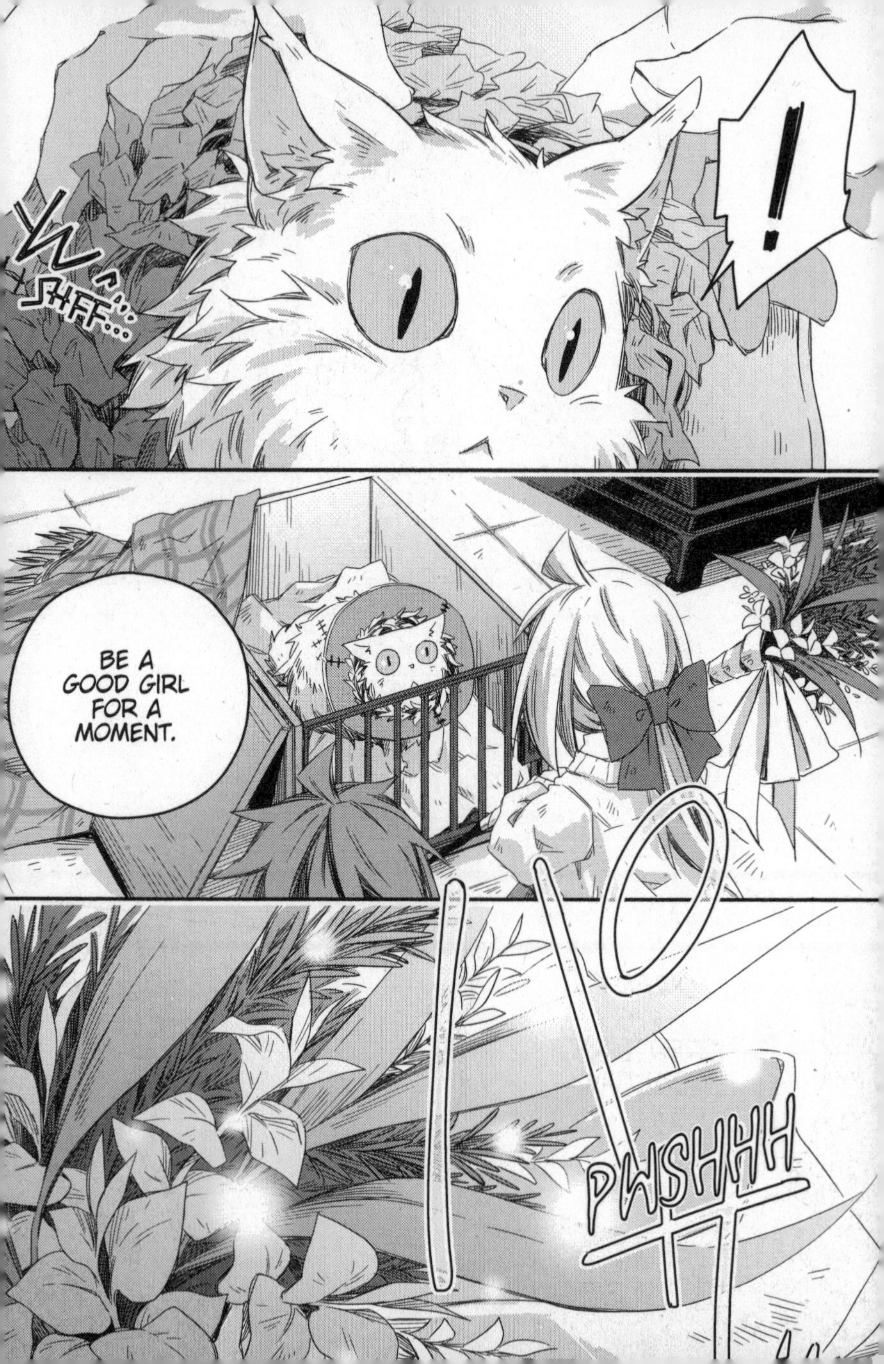
!!
SHFF...
BE A GOOD GIRL FOR A MOMENT.
PWSHHH

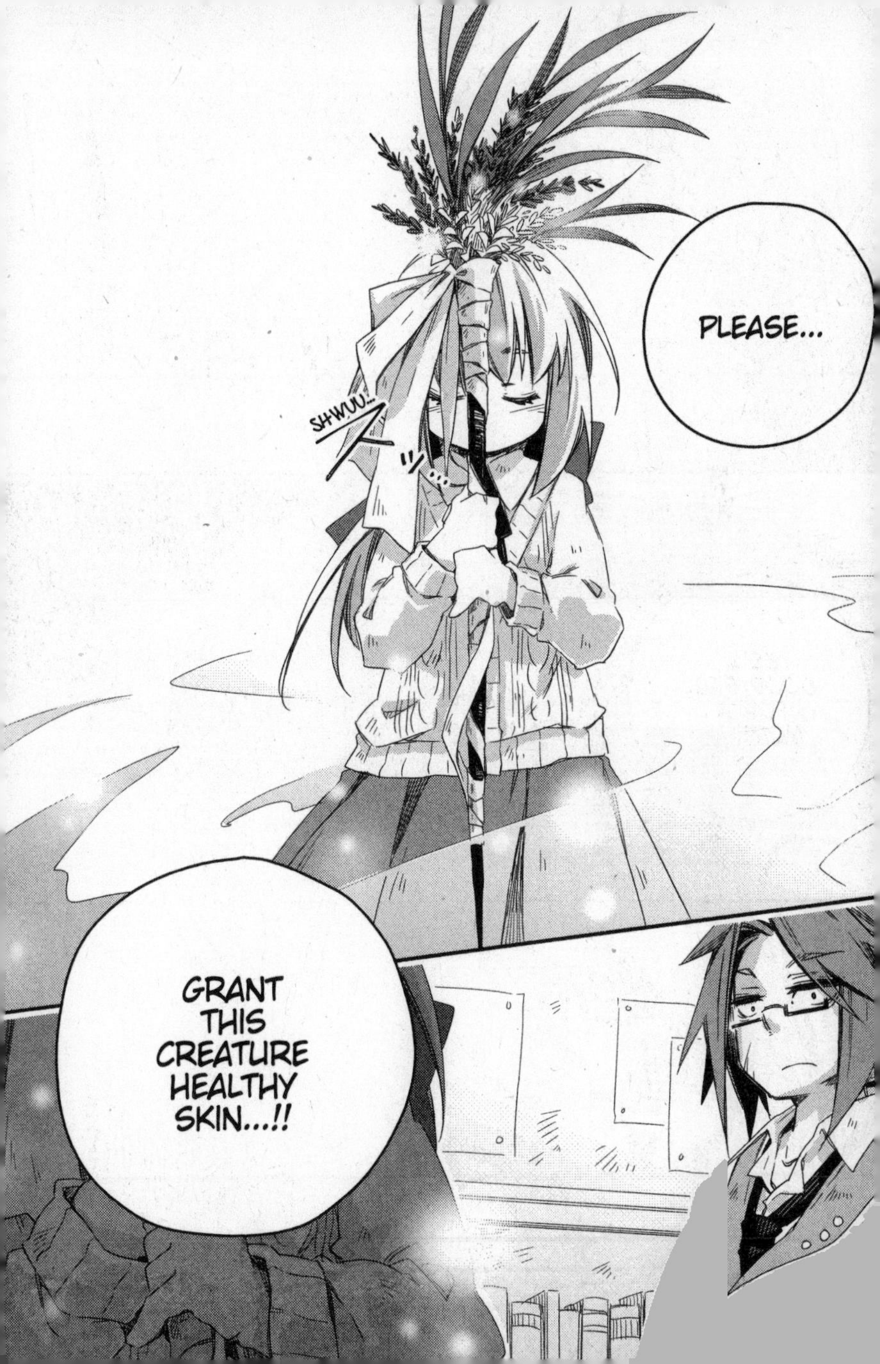
PLEASE...
SHWUU...
GRANT THIS CREATURE HEALTHY SKIN...!!

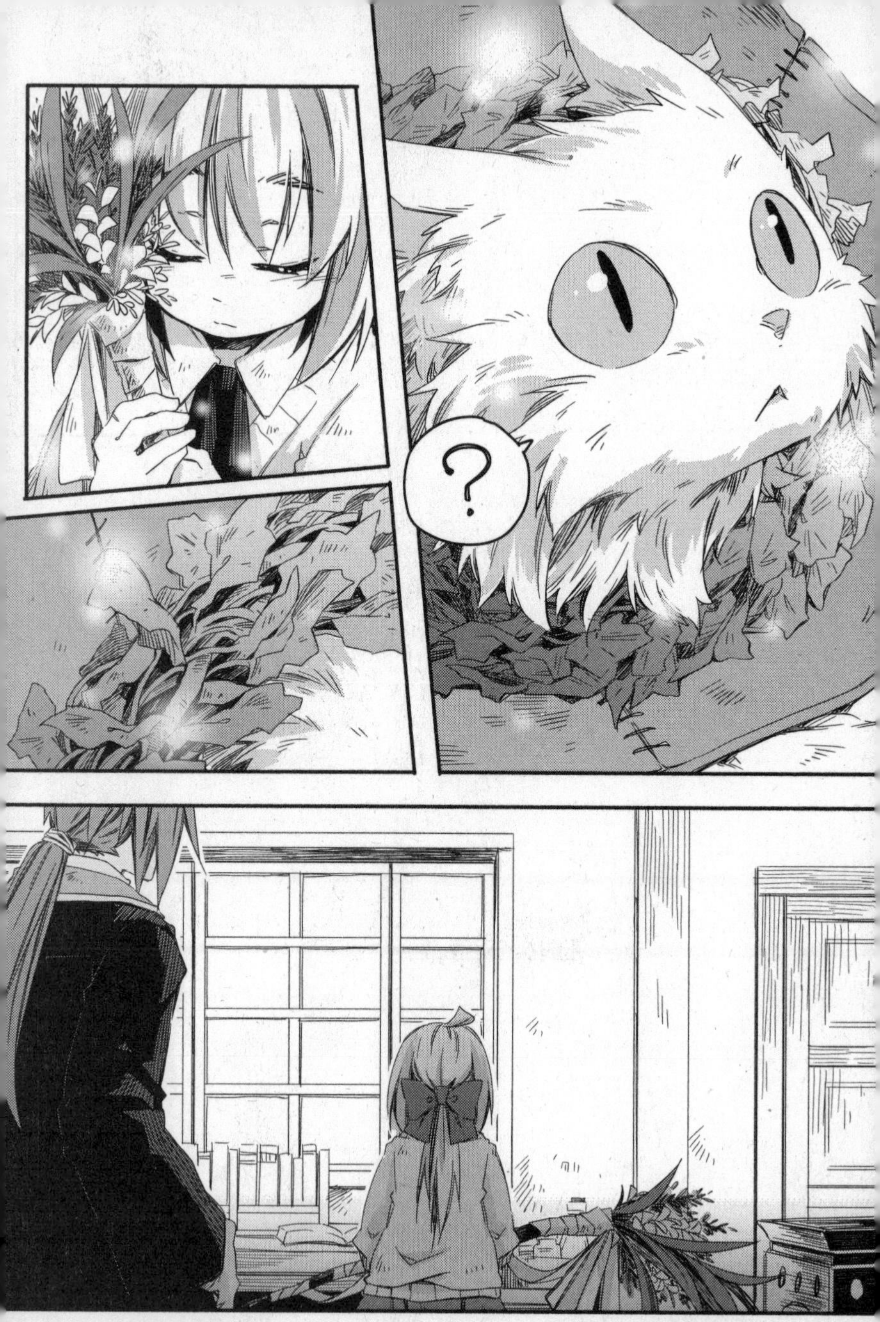
?

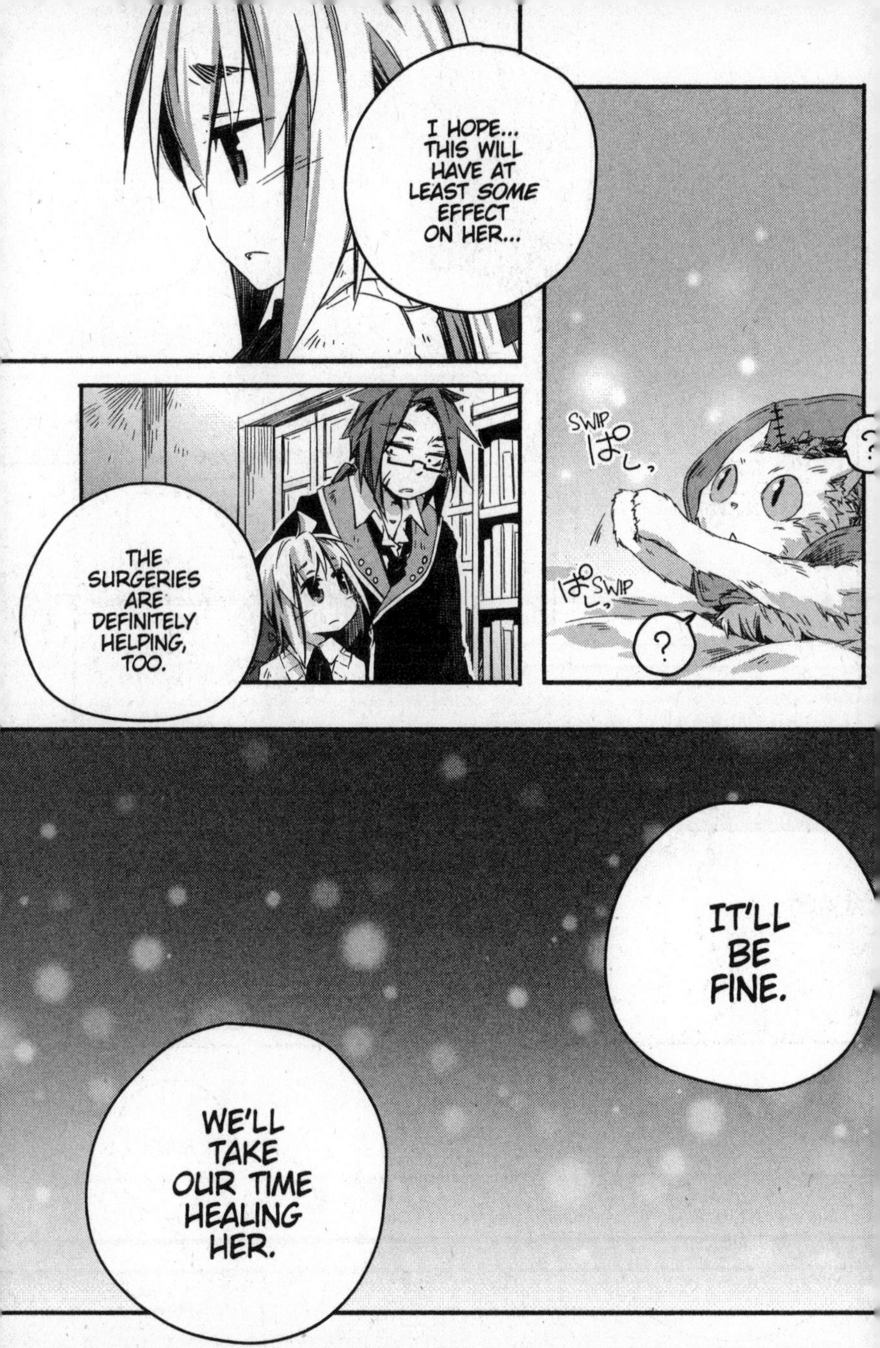
SWIP ぱしっ
?
ぱしっ SWIP
?
I HOPE... THIS WILL HAVE AT LEAST SOME EFFECT ON HER...
THE SURGERIES ARE DEFINITELY HELPING, TOO.
IT'LL BE FINE.
WE'LL TAKE OUR TIME HEALING HER.

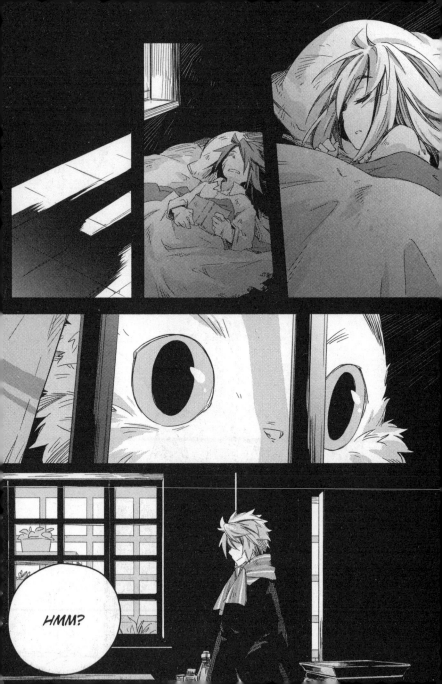

HMM?

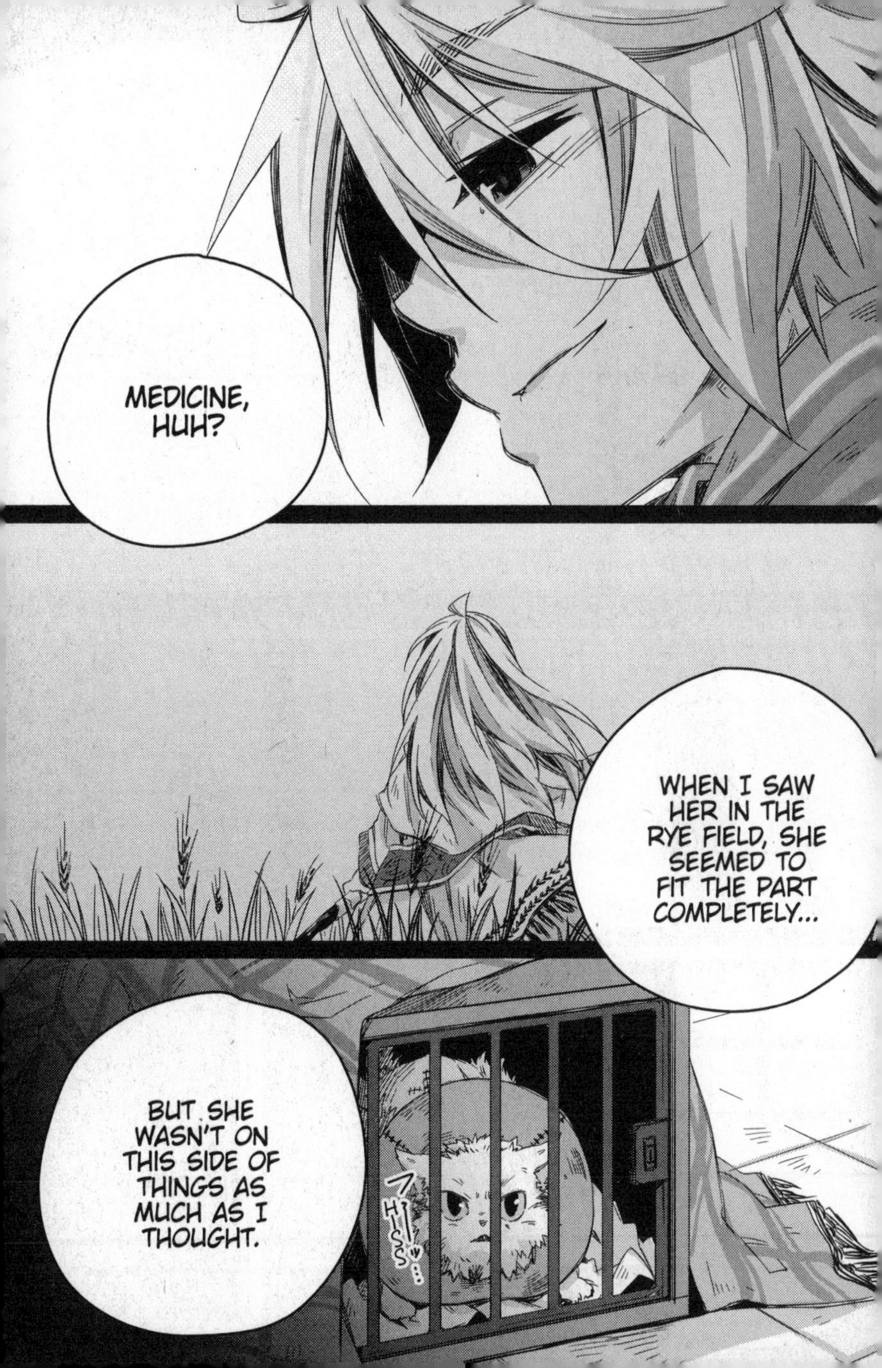
MEDICINE, HUH?
WHEN I SAW HER IN THE RYE FIELD, SHE SEEMED TO FIT THE PART COMPLETELY...
BUT SHE WASN'T ON THIS SIDE OF THINGS AS MUCH AS I THOUGHT.
HISS...

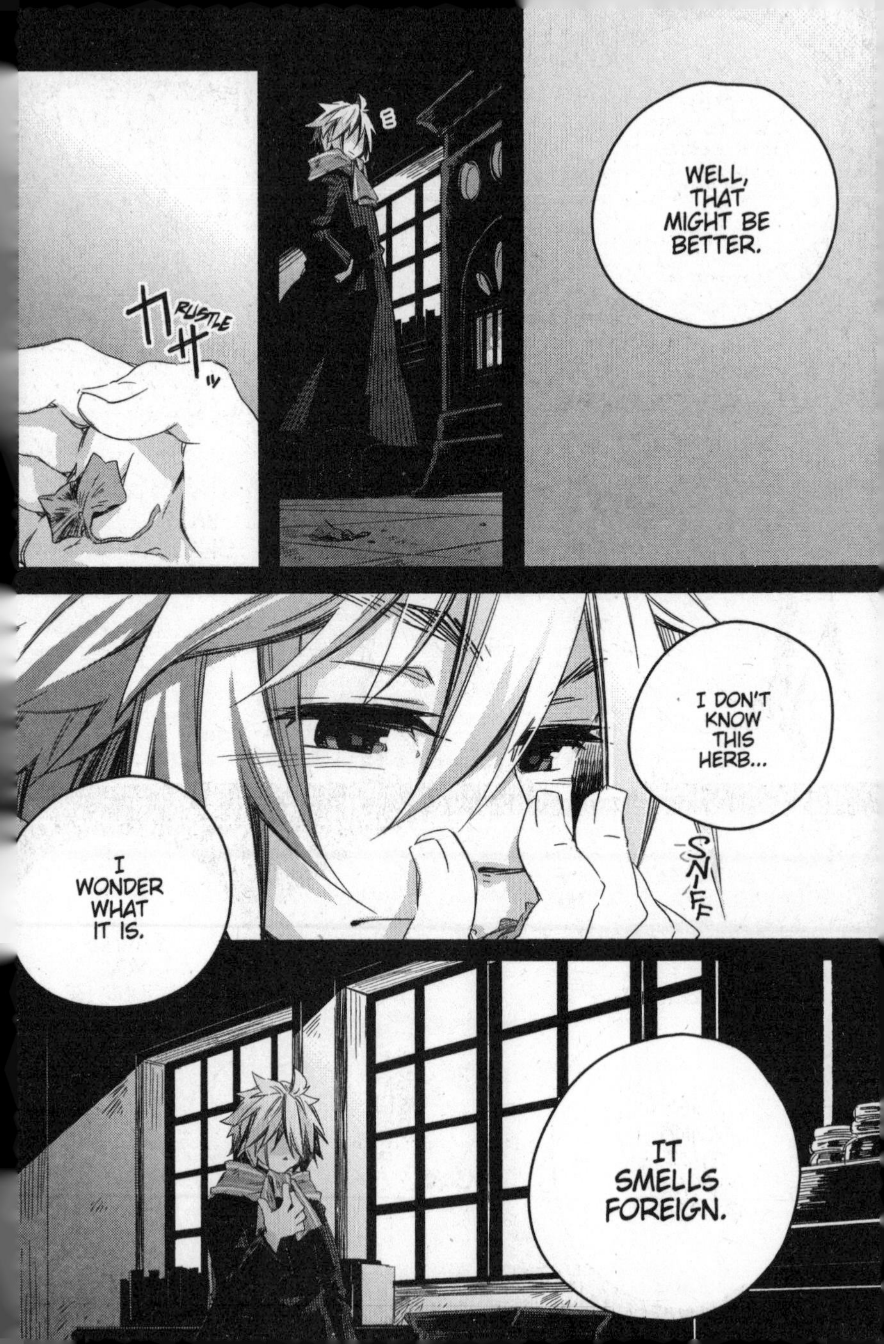
WELL, THAT MIGHT BE BETTER.
RUSTLE
I DON'T KNOW THIS HERB...
SNIFF
I WONDER WHAT IT IS.
IT SMELLS FOREIGN.

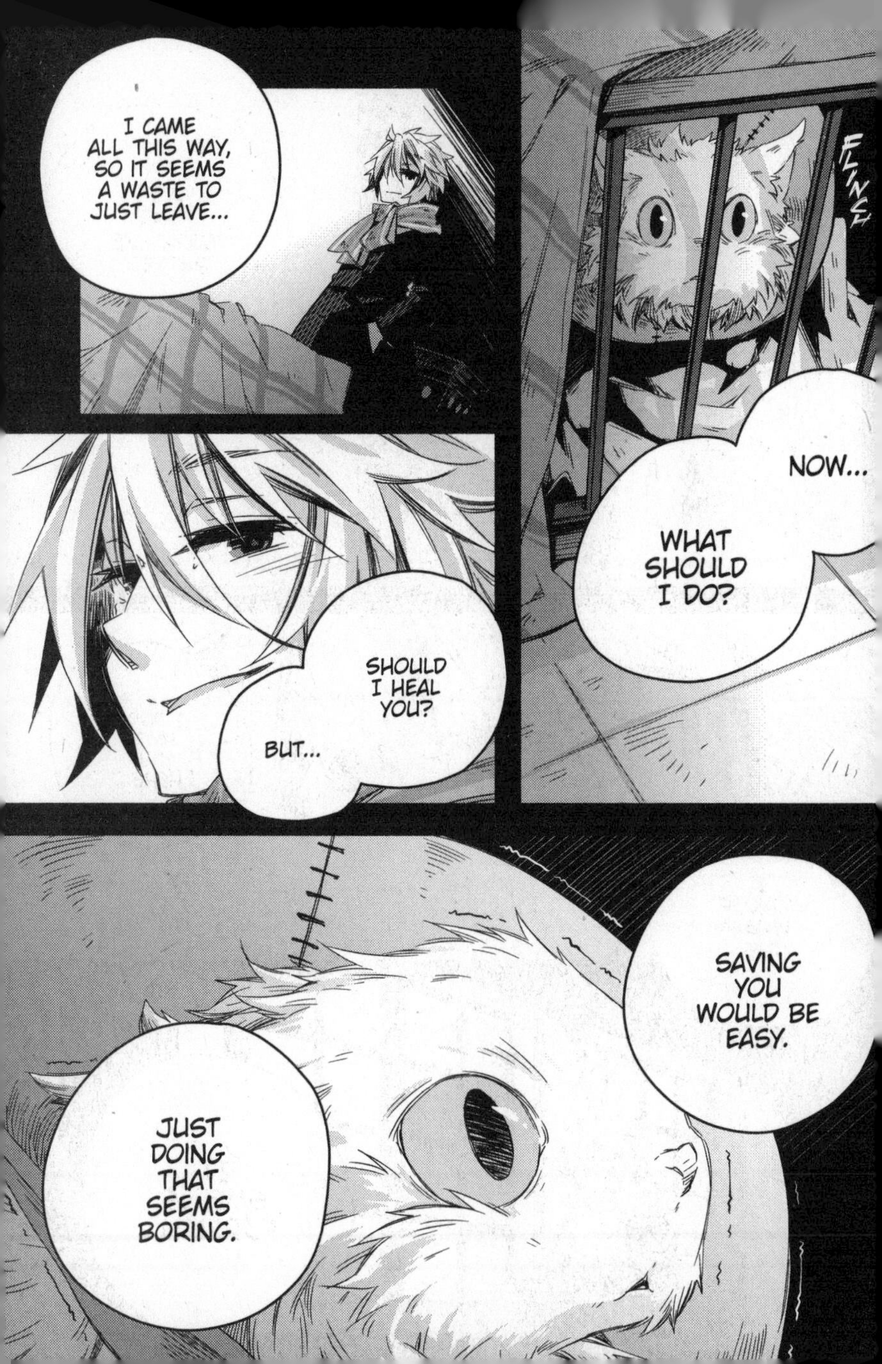
FLINCH
NOW...
WHAT SHOULD I DO?
I CAME ALL THIS WAY, SO IT SEEMS A WASTE TO JUST LEAVE...
SHOULD I HEAL YOU?
BUT...
SAVING YOU WOULD BE EASY.
JUST DOING THAT SEEMS BORING.

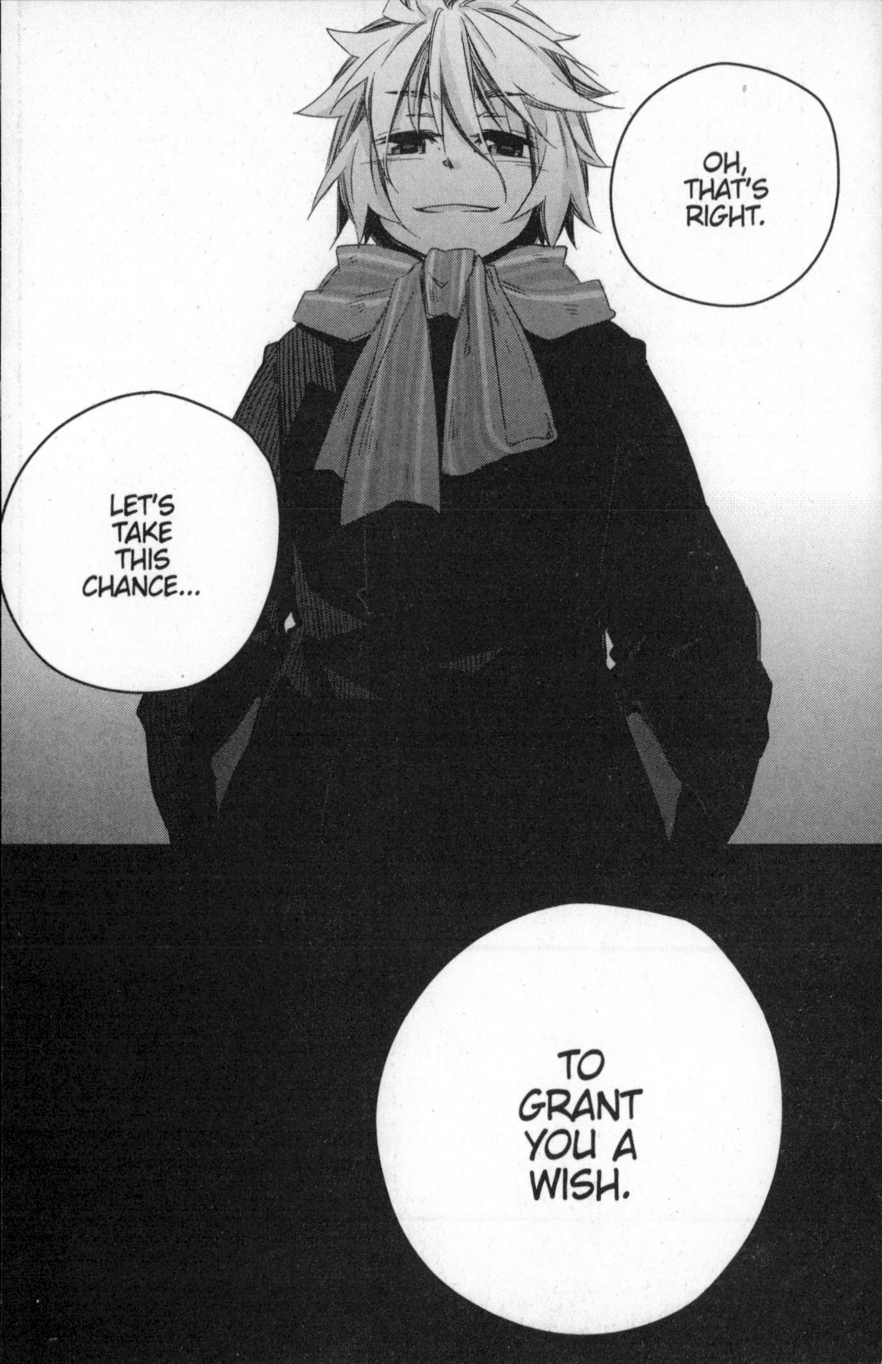
OH, THAT'S RIGHT.
LET'S TAKE THIS CHANCE...
TO GRANT YOU A WISH.

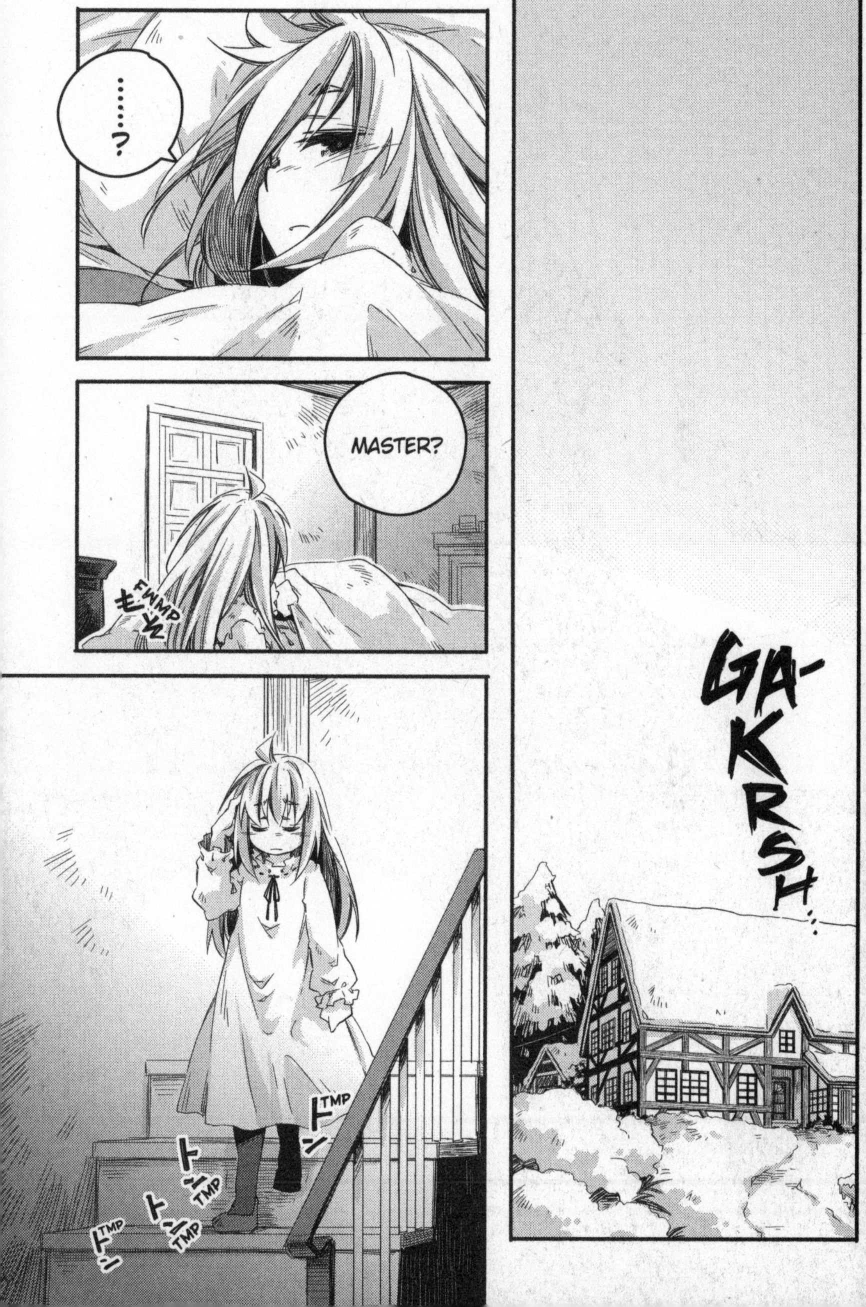

GA-KRSH...
......?
MASTER?
FWMP
TMP
TMP
TMP
TMP

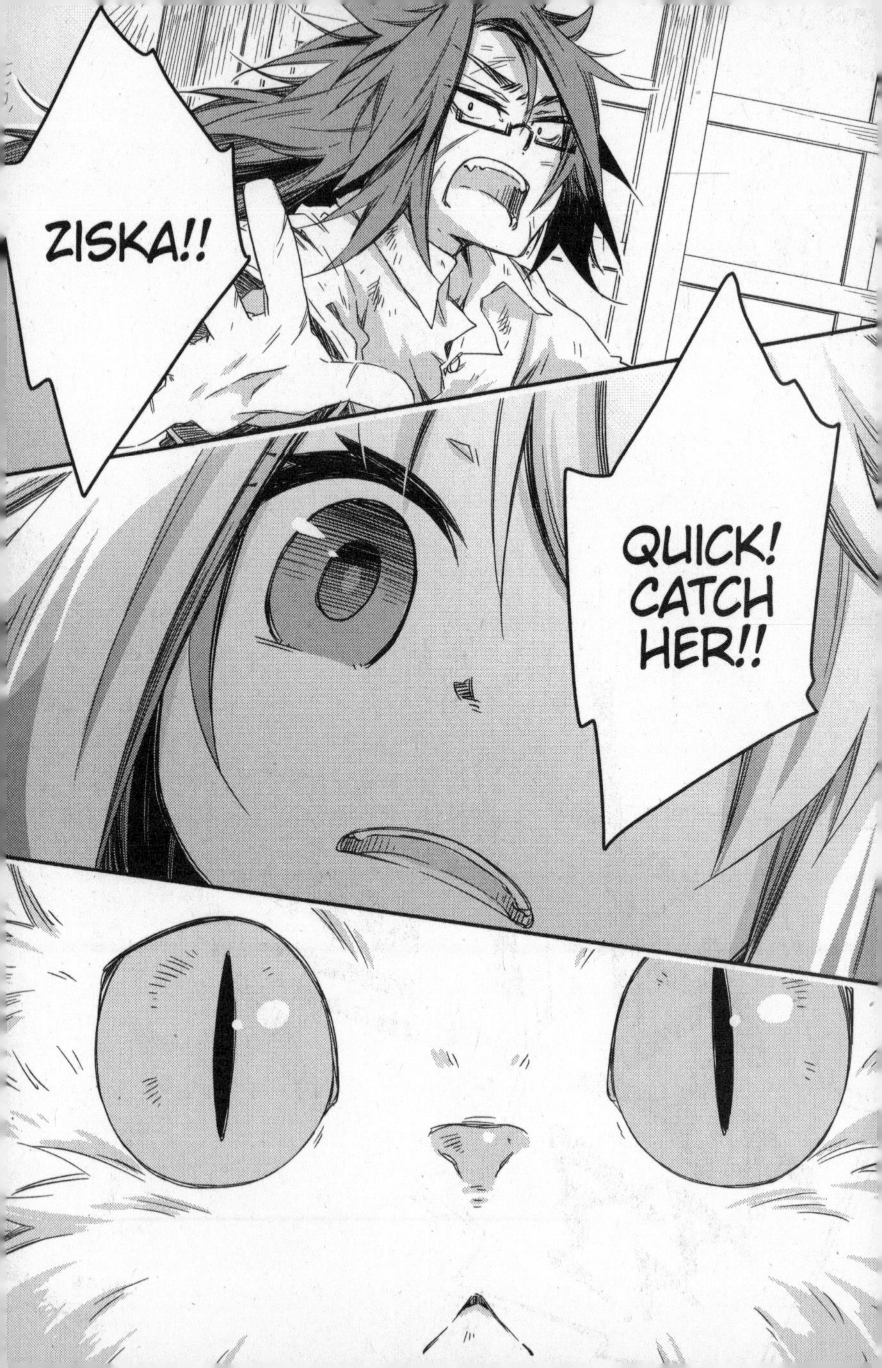
ZISKA!!
QUICK! CATCH HER!!

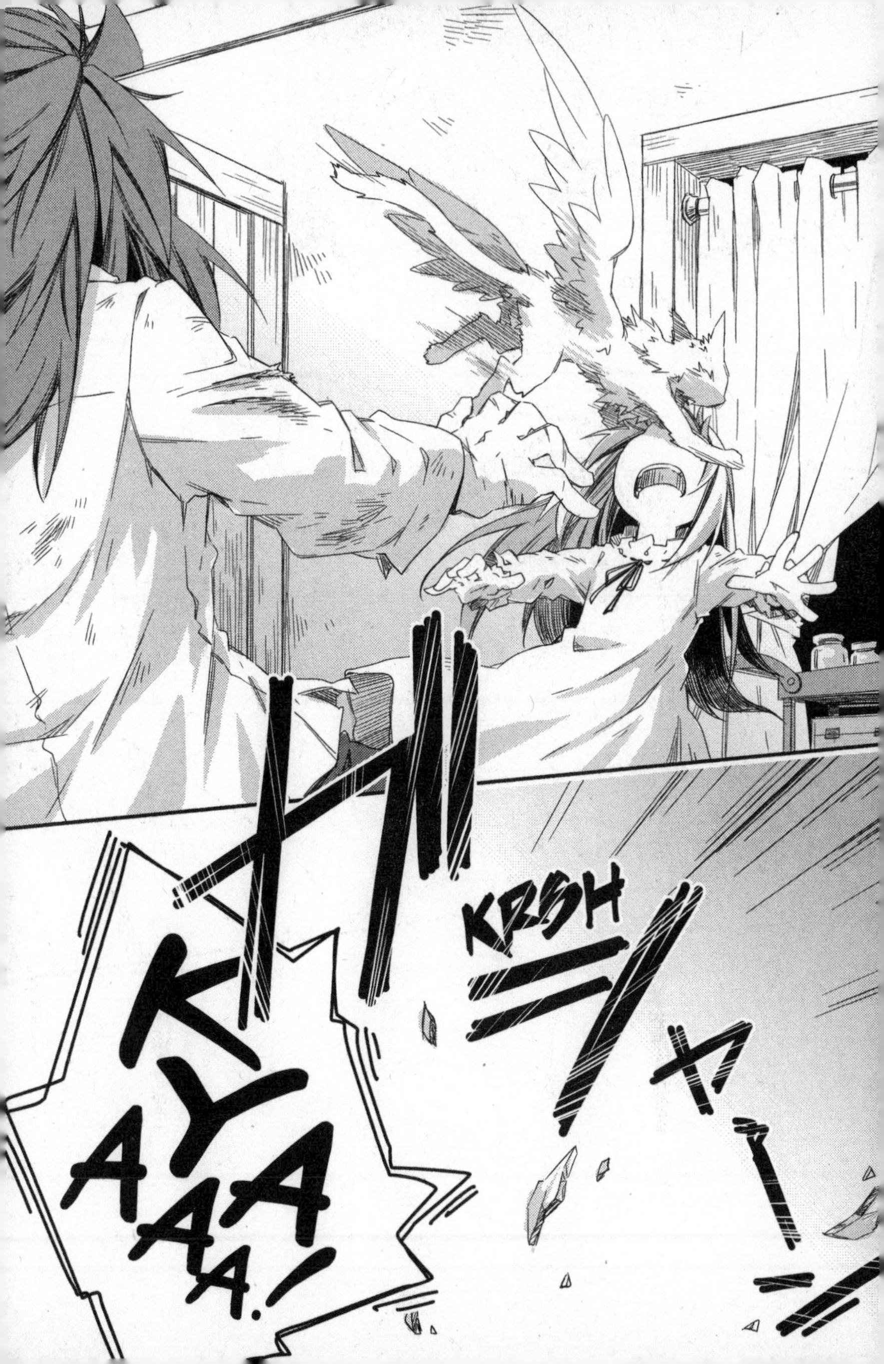
KRSH
KYAAAAA!

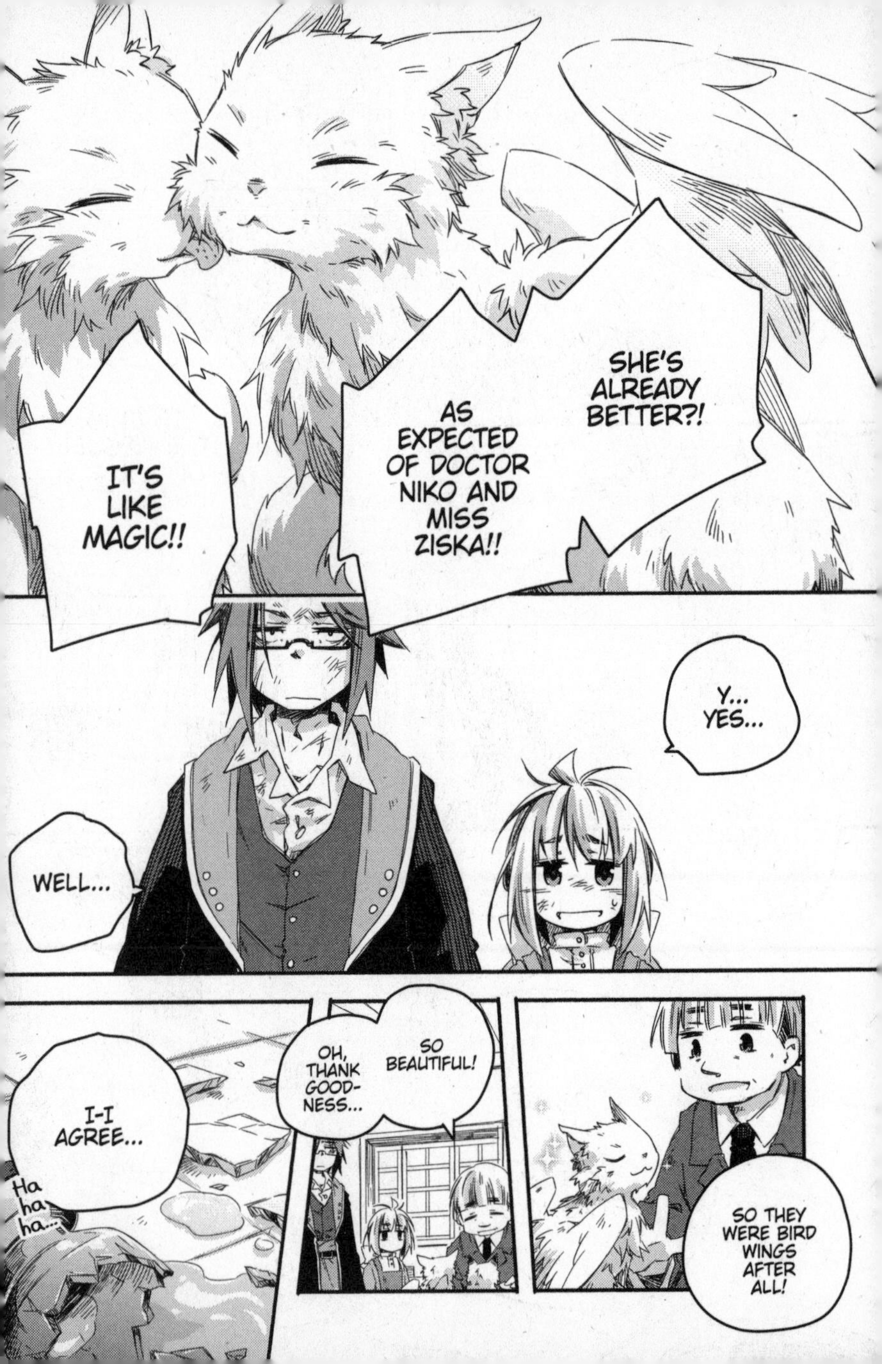
SHE'S ALREADY BETTER?!
AS EXPECTED OF DOCTOR NIKO AND MISS ZISKA!!
IT'S LIKE MAGIC!!
Y... YES...
WELL...
SO THEY WERE BIRD WINGS AFTER ALL!
SO BEAUTIFUL!
OH, THANK GOOD-NESS...
I-I AGREE...
Ha ha ha...

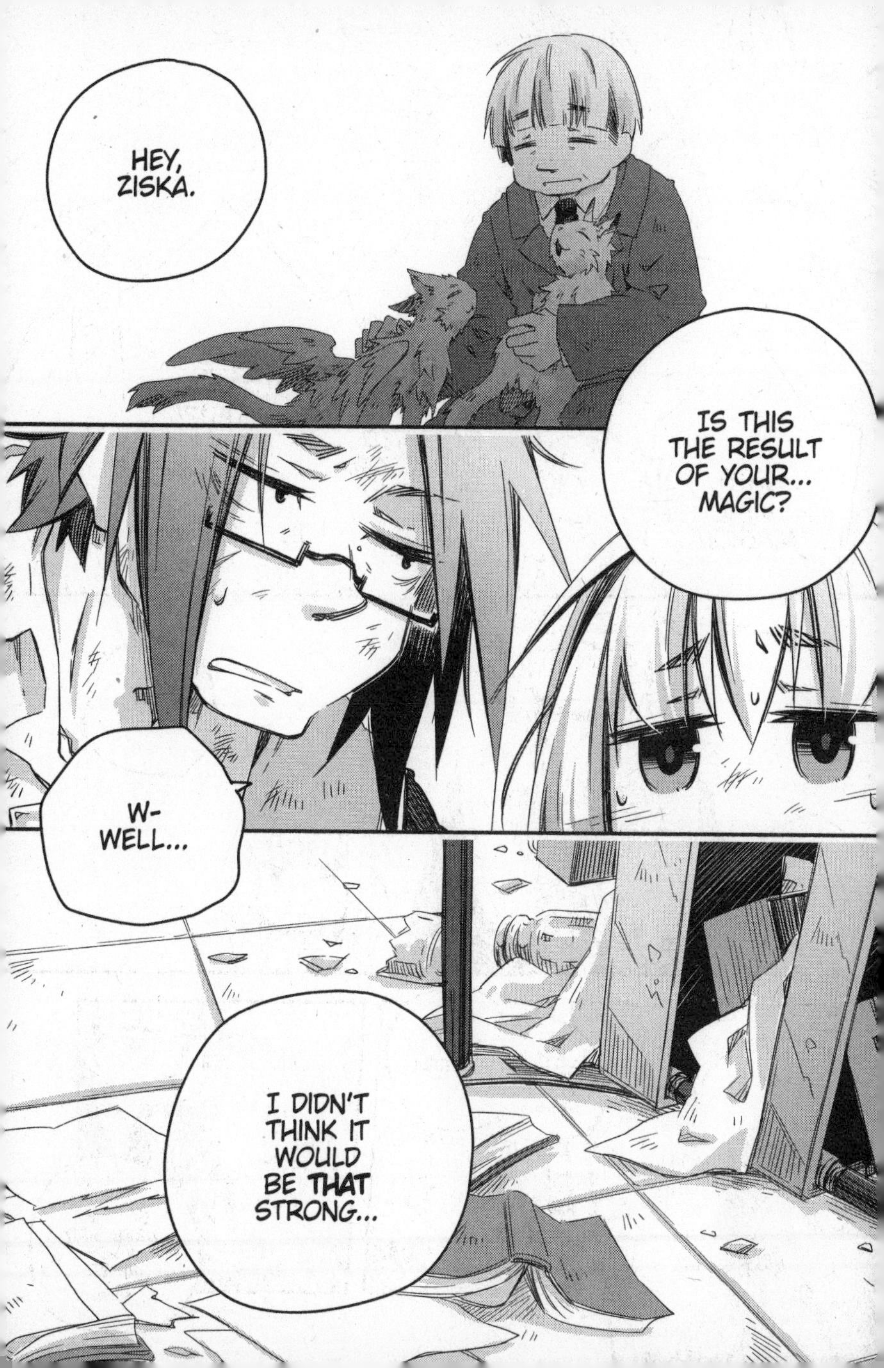
HEY, ZISKA.
IS THIS THE RESULT OF YOUR... MAGIC?
W- WELL...
I DIDN'T THINK IT WOULD BE THAT STRONG...

There is a puk hiding in every chapter!

Try to find them all.

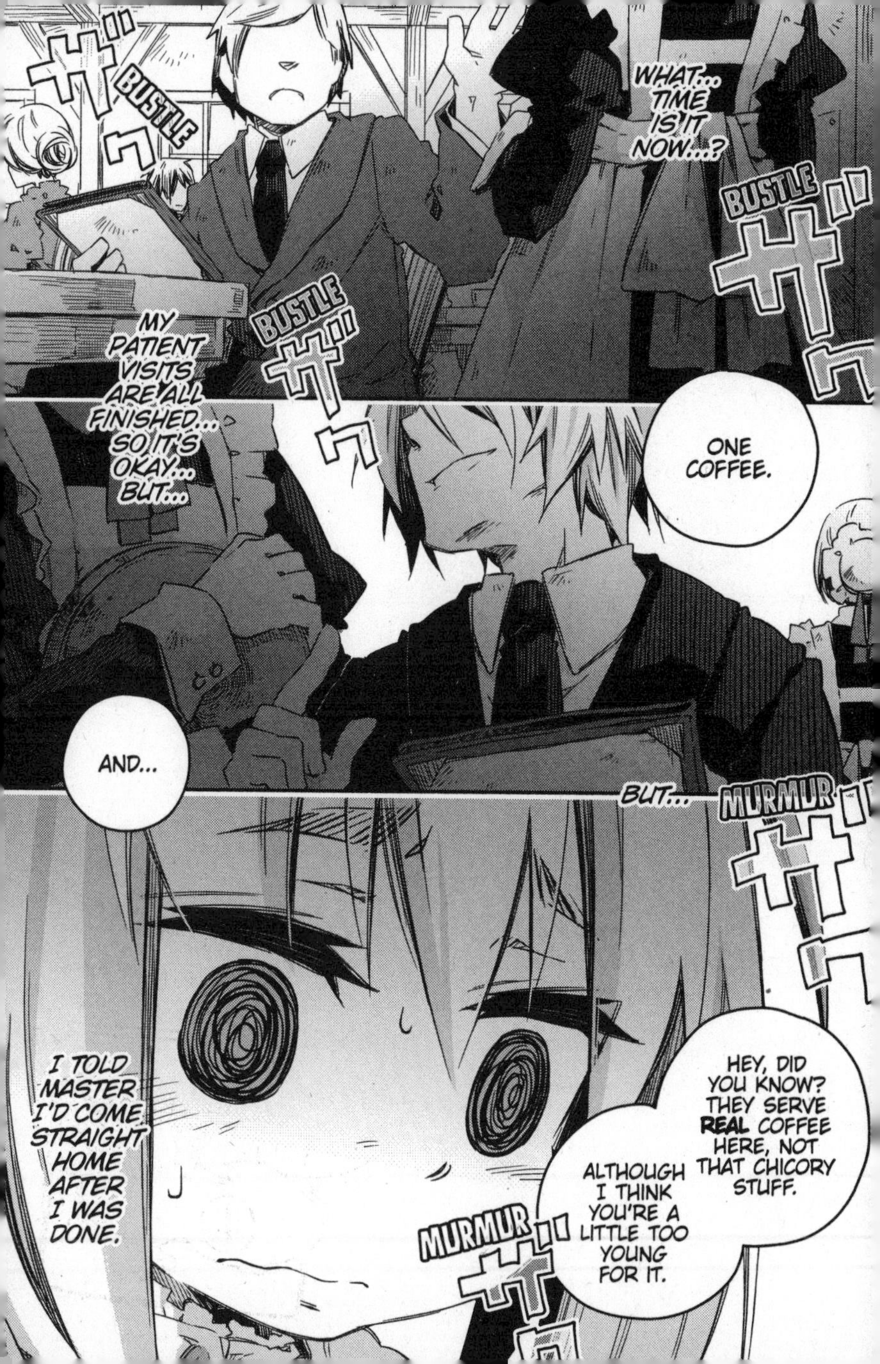
BUSTLE
WHAT... TIME IS IT NOW...?
BUSTLE
MY PATIENT VISITS ARE ALL FINISHED... SO IT'S OKAY... BUT...
BUSTLE
ONE COFFEE.
AND...
MURMUR
BUT...
HEY, DID YOU KNOW? THEY SERVE **REAL** COFFEE HERE, NOT THAT CHICORY STUFF.
ALTHOUGH I THINK YOU'RE A LITTLE TOO YOUNG FOR IT.
MURMUR
I TOLD MASTER I'D COME STRAIGHT HOME AFTER I WAS DONE.

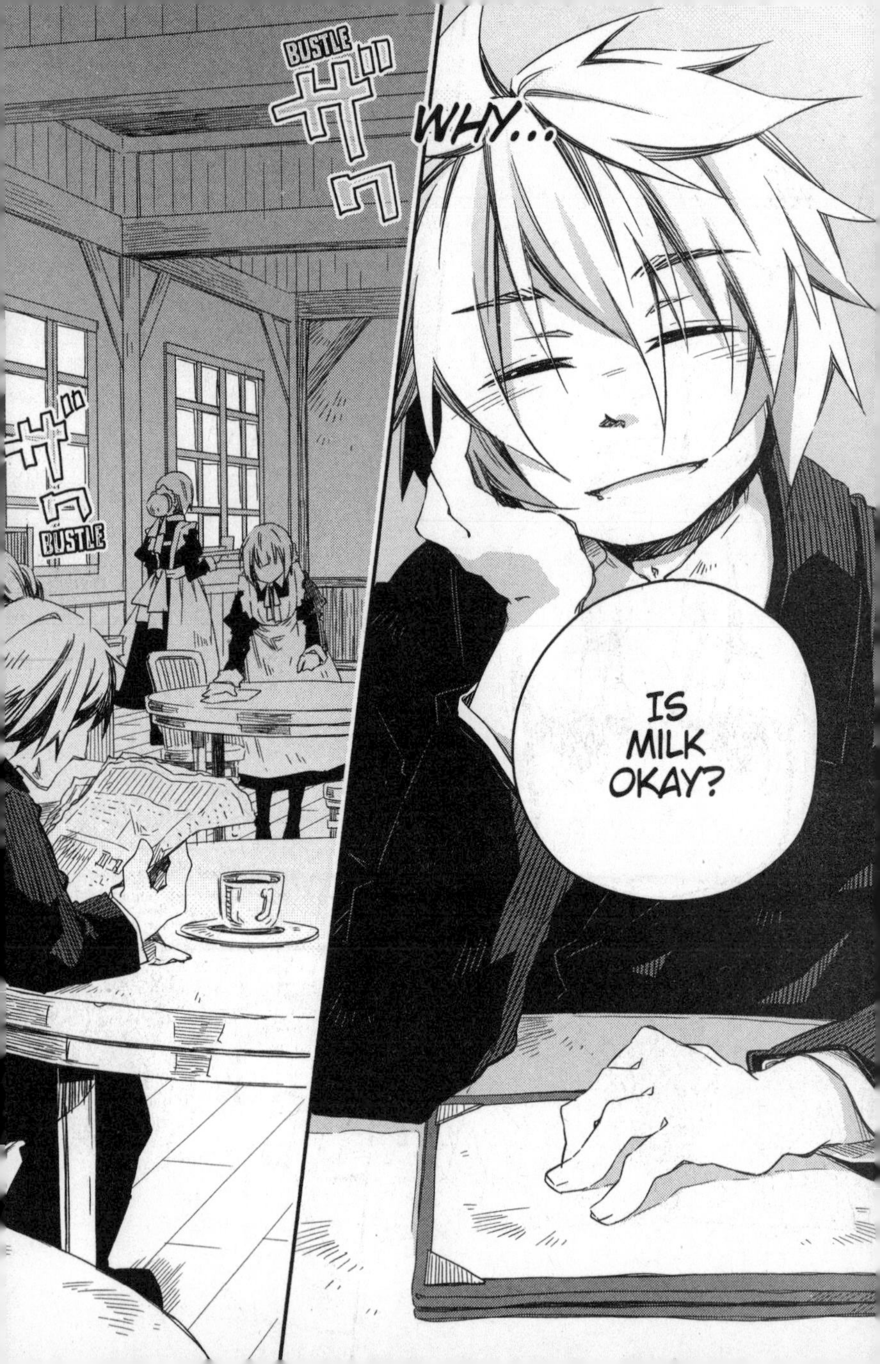
WHY...
IS MILK OKAY?
BUSTLE
BUSTLE

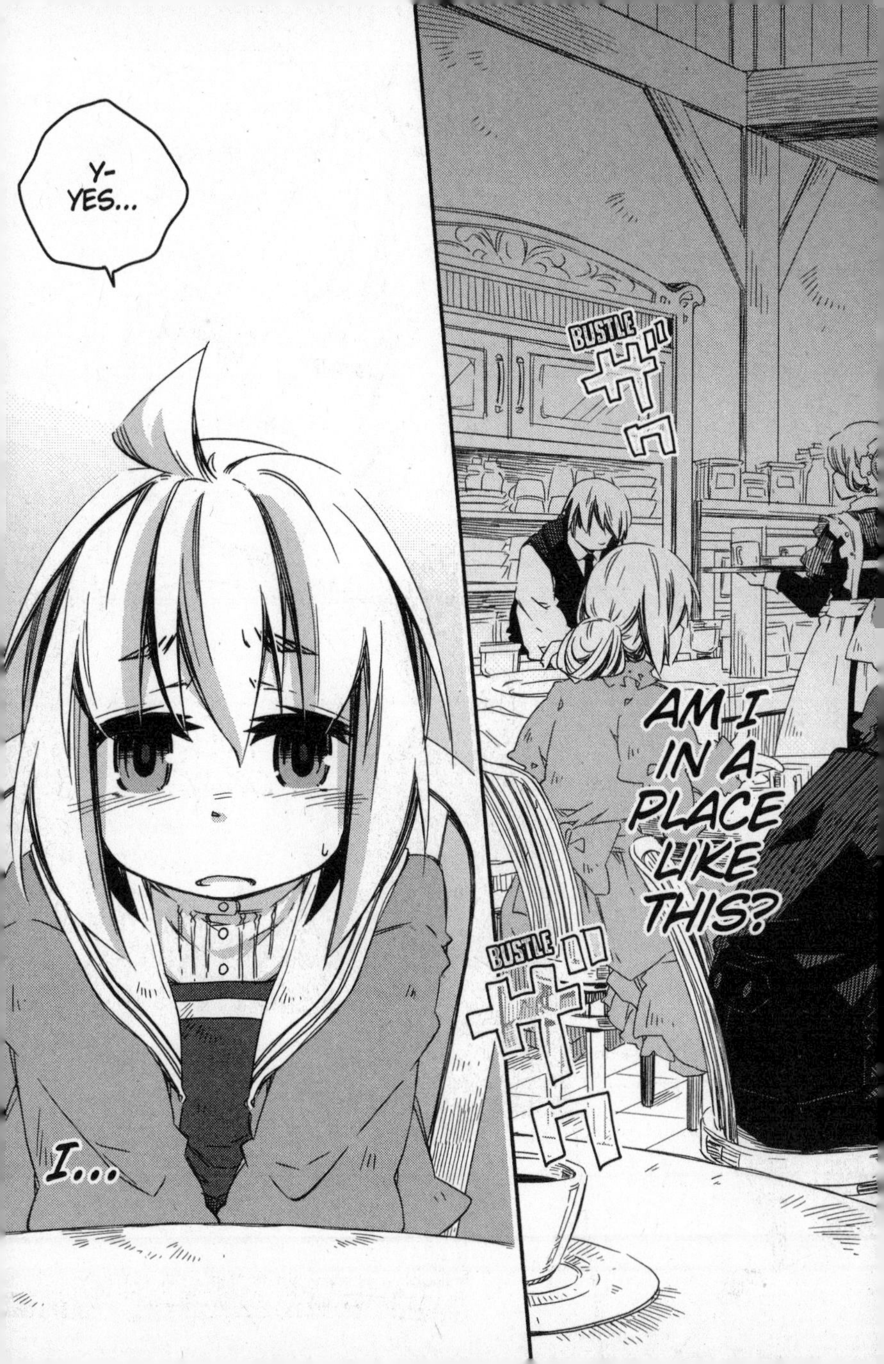
BUSTLE
BUSTLE
AM I IN A PLACE LIKE THIS?
Y-YES...
I...

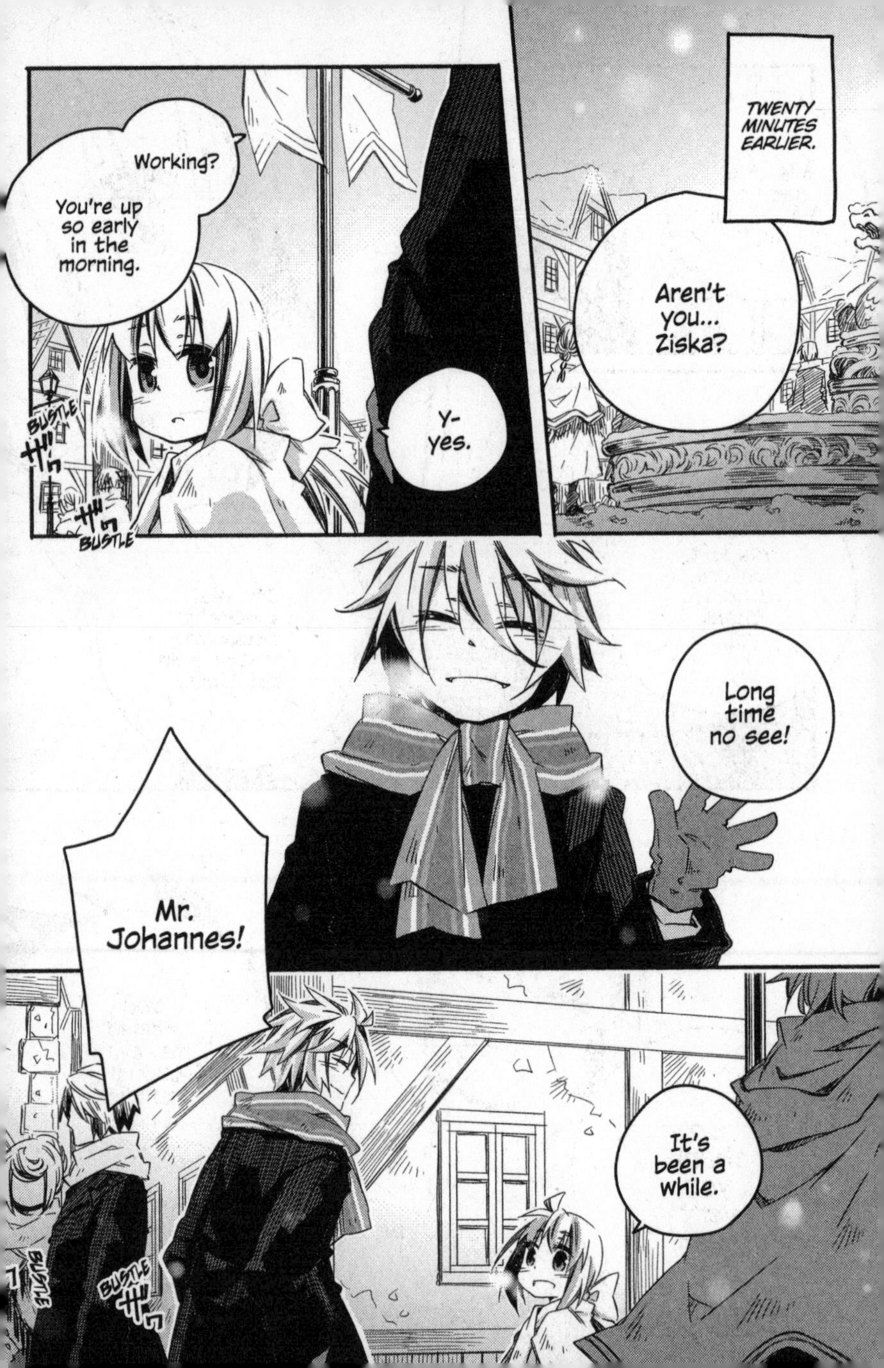
TWENTY MINUTES EARLIER.
Aren't you... Ziska?
Y-yes.
Working?
You're up so early in the morning.
BUSTLE
BUSTLE
Long time no see!
Mr. Johannes!
It's been a while.
BUSTLE
BUSTLE

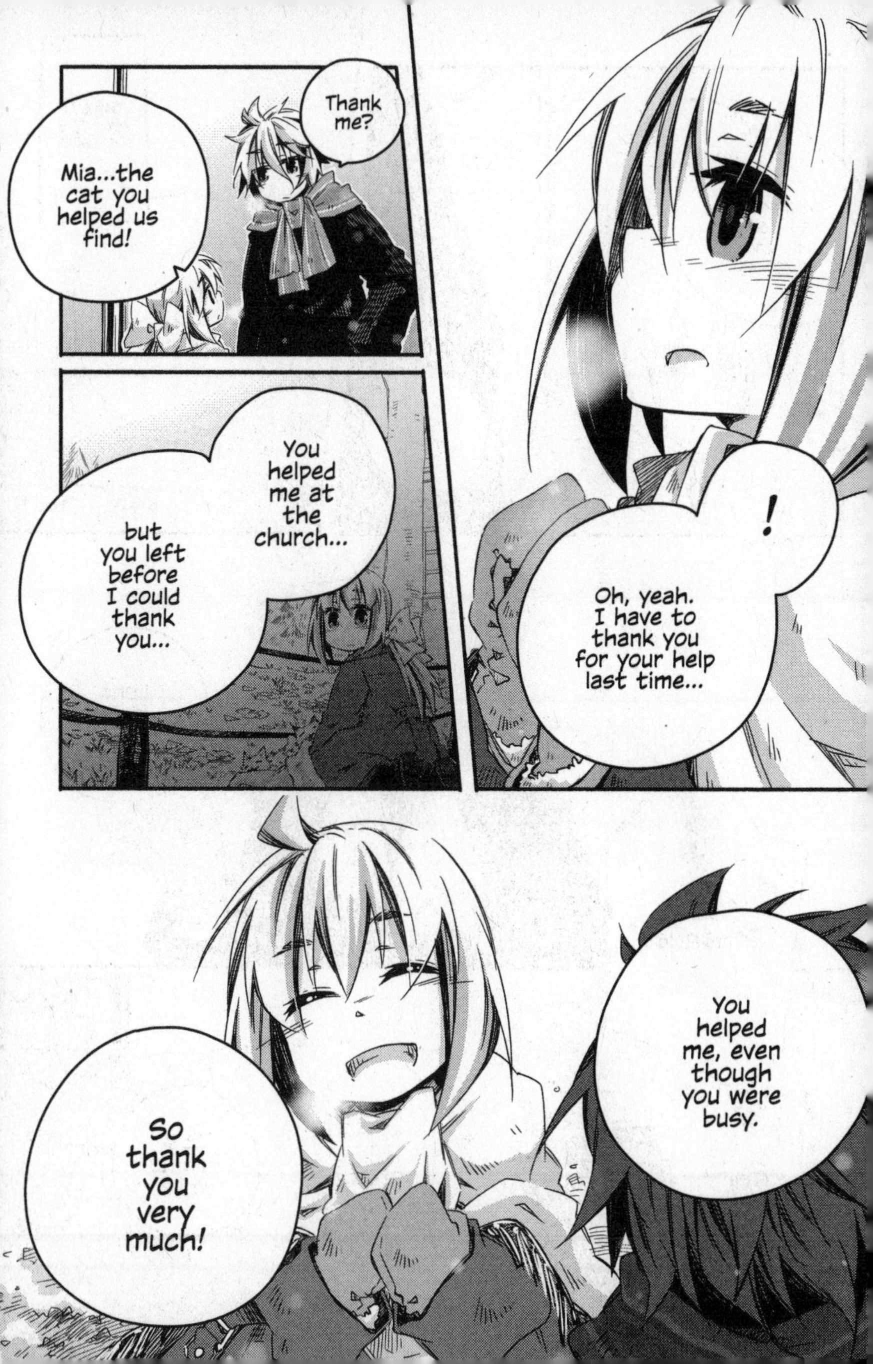
!
Oh, yeah. I have to thank you for your help last time...
Thank me?
Mia...the cat you helped us find!
You helped me at the church...
but you left before I could thank you...
You helped me, even though you were busy.
So thank you very much!

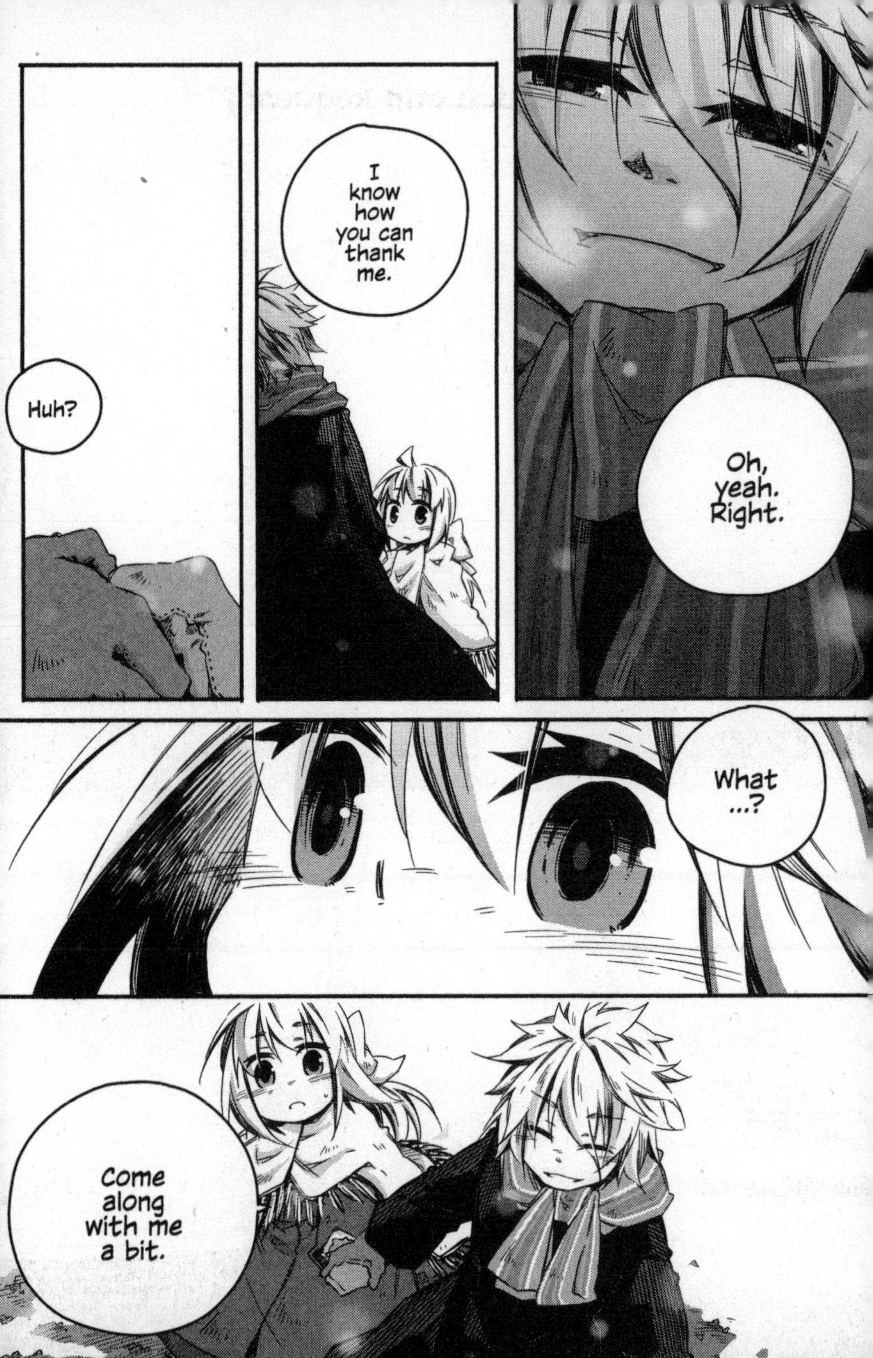
Oh, yeah. Right.
I know how you can thank me.
Huh?
What ...?
Come along with me a bit.

[Case 16: Reciprocation and Request]

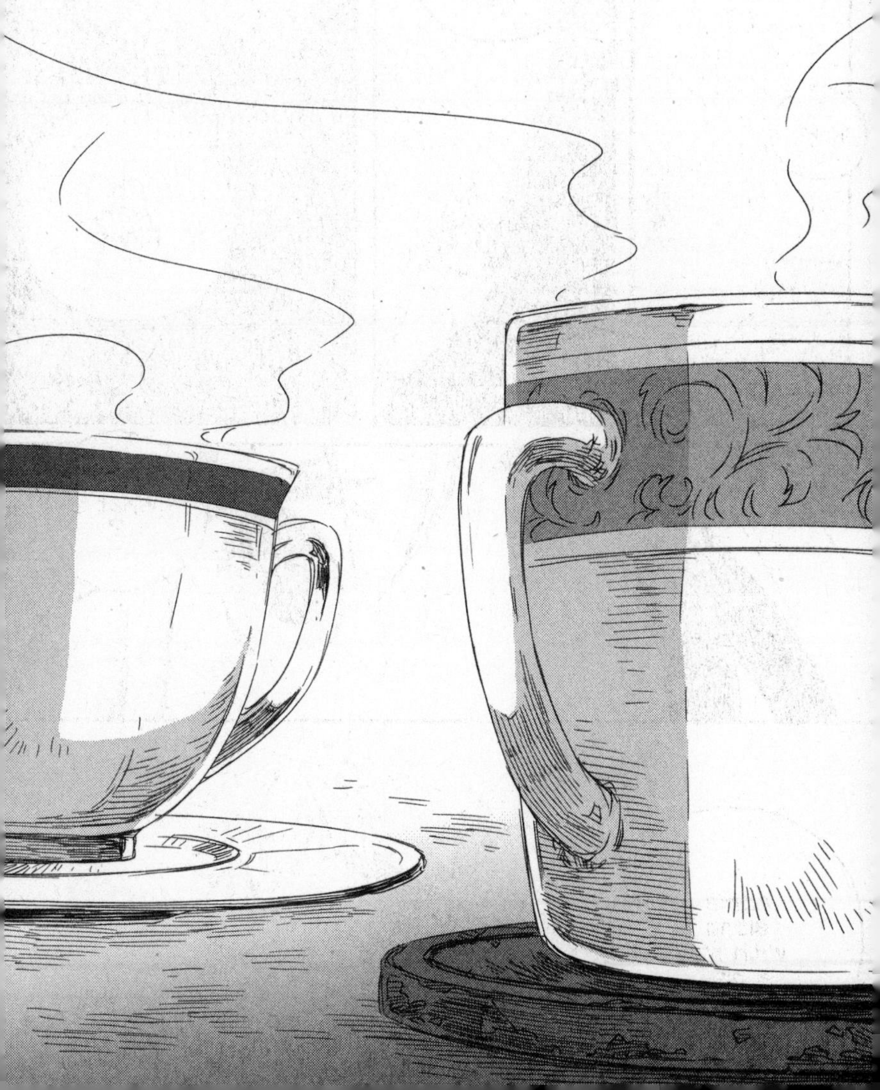

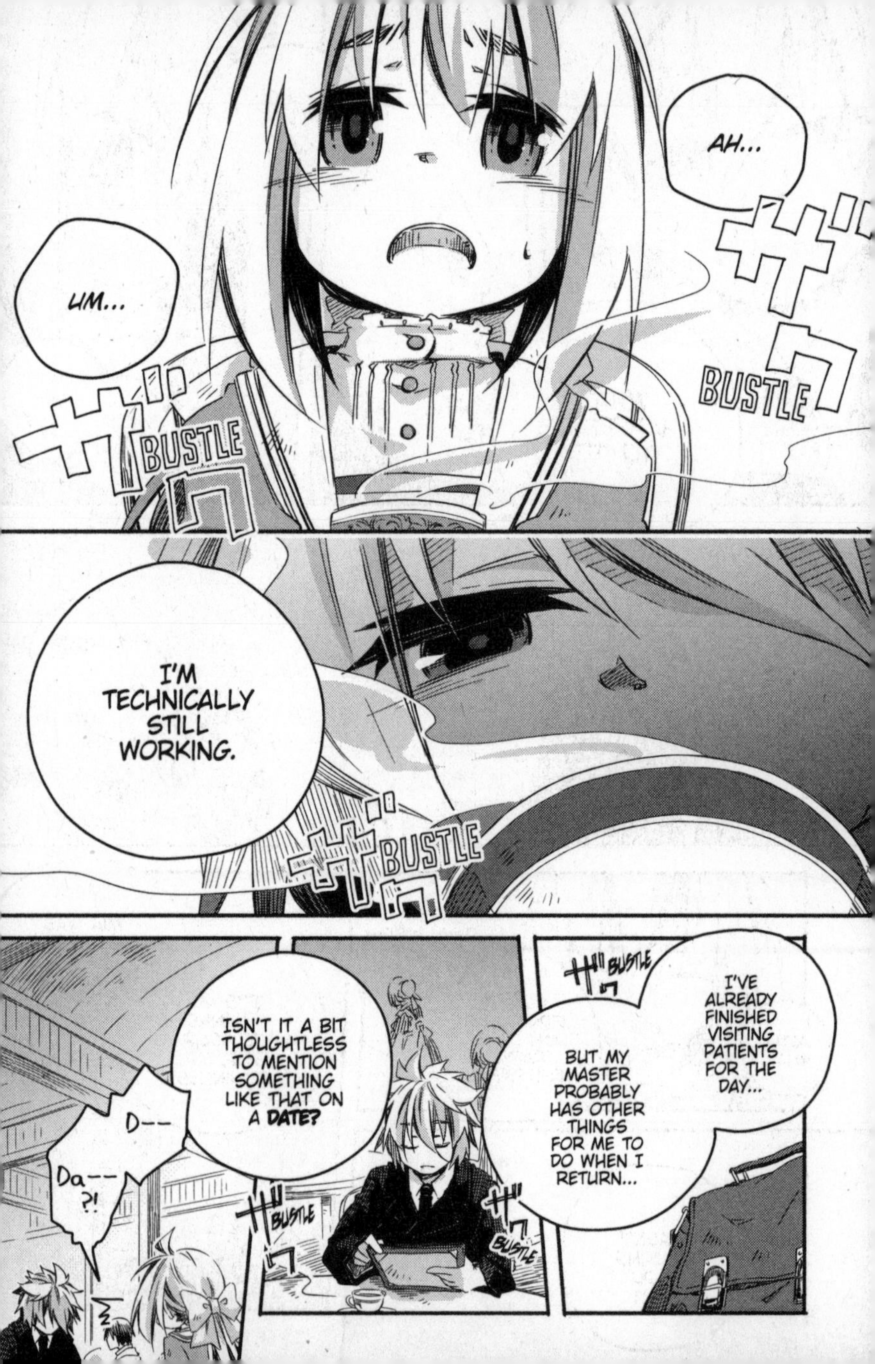
AH...
BUSTLE
UM...
BUSTLE
I'M TECHNICALLY STILL WORKING.
BUSTLE
I'VE ALREADY FINISHED VISITING PATIENTS FOR THE DAY...
BUT MY MASTER PROBABLY HAS OTHER THINGS FOR ME TO DO WHEN I RETURN...
BUSTLE
BUSTLE
ISN'T IT A BIT THOUGHTLESS TO MENTION SOMETHING LIKE THAT ON A **DATE?**
BUSTLE
D--
Da-- ?!

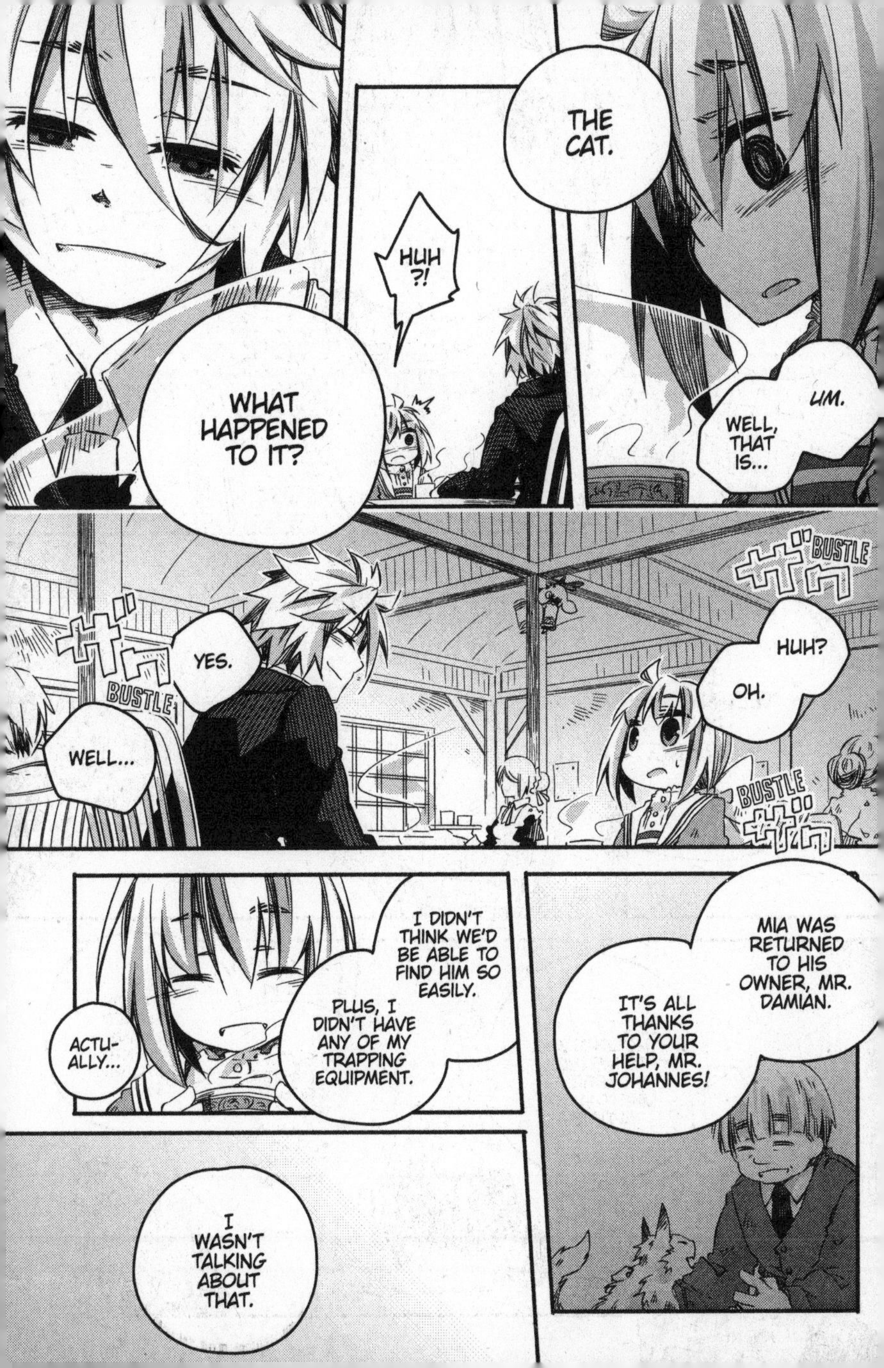
THE CAT.
UM.
WELL, THAT IS...
HUH ?!
WHAT HAPPENED TO IT?
BUSTLE
HUH?
OH.
BUSTLE
YES.
BUSTLE
WELL...
MIA WAS RETURNED TO HIS OWNER, MR. DAMIAN.
IT'S ALL THANKS TO YOUR HELP, MR. JOHANNES!
I DIDN'T THINK WE'D BE ABLE TO FIND HIM SO EASILY.
PLUS, I DIDN'T HAVE ANY OF MY TRAPPING EQUIPMENT.
ACTU-ALLY...
I WASN'T TALKING ABOUT THAT.

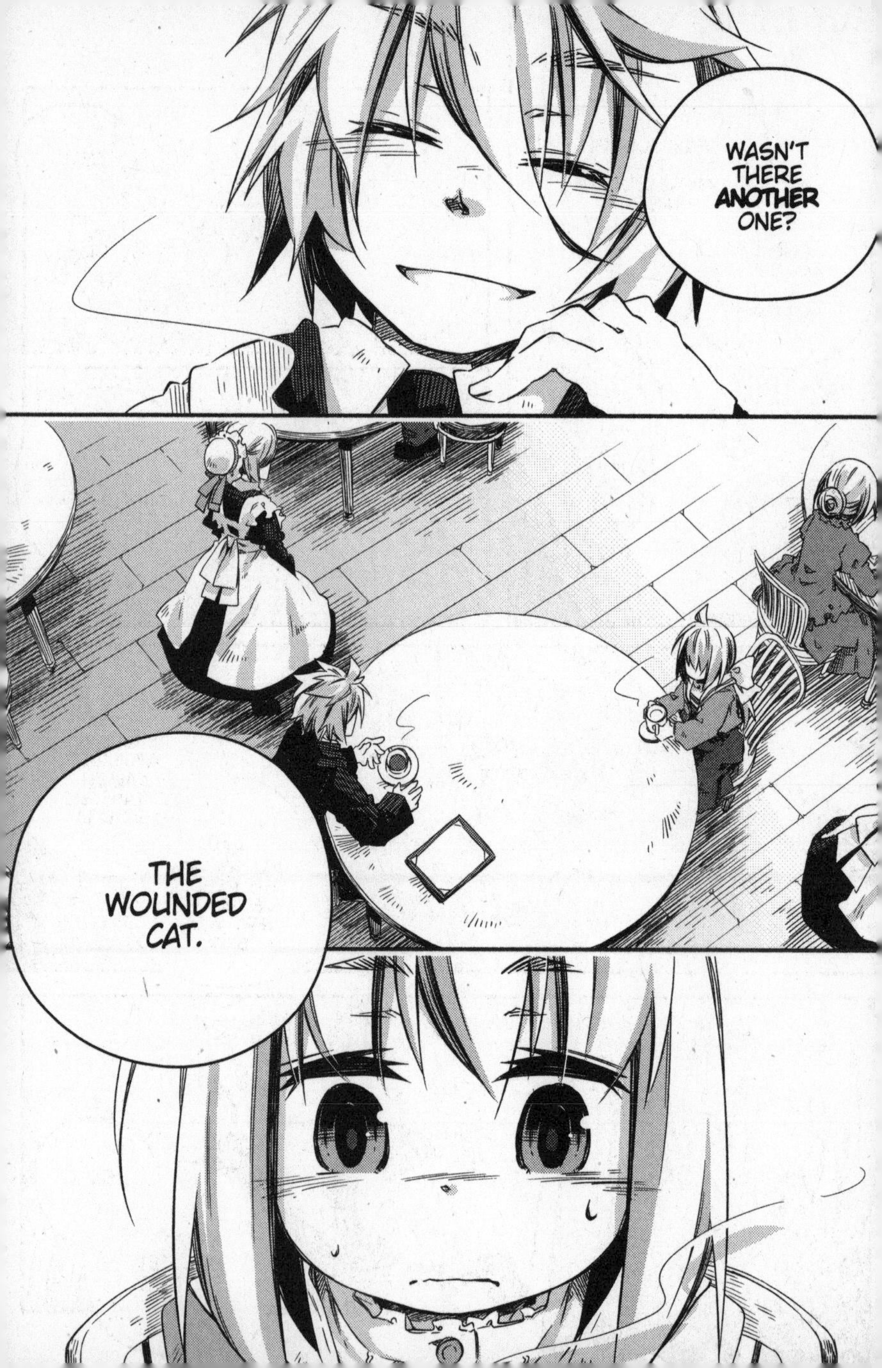
WASN'T THERE **ANOTHER** ONE?
THE WOUNDED CAT.

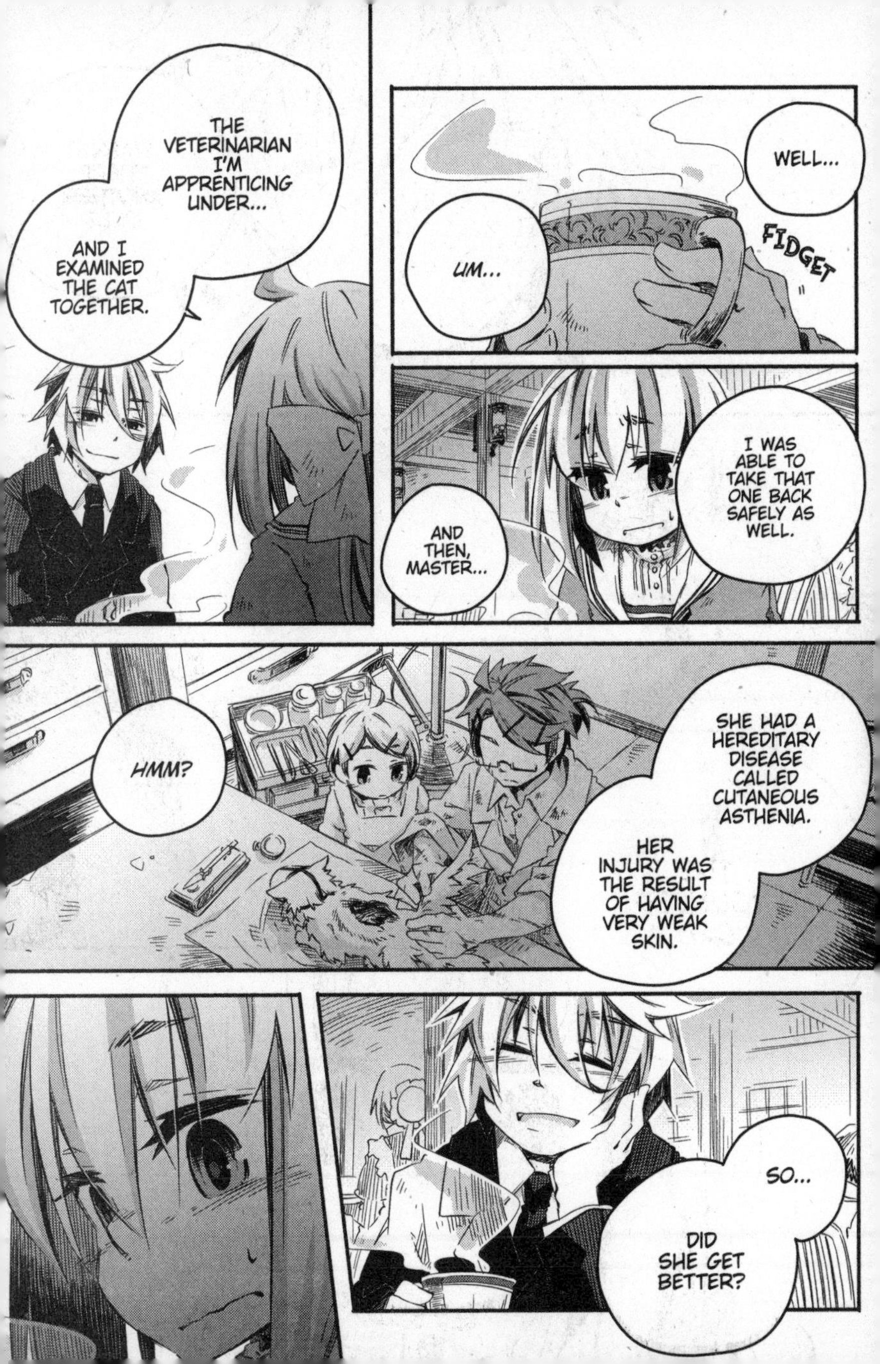
WELL...
FIDGET
UM...
I WAS ABLE TO TAKE THAT ONE BACK SAFELY AS WELL.
AND THEN, MASTER...
THE VETERINARIAN I'M APPRENTICING UNDER...
AND I EXAMINED THE CAT TOGETHER.
SHE HAD A HEREDITARY DISEASE CALLED CUTANEOUS ASTHENIA.
HER INJURY WAS THE RESULT OF HAVING VERY WEAK SKIN.
HMM?
SO...
DID SHE GET BETTER?

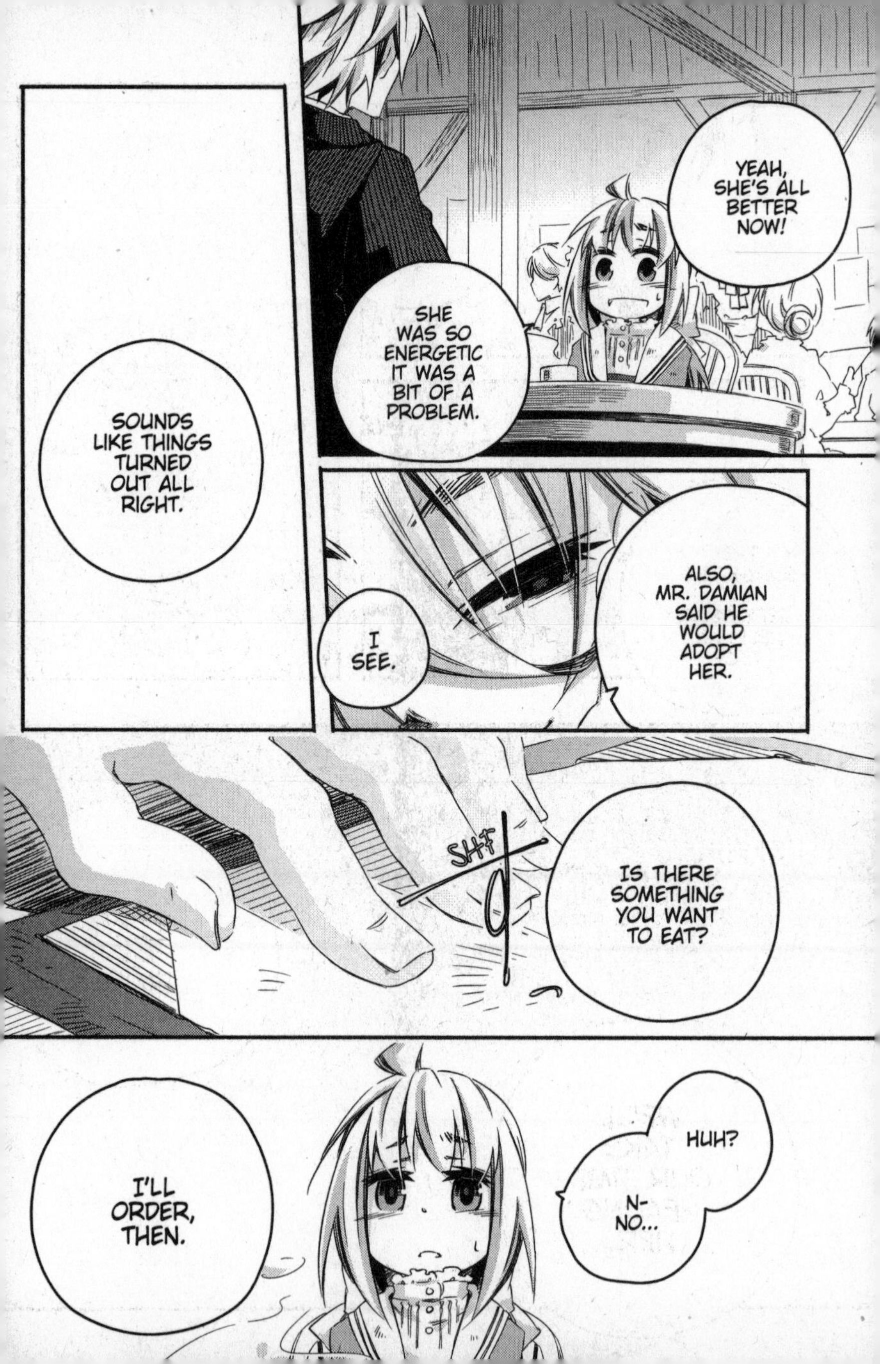
YEAH, SHE'S ALL BETTER NOW!
SHE WAS SO ENERGETIC IT WAS A BIT OF A PROBLEM.
ALSO, MR. DAMIAN SAID HE WOULD ADOPT HER.
I SEE.
SOUNDS LIKE THINGS TURNED OUT ALL RIGHT.
IS THERE SOMETHING YOU WANT TO EAT?
SHF
HUH?
N-NO...
I'LL ORDER, THEN.

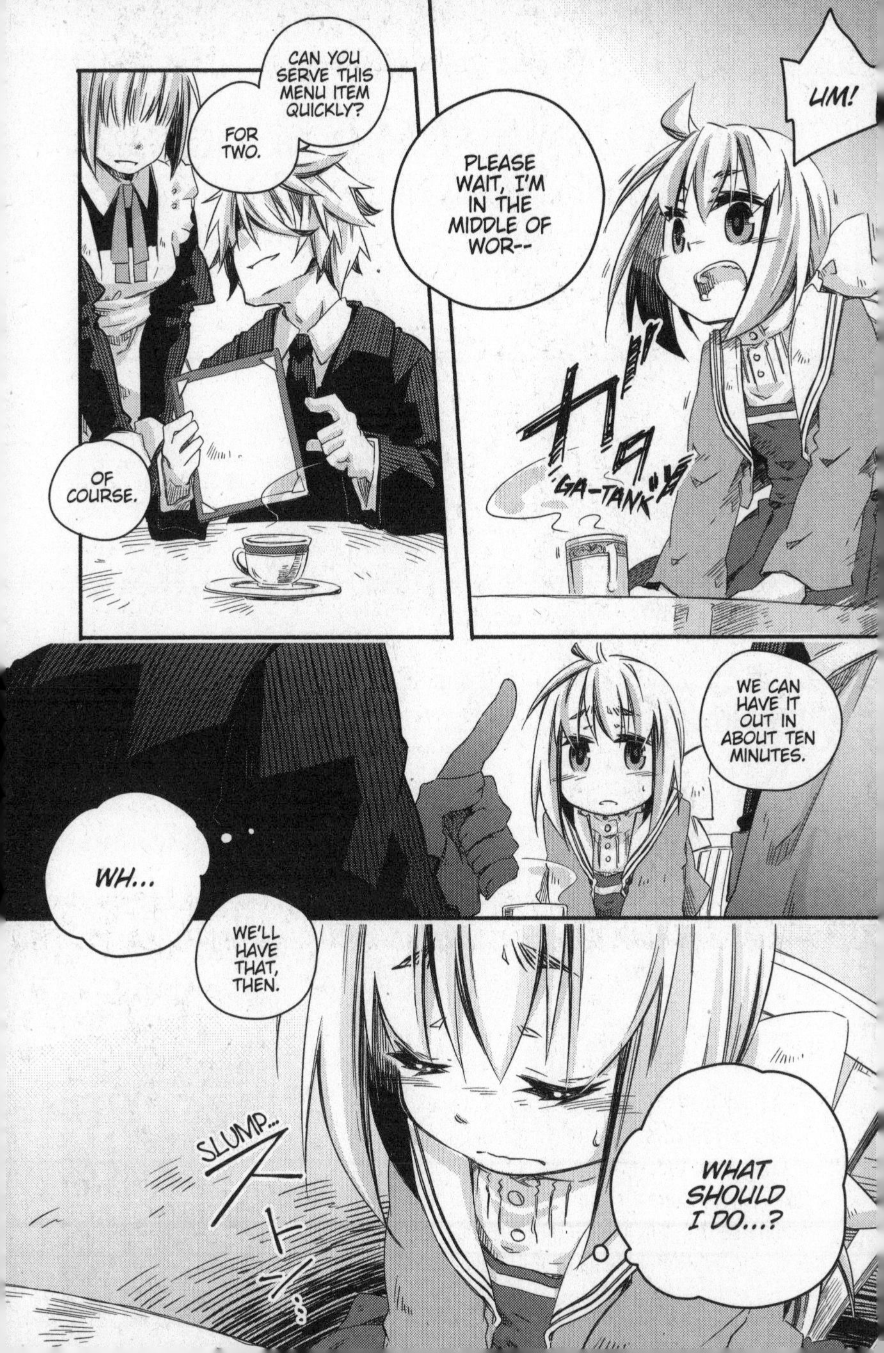
UM!
PLEASE WAIT, I'M IN THE MIDDLE OF WOR--
GA-TANK
CAN YOU SERVE THIS MENU ITEM QUICKLY?
FOR TWO.
OF COURSE.
WE CAN HAVE IT OUT IN ABOUT TEN MINUTES.
WH...
WE'LL HAVE THAT, THEN.
SLUMP...
WHAT SHOULD I DO...?

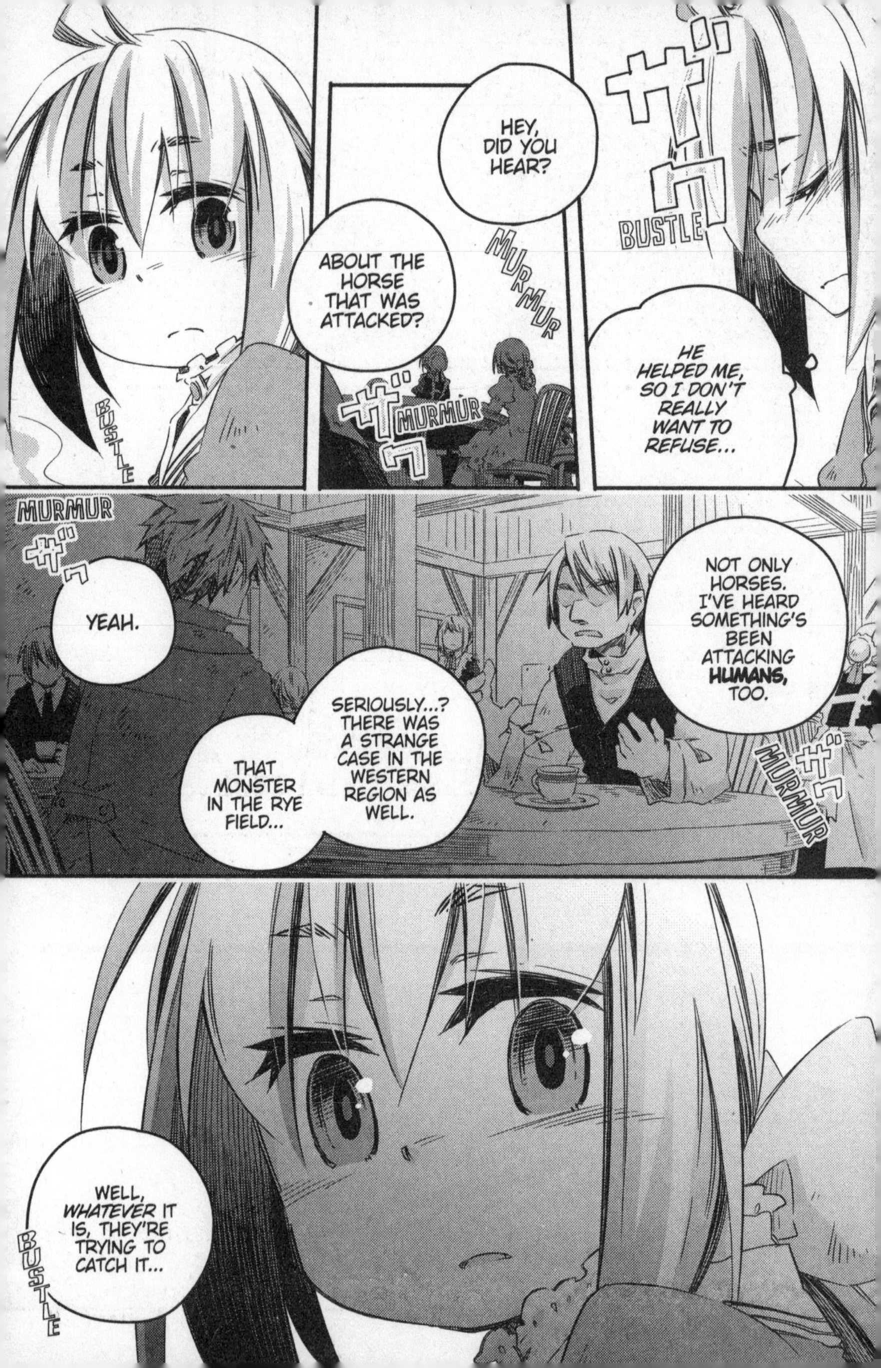
BUSTLE
HE HELPED ME, SO I DON'T REALLY WANT TO REFUSE...
HEY, DID YOU HEAR?
MURMUR
ABOUT THE HORSE THAT WAS ATTACKED?
MURMUR
BUSTLE
NOT ONLY HORSES. I'VE HEARD SOMETHING'S BEEN ATTACKING **HUMANS,** TOO.
MURMUR
SERIOUSLY...? THERE WAS A STRANGE CASE IN THE WESTERN REGION AS WELL.
THAT MONSTER IN THE RYE FIELD...
YEAH.
MURMUR
WELL, *WHATEVER* IT IS, THEY'RE TRYING TO CATCH IT...
BUSTLE

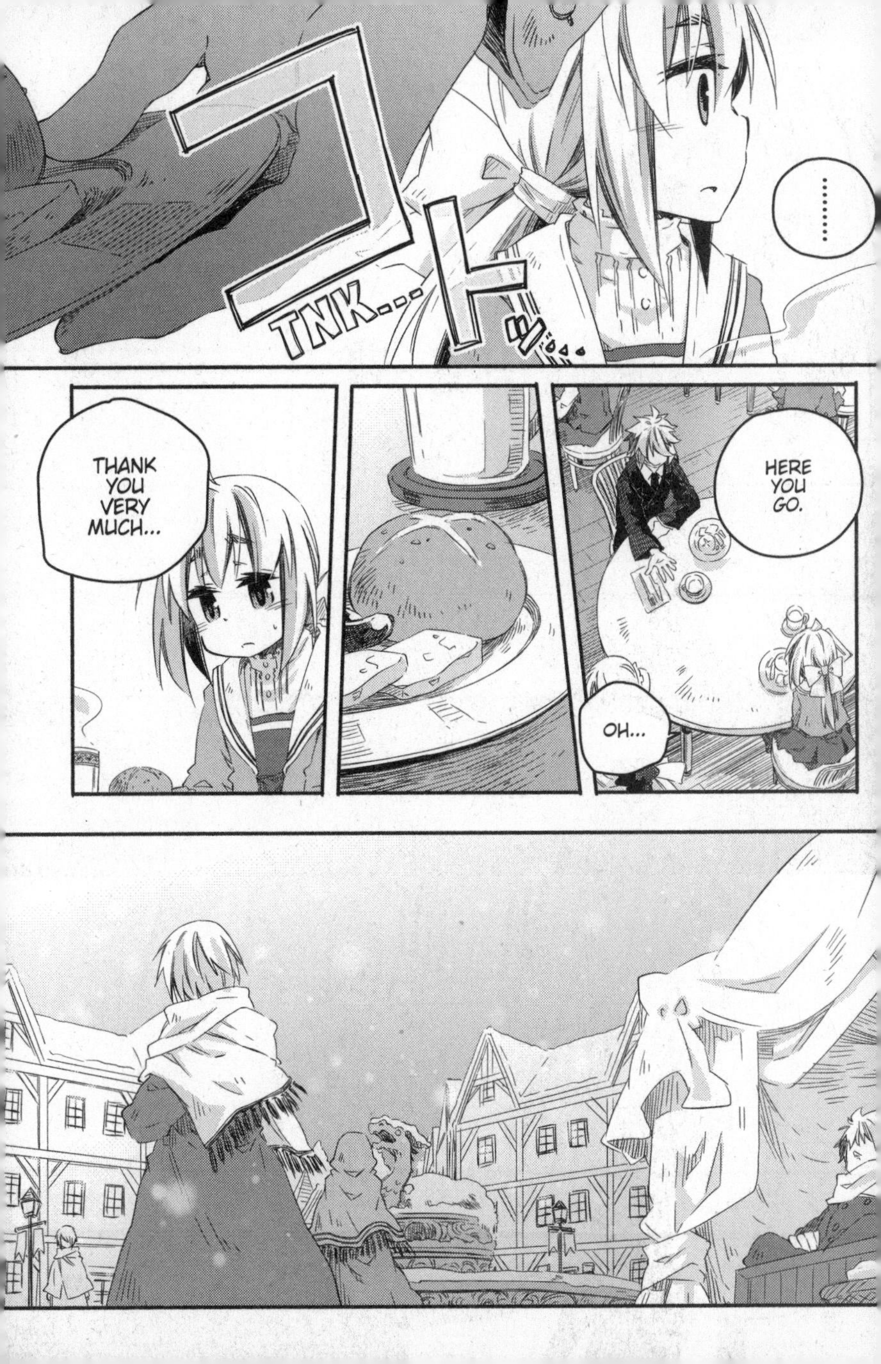
TNK...
......
HERE YOU GO.
OH...
THANK YOU VERY MUCH...

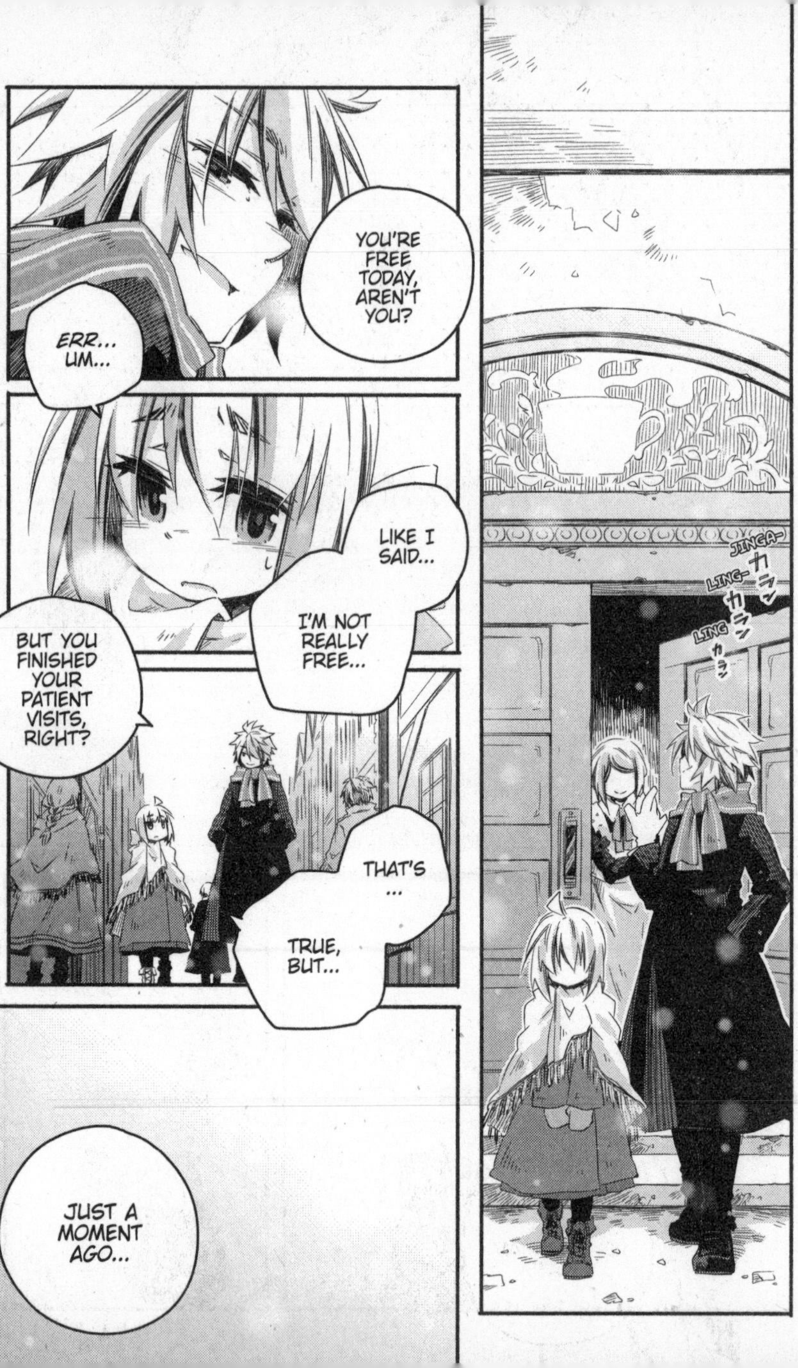
JINGA- カラン
LING- カラン
LING カラン
YOU'RE FREE TODAY, AREN'T YOU?
ERR... UM...
LIKE I SAID...
I'M NOT REALLY FREE...
BUT YOU FINISHED YOUR PATIENT VISITS, RIGHT?
THAT'S ...
TRUE, BUT...
JUST A MOMENT AGO...

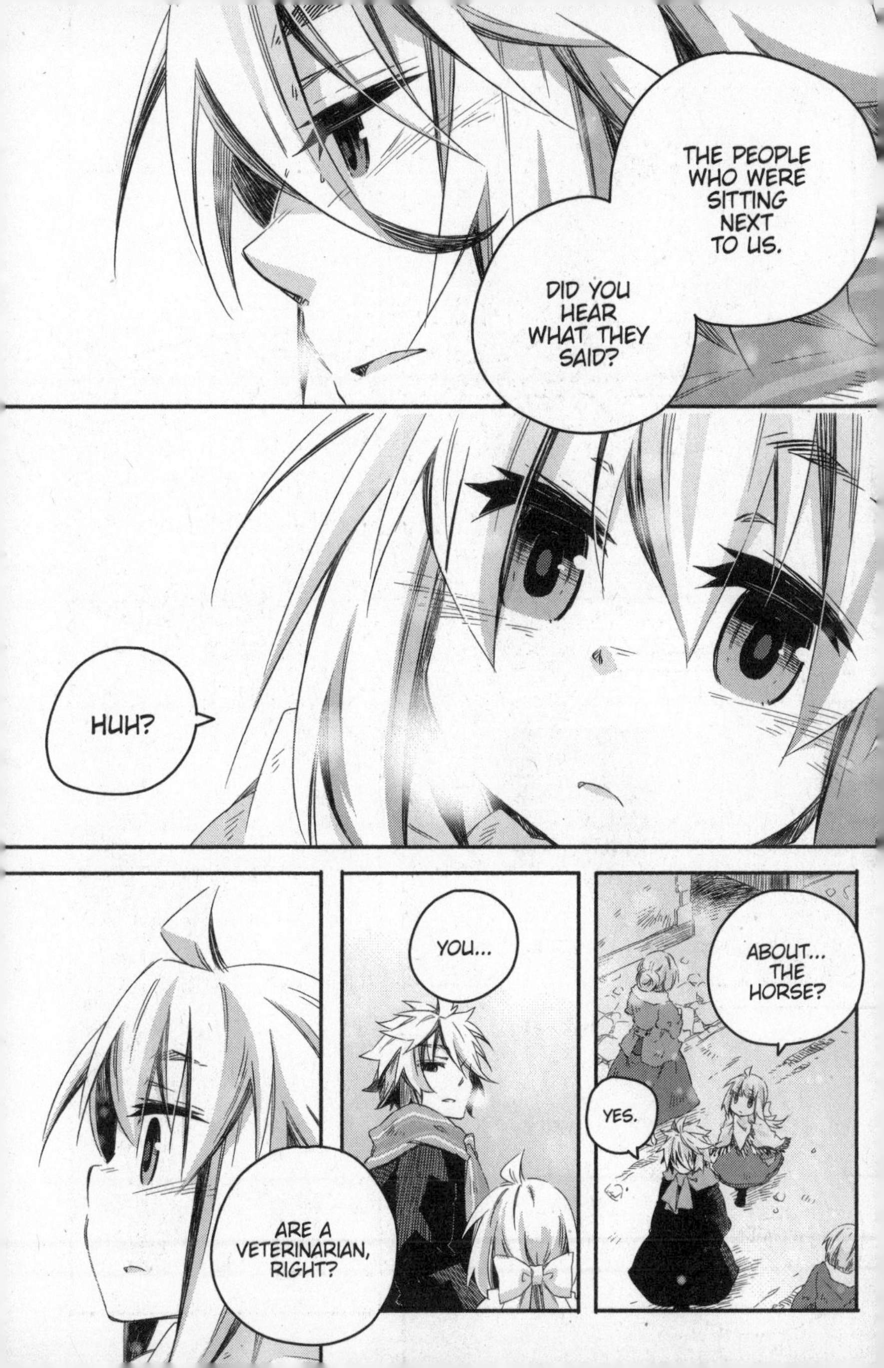
THE PEOPLE WHO WERE SITTING NEXT TO US.
DID YOU HEAR WHAT THEY SAID?
HUH?
ABOUT... THE HORSE?
YES.
YOU...
ARE A VETERINARIAN, RIGHT?

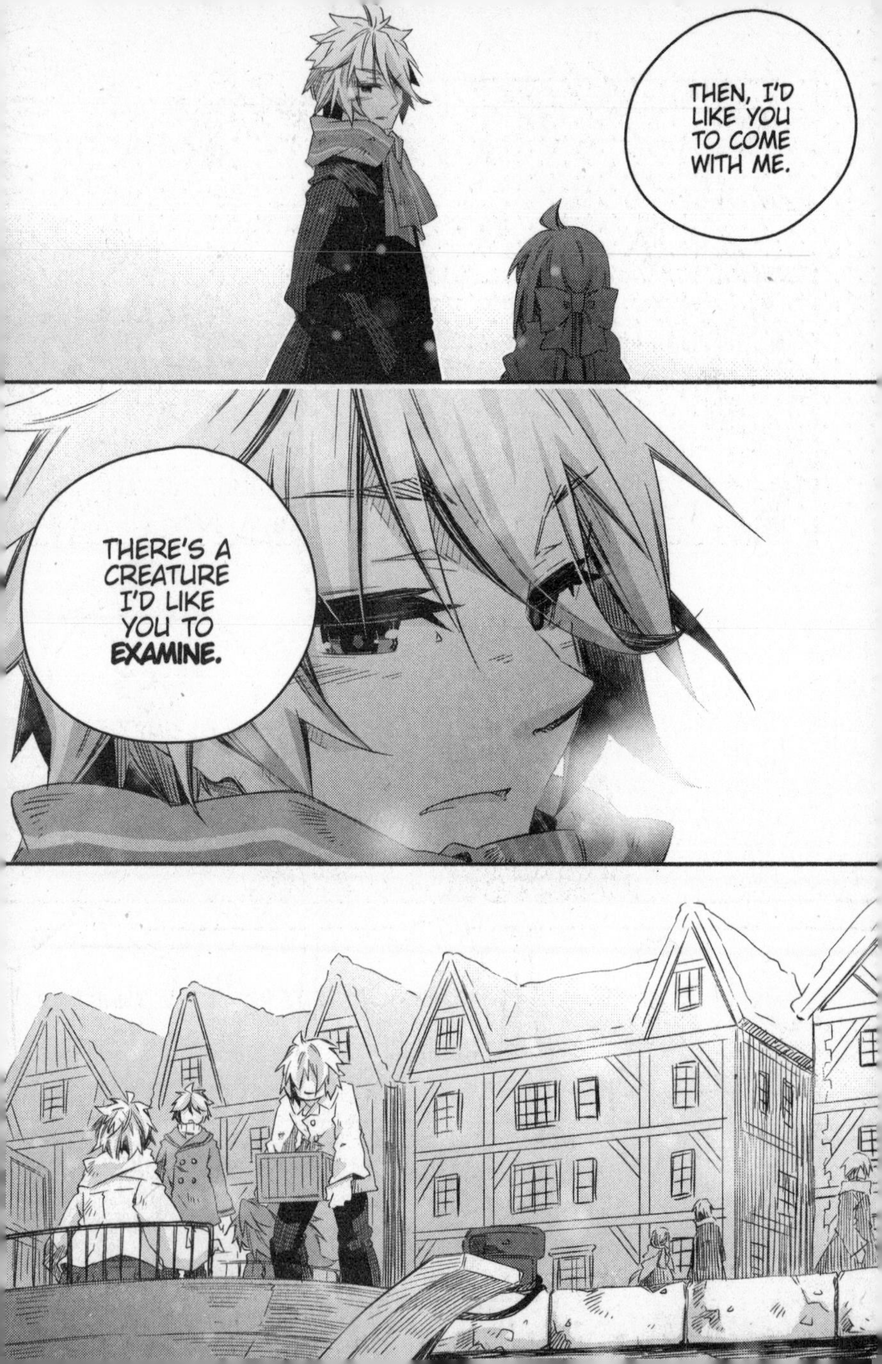
THEN, I'D LIKE YOU TO COME WITH ME.
THERE'S A CREATURE I'D LIKE YOU TO EXAMINE.

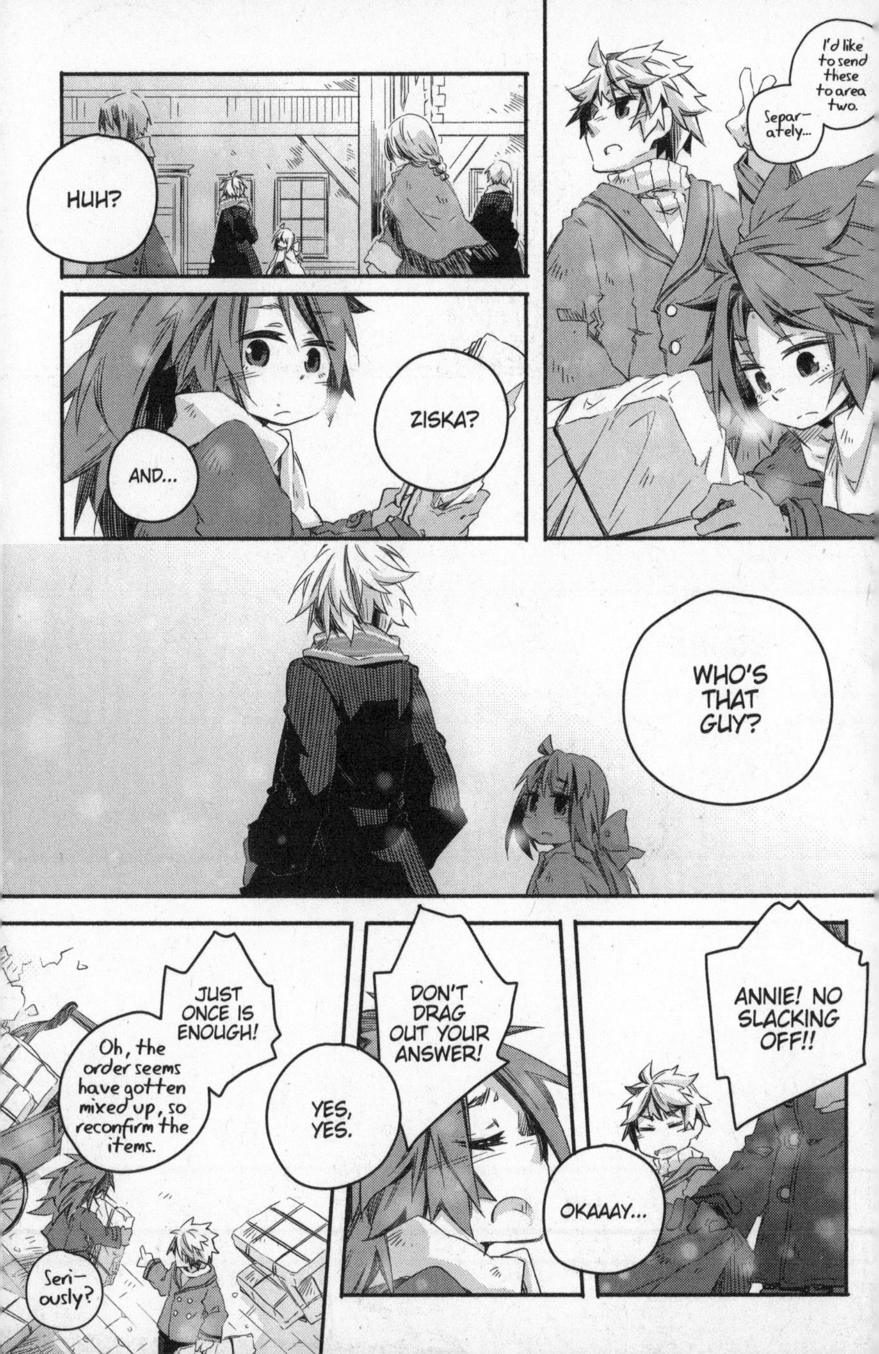
I'd like to send these to area two.
Separ-ately...
HUH?
ZISKA?
AND...
WHO'S THAT GUY?
ANNIE! NO SLACKING OFF!!
OKAAAY...
DON'T DRAG OUT YOUR ANSWER!
YES, YES.
JUST ONCE IS ENOUGH!
Oh, the order seems have gotten mixed up, so reconfirm the items.
Seri-ously?

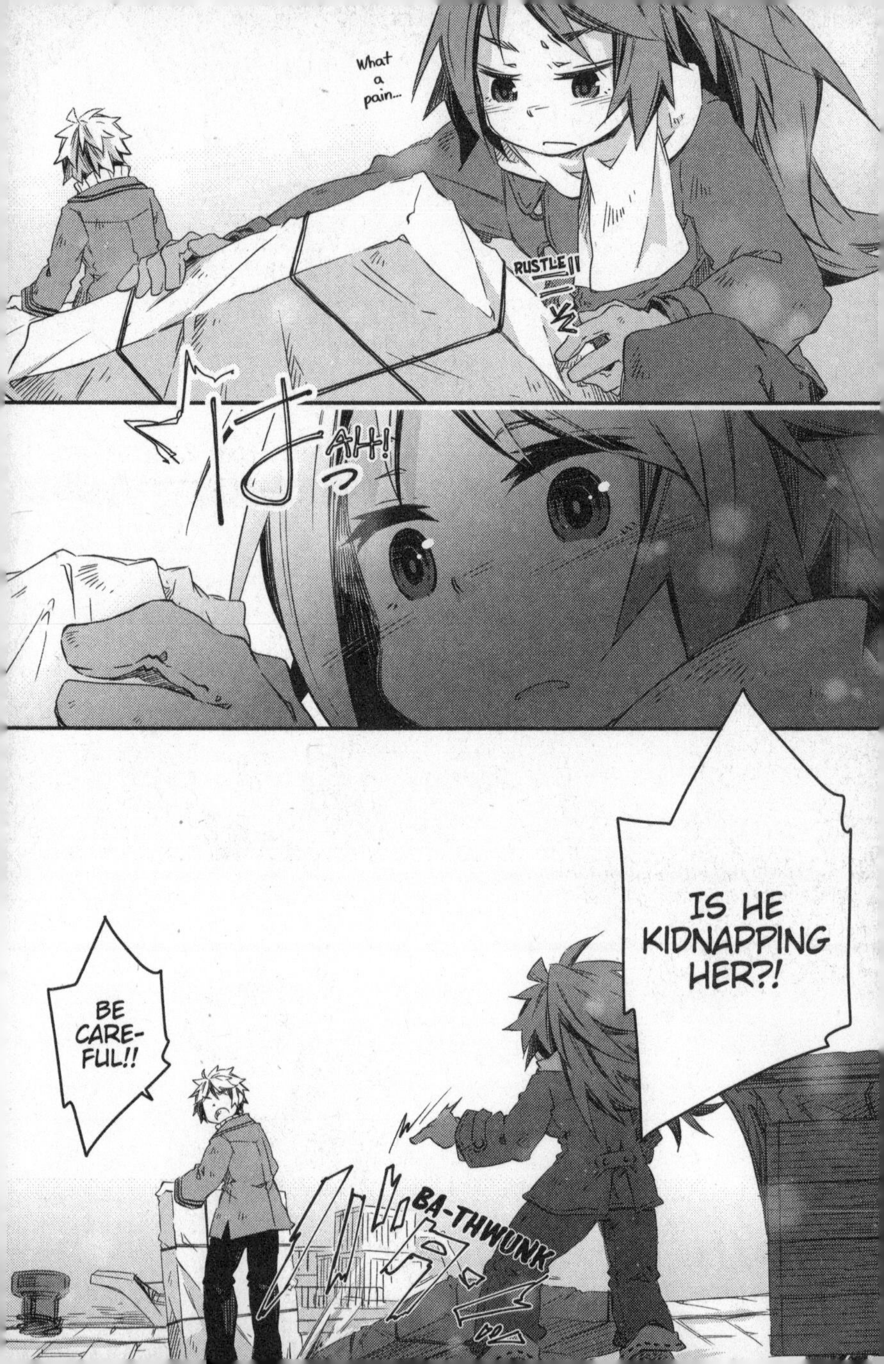
What a pain...
RUSTLE
AH!
IS HE KIDNAPPING HER?!
BE CARE-FUL!!
BA-THWUNK

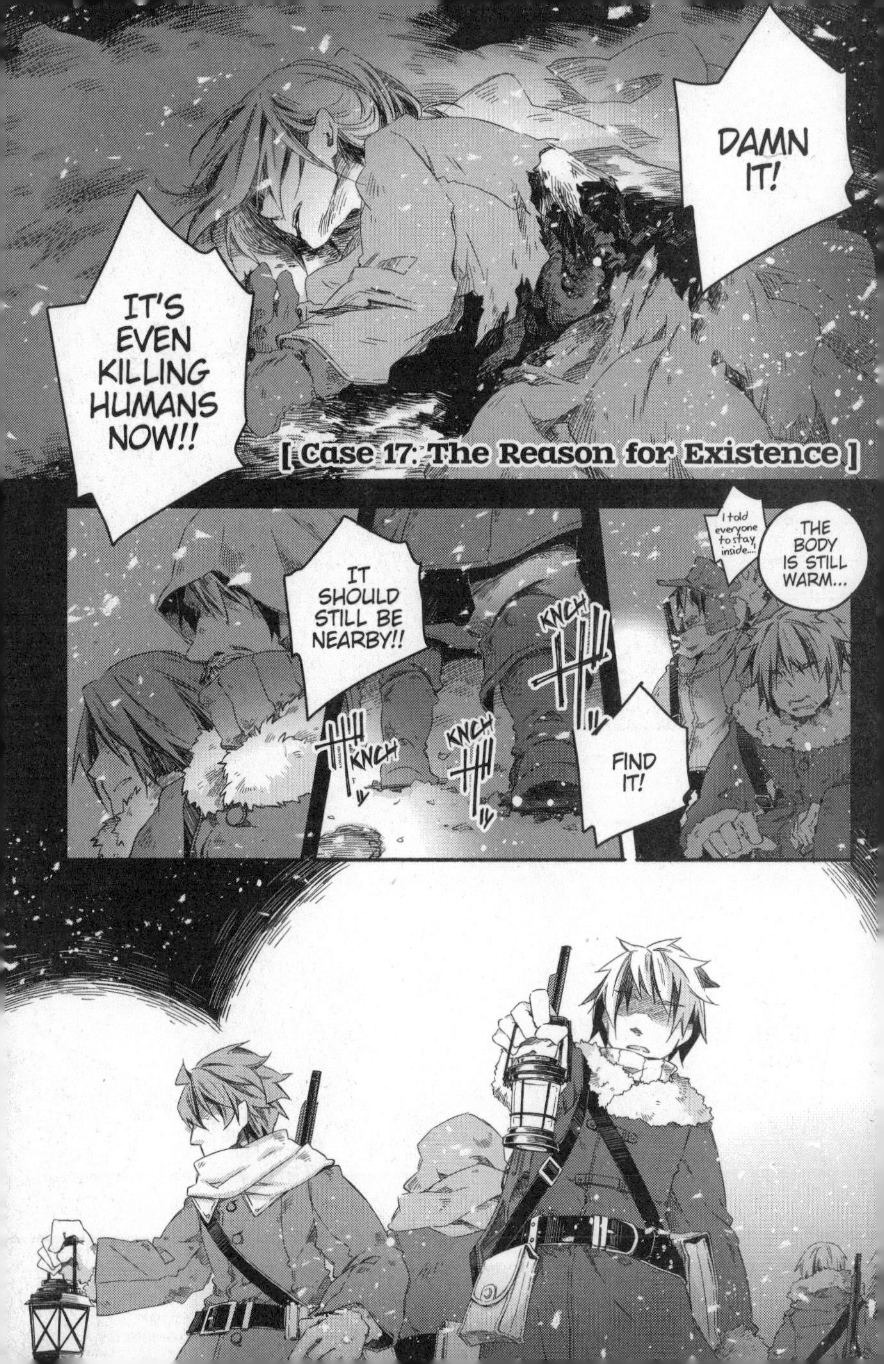
DAMN IT!
IT'S EVEN KILLING HUMANS NOW!!
[Case 17: The Reason for Existence]
I told everyone to stay inside...!
THE BODY IS STILL WARM...
KNCH
FIND IT!
KNCH
IT SHOULD STILL BE NEARBY!!
KNCH

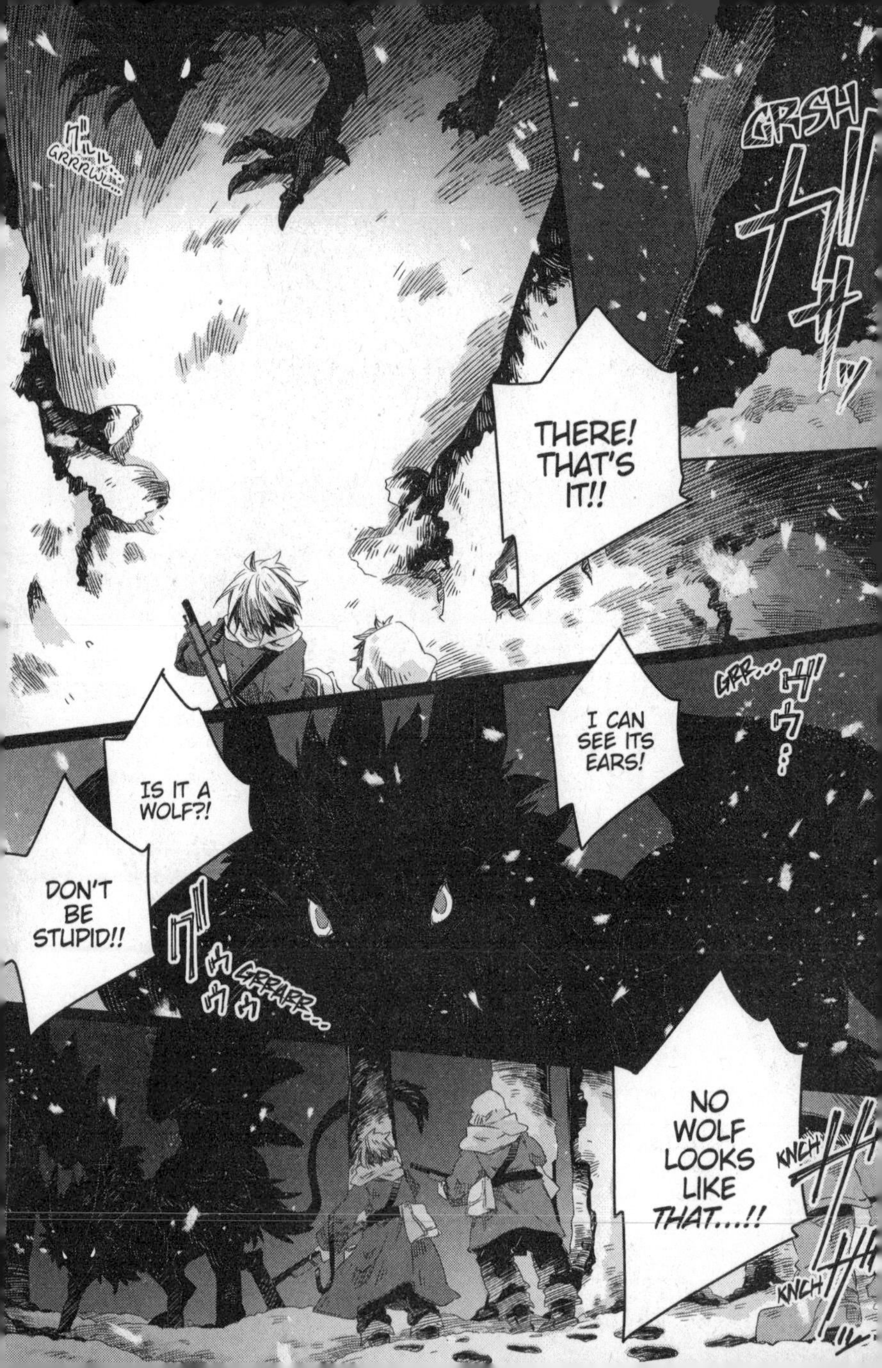
GRSH
THERE! THAT'S IT!!
GRRRWL...
GRR...
I CAN SEE ITS EARS!
IS IT A WOLF?!
DON'T BE STUPID!!
GRRARR...
NO WOLF LOOKS LIKE THAT...!!
KNCH
KNCH

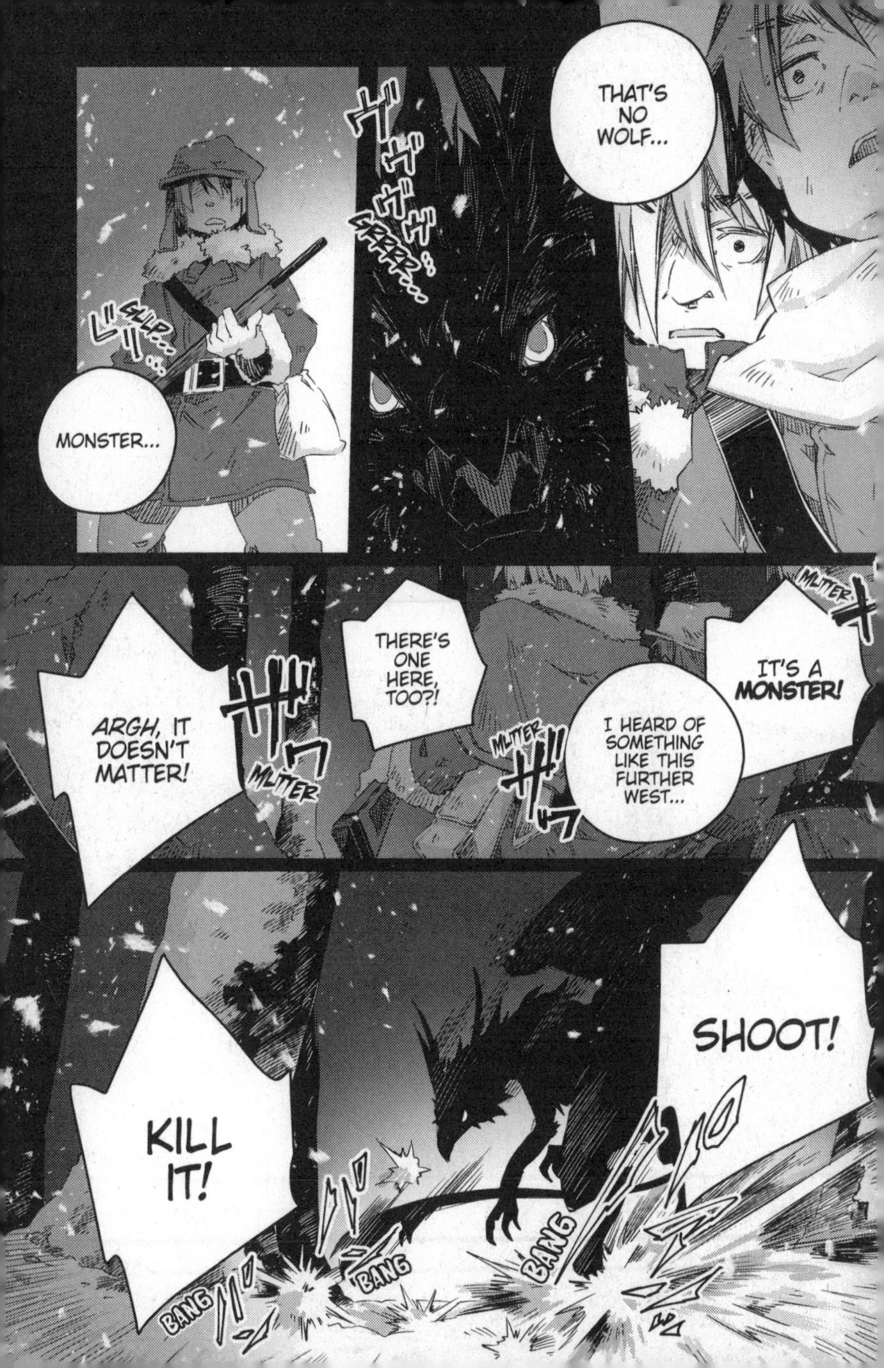
THAT'S NO WOLF...
GRRRR...
GULP...
MONSTER...
MUTTER
IT'S A MONSTER!
I HEARD OF SOMETHING LIKE THIS FURTHER WEST...
MUTTER
THERE'S ONE HERE, TOO?!
MUTTER
ARGH, IT DOESN'T MATTER!
SHOOT!
KILL IT!
BANG
BANG
BANG
BANG

IT'S DARK ALREADY...
CHA-CLANK
CHA-CLANK
CHA-CLANK
WHERE... IS THIS PLACE...?
CHA-CLANK
WE HAVEN'T CHANGED TRAINS...
SO I THINK WE'VE GONE STRAIGHT SOUTH...
Then, I'd like you to come with me.
There is a creature I'd like you to examine.

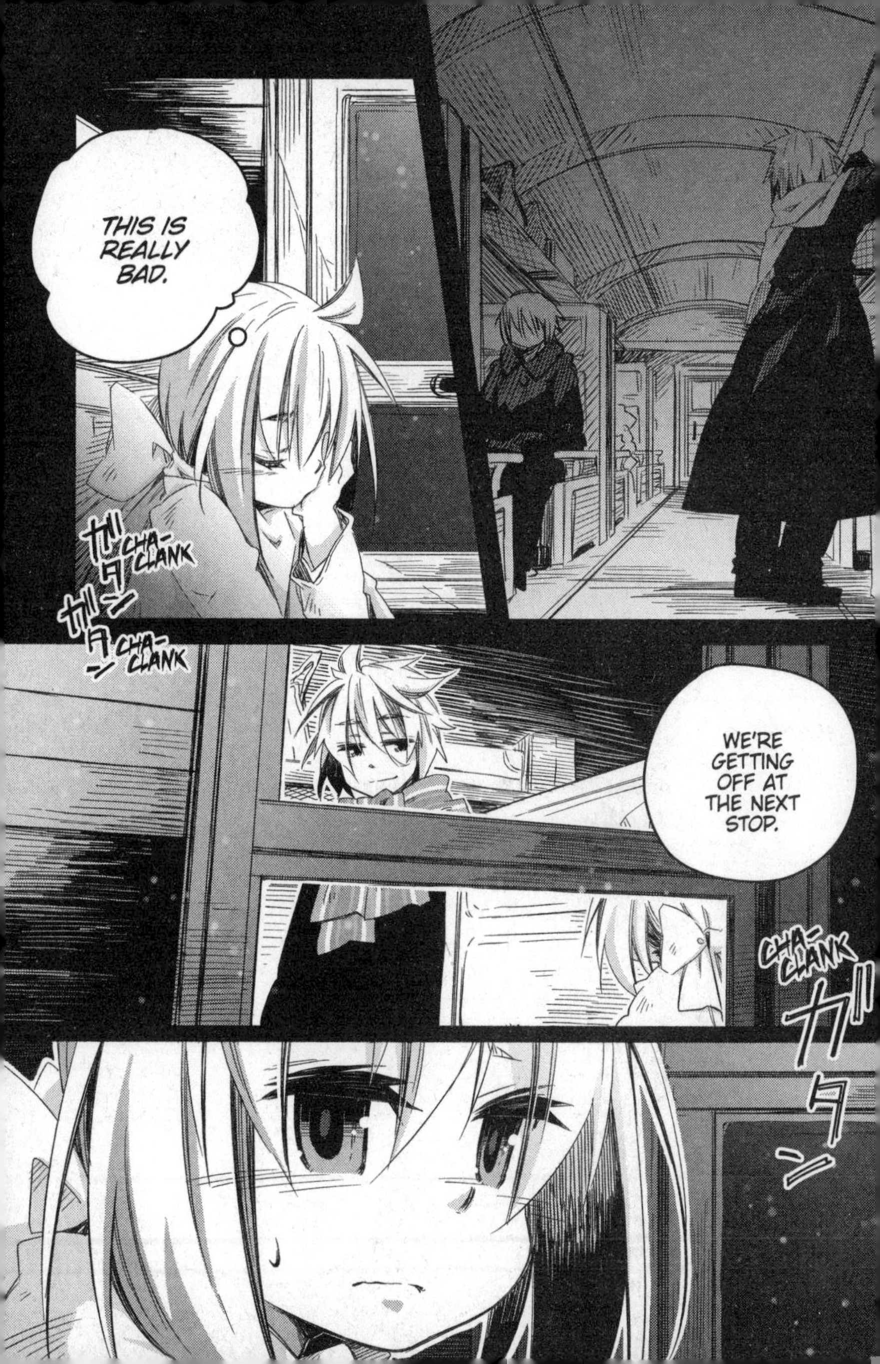
THIS IS REALLY BAD.
ガタン CHA-CLANK
ガタン CHA-CLANK
WE'RE GETTING OFF AT THE NEXT STOP.
CHA-CLANK ガタン

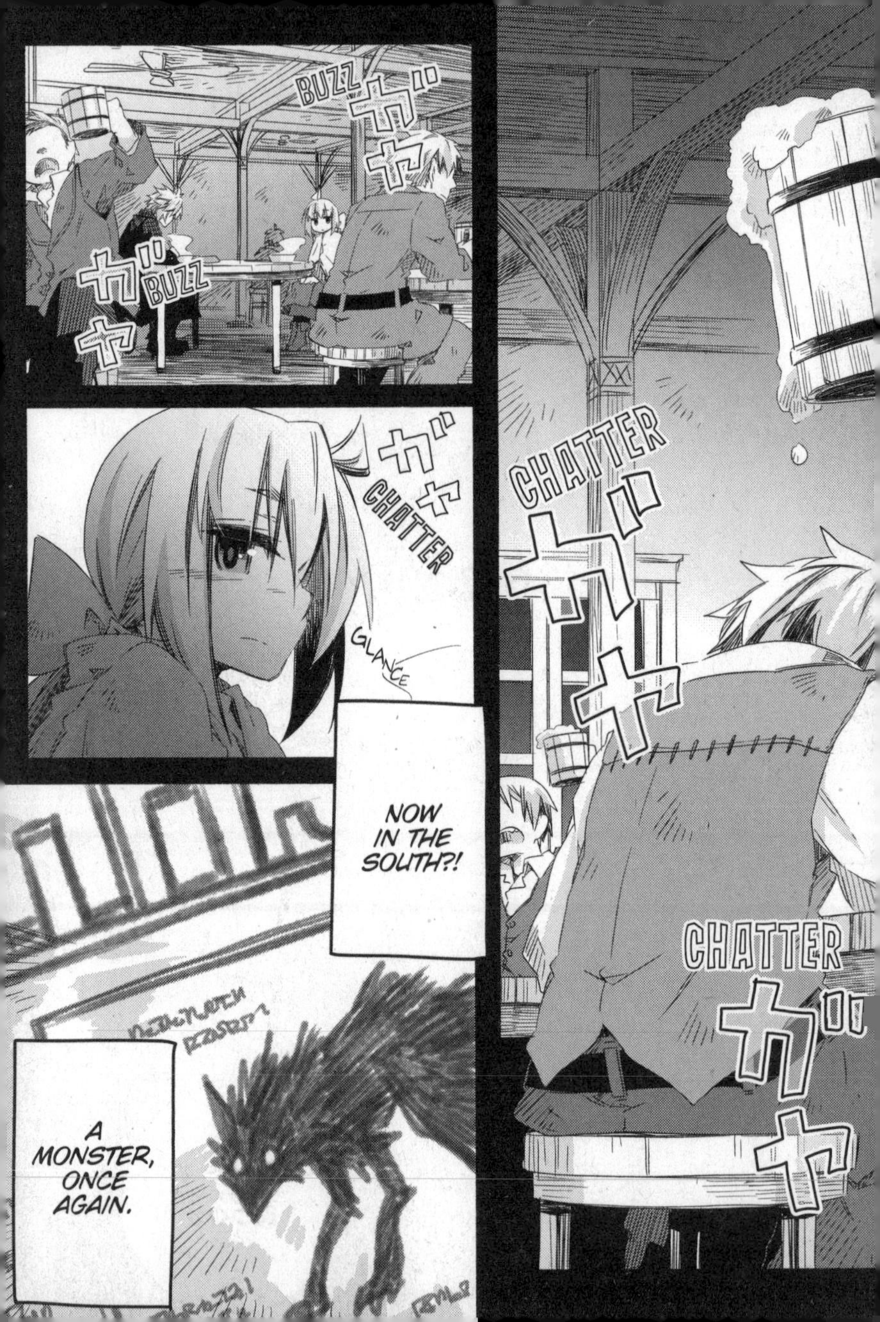
CHATTER
ガヤ
CHATTER
ガヤ
BUZZ
ガヤ
ガヤ
BUZZ
ガヤ
CHATTER
GLANCE
NOW IN THE SOUTH?!
A MONSTER, ONCE AGAIN.

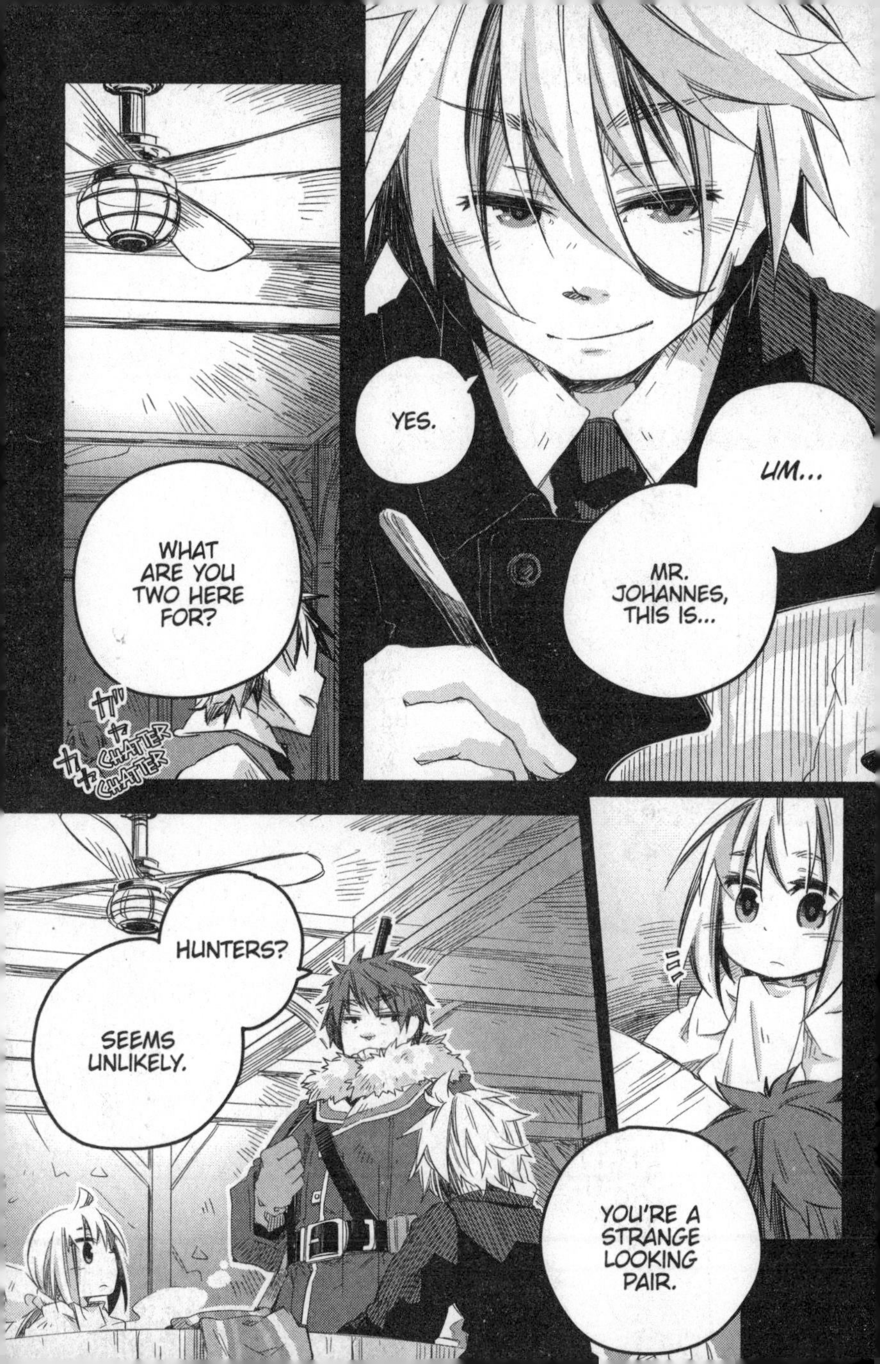
YES.
UM...
MR. JOHANNES, THIS IS...
WHAT ARE YOU TWO HERE FOR?
ガヤ ガヤ
CHATTER CHATTER
YOU'RE A STRANGE LOOKING PAIR.
HUNTERS?
SEEMS UNLIKELY.

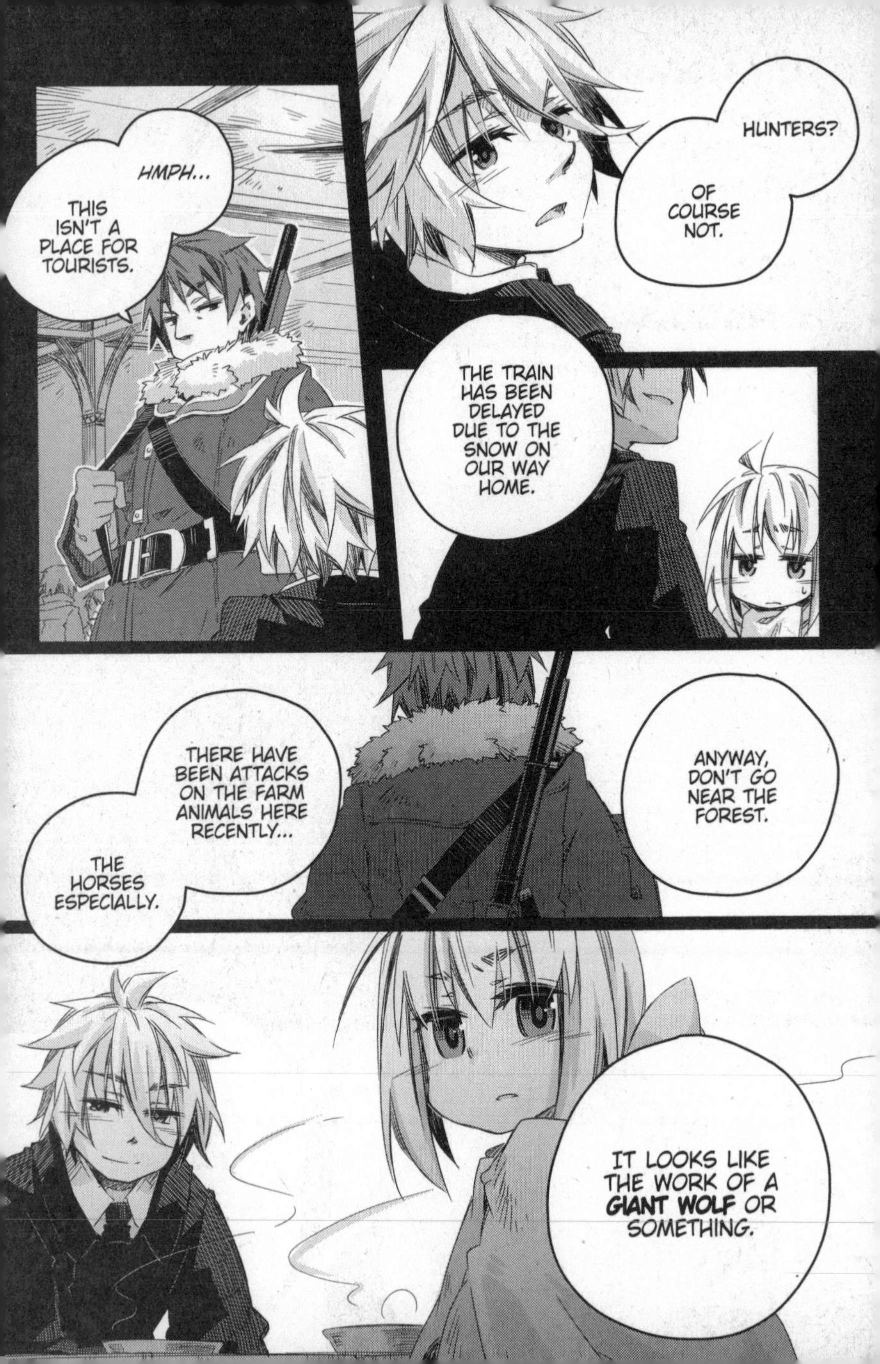
HUNTERS?
OF COURSE NOT.
THE TRAIN HAS BEEN DELAYED DUE TO THE SNOW ON OUR WAY HOME.
HMPH...
THIS ISN'T A PLACE FOR TOURISTS.
ANYWAY, DON'T GO NEAR THE FOREST.
THERE HAVE BEEN ATTACKS ON THE FARM ANIMALS HERE RECENTLY...
THE HORSES ESPECIALLY.
IT LOOKS LIKE THE WORK OF A **GIANT WOLF** OR SOMETHING.

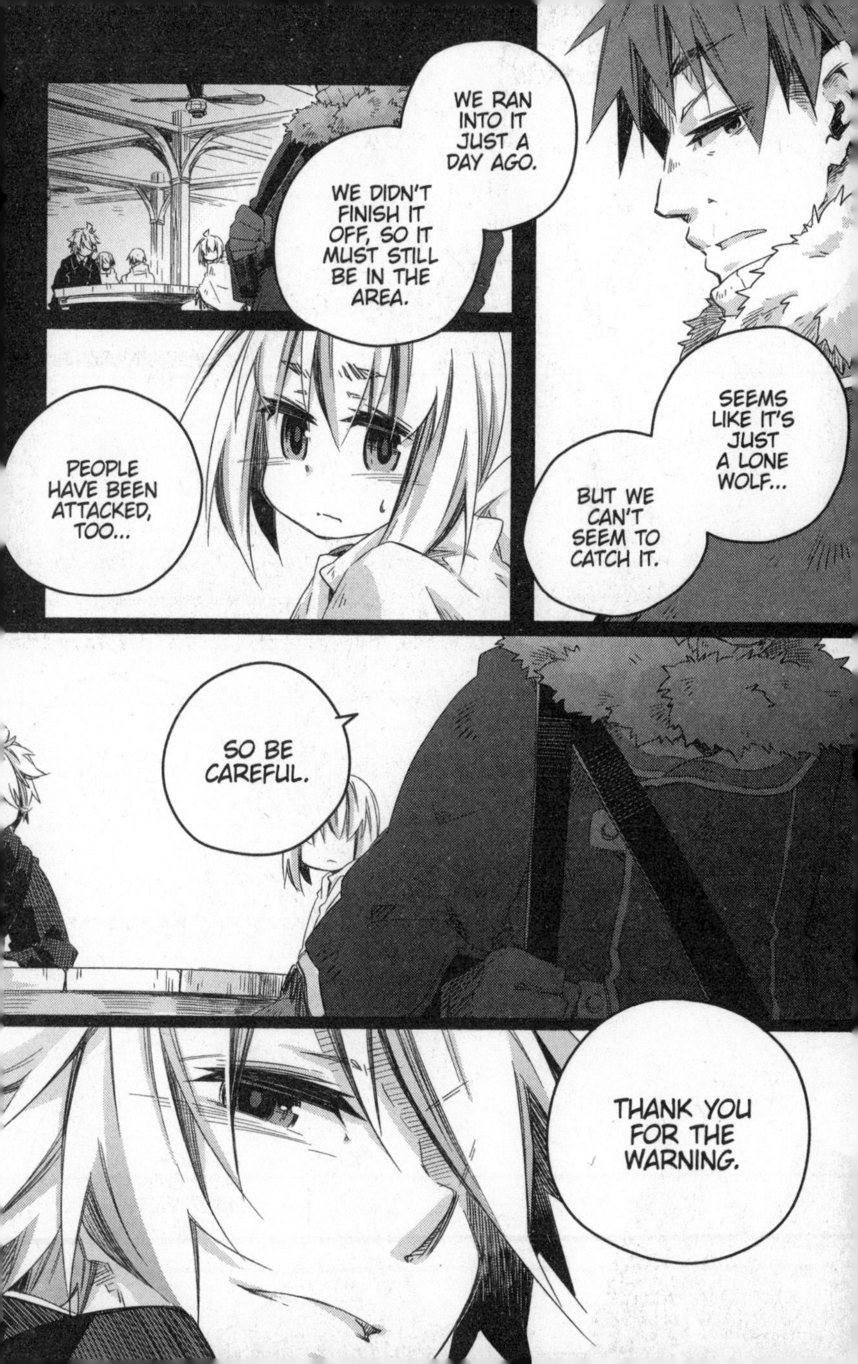
SEEMS LIKE IT'S JUST A LONE WOLF...
BUT WE CAN'T SEEM TO CATCH IT.
WE RAN INTO IT JUST A DAY AGO.
WE DIDN'T FINISH IT OFF, SO IT MUST STILL BE IN THE AREA.
PEOPLE HAVE BEEN ATTACKED, TOO...
SO BE CAREFUL.
THANK YOU FOR THE WARNING.

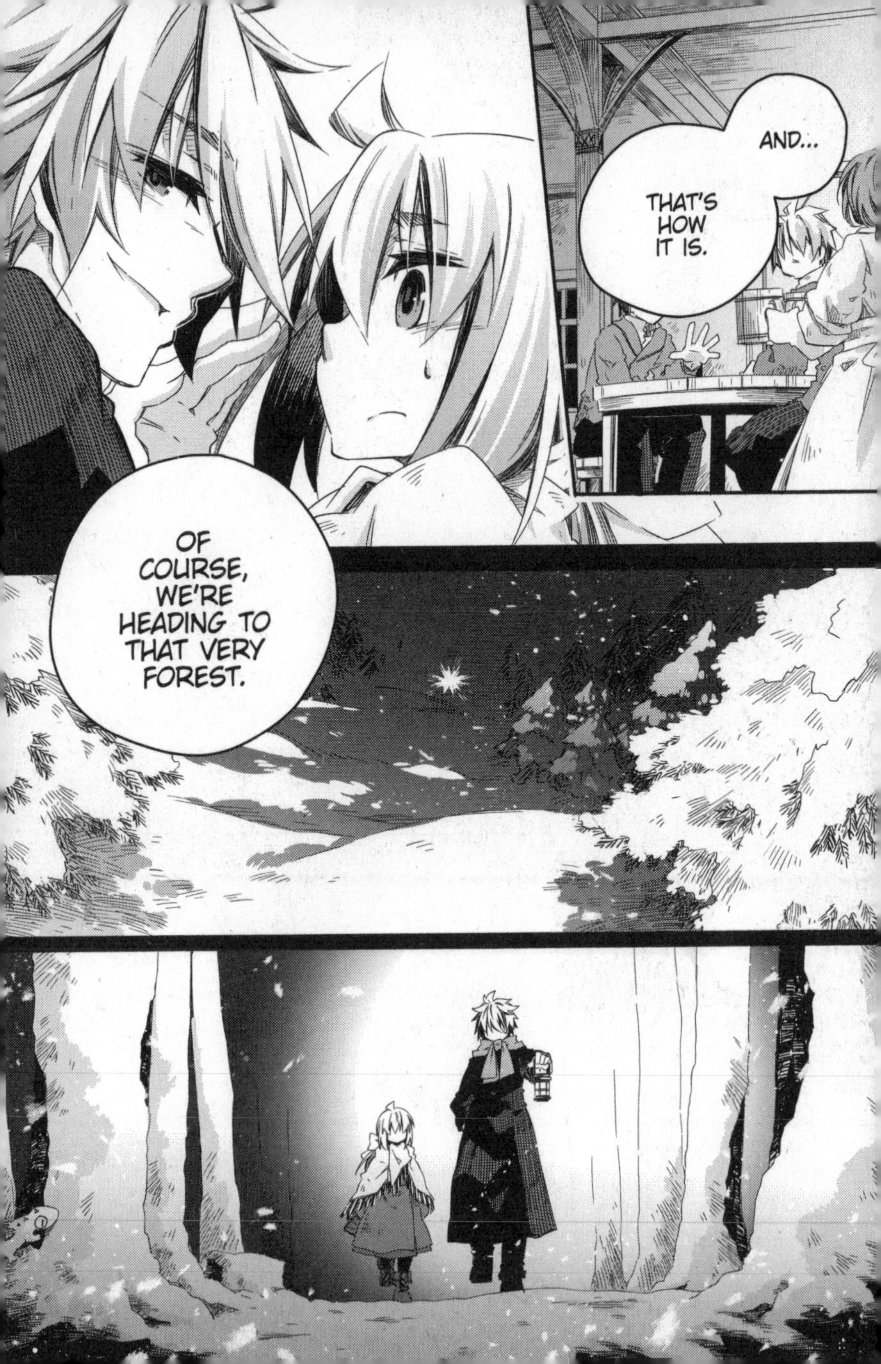
AND...
THAT'S HOW IT IS.
OF COURSE, WE'RE HEADING TO THAT VERY FOREST.

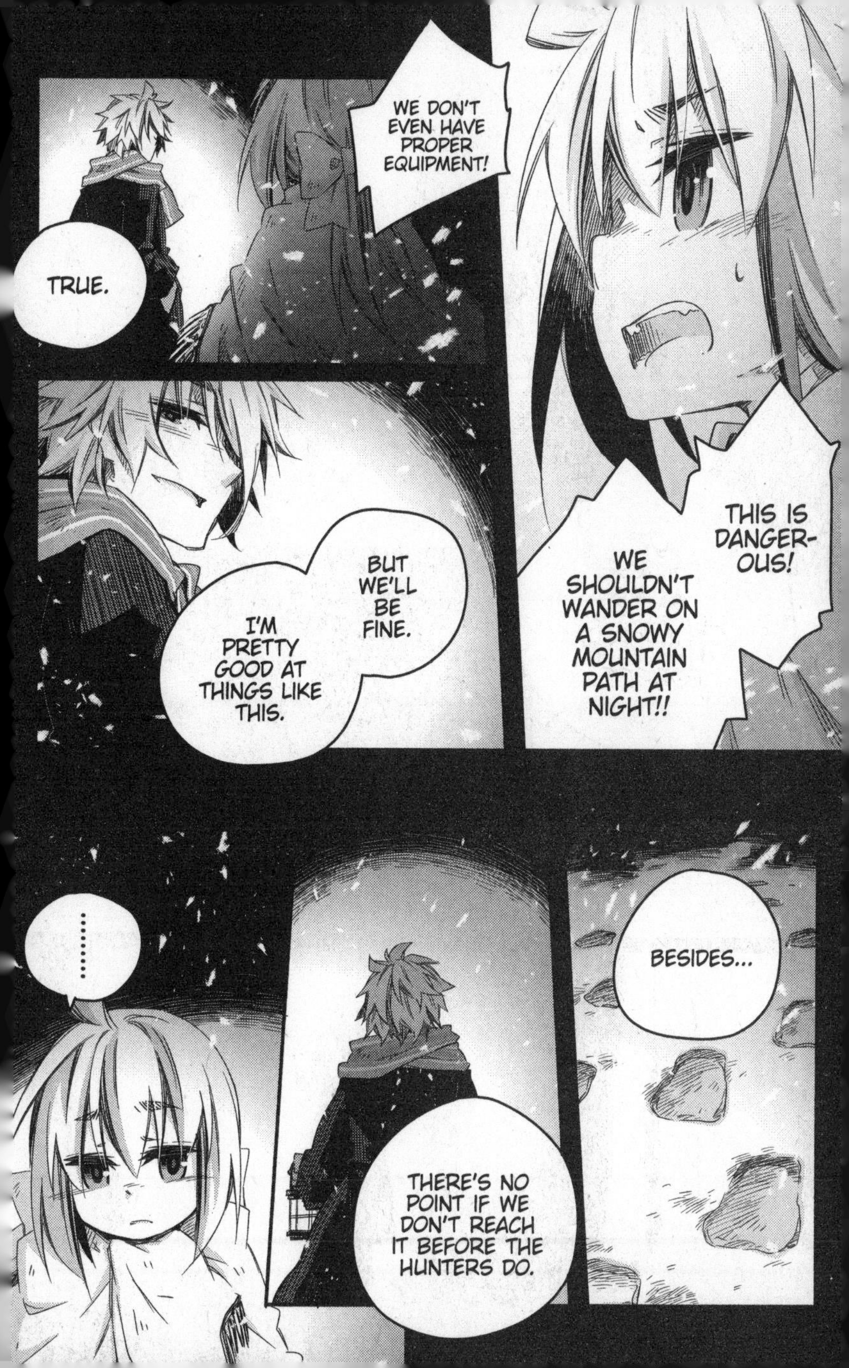
THIS IS DANGER-OUS!
WE SHOULDN'T WANDER ON A SNOWY MOUNTAIN PATH AT NIGHT!!
WE DON'T EVEN HAVE PROPER EQUIPMENT!
TRUE.
BUT WE'LL BE FINE.
I'M PRETTY GOOD AT THINGS LIKE THIS.
BESIDES...
THERE'S NO POINT IF WE DON'T REACH IT BEFORE THE HUNTERS DO.
....

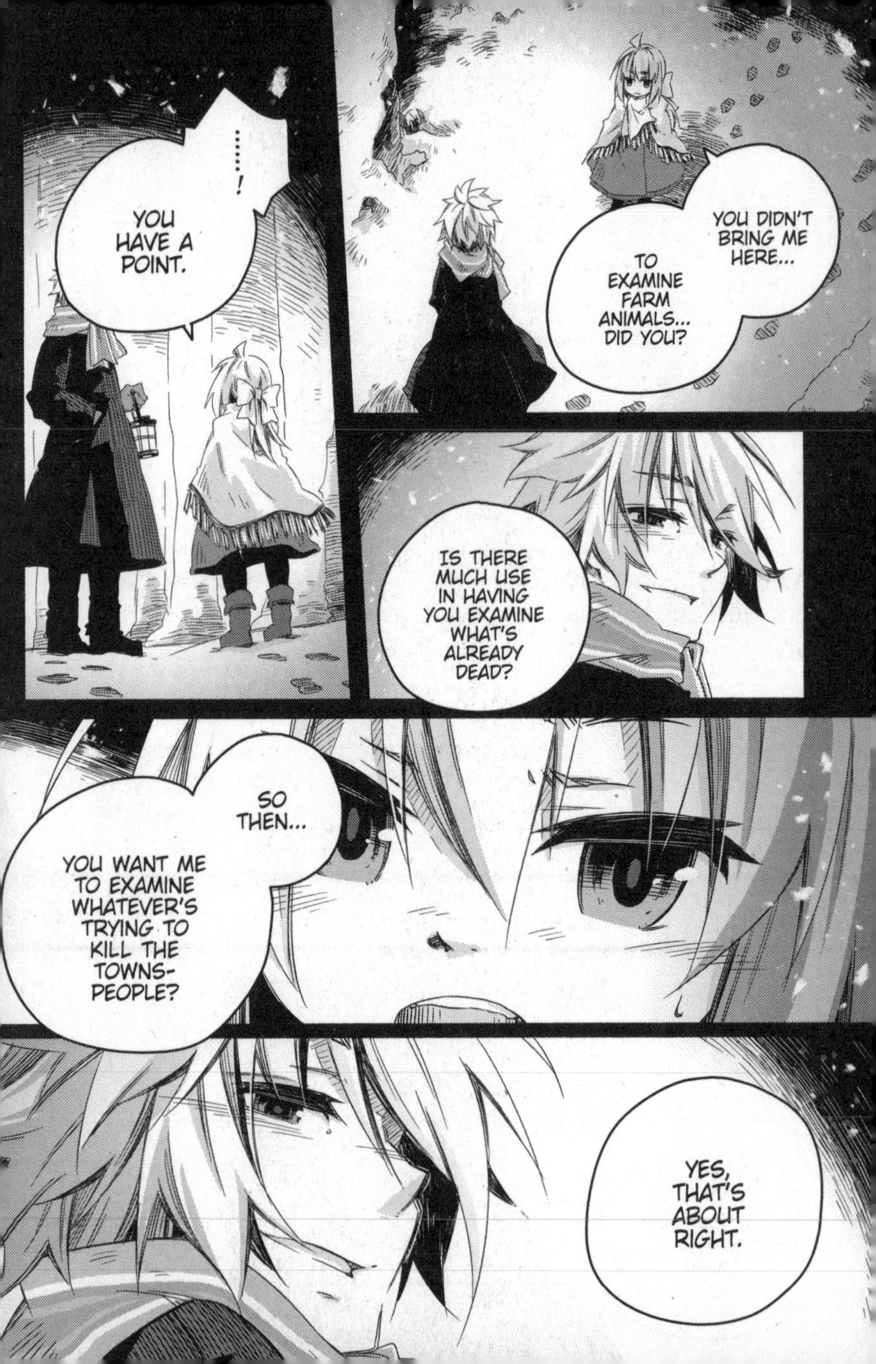
YOU DIDN'T BRING ME HERE...
TO EXAMINE FARM ANIMALS... DID YOU?
IS THERE MUCH USE IN HAVING YOU EXAMINE WHAT'S ALREADY DEAD?
......!
YOU HAVE A POINT.
SO THEN...
YOU WANT ME TO EXAMINE WHATEVER'S TRYING TO KILL THE TOWNS-PEOPLE?
YES, THAT'S ABOUT RIGHT.

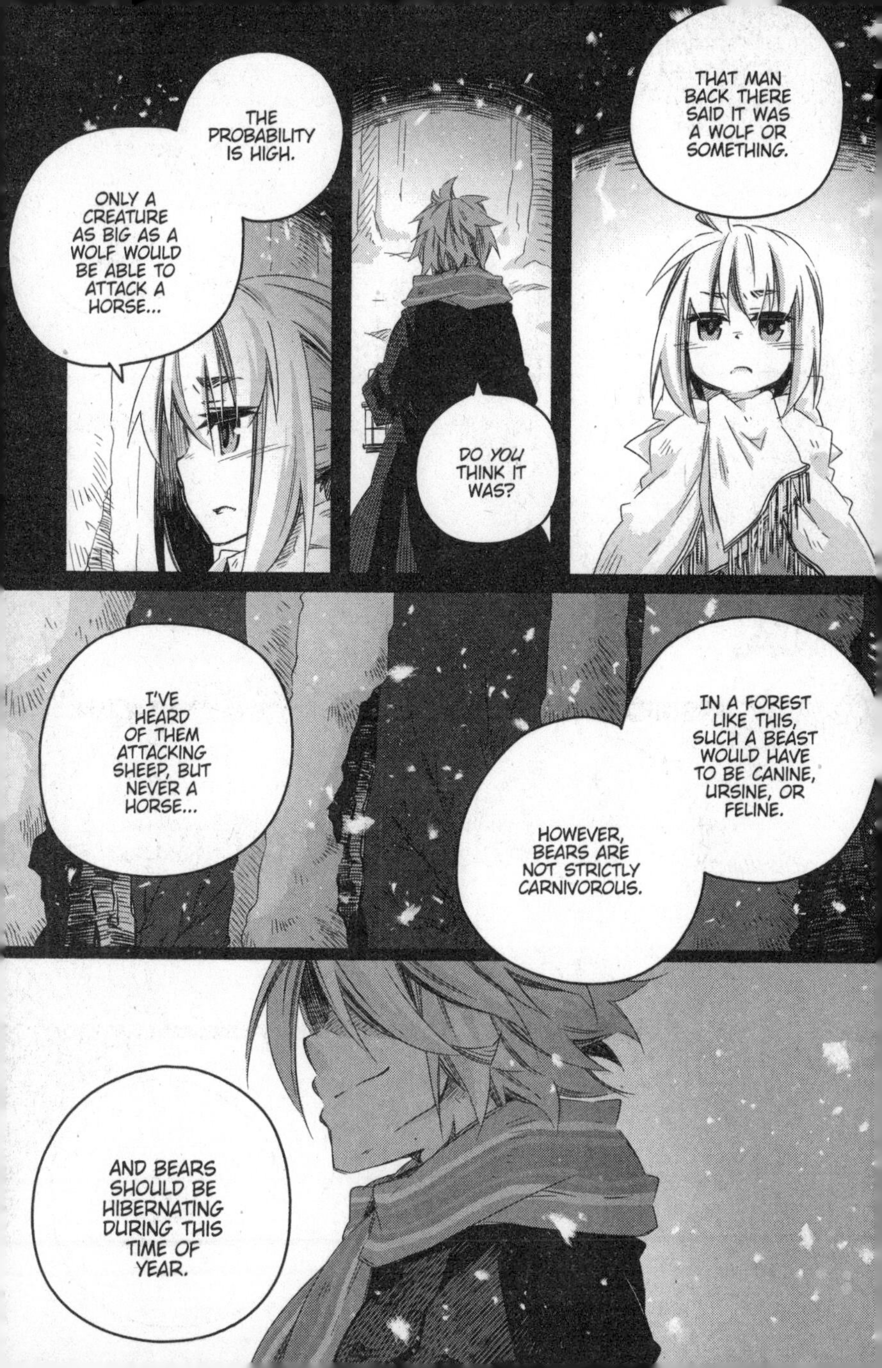
THAT MAN BACK THERE SAID IT WAS A WOLF OR SOMETHING.
DO YOU THINK IT WAS?
THE PROBABILITY IS HIGH.
ONLY A CREATURE AS BIG AS A WOLF WOULD BE ABLE TO ATTACK A HORSE...
IN A FOREST LIKE THIS, SUCH A BEAST WOULD HAVE TO BE CANINE, URSINE, OR FELINE.
HOWEVER, BEARS ARE NOT STRICTLY CARNIVOROUS.
I'VE HEARD OF THEM ATTACKING SHEEP, BUT NEVER A HORSE...
AND BEARS SHOULD BE HIBERNATING DURING THIS TIME OF YEAR.

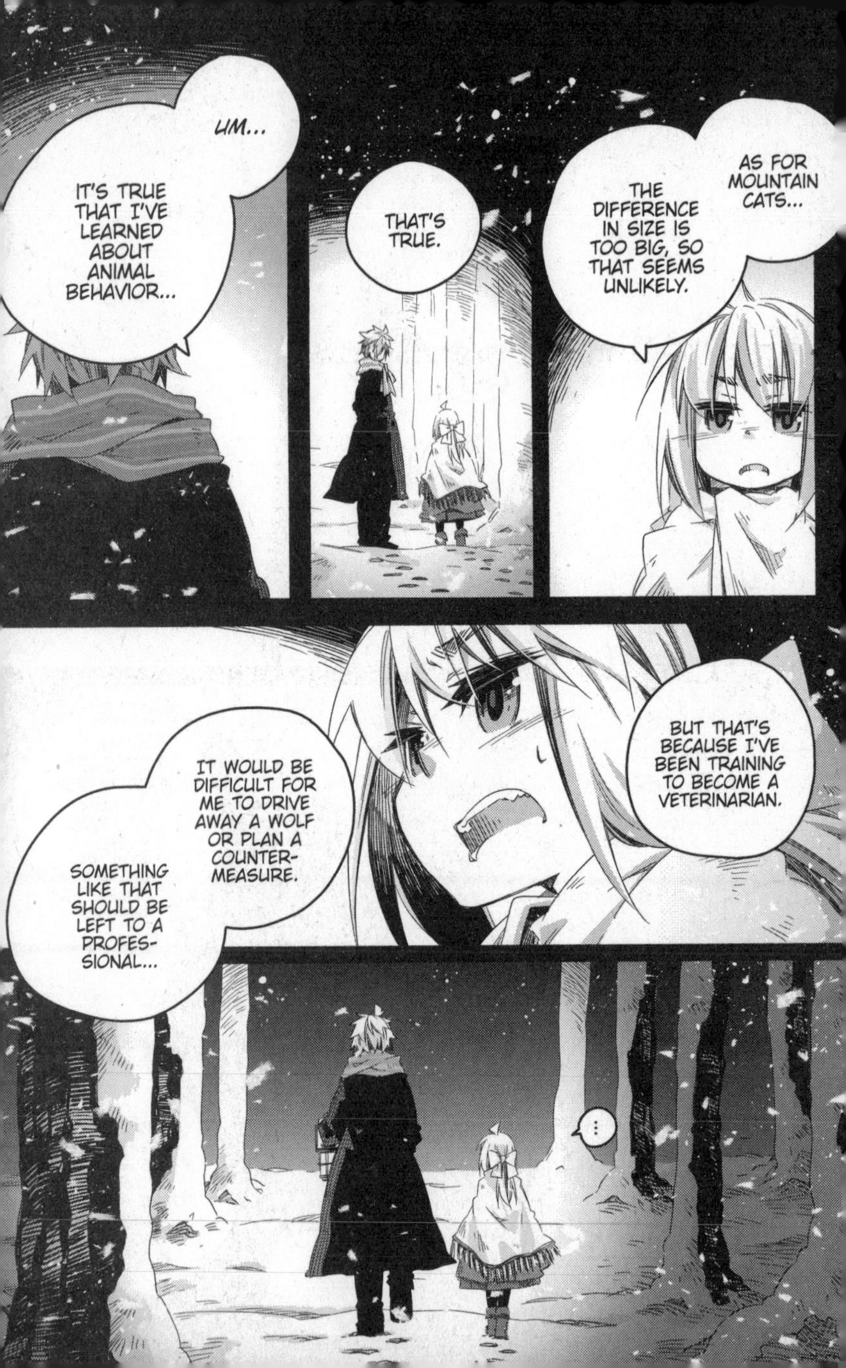
AS FOR MOUNTAIN CATS...
THE DIFFERENCE IN SIZE IS TOO BIG, SO THAT SEEMS UNLIKELY.
THAT'S TRUE.
UM...
IT'S TRUE THAT I'VE LEARNED ABOUT ANIMAL BEHAVIOR...
BUT THAT'S BECAUSE I'VE BEEN TRAINING TO BECOME A VETERINARIAN.
IT WOULD BE DIFFICULT FOR ME TO DRIVE AWAY A WOLF OR PLAN A COUNTER-MEASURE.
SOMETHING LIKE THAT SHOULD BE LEFT TO A PROFES-SIONAL...
...

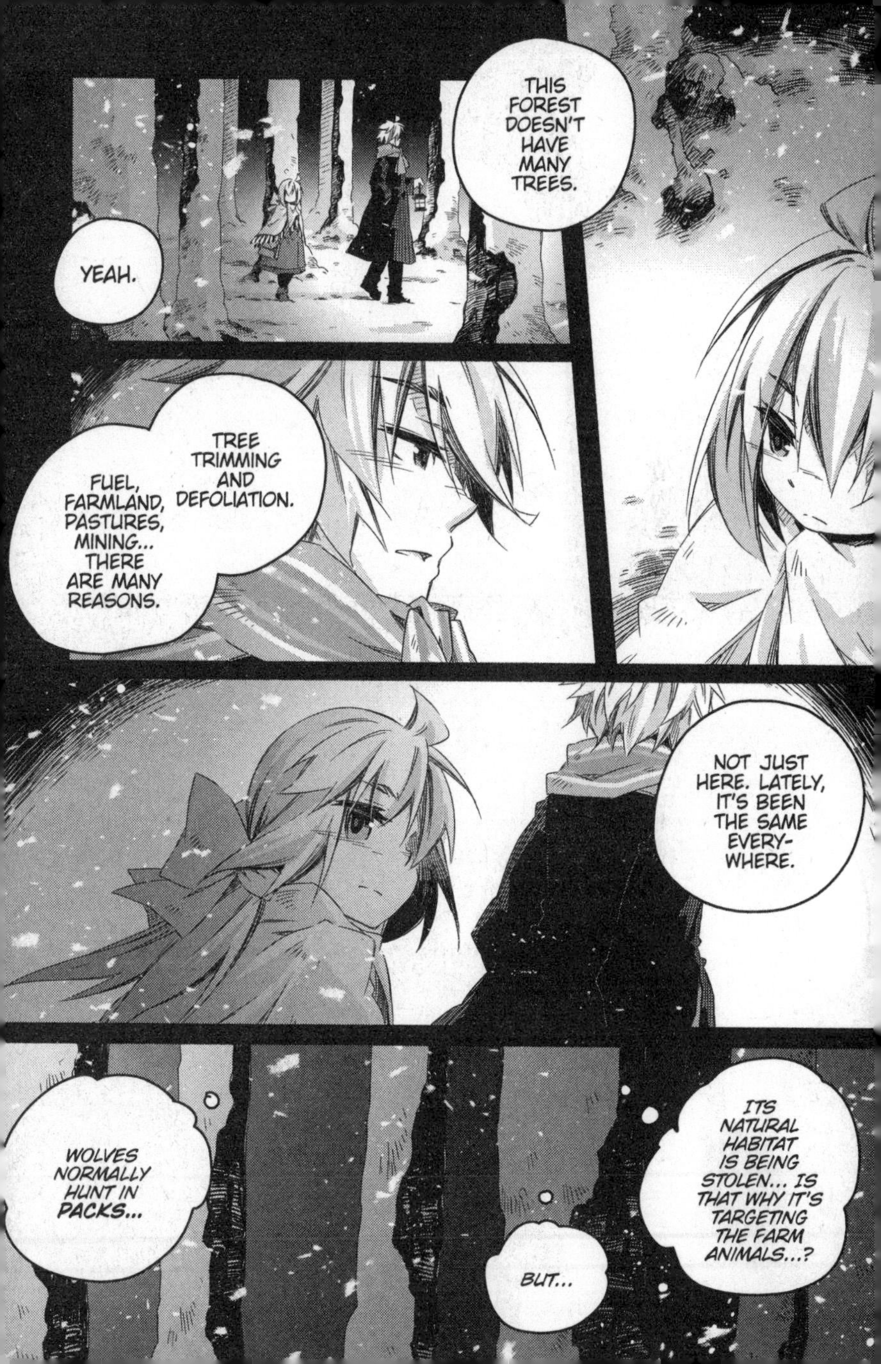
THIS FOREST DOESN'T HAVE MANY TREES.
YEAH.
TREE TRIMMING AND DEFOLIATION.
FUEL, FARMLAND, PASTURES, MINING... THERE ARE MANY REASONS.
NOT JUST HERE. LATELY, IT'S BEEN THE SAME EVERY-WHERE.
ITS NATURAL HABITAT IS BEING STOLEN... IS THAT WHY IT'S TARGETING THE FARM ANIMALS...?
BUT...
*WOLVES NORMALLY HUNT IN **PACKS**...*

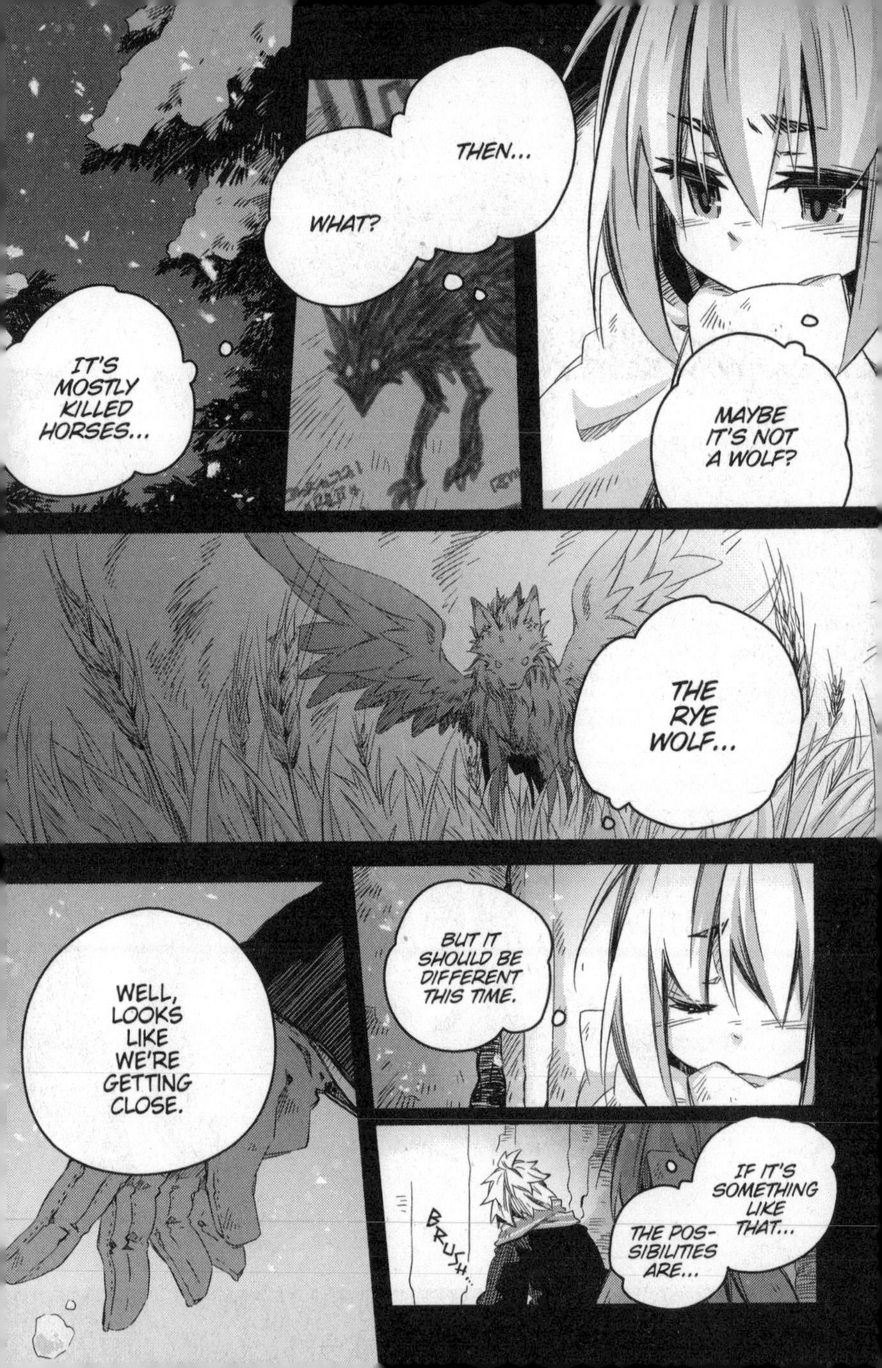
MAYBE IT'S NOT A WOLF?
THEN...
WHAT?
IT'S MOSTLY KILLED HORSES...
THE RYE WOLF...
BUT IT SHOULD BE DIFFERENT THIS TIME.
IF IT'S SOMETHING LIKE THAT...
THE POSSIBILITIES ARE...
BRUSH...
WELL, LOOKS LIKE WE'RE GETTING CLOSE.

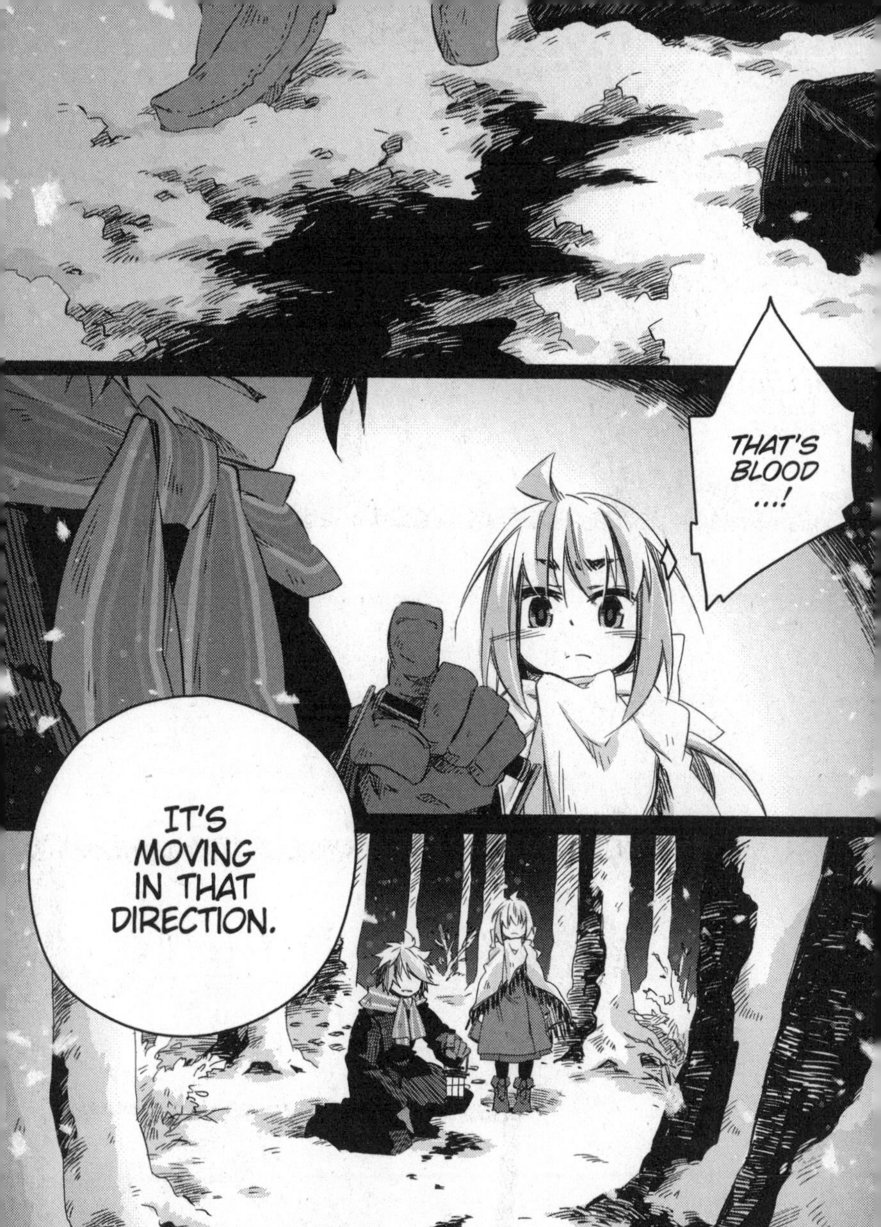
THAT'S BLOOD ...!
IT'S MOVING IN THAT DIRECTION.

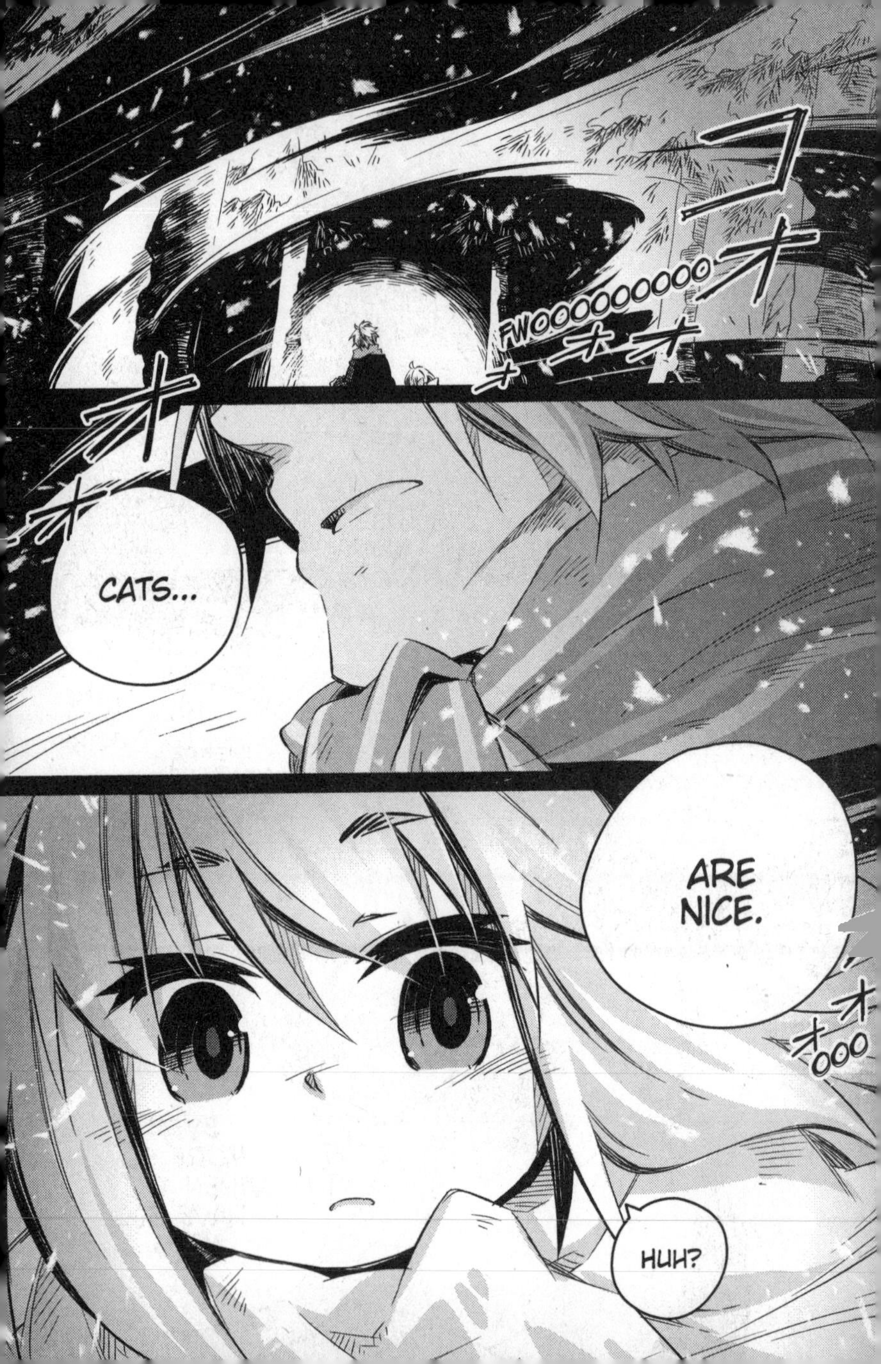
FWOOOOOOOOOO
CATS...
ARE NICE.
OOO
HUH?

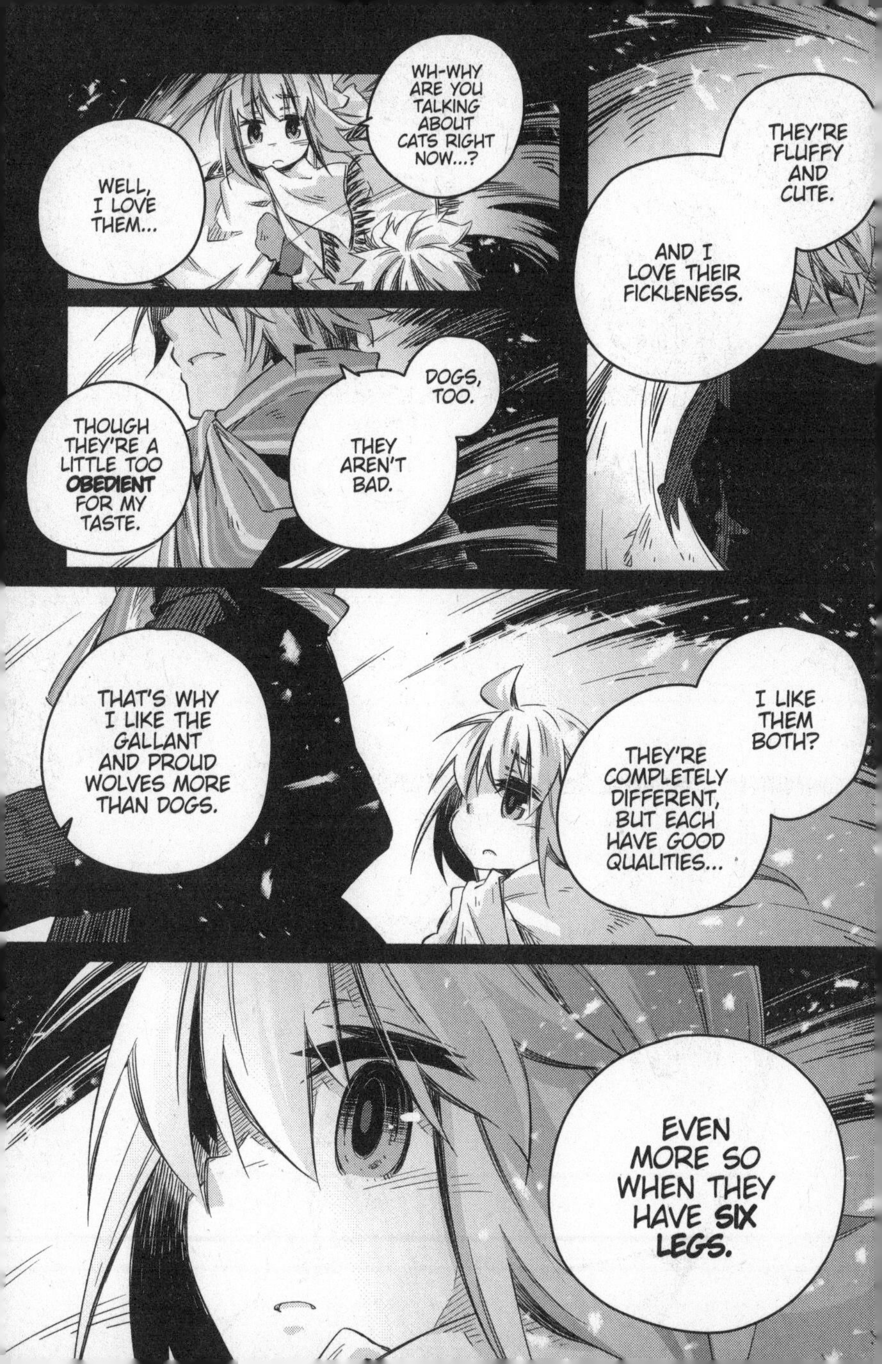
THEY'RE FLUFFY AND CUTE.
AND I LOVE THEIR FICKLENESS.
WH-WHY ARE YOU TALKING ABOUT CATS RIGHT NOW...?
WELL, I LOVE THEM...
DOGS, TOO.
THEY AREN'T BAD.
THOUGH THEY'RE A LITTLE TOO **OBEDIENT** FOR MY TASTE.
THAT'S WHY I LIKE THE GALLANT AND PROUD WOLVES MORE THAN DOGS.
I LIKE THEM BOTH?
THEY'RE COMPLETELY DIFFERENT, BUT EACH HAVE GOOD QUALITIES...
EVEN MORE SO WHEN THEY HAVE **SIX LEGS.**

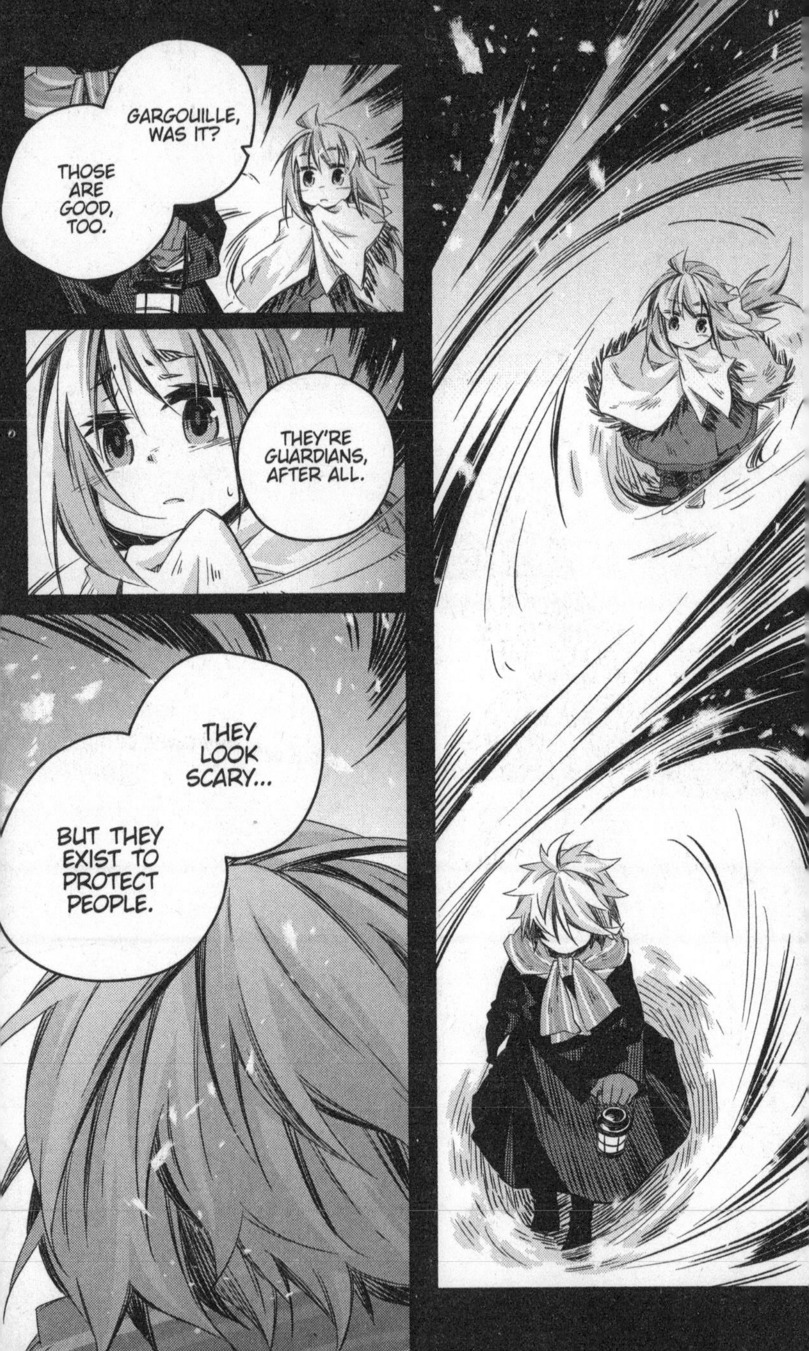
GARGOUILLE, WAS IT?
THOSE ARE GOOD, TOO.
THEY'RE GUARDIANS, AFTER ALL.
THEY LOOK SCARY...
BUT THEY EXIST TO PROTECT PEOPLE.

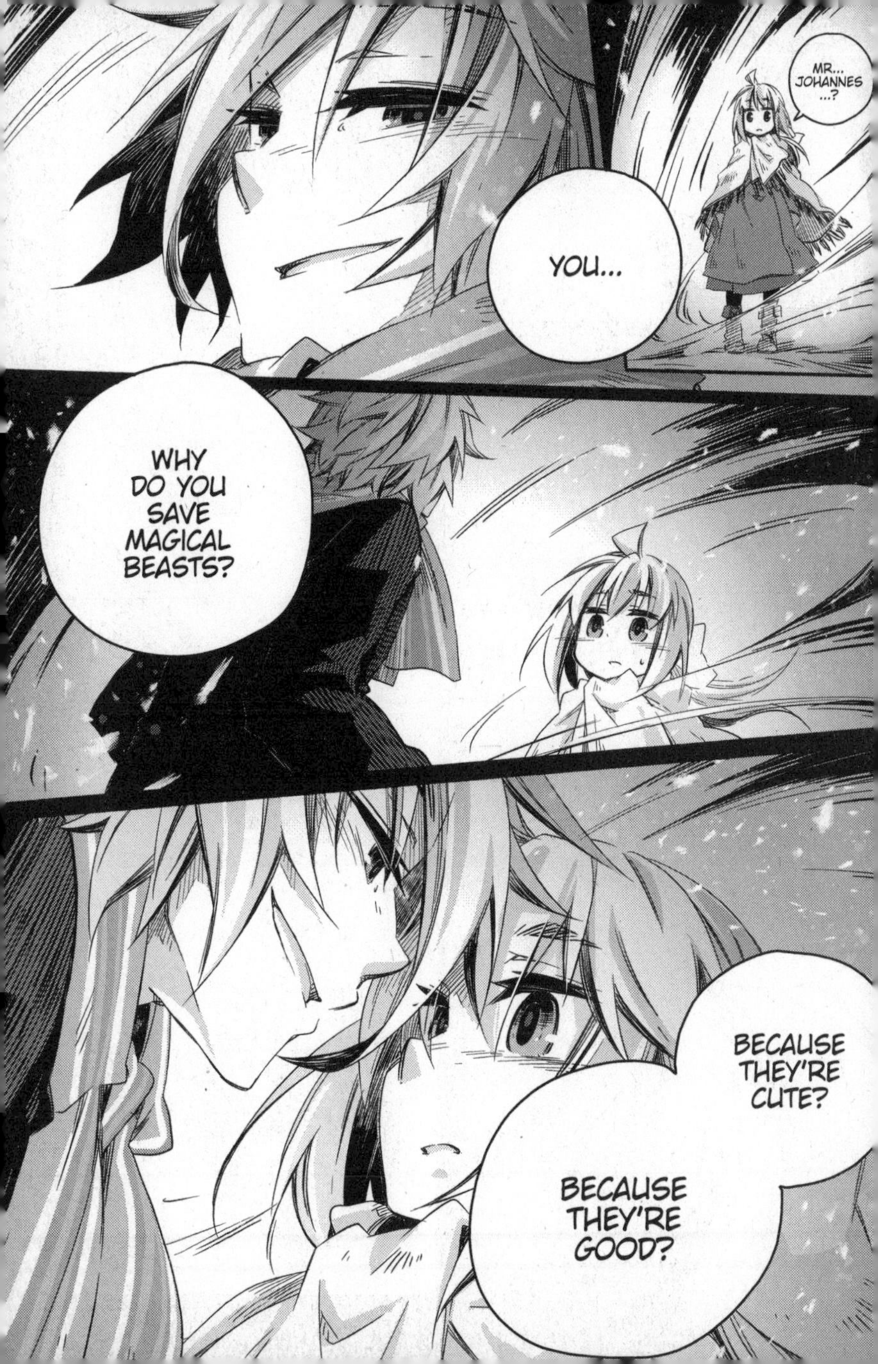
MR... JOHANNES ...?
YOU...
WHY DO YOU SAVE MAGICAL BEASTS?
BECAUSE THEY'RE CUTE?
BECAUSE THEY'RE GOOD?

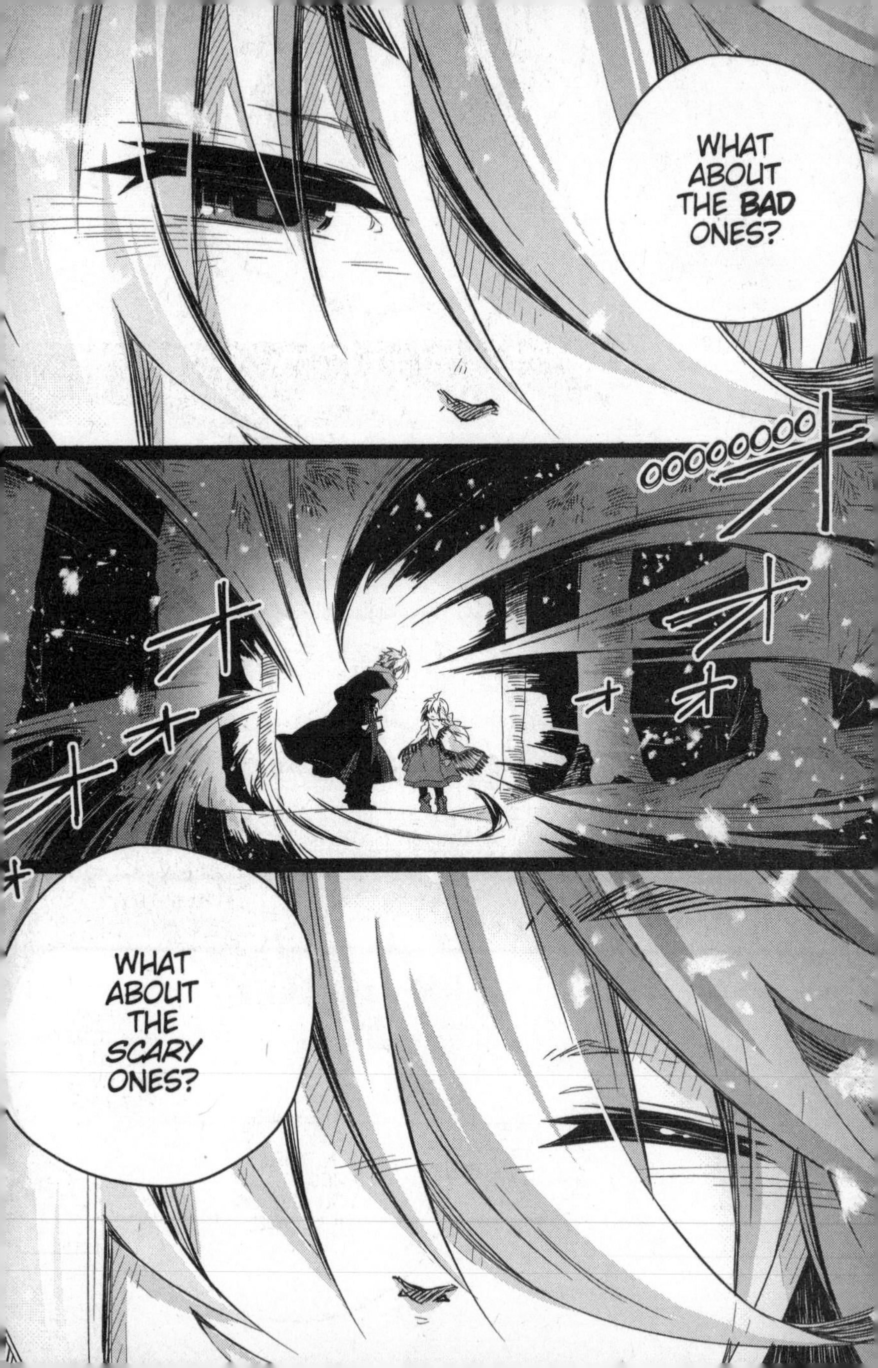
WHAT ABOUT THE BAD ONES?
OOOOOOOO
WHAT ABOUT THE SCARY ONES?

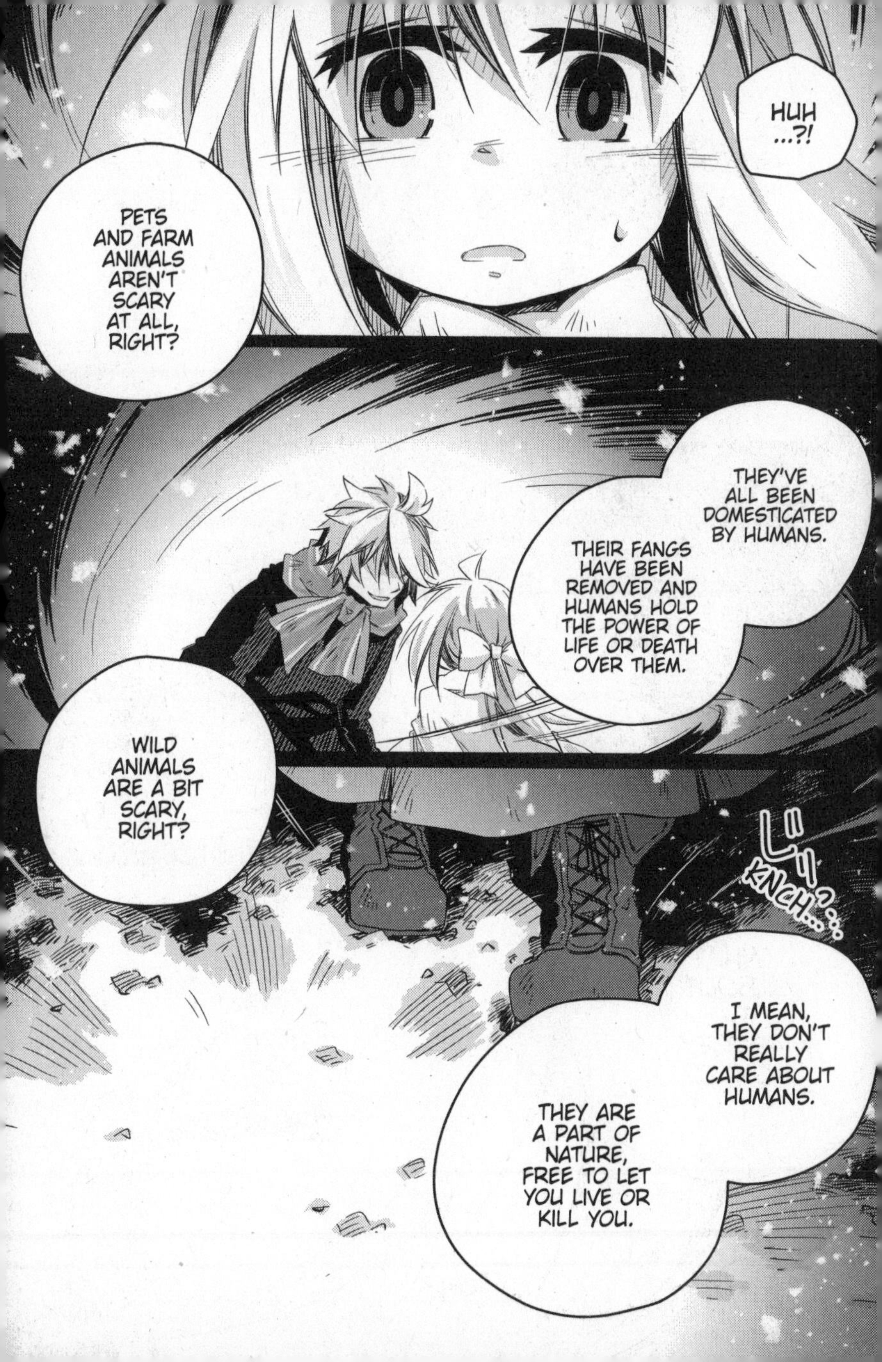
HUH ...?!
PETS AND FARM ANIMALS AREN'T SCARY AT ALL, RIGHT?
THEY'VE ALL BEEN DOMESTICATED BY HUMANS.
THEIR FANGS HAVE BEEN REMOVED AND HUMANS HOLD THE POWER OF LIFE OR DEATH OVER THEM.
WILD ANIMALS ARE A BIT SCARY, RIGHT?
KNCH...
I MEAN, THEY DON'T REALLY CARE ABOUT HUMANS.
THEY ARE A PART OF NATURE, FREE TO LET YOU LIVE OR KILL YOU.

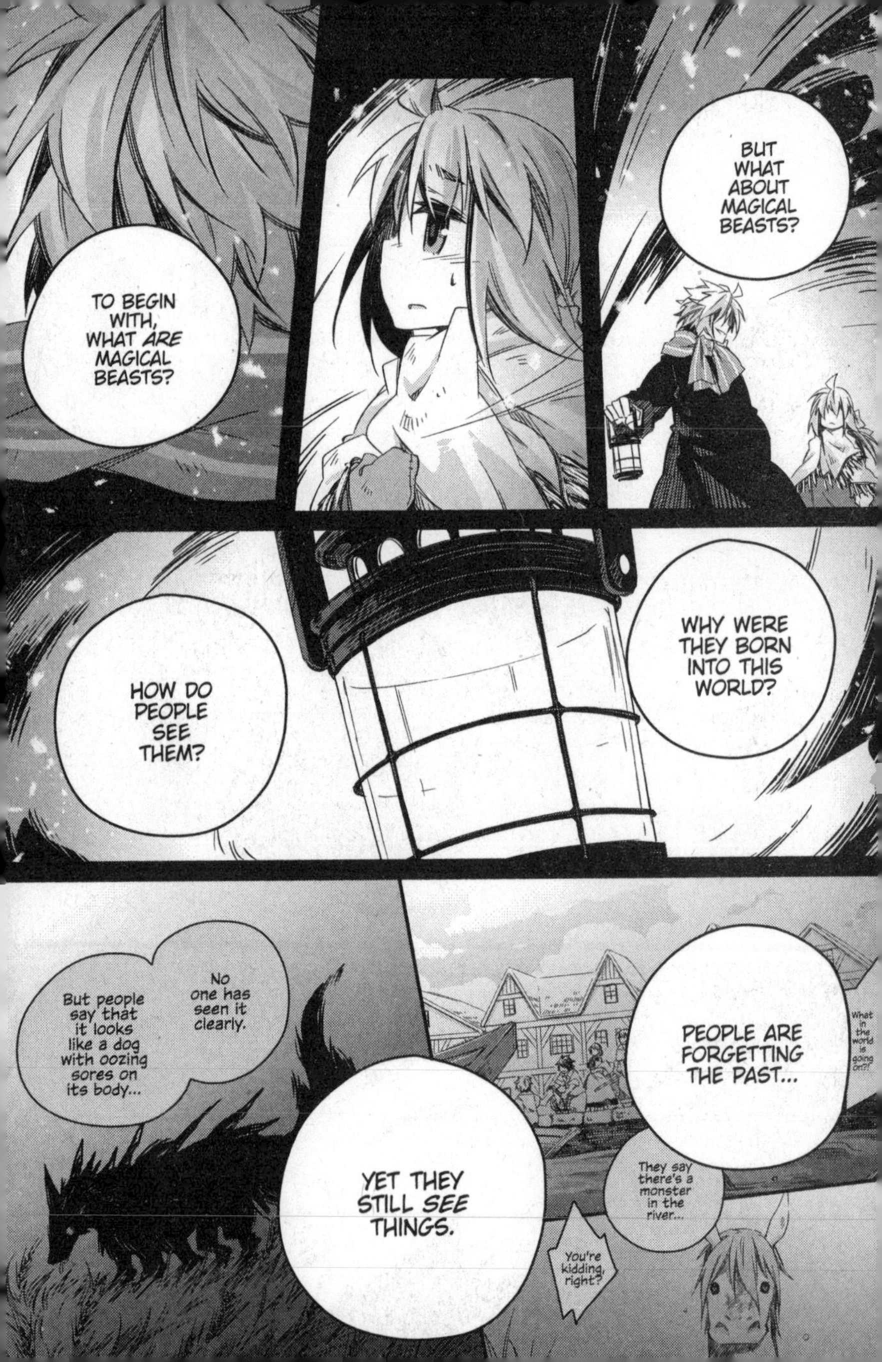
BUT WHAT ABOUT MAGICAL BEASTS?
TO BEGIN WITH, WHAT ARE MAGICAL BEASTS?
WHY WERE THEY BORN INTO THIS WORLD?
HOW DO PEOPLE SEE THEM?
PEOPLE ARE FORGETTING THE PAST...
What in the world is going on?!
They say there's a monster in the river...
You're kidding, right?
YET THEY STILL SEE THINGS.
No one has seen it clearly.
But people say that it looks like a dog with oozing sores on its body...

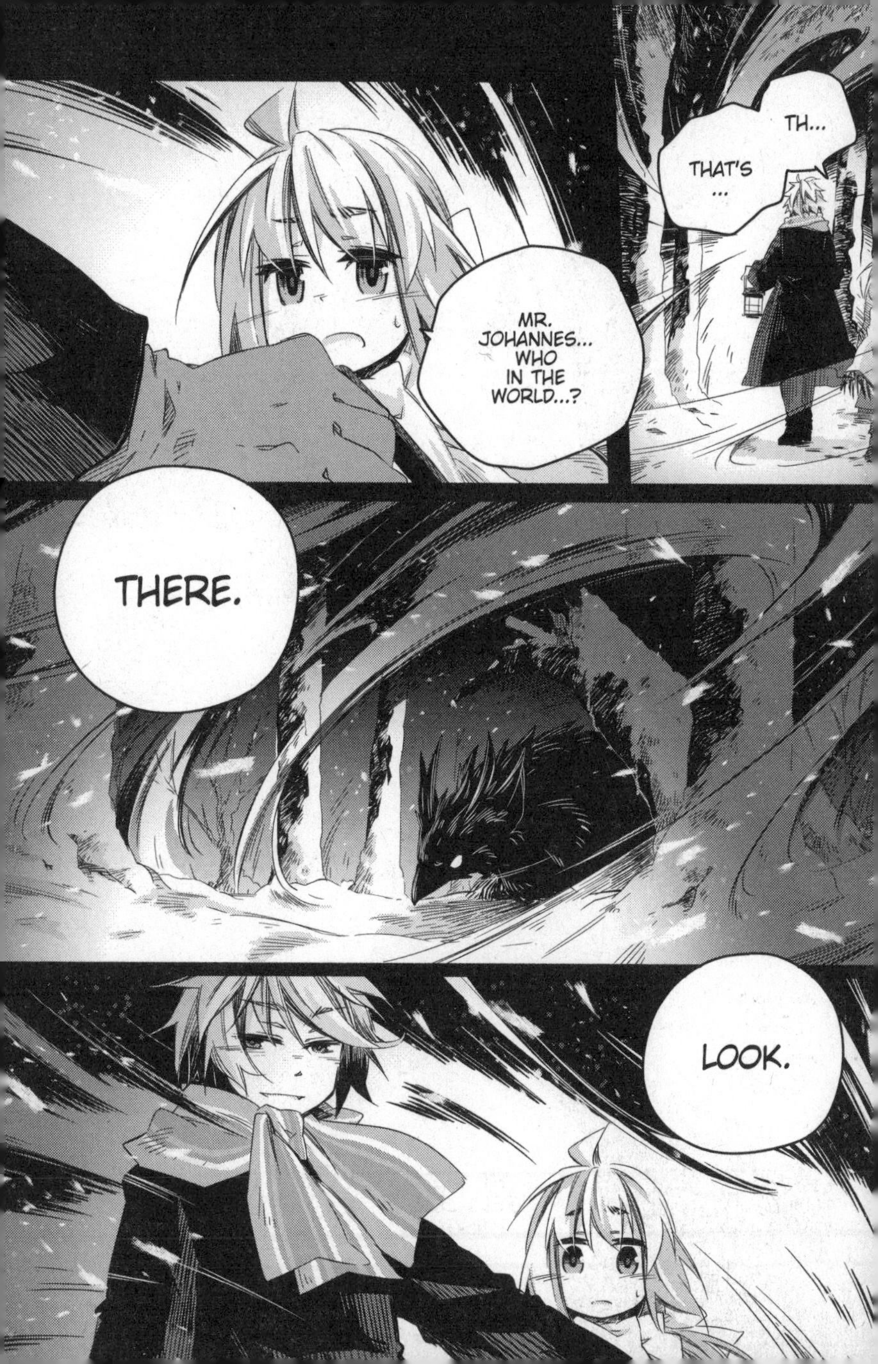
TH...
THAT'S ...
MR. JOHANNES... WHO IN THE WORLD...?
THERE.
LOOK.

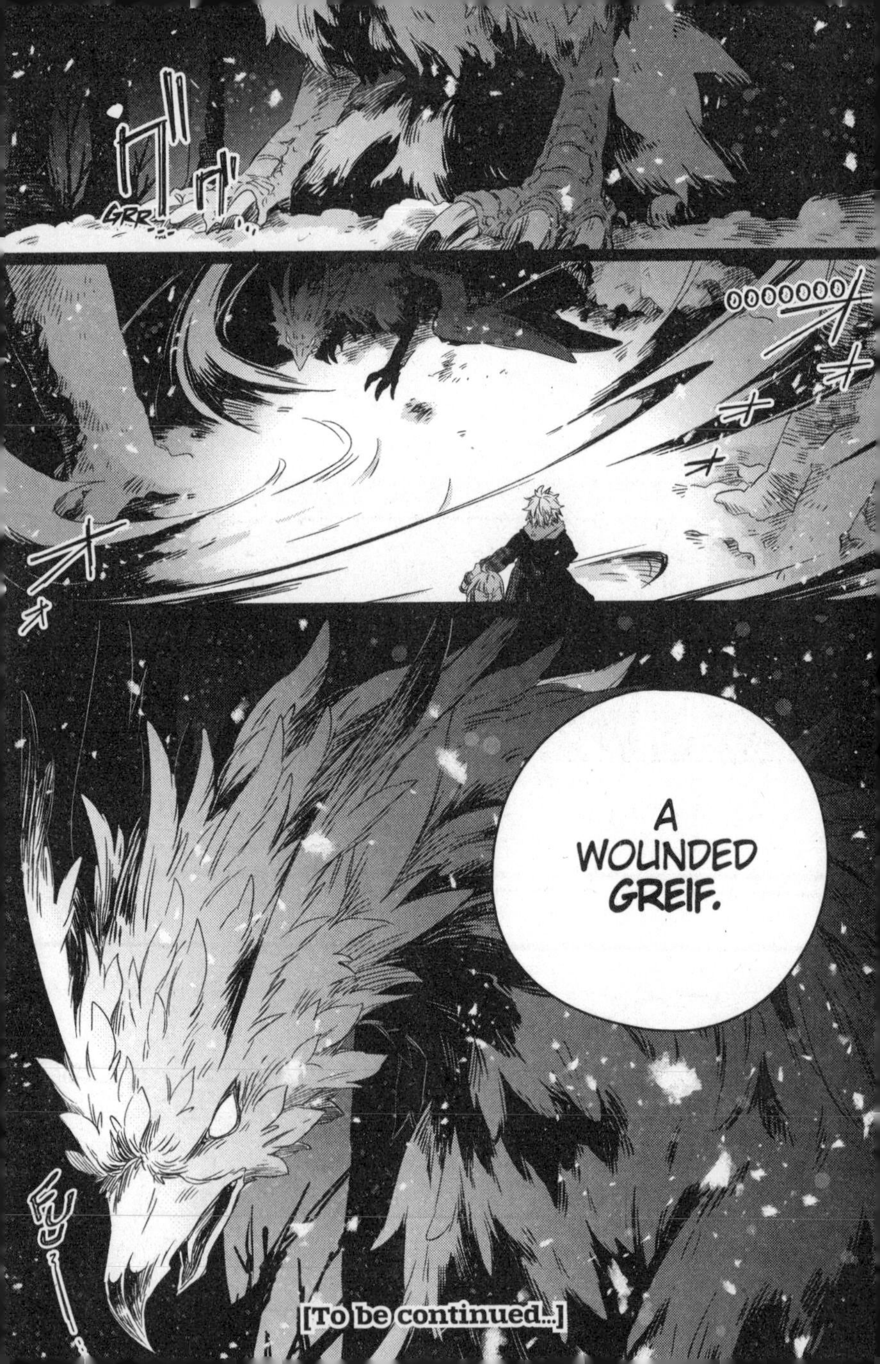
GRR
OOOOOOO
A WOUNDED GREIF.
[To be continued...]

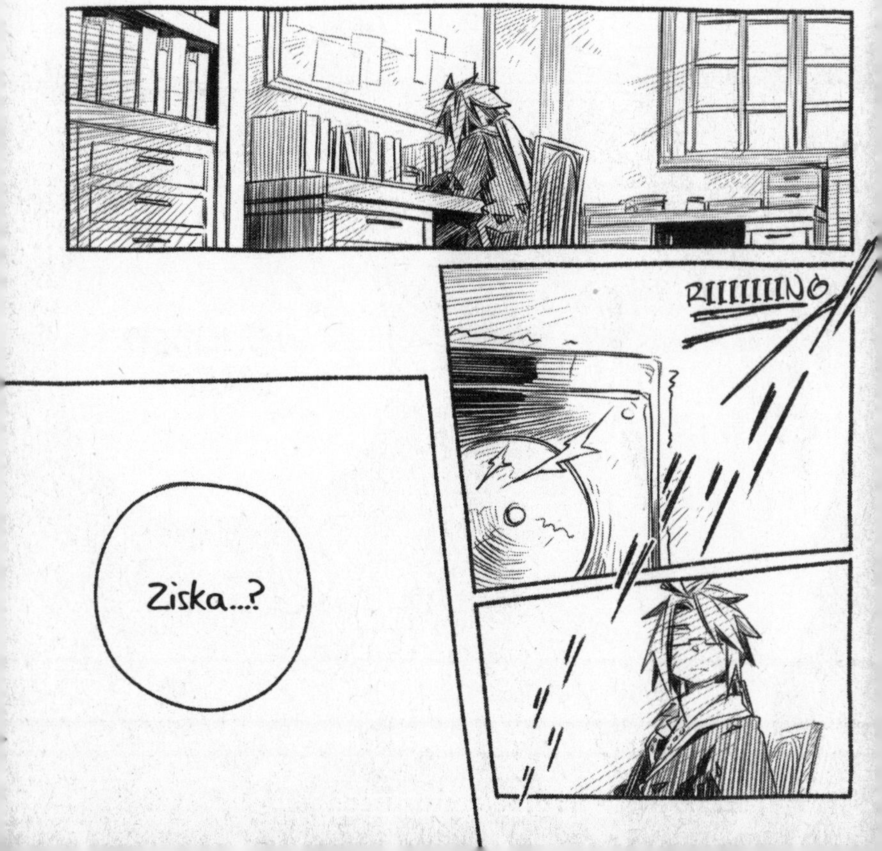
RIIIIIIING
Ziska...?

Assistant (Chapters 16 ~ 17): Morino Hiroshi-sama

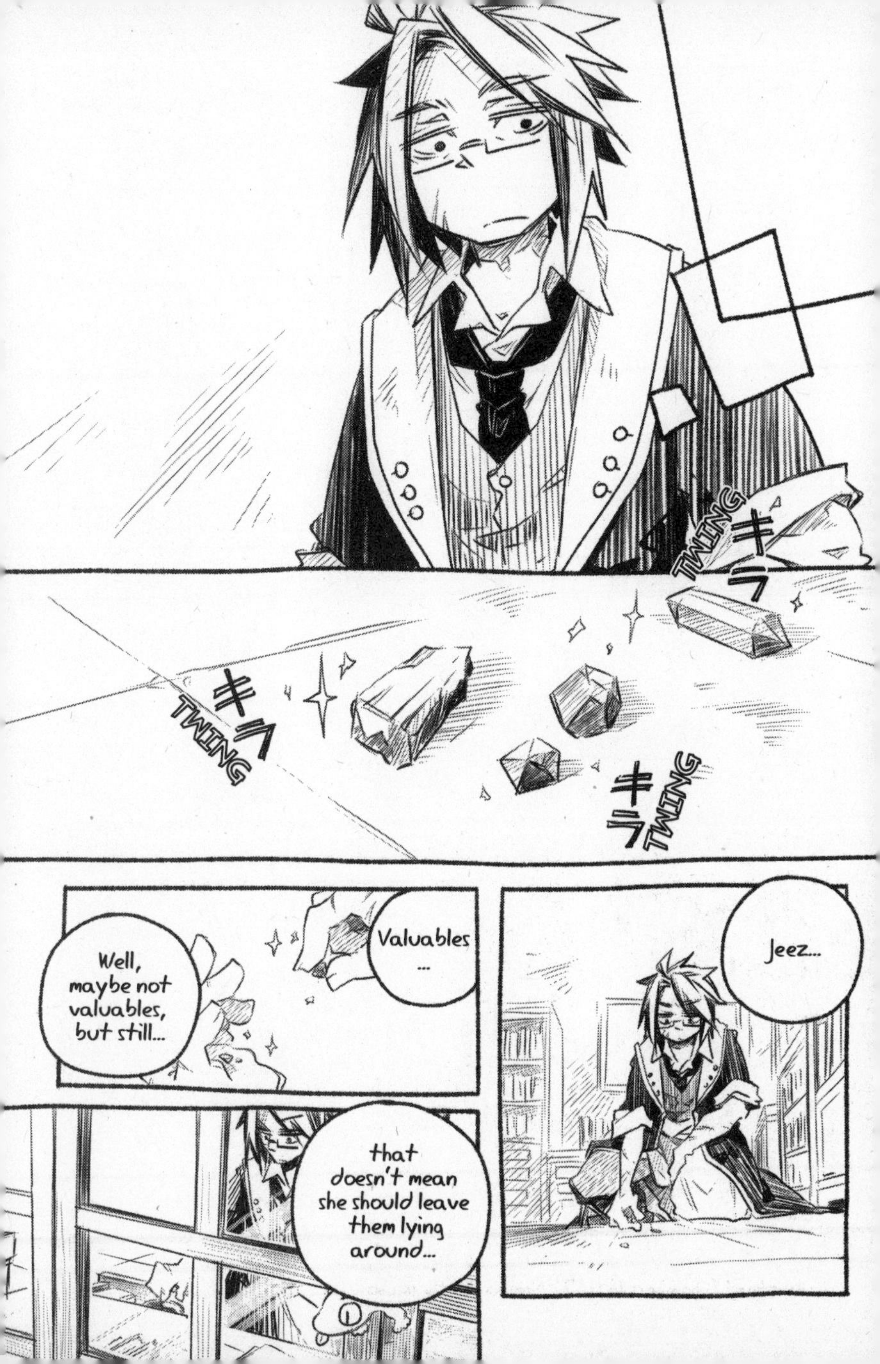

キラ
TWING
キラ
TWING
キラ
TWING
Jeez...
Valuables...
Well, maybe not valuables, but still...
that doesn't mean she should leave them lying around...

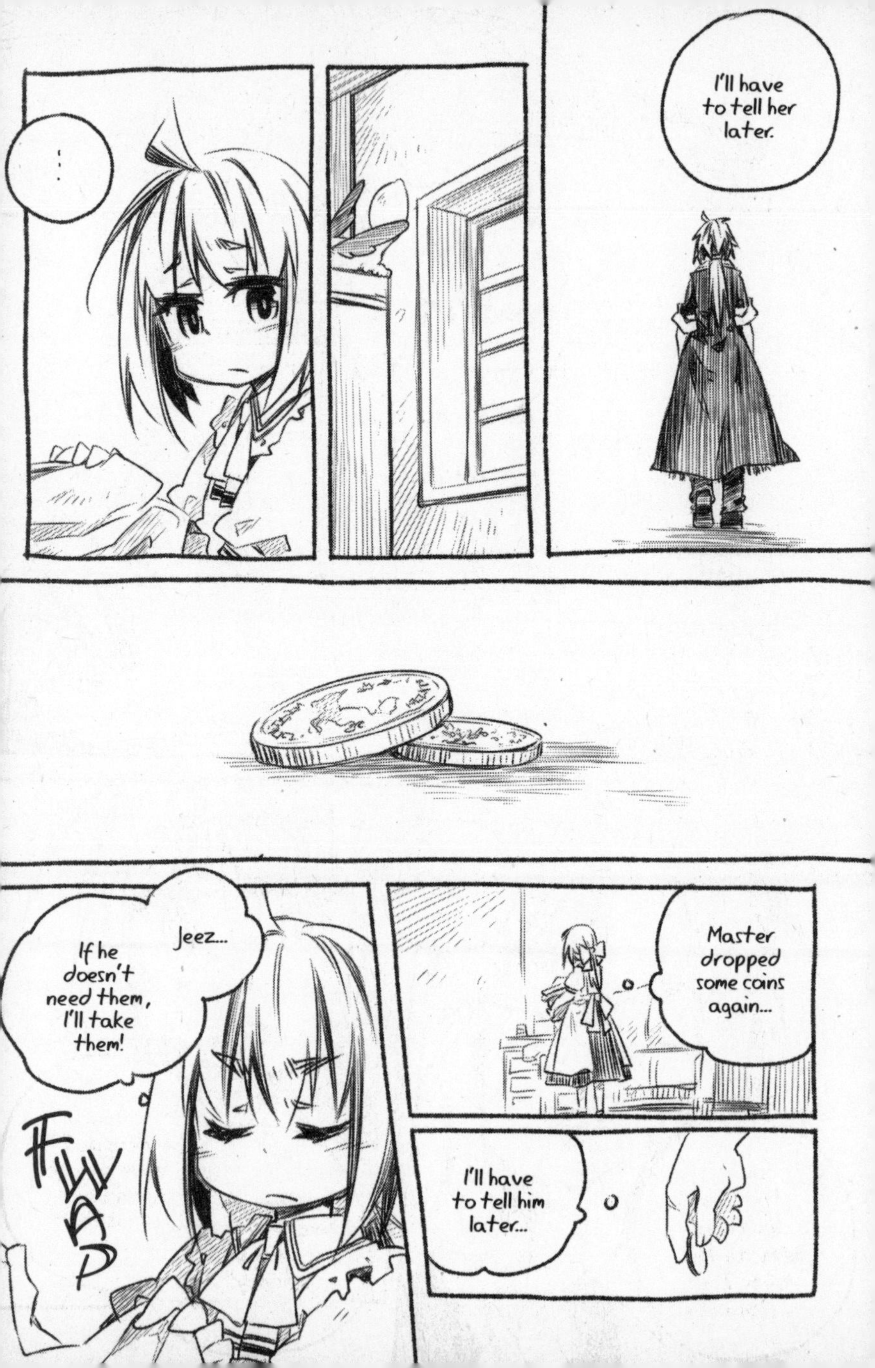
I'll have to tell her later.
...
Master dropped some coins again...
I'll have to tell him later...
Jeez... If he doesn't need them, I'll take them!
FWAP

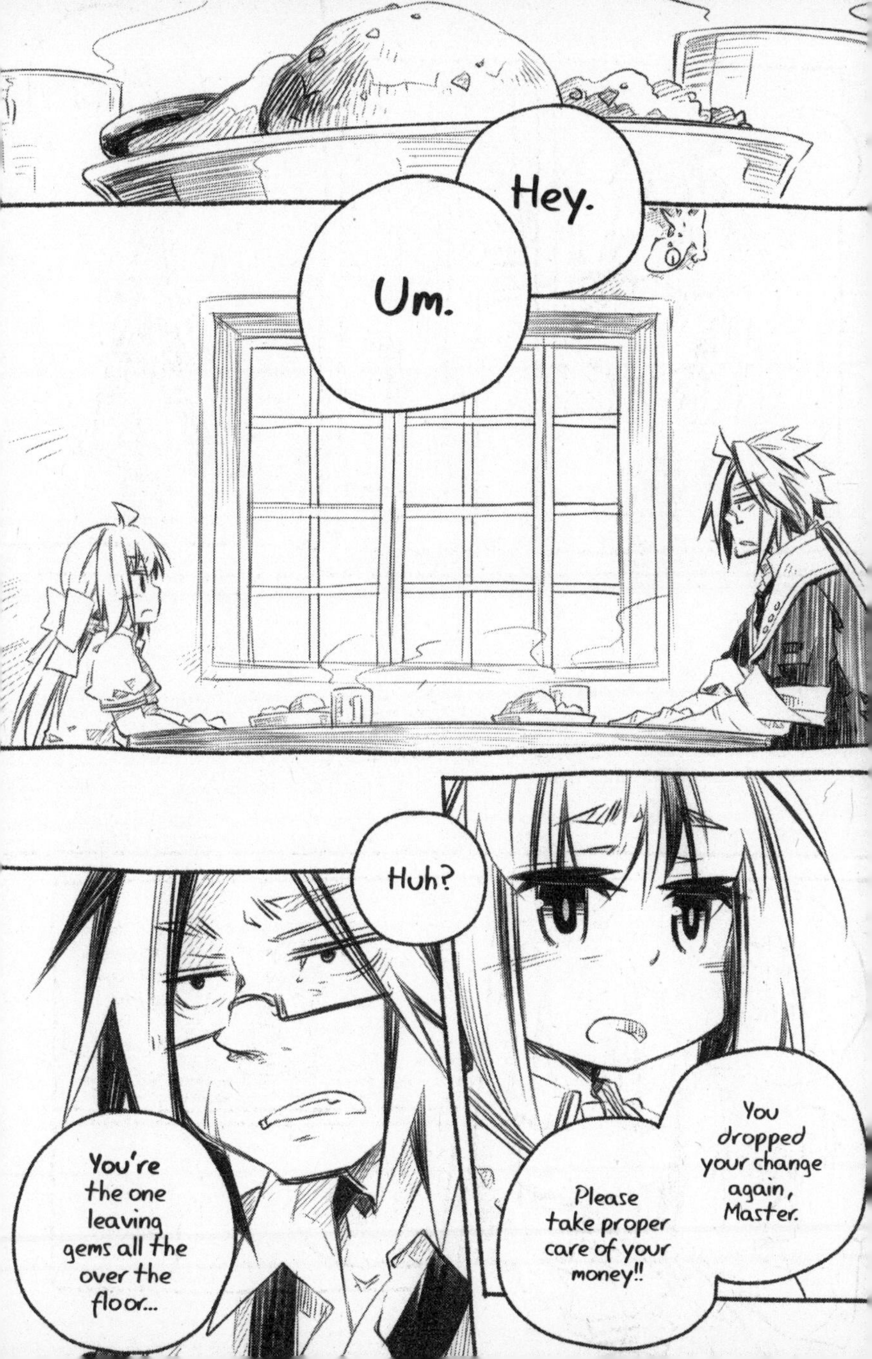
Hey.
Um.
Huh?
You dropped your change again, Master.
Please take proper care of your money!!
You're the one leaving gems all the over the floor...

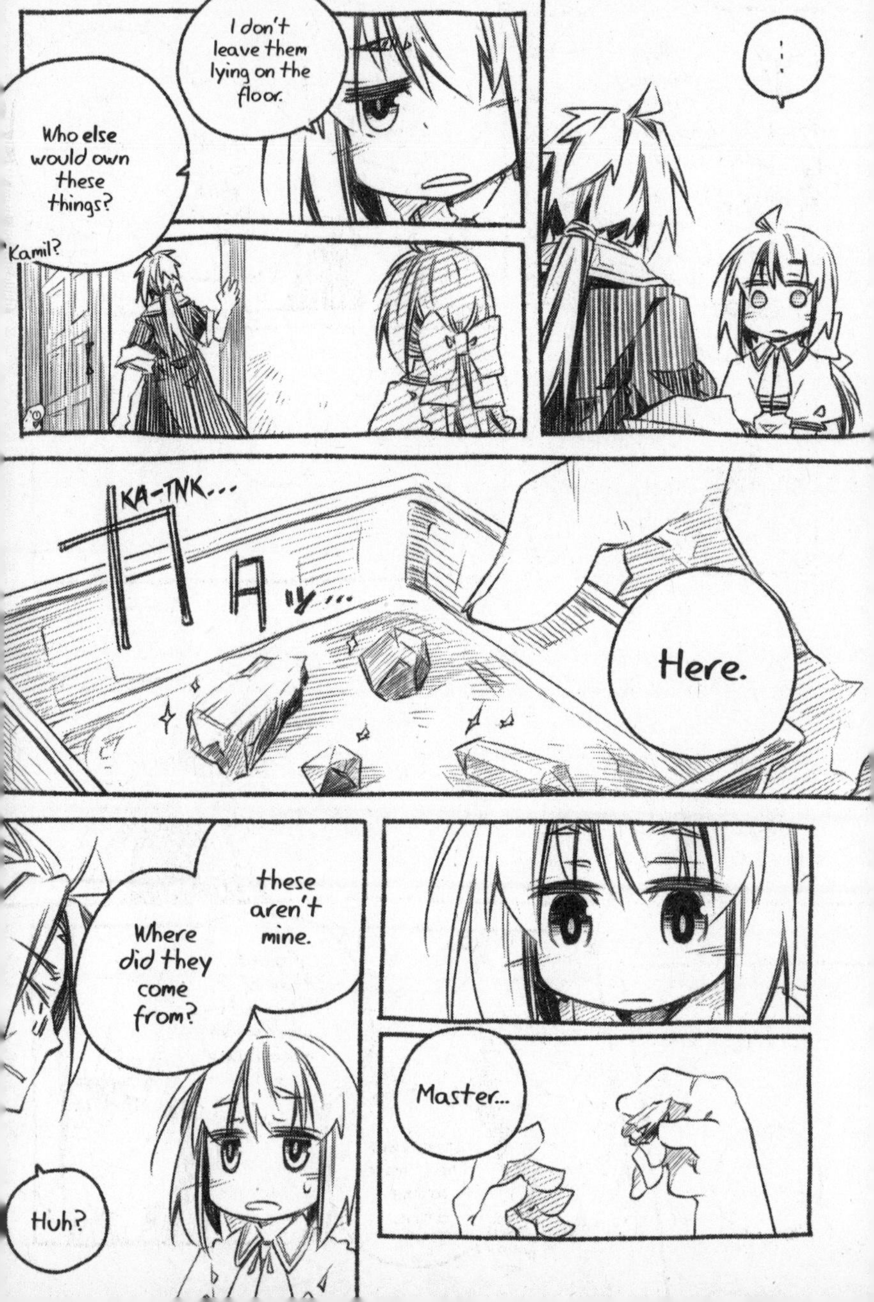
...
I don't leave them lying on the floor.
Who else would own these things?
Kamil?
KA-TNK...
Here.
Master...
these aren't mine.
Where did they come from?
Huh?

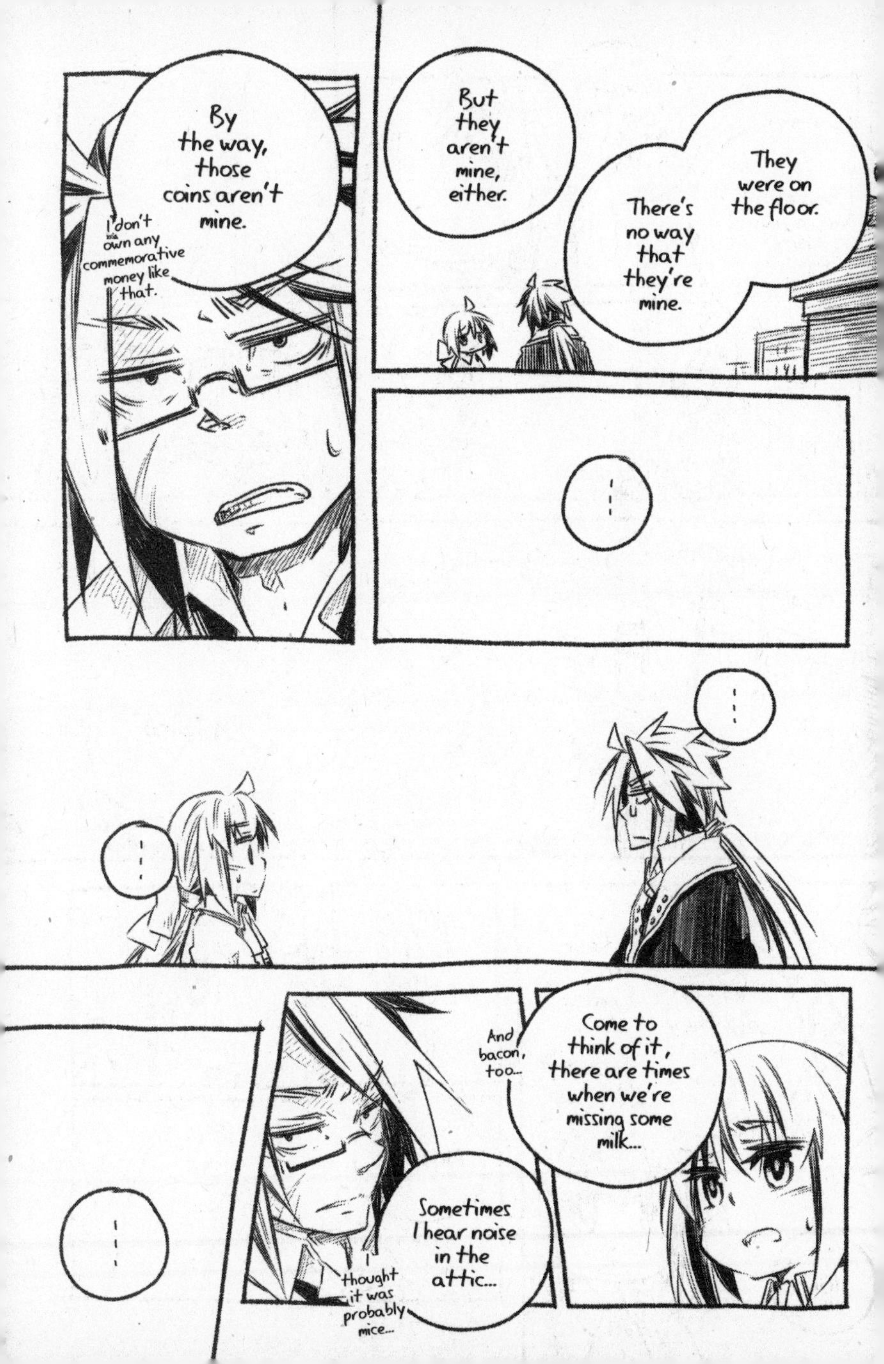
They were on the floor.
There's no way that they're mine.
But they aren't mine, either.
...
By the way, those coins aren't mine.
I don't own any commemorative money like that.
...
...
Come to think of it, there are times when we're missing some milk...
And bacon, too...
Sometimes I hear noise in the attic...
I thought it was probably mice...
...

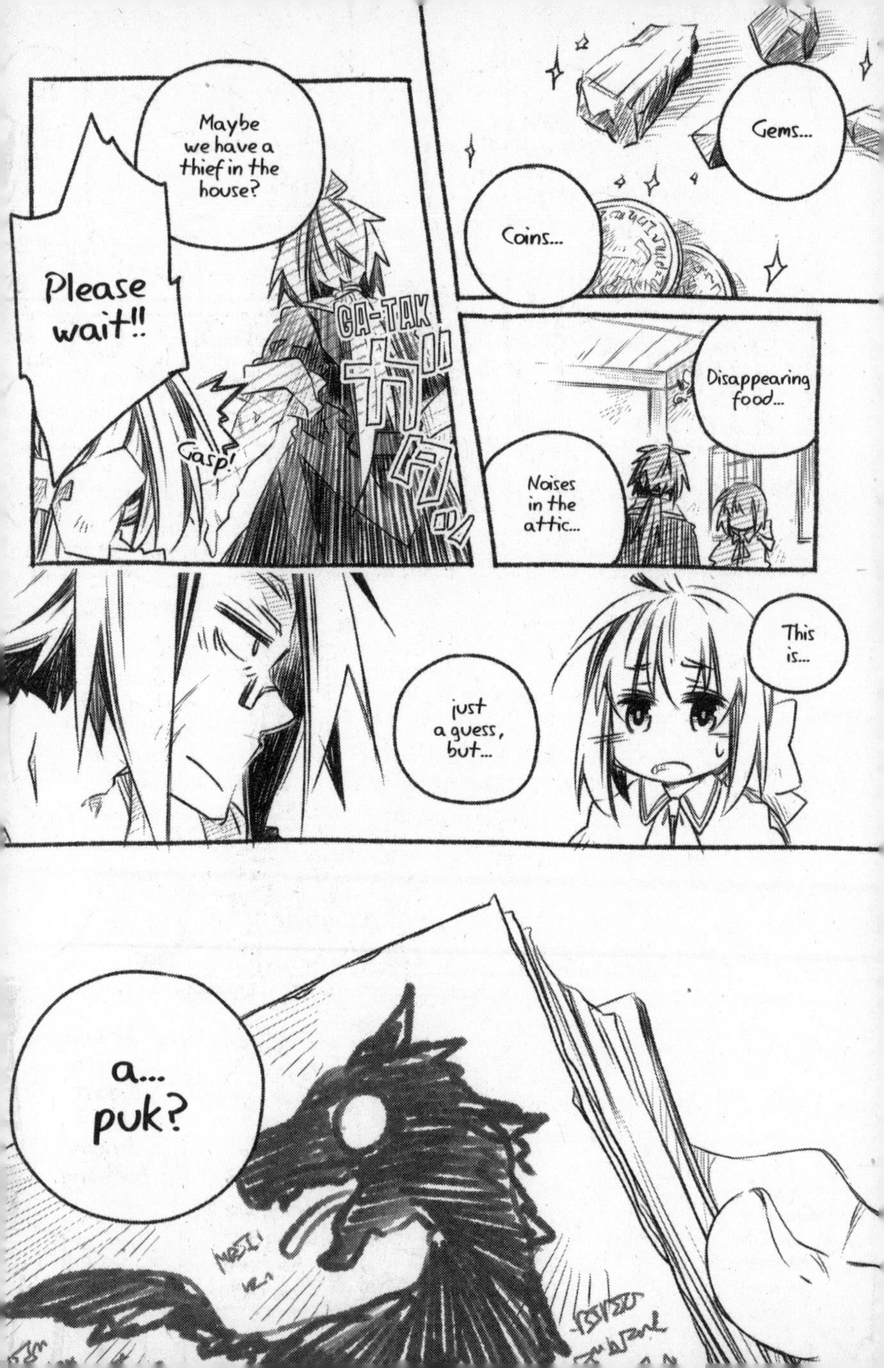
Gems...
Coins...
Disappearing food...
Noises in the attic...
Maybe we have a thief in the house?
GA-TAK
Please wait!!
Gasp!
This is...
just a guess, but...
a... puk?

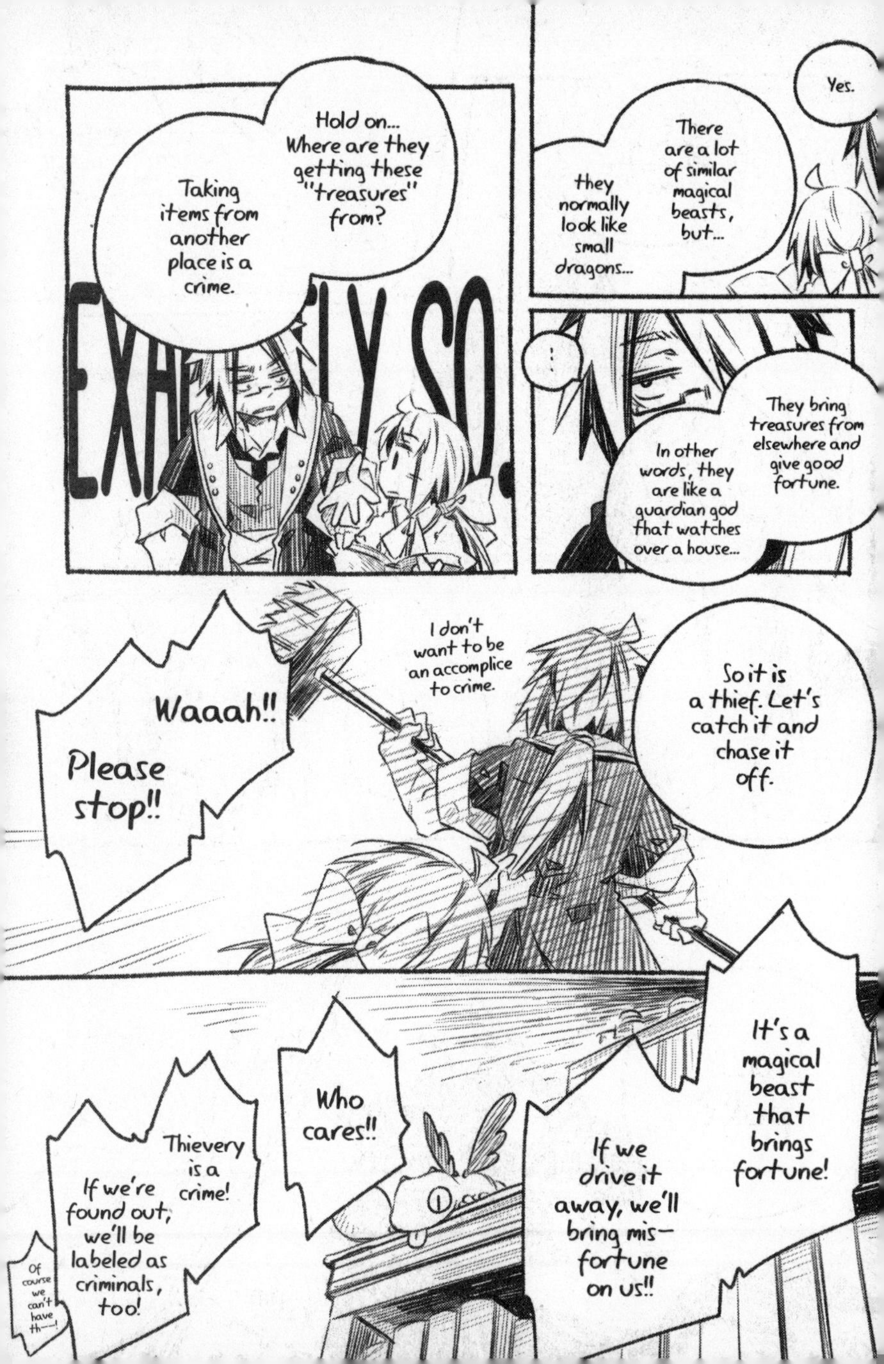
Yes.
There are a lot of similar magical beasts, but...
they normally look like small dragons...
!
They bring treasures from elsewhere and give good fortune.
In other words, they are like a guardian god that watches over a house...
Hold on... Where are they getting these "treasures" from?
Taking items from another place is a crime.
So it is a thief. Let's catch it and chase it off.
I don't want to be an accomplice to crime.
Waaah!!
Please stop!!
It's a magical beast that brings fortune!
If we drive it away, we'll bring mis-fortune on us!!
Who cares!!
Thievery is a crime!
If we're found out, we'll be labeled as criminals, too!
Of course we can't have th—!

Just as Niko and the others are worrying for Ziska's safety, a woman appears!

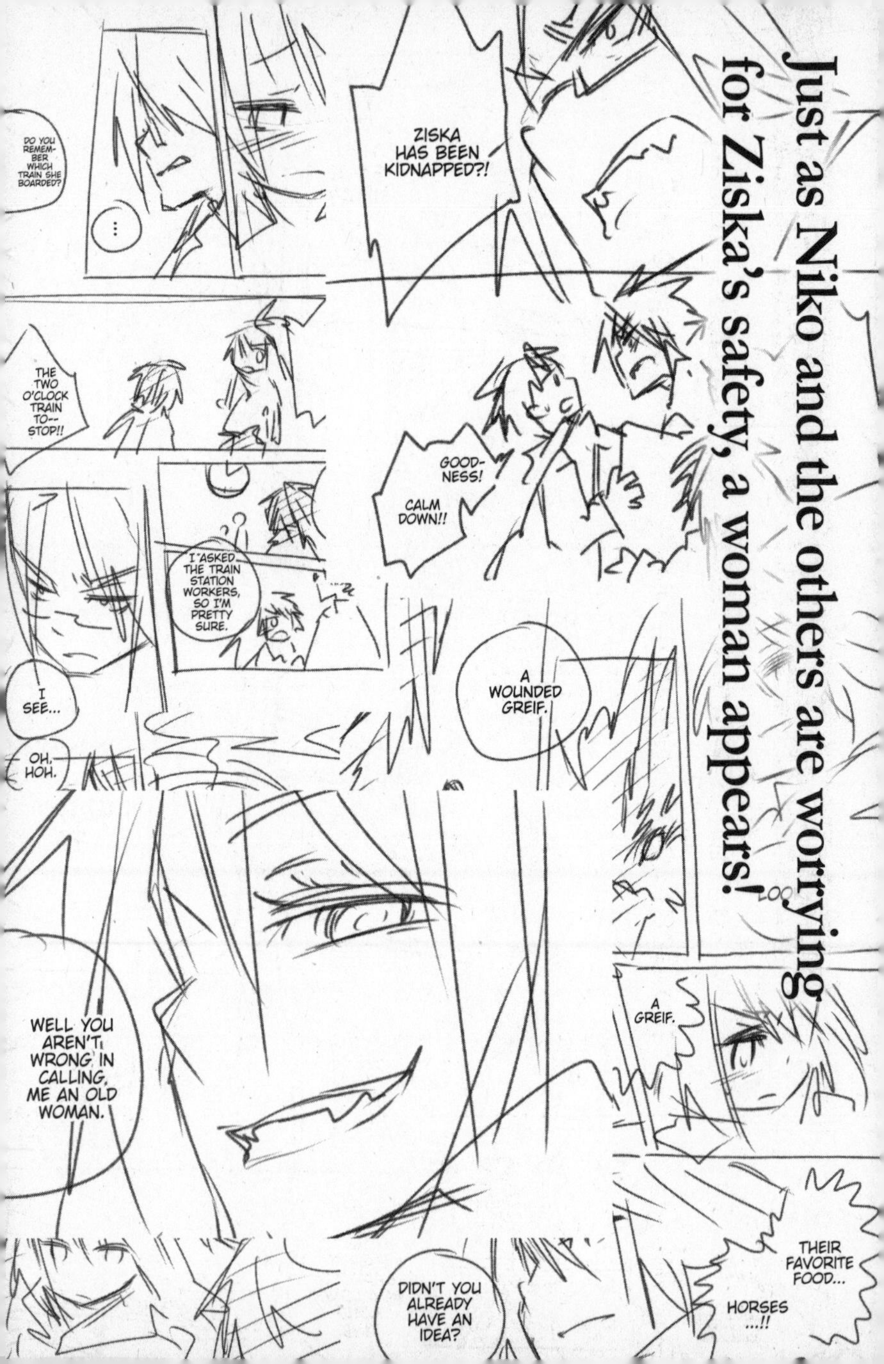
ZISKA HAS BEEN KIDNAPPED?!
DO YOU REMEMBER WHICH TRAIN SHE BOARDED?
...
GOODNESS!
CALM DOWN!!
THE TWO O'CLOCK TRAIN TO--STOP!!
I ASKED THE TRAIN STATION WORKERS, SO I'M PRETTY SURE.
I SEE...
OH, HOH.
A WOUNDED GREIF.
A GREIF.
WELL YOU AREN'T WRONG IN CALLING ME AN OLD WOMAN.
THEIR FAVORITE FOOD...
HORSES...!!
DIDN'T YOU ALREADY HAVE AN IDEA?

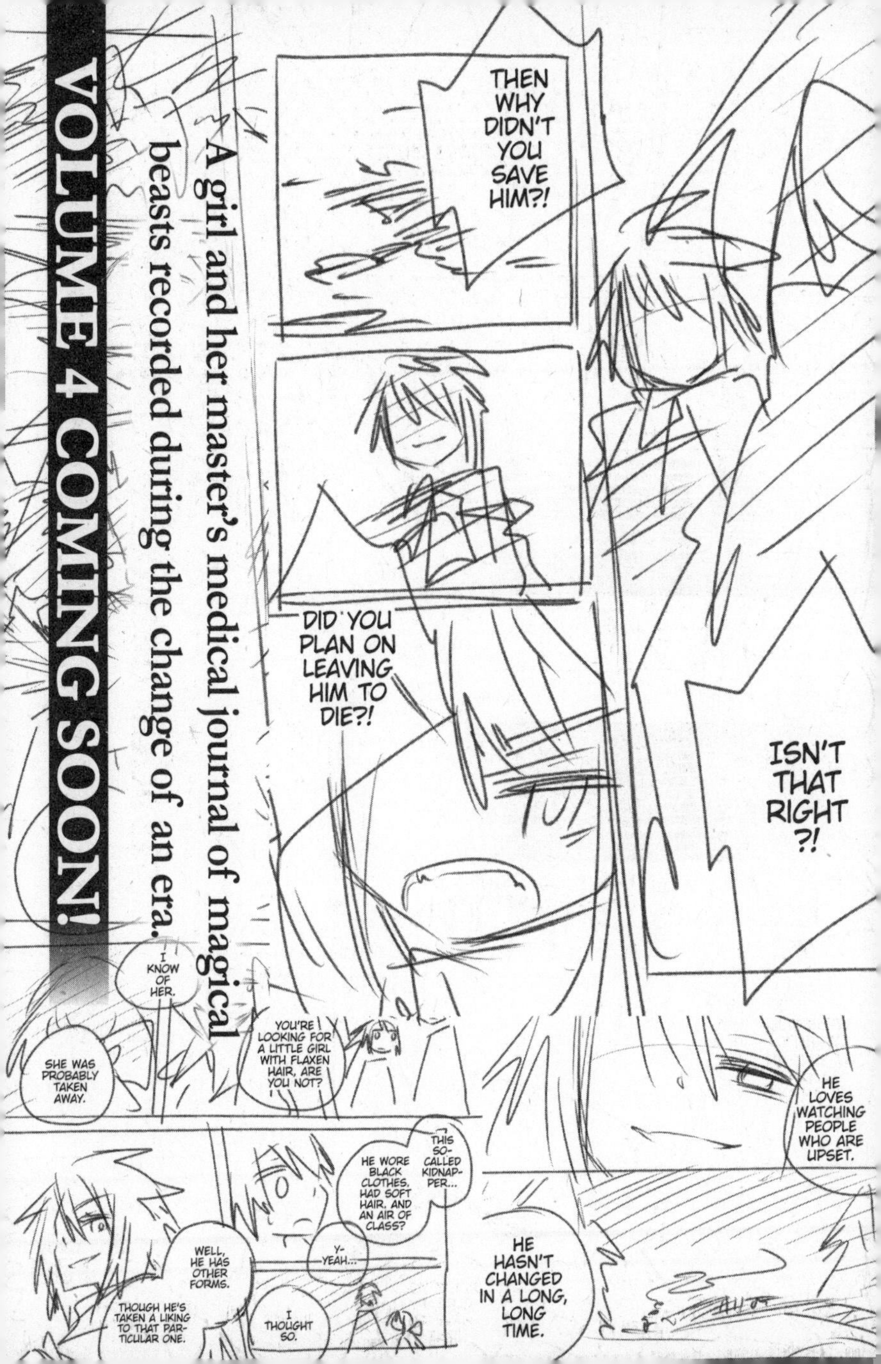
VOLUME 4 COMING SOON!
A girl and her master's medical journal of magical beasts recorded during the change of an era.
ISN'T THAT RIGHT?!
THEN WHY DIDN'T YOU SAVE HIM?!
DID YOU PLAN ON LEAVING HIM TO DIE?!
HE LOVES WATCHING PEOPLE WHO ARE UPSET.
YOU'RE LOOKING FOR A LITTLE GIRL WITH FLAXEN HAIR, ARE YOU NOT?
I KNOW OF HER.
SHE WAS PROBABLY TAKEN AWAY.
HE HASN'T CHANGED IN A LONG, LONG TIME.
THIS SO-CALLED KIDNAP-PER...
HE WORE BLACK CLOTHES, HAD SOFT HAIR, AND AN AIR OF CLASS?
Y-YEAH...
WELL, HE HAS OTHER FORMS.
I THOUGHT SO.
THOUGH HE'S TAKEN A LIKING TO THAT PAR-TICULAR ONE.

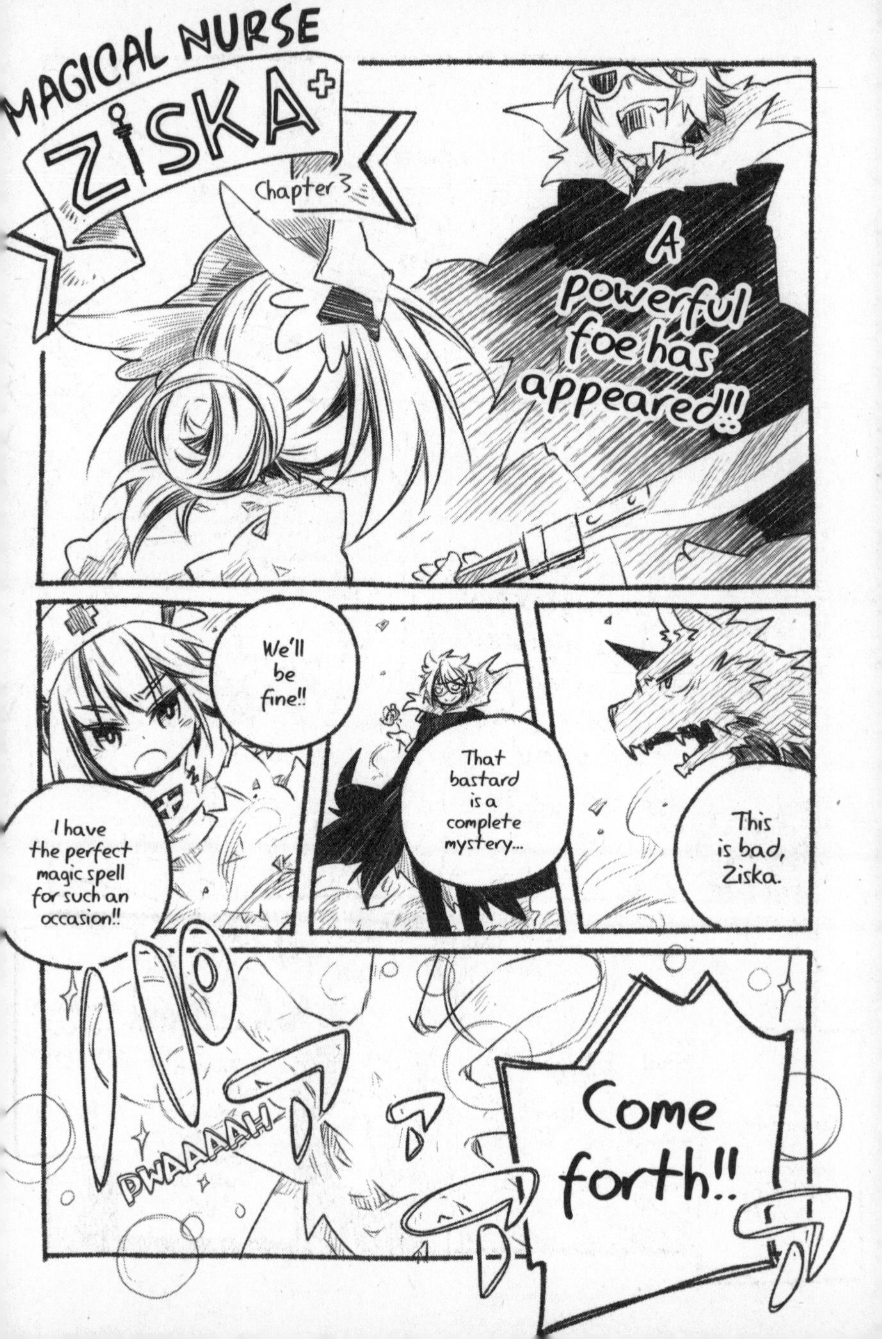
MAGICAL NURSE ZISKA+
Chapter 3
A powerful foe has appeared!!
This is bad, Ziska.
That bastard is a complete mystery...
We'll be fine!!
I have the perfect magic spell for such an occasion!!
Come forth!!
PWAAAAH

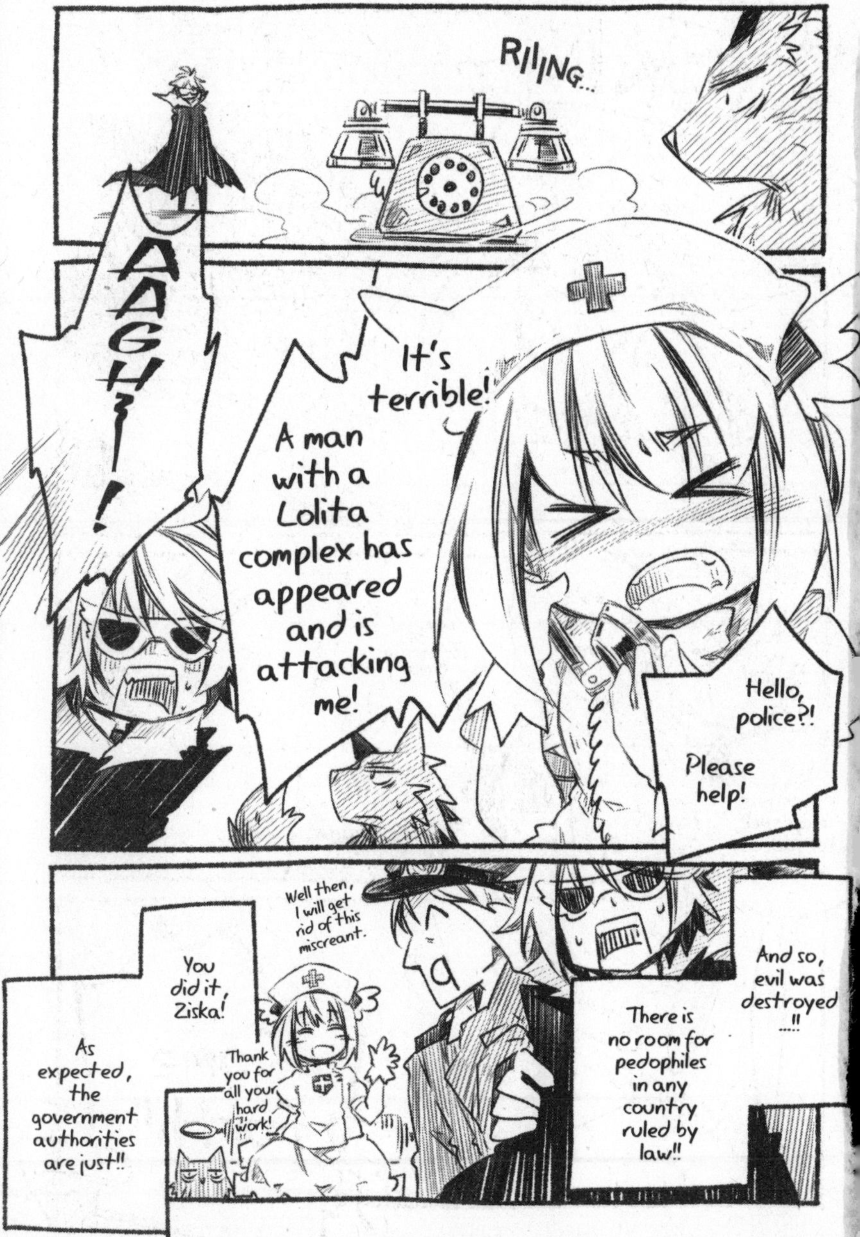
RIIING...
Hello, police?!
Please help!
It's terrible!
A man with a Lolita complex has appeared and is attacking me!
AAGH!!
And so, evil was destroyed.....!!
There is no room for pedophiles in any country ruled by law!!
Well then, I will get rid of this miscreant.
You did it, Ziska!
Thank you for all your hard work!!
As expected, the government authorities are just!!

SEVEN SEAS ENTERTAINMENT PRESENTS

How to Treat Magical Beasts
Mine and Master's Medical Journal

story and art by **KAZIYA** **VOLUME 3**

TRANSLATION
Angela Liu

ADAPTATION
Jaymee Goh

LETTERING AND RETOUCH
Annaliese Christman

COVER DESIGN
KC Fabellon

PROOFREADER
Cae Hawksmoor
Holly Kolodziejczak

EDITOR
Jenn Grunigen

PRODUCTION MANAGER
Lissa Pattillo

MANAGING EDITOR
Julie Davis

EDITOR-IN-CHIEF
Adam Arnold

PUBLISHER
Jason DeAngelis

WATASHI TO SENSEI NO GENJUU SHINRYOUROKU VOL. 3

Originally published in Japan in 2018 by MAG Garden Corporation, Tokyo. English translation rights arranged through TOHAN CORPORATION, Tokyo.

Seven Seas press and purchase enquiries can be sent to Marketing Manager Lianne Sentar at press@gomanga.com. Information regarding the distribution and purchase of digital editions is available from Digital Manager CK Russell at digital@gomanga.com.

ISBN: 978-1-642750-05-8

Printed in Canada

First Printing: April 2019

10 9 8 7 6 5 4 3 2 1

READING DIRECTIONS

This book reads from ***right to left***, Japanese style. If this is your first time reading manga, you start reading from the top right panel on each page and take it from there. If you get lost, just follow the numbered diagram here. It may seem backwards at first, but you'll get the hang of it! Have fun!!

1
2
3
4
5
6
7
8
9

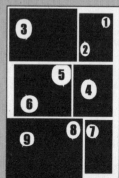